LAND DIVIDED BY LAW

LAND DIVIDED BY LAW

THE YAKAMA INDIAN NATION AS ENVIRONMENTAL HISTORY, 1840-1933

by

Barbara Leibhardt Wester

QUID PRO BOOKS
New Orleans, Louisiana

Copyright © 1990, 2014 by Barbara Liebhardt Wester. Foreword copyright © 2014 by Harry N. Scheiber. All rights reserved. This book may not be reproduced or retransmitted in any form, including digital reproductions and photocopies, without written permission from the publisher.

Published in 2014 by Quid Pro Books.

ISBN 978-1-61027-839-3 (hardcover)
ISBN 978-1-61027-140-0 (paperback)
ISBN 978-1-61027-141-7 (ebook)

QUID PRO, LLC
5860 Citrus Blvd., Suite D-101
New Orleans, Louisiana 70123
www.quidprobooks.com

qp

Publisher's Cataloging-in-Publication

Wester, Barbara Leibhardt.
  Land divided by law : the Yakama Indian Nation as environmental history, 1840-1933 / Barbara Leibhardt Wester.
      p. cm. — (Classic dissertation series)
  Includes bibliographical references.
  ISBN: 978-1-61027-839-3 (hbk)

1. Human ecology—United States—History. 2. Yakama Indians—Treaties. 3. Yakama Indians—Fishing—Law and legislation. 4. Salmon—Columbia River. I. Title. II. Series.
GF502.W23 2014   2014577359

Cover image, depicting "Wishram early style cornhusk bag, dogbane foundation, cornhusk overlay, leather patches, holes remain from former drawstring, UOMNCH Cat. #2-746, University of Oregon Museum of Natural and Cultural History, by photographer Chris White," copyright © 2012 by UOMNCH, used by permission. Interior photographs are under copyright as indicated with their captions, and used by permission and under license from the sources there credited. Author photograph on back cover inset courtesy of Stephen N. Wester.

LAND DIVIDED BY LAW:
THE YAKAMA INDIAN NATION AS ENVIRONMENTAL HISTORY,
1840-1933

by
Barbara Leibhardt Wester

Abstract

This study examines natural resource use disputes between Euro-Americans and the Confederated Tribes and Bands of the Yakama Indian Nation from 1840 to 1933. The Yakama Nation is comprised of fourteen separate bands that were resettled on the Yakama Reservation in eastern Washington State following an 1855 treaty with the United States. During the 93 years of this study, Yakama fought to retain control over subsistence resources that Euro-Americans sought to channel into capitalist markets. The ensuing struggle between the two cultures has continued into the present. This study explores its distinctive social, legal, and ecological dimensions.

Part I of this study examines how Yakama and Euro-American peoples organized their relationships to land. As the two groups came into sustained contact, it was the Euro-American notion of individual rights in private property, especially as advanced through federal allotment policy, that displaced the Yakamas' own concept of individual entitlements to communally-held use rights.

Part II considers conflicts between Yakama and neighboring settlers over control of the waters bordering the reservation. Yakama were well aware of the injustice of federal reclamation law and sought to increase their water claims under terms of the U.S. Supreme Court's *Winters v. United States* decision in 1908.

Part III examines conflicts over Yakama salmon fisheries, hunting grounds, and berry- and root-gathering grounds, upon whose proceeds tribal members continued to rely especially when farming failed. Yakama won access to important Columbia River fishing sites in *United States v. Winans* (1905), and they unsuccessfully tried to apply this decision to off-reservation game.

Law and legal institutions play a crucial role in the Yakamas' collective history. First, Euro-Americans regulated their relationship with Native Americans and with nature primarily through the legal system. Second, Euro-Americans wanted to control Native American resources, but law was an imperfect instrument of conquest. As this study shows, Native Americans learned to manipulate law and employed it—sometimes successfully—to press their own claims.

To William

Contents

Foreword i

Preface iii

Acknowledgments vii

Abbreviations Used in the Notes ix

Map of the State of Washington xi

1 · Introduction: Indians, Law, Environment, and History 1

PART I • EARTH'S BODY: LAND

2 · Sacred Bundles 15

3 · Goods and the Earth 37

4 · "Shall I Tear My Mother's Bosom?" 65

5 · "The Indian Belongs To The Earth" 93

PART II • EARTH'S HEART: WATER

6 · Sacred Water 123

7 · Command of the Waters 149

PART III • LIFE AND BREATH OF THE EARTH: FISH AND WILDLIFE

8 · Seated Together at the Great Table of the Columbia River 177

9 · Foragers in a Farmers' World 211

10 · Conclusion 239

Appendix 245

Bibliography 257

FOREWORD

Barbara Wester's book is a masterful study of the complex, extended series of confrontations between the native Indian cultures of the Yakima region and the regime of the conquering white nation. Her analysis is based on a blending of materials from rich archival sources and from the literatures of legal history, administrative history, anthropology, ecology, and cultural theory. Most remarkably, the book makes important new contributions to all these fields of scholarship. Above all, in fresh and intriguing ways, it weaves the topic of native culture into the tapestry of American legal history.

Wester eschews any simplistic two-party model of legal contestations. Her book provides instead an intriguing portrayal of the clashes of hierarchy, substantive objectives, and power on both sides—but especially within the Yakama community itself, shaping its varied responses over time to American cultural values, legal and religious norms, and judicial procedures. In this respect, her work is of special value in advancing our understanding of Indian-white relations from the 1840s to the present day.

A theme brightly illuminated throughout is the conflicting set of fundamental values that undergirded the claims of two cultures regarding what is sacred—access to natural resources as a community right, for the native culture, in contrast to the claims of private property rights traditionally embedded in the Anglo-American law of the conquerors.

This book is commended to historians and environmentalists alike, as a study bridging disciplines and bringing understanding of how, over nearly a century of life and legal conflict, two competing cultures had very different relationships with and effects on their environments. Naturally, those effects continue today.

HARRY N. SCHEIBER
Chancellor's Professor of Law and History, Emeritus
University of California, Berkeley

Berkeley, California
September 2014

PREFACE

More than 25 years ago I set out to figure out what happens to real people's everyday lives when two cultures collide and mediate their relationships over shared land, water, and other natural resources through the language and the tools of the U.S. legal system. At the time, I was a graduate student at the University of California at Berkeley, passionate about the study of Native American cultures and how these cultures had adapted and survived in the world of post-Euro-American contact. Although the interaction between Native American cultures and European colonizers occurred through capitalist markets, violent conflict, and various forms of voluntary and forced acculturation, my particular interest was law. Law and the courts: instruments of a conquering people, loaded with the values and calculus of this conquering people, but carrying also the power and protection of legally defined and defensible rights.

My undergraduate and graduate studies coincided with a unique time in American historical study: the self-conscious emergence of environmental history as its own field of study, separate from historical geography and different from the history of the science of ecology. For the first time, environments and ecologies became actors in the historical narrative. For me, the focus on environment as historical actor resonated with a desire to highlight how Native American peoples might also be viewed as proactive actors in history.

The law defines Native peoples as "domestic dependent nations,"[1] and in the 1980s historians were writing of "cultures of dependency," circumscribing an historical arc in which Native peoples were conquered militarily, economically, socially. Environmental historians had contributed to this theme with an added layer of ecological conquest.[2] Native Americans as historical subjects seemed destined to end as mere subordinates whose actions must always be subsumed by dominant forces, now including the destruction of their environments. But while numerous histories suggested how compelling this historical arc might be, I wondered if it were true, especially if one studied cultural interactions in terms of individual lives changing over time. What if one added law to the mix? Could access to the legal system make a difference—either at the level of the individual or at the level of an entire society?

How do you study changes in individual lives over time when everyone involved has long passed into distant memory? I needed records. While many Native American peoples have rich oral traditions, my focus on law and the

---

[1] *Cherokee Nation v. Georgia*, 30 U.S. 1 (1831).

[2] See Richard White, *The Roots of Dependency: Subsistence, Environment, and Social Change Among the Choctaws, Pawnees, and Navajos* (Lincoln: University of Nebraska Press, 1983).

courts required studying a people who had developed written traditions as well, and I found a far richer historical record than I could ever have imagined when I began my study of the Confederated Tribes and Bands of the Yakama Indian Nation, whose reservation is situated in central Washington state.

Letters written by Yakama tribal members have been preserved in the hundreds of correspondence files in the National Archives records of the Commissioner of Indian Affairs. Through a hot summer in 1988 in Washington, D.C., I studied the letters written to the Commissioner by many individual Yakama who told of their daily battles to secure access to treaty reserved fishing areas, to collect water at sacred springs, and to gather roots and other subsistence and medicinal plants. Many of these individuals played a role in the tribe's long legal battles to secure the full measure of their treaty rights (still ongoing today). Many realized that their battles really only had begun once they had won rights to fish or obtain an appropriated share of water from the area's large federally-funded irrigation projects. In reading the words of these Yakama members, I was struck over and over by how firmly they asserted their rights—rights which then (and still now) are not readily affirmed.

Native American uses and claims to natural resources, as I explored in detail in my research, do not easily fit within the language of the Anglo-American legal tradition. That legal tradition, the long-time spouse of capitalism, is an efficient tool for translating resources into property, and property and other rights into cash. There is no ready mechanism—in the nineteenth century during the time of my study, or in the present—for accounting for the non-monetary value of anything. The legal system, while efficient in keeping capitalist markets employed in the conversion of natural resources into goods and cash, is very inefficient for valuing, say, the right to continue to harvest a share of salmon at a traditional fishing cliff during the spring salmon run, or the desire to protect a forest for "seven generations" to come. The legal battles the Yakama fought became, then, an exercise in translating their cultural values in natural resources into legally defensible rights, but at the cost of defining that value in terms understandable by law.

This battle continues right into the present, and the questions on which battle lines are drawn are, if anything, more complex than anything that nineteenth-century policymakers could have imagined: what share of water should be allocated to protect salmon runs? What are the appropriate water quality standards needed to protect subsistence rights to harvest fish or wild rice? How do the footprints of hard rock mines coexist with protection of migration corridors for game that tribal members can take pursuant to their subsistence hunting rights? In what many perceive to be the twilight of New Deal-inspired environmental protection, what is the role of law in environmental protection and what should it be? As scholars and policymakers analyze and debate, practitioners are left to work things out on the ground.

In looking back over my research and writing—now more than a quarter century old—there is a certain amusement in reading my descriptions of federal policymakers, lawyers, and judges who appear at many points of my story.

During the past same quarter century I have worked as a lawyer for a federal agency, in which position I've had the opportunity to study firsthand how federal policymakers, lawyers, and judges work in real life. In my practice, which has included the Agency's programs in Indian country, I see every day—at the level of individual citizens; tribal, state, and local governmental representatives; industry; and other stakeholders—the tension between law as a powerful tool for defining and regulating rights to use resources responsibly and law's chronic inability to fully value rights and resources.

Yet, like the Yakama plaintiffs and the federal prosecutors who represented them, and like all the other citizens, farmers, ranchers, and other stakeholders I wrote about who put their faith in this same legal system—and after all these years of practicing law since I completed the original dissertation—I still believe that the arc of history, and of law, "bends toward justice."[3]

A note on usages: at the time of the original study, and throughout most (but not all) of the historical records I examined, the term "Yakima" was in vogue to describe not only geography, river, basin, valley, city, and county, but also a tribe and a people. I have changed the latter human and organizational uses of the word to the more modern, accepted "Yakama" throughout, except when referring to the uses previously put (such as the Yakima Tribal Council of the time, or in the historical records, or quoting writers or speakers) and of course to the continued spelling of geographic features and political structures (such as the Yakima River or Yakima County).

There were other usages, sources, and observations that I would have preferred to update as well. But the nature of this project, included in a series of "classic dissertations" that asks the writer to preserve as much as possible the original research and structure for readers and researchers, rather than attempting to create a thoroughly revised narrative, necessarily left some such usages and terms frozen in the perspective of late twentieth century culture and scholarship. Still, themes, concepts, and relationships described in the narrative remain vital elements in contemporary resources disputes in and affecting Indian country, including the modern-day progeny of the lawsuits and legal disputes begun in the nineteenth century.

The format of the series also allowed me to include appendices, abstract, and acknowledgments from the original, and in the form I created or reported them at the time. I remain grateful today to the many people I thanked in 1990, but could not countenance expending the trees it would take to thank the people since then who have generously supported me in all my endeavors.

BARBARA LEIBHARDT WESTER

Naperville, Illinois
October 2014

---

[3] Martin Luther King, Jr., "Where do we go from here," Address to the Southern Christian Leadership Conference, August 16, 1967: "Let us realize the arc of the moral universe is long, but it bends toward justice."

ACKNOWLEDGMENTS

Many hands and hearts have helped me to write this history. My advisor, Professor Harry N. Scheiber of the Jurisprudence and Social Policy Program at the University of California, Berkeley, gave very generously of his time and expertise, and he fully encouraged me and supported my work in all respects. Professor Carolyn Merchant, of the Conservation and Resource Studies Program, University of California, Berkeley, gifted me with me her enthusiasm and conviction of the importance of "doing" environmental history, and in the process shared with me her own extensive knowledge of the field. Professor John P. Dwyer, of Boalt Hall Law School, was a supportive and critical reader of my work throughout.

Dr. John A. Bower blessed me with his love for historical research and his knowledge of Yakama history; he was a willing and critical reader of many drafts of this work. Professor Arthur F. McEvoy, currently of Northwestern University and Research Fellow at the American Bar Foundation, sowed early seeds of this project when he added me into his environmental history seminar at Northwestern; his influences on my work are both numerous and a lasting gift. Professor Donald J. Pisani, currently of Texas A&M University, generously loaned me rolls of his own microfilm research on Native American water rights correspondence and made helpful suggestions.

I was fortunate to receive support for this project from many sources. A Charlotte W. Newcombe Doctoral Dissertation Fellowship, from the Woodrow Wilson National Fellowship Foundation, made possible the luxury of an entire year of research and writing during 1989-90. I received two Humanities Graduate Research grants from the Graduate Division at the University of California, Berkeley, during 1988 and 1989, which funded research trips to Washington, D.C. and to Washington State. The Center for the Study of Law and Society, at the University of California, Berkeley, provided travel funds for a conference. Additionally, the staff at the Jurisprudence and Social Policy Program, especially Margo Rodriguez and Rod Wantanabe, provided both administrative and moral support. William Wester kindly ventured away from his particle physics research to create the map of the state of Washington that appears on the page following Abbreviations Used in the Notes.

Many librarians and archivists assisted me in locating the materials for this study. Joyce Justice, at the National Archives, Seattle Branch; and Mary I. Ronan, Donald W. Jackanicz, and Elizabeth K. Lockwood at the National Archives in Washington, D.C., all provided patient, knowledgeable assistance with the extensive Bureau of Indian Affairs records and other collections. Dianne Tufts, at the Yakima Valley Regional Library, and Agnes Tulee, at the Yakima Indian Nation Cultural Center, supplied advice about local collections.

The law library staff at Boalt Hall Law School was helpful and good humored through many queries about obscure historical legal points and documents.

I have been lucky to have many staunch supporters throughout this long process. My friends and colleagues at the Jurisprudence and Social Policy Program and at Boalt both challenged and sustained me: Carl Bauer, Gillian Dutton, Charles Lester, Martha Matthews, Roger Rabb, and especially Lucy Salyer. Victoria Saker shared with me her love of history and life, and her tremendous faith. Janie Lee was an enthusiastic and tireless listener to my research trials and treasures, and I have learned much from her. Michael Allen and Thais Winsome also offered helpful insights at various stages of my project.

My family has provided unfailing emotional, academic, and financial support. My parents blessed me with a love for nature, respect for life, and curiosity about the world which are threads woven throughout this work. William Wester has been my dearest friend, my refuge, and my companion on many hikes, and his imprint is here too.

Finally, the stories, preserved in letters, of many Yakama men and women appear in this history, and for them and for others whose stories remain alive only in the hearts of their descendents, I hope that this work helps to illuminate their rich collective history.

B.L.

Berkeley, California
October 1990

Abbreviations Used in the Notes

ABCFM	American Board of Commissioners for Foreign Missions
AG U.S.	Attorney General
AGLR	U.S. Attorney General, Letters Received, Record Group 60, Records of the Department of Justice, National Archives, Washington, D.C.
BIA	U.S. Bureau of Indian Affairs (1921-)
CIA	U.S. Commissioner of Indian Affairs (1832-)
c.f.s.	cubic feet per second
CIA-AR	U.S. Commissioner of Indian Affairs, Annual Report
CRP	Click Relander Papers; Yakima Valley Regional Library, Yakima, Washington (box:file)
DOJ	U.S. Department of Justice
DOI	U.S. Department of Interior
FS	U.S. Forest Service
HJSP	Henry J. Snively Papers, University of Washington, Library Manuscripts Division, Seattle (box:file)
NA	National Archives and Record Service, Washington, D.C.
NwARN	Northwest Anthropological Research Notes
NA-Seattle	National Archives and Record Service, Seattle Branch, Seattle, Washington
OIA	U.S. Office of Indian Affairs (1832-1921)
OIA-IIS	Office of Indian Affairs, Indian Irrigation Service (1887-)
WDG	Washington Department of Game
WDF	Washington Department of Fisheries
YTC-WS	Yakima Tribal Council, White Swan, Washington
YA	Yakima Indian Agency, Yakima, Washington

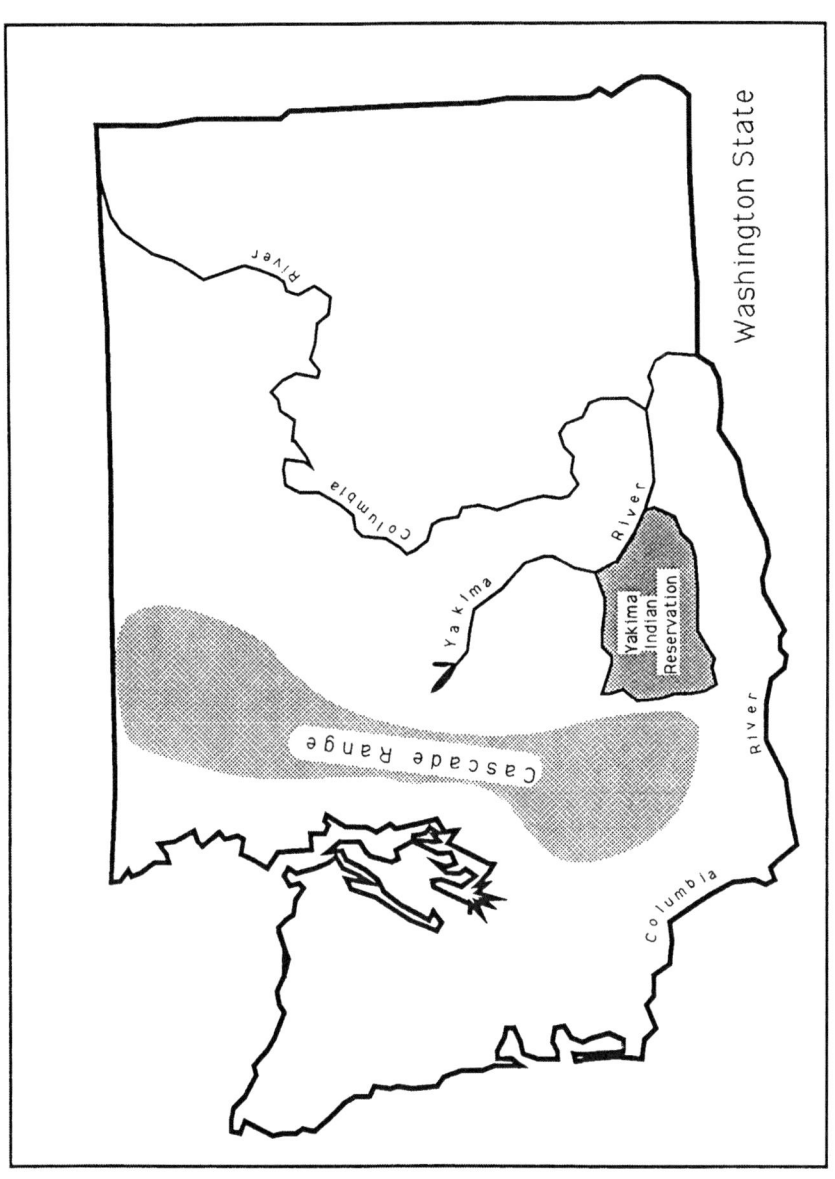

Map of the State of Washington

Land Divided by Law

1

INTRODUCTION:
INDIANS, LAW, ENVIRONMENT, AND HISTORY

> Let my people live in their own way.
> —Louis Mann (1916)[1]

The Columbia Plateau is an arid plain lying low in the shadow of the Cascade range to the east and bounded on its other side by the mountains of western Idaho. The landscape is varied. The Columbia River slices through deep basalt canyons to the sea. Beige, sage-dotted "benchlands" rise above the old lava plain. Just north of Columbia's "Big Bend," the Yakima River cuts west and then north toward the hills, creating its own canyons where its course pushes through the ridged hills of the Yakima Basin.[2] Yakama Indian peoples say that the ridges are scars left from Coyote's long ago battle with the Great Beaver God; their wrestling tore the hills apart and formed Naches Gap and Union Gap. When Coyote killed the Beaver God, he cut the different Plateau peoples from the body. Yakama came from the ribs.[3]

When Euro-Americans arrived in the Plateau around the turn of the eighteenth century, Plateau peoples remembered their light skin and foreign goods, but also that they brought a new law. Nez Perce Chief Lawyer recounted: "Those children that he [Christopher Columbus] had placed in this country among the Red people from them the blood ran on both sides. That is when the laws came into the country to these poor people."[4] Plateau peoples both feared

---

[1] Mann to Commissioner of Indian Affairs, n.d., but ca. 1916, quoted in Lucillus Virgil McWhorter, n.d., but ca. Feb. 1916, newspaper clipping in file 20332-16-115, Yakima Agency, Central Classified Files, General Records, 107-39, Bureau of Indian Affairs, National Archives, Washington, D.C. (See "Abbreviations Used in the Notes" in introductory material.)

[2] On the geography and ecology of the Columbia Plateau and the Yakima Basin, see Donald W. Meinig, *The Great Columbia Plain, A Historical Geography, 1805-1910*, The Emil and Kathleen Sick Lecture-Book Series in Western History and Biography (Seattle: University of Washington Press, 1968): 3-20; George Otis Smith, *Geology and Water Resources of a Portion of Yakima County, Wash.*, Department of the Interior, Water Supply and Irrigation Papers of the U.S. Geological Survey, no. 55 (Washington, D.C.: Government Printing Office, 1901); Morris L. Uebelacker, "Geographic Explorations in the Southern Cascades of Eastern Washington: Changing Land, People, and Resources" (Ph.D. diss., University of Oregon, 1986): 12-80ff.

[3] Yohyowan, "Legend of the Origin of the Yakimas," m.s., n.d., folder "Indians-Yakima-History," Yakima Valley Museum, Yakima, WA [hereafter YVM].

[4] Isaac Ingalls Stevens, *A True Copy of the Record of the Official Proceedings at the Council in the Walla Walla Valley 1855*, Darrell Scott, ed. (Fairfield, WA: Ye Galleon Press, 1985): 74. Lawyer explicitly referred to Columbus.

and wanted to know more of this law. Some wanted to incorporate the newcomers' exotic teachings of Christianity into their own world. Others feared that white persons and their land laws for "poor people"—such as Indians—would destroy Native societies in the relentless campaign to clear the land for settlement.

To Plateau peoples at the beginning of the nineteenth century—especially those living in the Yakima Basin—such fears remained blurred in the still-hazy future. Treaties and full-scale war with Euro-Americans were more than a half-century away. Non-indians at that time were still only visitors who came for furs, traded for food, and went away again; homesteaders would not be a permanent presence in the region until the late 1830s. Yet as increasing numbers of Euro-Americans made their way west across the Great Plains in search of riches, open land, or new beginnings, Plateau peoples recognized the threat that Euro-Americans posed to their world. At stake in the resulting inter-cultural conflict was each people's way of life. The ensuing struggle between Indians and Euro-Americans has continued into the present, and this research explores its distinctive social, legal, and ecological dimensions.

This study focuses particularly on natural resource use disputes between Euro-Americans and the Confederated Tribes and Bands of the Yakama Indian Nation during the period 1840 to 1933. The Confederated Yakama are an amalgamation of fourteen or more separate Indian groups that were resettled on the present-day Yakama Indian Reservation in south-central Washington State as a result of an 1855 treaty with the United States (see Map, reprinted in front matter). The reservation presently encompasses about 1.3 million acres, of which the federal government holds about 80 percent in trust whereas Indians and non-Indians own the other 20 percent in fee.[5] Historically, the Indian groups of the Yakima River basin relied on a broad range of resources for their well-being: fish, roots, and berries, game, and the land and water that gave life to all. This subsistence complex not only sustained life but defined the cultural identities of Indian peoples.

During the nearly 100 years covered in this study, every resource of importance to the Yakama became the subject of interracial conflict as Euro-Americans attempted to bring Indian resources into capitalist markets and marginalize or even purposefully exterminate Indian peoples. During a time when American courts denied Indians legal standing to bring suit, the Yakama continually asserted their resource claims through the courts and political forums by pressuring local, state, and federal officials to act on their behalf. Often they did not win; and when they did, officials almost invariably fashioned remedies that ensured that Yakama victories would be limited ones.

---

[5] The fourteen bands covered by the treaty were the Yakama, Palouse, Pisquouse, Wenatshapam, Wishram, Skin, Klickitat, Linquit, Kow-was-say-ce, Li-ay-was, Shyiks, Ochechotes, Kay-milt-pah, and Se-ap-cat. Treaty between the United States and Yakima Nation, 12 Stat. 951. Land holding statistics cited in *Brendale v. Confederated Tribes and Bands of Yakima Indian Nation*, 492 U.S. 408 (1989).

Introduction • 3

While the Yakama sought vindication of rights to resources because they wanted to secure the economic well-being of their culture, the American legal system functioned to deny or destroy the cultural component of resource use and to redefine economic entitlements in limited Euro-American terms of exchange.

The Importance of Legal and Environmental History

Yakama resource use conflicts involved (and today still involve) two broad, related political questions: What powers of self-determination should Indian societies have? And what is the relationship among state, federal, and tribal authority in the U.S. federal system? The legal system, however, hid those large questions by forcing resource disputes into narrowly defined categories that emphasized individual entitlements to particular resources located in a particular place and at a particular time.[6] By thus confining the controversies at issue to discrete, abstract, legal questions, judges and other federal officials perpetuated a system in which the real political issues were successfully diffused or disguised for long periods of time: Yakama claims to a tribal share of Ahtanum Creek and the Yakima River's water, for example, were adjudicated for the first time only in the 1950s and are still at issue. Similarly, Yakama claims to a tribal allocation of a percentage of the Columbia River salmon fisheries were not recognized until 1979; and in 1989 the U.S. Supreme Court denied the tribe's authority to make important on-reservation zoning decisions.[7]

Much historical work on Native American resource use and on resource use conflicts between cultures has come from the relatively new field of environmental history. Environmental historians examine the interactions over time between societies and the ecology of their habitats. Included among

---

[6] James Willard Hurst, *Law and Markets in United States History, Different Modes of Bargaining Among Interests*, The Curti Lectures, the University of Wisconsin-Madison, April 1981 (Madison: University of Madison Press, 1982): 132-41, discussing the problems that have characterized both American legal and economic organization over the nineteenth and twentieth centuries, including a narrow focus of interests, a "monetized calculus," a tendency toward incremental change, and a tendency to foster inequality among interest groups. Scholars of the Critical Legal Studies school have examined some of the ways in which law may be used to de-politicize and narrow social conflicts. See David Kairys, "Legal Reasoning," in Kairys, ed. *The Politics of Law, A Progressive Critique* (New York: Pantheon Books, 1982): 11-17; Roberto Mangabeira Unger, *Knowledge and Politics* (New York: The Free Press, 1975): 72-76ff; Peter Gabel and Paul Harris, "Building Power and Breaking Images: Critical Legal Theory and the Practice of Law, *New York University Review of Law and Social Change* 11 (1982): 372-73.

[7] The cases involving Yakama resource use rights are: for water, *United States v. Ahtanum Irr. Dist.*, 124 F. Supp. 818 (1953), *United States v. Ahtanum Irr. Dist.*, 330 F.2d 897 (9th Cir. 1964), and *Department of Ecology v. Acquavella*, 100 Wash. 2d 651 (1983); for fisheries, *Washington v. Washington State Commercial Passenger Fishing Vessel Association*, 443 U.S. 658 (1979); for zoning, *Brendale v. Confederated Yakima Indian Nation*, 492 U.S. 408 (1989).

the elements of the environmental historian's craft are a knowledge of the dynamics of ecological change and the belief that human societies both influence and are themselves influenced by the environments in which they live. Thus nature emerges from the backdrop of human history to take its place as an historical actor in its own right.[8] Consequently, human societies may be examined in light of their relations with nature, which makes environmental history a particularly well-adapted approach to the study of inter-cultural conflicts where resources are at issue.

Environmental historians still are exploring the factors relevant to human and ecological change. Past works have focused on the relationship of economics, technology, biological reproduction, ideology, religion, and ecology to the construction of human relations with nature. Law, too, is an important, component of human-ecological relations.[9] Especially in Euro-American society, people historically have used written law to shape their relations, which in turn have environmental consequences. Two examples of such legal schemes are state resource-management regimes such as fishing regulations and property laws that define individual rights to private property. Unwritten laws, or customs, also delimit human-environmental relations: for example, rules governing the inheritance of certain fishing locations or root-gathering grounds were an important Yakama Indian method for regulating access to resources. By comparing such different systems for organizing human-nature relations, historians may better understand the origins and dynamics of inter-cultural conflict.

Environmental historians argue that Native Americans lost their autonomy because Euro-Americans systematically deprived them of culturally and economically important natural resources and destroyed the ecological conditions on which their independence rested.[10] Euro-American domination of

---

[8] A sampler of environmental historiographical scholarship would include the following: Symposium, "Theories of Environmental History," *Environmental Review* 11 (Winter 1987): 251-305; Donald Worster, ed., *The Ends of the Earth: Perspectives on Modern Environmental History* (Cambridge, MA: Cambridge University Press, 1988); "A Round Table: Environmental History," *Journal of American History* 76 (1990): 1087-1147; Barbara Leibhardt, "Interpretation as an Alternative to Causal Analysis: The Use of Theories in Environmental History," *Environmental Review* 12 (1988): 23-36. See also Richard White, "Native Americans and the Environment," in W. R. Swagerty, ed., *Scholars and the Indian Experience: Critical Reviews of Recent Writing in the Social Sciences*, Bibliographical Series, D'Arcy McNickle Center for the History of the American Indian (Bloomington, IN: published for the D'Arcy McNickle Center for the History of the American Indian, Newberry Library by Indian Press, 1984): 179-204.

[9] Arthur F. McEvoy, *The Fisherman's Problem: Ecology and Law in the California Fisheries, 1850-1980* (Cambridge, MA: Cambridge University Press, 1986): 13-14; McEvoy, "Toward an Interactive Theory of Nature and Culture: Ecology, Production, and Cognition in the California Fishing Industry," *Environmental Review* 11 (1987): 289-305, esp. 289-92.

[10] See for example William Cronon, *Changes in the Land: Indians, Colonists, and the Ecology of New England* (New York: Hill and Wang, 1983); Richard White, *The Roots of Dependency:*

Native American societies has an important ecological component because political autonomy is closely related to economic self-determination.[11] Because Euro-Americans used law to structure and to regulate their relationship with Native Americans, it is important to analyze law as a component of the Euro-American effort to gain control of Native American land, resources, and lives.

Federal Indian law is not law made by Indian peoples; rather it is law constructed by Euro-Americans to control Native societies, and it has served largely to channel Indian wealth into the dominant society. During the period covered by this study, the U.S. economy was undergoing dramatic, rapid change. The period of industrialization and the changes in the legal system that accompanied it have been termed the "release of energy," signifying American society's collective commitment to encourage individuals, corporations, and governments to use their capital and creative energies to develop the continent's natural resources for both individual and public benefit.[12]

One continuing question is the degree to which minority groups were affected by or shared in this process.[13] The Yakamas' experience show that they clearly were an economically marginalized people during this period. Yet tribal members continued to struggle to control their resources; and occasionally they succeeded because they were well-organized and many of them retained a collective sense of culture, rooted in the continuing importance of subsistence

---

Subsistence, Environment, and Social Change Among the Choctaws, Pawnees, and Navajos (Lincoln, NE: University of Nebraska Press, 1983); Carolyn Merchant, *Ecological Revolutions: Nature, Gender, and Science in New England* (Chapel Hill, NC: University of North Carolina Press, 1989): 29-111.

[11] White, *The Roots of Dependency*, xv-xix; Annette Hamilton, "The Unity of Hunting-Gathering Societies: Reflections on Economic Forms and Resource Management," in Nancy M. Williams and Eugene Hunn, eds., *Resource Managers: North American and Australian Hunter Gatherers*, AAAS Selected Symposium 67 (Boulder, CO: Westview Press, 1982): 229-47.

[12] James Willard Hurst, *Law and the Conditions of Freedom in Nineteenth United States History* (Madison: University of Wisconsin Press, 1956); Harry N. Scheiber, "Property Law, Expropriation, and Resource Allocation by Government, 1789-1910," *Journal of Economic History* 33 (1973): 232-51; Harry N. Scheiber, "The Road to Munn: Eminent Domain and the Concept of Public Purpose in the State Courts," *Perspectives in American History* 5 (1971): 287-328. See also Scheiber, "At the Borderland of Law and Economic History: The Contributions of Willard Hurst," *American Historical Review* 75 (1970): 744-56.

[13] For a detailed study of how resources, particularly land, moved out of the possession of Choctaw, Chickasaw, and Creek tribes during the nineteenth century, see Mary E. Young, *Redskins, Ruffleshirts and Rednecks: Indian Allotments in Alabama and Mississippi, 1830-1860*, Civilization of the American Indian Series (Norman, OK: University of Oklahoma Press, 1961); and Angie Debo, *And Still the Waters Run: The Betrayal of the Five Civilized Tribes* (Princeton, N.J.: Princeton University Press, 1940, 1972). For a discussion and case study of the difficulties of defining "public good"—even solely among Euro-American communities, corporations, and governments—see Louis Hartz, *Economic Policy and Democratic Thought: Pennsylvania 1776-1860*, revised ed. (Cambridge, MA: The Belknap Press, 1969).

to their daily lives, which inspired their struggle against the dominant U.S. society.

During especially the period preceding 1934 and the Indian's "New Deal" in the Indian Reorganization Act, federal policies sought to destroy the tribal organization and cultural integrity of Native peoples.[14] One legal scholar has noted that Indian law may be characterized by its duality: At times the law has viewed Indians as sovereign nations and at other times it has treated Indians as dependent wards of the State.[15] Indian tribes have power to define membership and have jurisdiction to regulate and sanction the activities of members. Tribes, however, still do not have autonomy over their land base, natural resources belonging to the tribe, or many off-reservation activities in which members participate.[16] The duality disappears if we look at federal Indian law as law that Native peoples did not write for themselves. In every important aspect of interaction between Native peoples and Euro-Americans, Euro-Americans have controlled the terms of the relationship.

Historically, Euro-Americans have viewed law as their chief means of bringing Native peoples and their resources under Euro-American control. Not only did Euro-Americans use law to legitimate their domination of Native societies, law became the primary medium which governed relations between the two cultures.[17] As Native peoples were forced to express their economic and political claims through the U.S. legal system, they came to speak in a language that was not their own and one that was not designed to acknowledge or protect the culturally distinct nature of their demands. Common property rights to land, or resource use rights that changed from season to season or year to year were difficult protect under laws that valued rights that were well-defined in time and space. Moreover, for most of the period examined here,

---

[14] This is the first episode in which U.S. Indian policy actively sought to "assimilate" the tribes. Between 1943 and 1961, the federal government embarked on another campaign to "terminate" tribes. See generally, Felix S. Cohen, *Handbook of Federal Indian Law,* 1982 ed. (Charlottesville, VA: The Michie Co., 1982): 47-206; Robert A. Williams, Jr., "Documents of Barbarism: The Contemporary Legacy of European Racism and Colonialism in the Narrative Traditions of Federal Indian Law," *Arizona Law Review* 31 (1989): 237-78; Williams, The *American Indian in Western Legal Thought: The Discourses of Conquest* (New York: Oxford University Press, 1990).

[15] Charles F. Wilkinson, *American Indians, Time, and the Law: Native Societies in a Modern Constitutional Democracy* (New Haven: Yale University Press, 1987): 13ff; Wilkinson terms the two conflicting policies separatism and assimilation.

[16] See generally Cohen, *Handbook of Federal Indian Law.* See also Vine Deloria, Jr. and Clifford Lytle, *The Nations Within: The Past and Future of American Indian Sovereignty* (New York: Pantheon Books, 1984), for a discussion of the issue of Native sovereignty and a history of Native American attempts to gain political freedom and the right to self-determination in the United States. Russel Lawrence Barsh and James Youngblood Henderson cover some of the same history in their study, *The Road: Indian Tribes and Political Liberty* (Berkeley: University of California Press, 1980).

[17] Williams, *American Indian in Western Legal Thought,* 6-8.

legislators shaped law expressly to destroy tribally based methods of resource use. Yet, despite all this, the law proved to be an imperfect instrument for achieving Euro-American domination of Native peoples.

The Yakama Nation's experience illuminates how this Tribe empowered themselves through their legal and political struggles: first, because Yakama plaintiffs occasionally won their suits; and second, because rights recognized by the courts or legislature created new bases for taking action.[18] Yakama throughout the period continued to assert their 1855 treaty with the United States as the basis for all their natural resource claims, and kept the terms of the treaty alive in political disputes over their entitlements where state and federal officials often seemed very willing to forget them altogether. A focus on law in Native American lives thus reveals the active (as opposed to passive) role of Native peoples in shaping their own histories and shows that culture can survive economic dependence.

Native Americans as Actors in History

Historians of Native American and Euro-American conflict must strive to avoid treating Native Americans as passive objects and instead to view them as historical subjects and actors, much as environmental historians work to treat nature as an active force in historical change.[19] The best legal scholarship in the past has focused on the actions of both Euro-Americans and Native Americans in developing methods of sharing land and other natural resources over time.[20]

---

[18] See, e.g., Gabel and Harris, "Building Power," 387; Diane Polan, "Toward a Theory of Law and Patriarchy," in Kairys, ed., *The Politics of Law*, 299-300, noting that an oppressed group that comes to see the legal system as an effective arena in which to obtain relief is at risk of supporting—or at least tacitly approving—the very system that oppresses it. On the development of nationalist movements generally among Native peoples in the Columbia Basin, see Jeffery C. Reichwein, "Native American Response to Euro-American Contact in the Columbia Plateau of Northwestern North America, 1840-1914: An Anthropological Interpretation Based on Written and Pictorial Ethnohistorical Data" (Ph.D. diss., Ohio State University, 1988).

[19] Although a society's economy may become dependent upon the larger, dominant society, members of the society may retain particular cultural traits that continue to structure their behavior and values, as the example of Yakama interaction with Euro-American society indicates. By including Native Americans in our histories only up to the point at which they become economically dependent upon the dominant society, however, we reinforce the notion that those people could make no meaningful contributions to their own or Euro-American history after a point at which they apparently lost the ability to control their economies. For example, White, in *Roots of Dependency*, examines the pre-and post-Euro-American contact histories of the Choctaws, Pawnees, and Navajos and concludes each group's history respectively: "The Collapse of the Traditional Economy," "The Pawnee Decline," and "The Navajos Become Dependent"—and after which his historical interest ends. Cronon and Merchant each end their discussion of Native Americans after the "transition" [Cronon] or "transformation" [Merchant] from subsistence to capitalist economy in the region was complete. See Cronon, *Changes in the Land*, 159-70; Merchant, *Ecological Revolutions*, 108-11.

[20] For studies of Native American legal systems and societies, see Karl N. Llewellyn and E. Adamson Hoebel, *The Cheyenne Way: Conflict and Case Law in Primitive Jurisprudence*

Such scholarship avoids the mistake of portraying Native Americans as passive objects of congressional Indian policy or the decisions of the U.S. Supreme Court. Still, detailed studies of the day-to-day relevance of law to Native American lives are scarce, and consequently we still have much to learn about how Native Americans themselves historically experienced the American legal system.[21]

Historians of inter-cultural conflict must, wherever possible, allow peoples of both cultures to speak and be heard in their own voices. Louis Mann, a Yakama who lived on the reservation in the early nineteenth century, tirelessly petitioned federal and state officials to "Let my people live in their own way."[22] Although it is difficult to document the experiences of Native peoples, many of whom did not leave written records, rich historical materials may be found in oral interviews, myths, and documents written by Native peoples in their own or other languages. Yakama peoples, some of whom were English-literate, for example, have left a detailed written record of their experiences.[23] Anthropologists who have studied Native cultures of the Columbia Plateau, and the Yakama in particular, have produced accounts of the rituals, stories, and material cultures of these peoples.[24] Environmental historians find additional source materials bearing on a culture's resource use by "reading" a landscape over time and tracing the roots of the present patterns of human occupation in a particular place.

(Norman: University of Oklahoma Press, 1941); John Phillip Reid, *A Better Kind of Hatchet: Law, Trade, and Diplomacy in the Cherokee Nation During the Early Years of European Contact* (University Park: Pennsylvania State University Press, 1976); Reid, *A Law of Blood: The Primitive Law of the Cherokee Nation* (New York: New York University Press, 1970); Rennard Strickland, *Fire and the Spirits: Cherokee Law from Clan to Court* (Norman: University of Oklahoma Press, 1975). For excellent case studies of Euro-American and Native American interactions over land use during the nineteenth century, see Young, *Rednecks and Ruffleshirts*, and Debo, *And Still the Waters Run*.

[21] Frederick E. Hoxie, "Towards a 'New' North American Indian Legal History," *American Journal of Legal History* 30 (1986): 351-57. See also Rennard Strickland, "Genocide-at-Law: An Historic and Contemporary View of the Native American Experience," *University of Kansas Law Review* 34 (1986): 713-55; Vine Deloria, Jr. and Clifford M. Lytle, *American Indians, American Justice* (Austin: University of Texas Press, 1983).

[22] Mann to Commissioner, ca. Feb. 1916; see this chapter's introductory inscription.

[23] The voices of many others have been preserved in written transcripts taken as part of the discovery process in late nineteenth and twentieth century litigation over water and fishing rights. It is certainly necessary to take into account the fact that literate Native Americans during the time were educated in government schools and may not have shared the same values or motivations as those who were not sent away to school.

[24] Anthropological studies have their own limitations as well. For a general discussion of methods and problems encountered by anthropologists, see Clifford Geertz, *The Interpretation of Cultures: Selected Essays* (New York: Basic Books, Inc., 1973); Geertz, *Local Knowledge: Further Essays in Interpretive Anthropology* (New York: Basic Books, Inc., 1983).

Over the course of the nineteenth and early twentieth centuries, Yakama, as well as other Plateau peoples, came to share the resources of the Columbia River Basin with Euro-Americans. This study examines the ways in which the two groups together worked out the structure of their use "in common" of many important Basin resources.[25] Although during the period Euro-Americans came to dominate many aspects of Yakama life, the tribe actively sought to retain control over important subsistence resources, including land, water, fish, and roots and berries.

The first part of this study focuses on the different ways in which Native Plateau peoples, including the Yakama, and Euro-American settlers to the Plateau region organized their relationships to land. Both cultures believed that their own relationship to the land was divinely ordained, and as the two groups came into sustained contact, it was the Euro-American notion of individual rights in private property that took precedence over the Plateau peoples' less rigidly defined concept of individual entitlements to communally-held rights of access and use. The 1855 treaty between the Yakama peoples and the U.S. government, with its provisions for dividing tribal lands into individually owned holdings set the stage for later federal legislation that attempted to transform Native peoples into yeoman farmers, after the Jeffersonian ideal. Yakama sought to use federal land laws to maintain as much control over tribal property as possible, and occasionally they met with success.

The second part of this study concerns the conflict between Yakama peoples, now largely confined to their reservation, and neighboring settlers over control of the waters of the Yakima River Basin. Yakama farmers, just as their Euro-American counterparts, required water to irrigate their lands if they were to grow crops. Federal reclamation policies, however, consistently favored non-Indian farmers at the expense of Indians. Yakama were well-aware of the injustice of these policies and sought to increase their share of water from rivers bordering the reservation. Despite their efforts, Yakama farmers throughout the period maintained smaller, less water-intensive operations that produced less valuable crops, and many tribal members continued to supplement their diets and incomes with more traditional subsistence resources such as fish, game, and roots and berries.

The third, and final, part of this study examines the ways in which Euro-Americans increasingly encroached on the salmon fisheries, hunting grounds, and berry- and root-gathering grounds of Yakama peoples, and how Yakama sought to maintain access to these resources through the courts and by lobbying state and federal officials. Yakama successfully won access to historic fishing sites along the Columbia River and tried to apply their entitlements of access, to off-reservation resources to hunting game beyond the reservation border as well.

---

[25] Treaty with the Yakima, 12 Stat. 951, art 3.

This study assumes that because the use of particular resources was an important part of the Yakama Nation's tribal definition, we can understand how federal, state, and tribal governments worked out the meaning of Native sovereignty by examining how well Yakama were able to protect access to those resources. The resources that the Yakama depended upon for their subsistence had more than economic importance: Subsistence provided nourishment, but it also formed the frame within which tribal members wove every aspect of their lives. Seasonal journeys, religious ritual, personal and communal relationships obtained significance and definition because they connected social life with that of-non-human nature.[26] Even as Euro-American political and economic institutions came to dominate Yakama life, many tribal members continued to assert the importance of subsistence to personal and cultural identity.

Subsistence was not a monolithic or static institution. During the period of this study, Yakama life changed in many profound ways. U.S. government officials increasingly attempted to confine tribal members to the reservation, curtailing annual subsistence journeys even as encroachment of non-Indians into the region made ever scarcer the resources necessary to sustain the older way of life. Some Yakama took up farming, under the pressured guidance of federal officials eager to set Indians on an agricultural path. Many more became sharecroppers and day laborers, working in Washington's hop fields and orchards. Even thus tied to the market, many Yakama hungered for subsistence. Fish, berries, and game tasted better than "white" foods and provided medicine for weary souls, and access to subsistence meant freedom—no matter how small a measure of it—from Euro-American control.

A contemporary Yakama Washat, or Long House religion, prayer teaches:

> Earth's body is everlasting;
> Earth's heart is everlasting;
> There is everlasting life and breath in earth.[27]

The song acknowledges the spirit infusing the earth and all life upon it, a spirit that binds humans and nature together just as it binds the past and future to the present. The Washat song represents not the unchanging nature of Yakama society but a continuity between past and present, a sense of history.

Subsistence practices changed during the period from 1840 to 1933; and Yakama society changed as well. Yet a particular tie between these peoples and the place in which they live connects the present to the past. Today, Yakama

---

[26] Morris L. Uebelacker, *Time Ball: A Story of the Yakima People and the Land* (Toppenish, WA: Yakima Indian Nation, 1984); Sue Whalen, "The Nez Perces' Relationship to their Land," *The Indian Historian* 2d ser., 4 (1971): 30-33.

[27] Helen Hersh Schuster, "Yakima Indian Traditionalism: A Study in Continuity and Change" (Ph.D. diss., University of Washington, 1975): 418.

often symbolize this connection in their sacramental treatment of key subsistence resources such as water, salmon, and certain roots. We may think of this link between humans and nature as a distinct and collective consciousness of place, a consciousness that largely was absent from the Euro-Americans' view of the world. Although American law was instrumental in undermining this particular collective consciousness, it ultimately failed to destroy it.

I

**EARTH'S BODY:
LAND**

2

SACRED BUNDLES

> Speak straight, I have ears to hear you and here is my heart. Suppose you show me goods, shall I run up and take them? That is the way we are, we Indians, as you know us. Goods and the Earth are not equal; goods are for using on the earth. I do not know where they have given lands for goods.
> —Cayuse Chief Five Crows (1855)[1]

Native people inhabited the Columbia Plateau long before Euro-Americans arrived there. During the time before contact between the cultures, there was no single "traditional" pattern of settlement or subsistence. Rather, people constantly adapted to and actively modified the world around them. Plateau peoples, including the Yakama, understood their place in the world through the stories and myths they passed down to their children and through religious beliefs that showed the complex connections between humans and nature. Native economies, based on gathering, fishing, hunting, trading, and occasionally gardening, made manifest these beliefs in the world. Similarly, Euro-Americans perceived their place in the world through particular beliefs about their race, their culture, and their Judeo-Christian religion. They organized their economies and society to reflect those beliefs, thereby setting into motion a very different set of relations to nature than Native Plateau peoples historically had practiced in the area.

One way to understand the changes generated by the initial encounter of these two cultures is to look at the "sacred symbols" employed by each, for these symbols embody "the picture they have of the way things in sheer actuality are, their most comprehensive ideas of order."[2] For both Plateau peoples and Euro-Americans a "sacred bundle" was such a symbol. Through that symbol we may better understand each culture's attitudes toward society and nature.

---

[1] Quoted in Isaac Ingalls Stevens, *A True Copy of the Record of the Official Proceedings at the Council in the Walla Walla Valley, 1855*, ed. by Darrell Scott (Fairfield, WA: Ye Galleon Press, 1985): 57.

[2] Cultures, according to Clifford Geertz, are "socially established structures of meaning." *The Interpretation of Cultures: Selected Essays* (New York: Basic Books, 1977): 12-15. On Sacred Symbols, see ibid., 89-90; 126-41. "In religious belief and practice," for example, Geertz writes, "a group's ethos is rendered intellectually reasonable by being shown to represent a way of life ideally adapted to the actual state of affairs the world view describes, while the world view is rendered emotionally convincing by being presented as an image of an actual state of affairs peculiarly well-arranged to accommodate such a way of life," ibid., 89-90.

Native Plateau dwellers, like many other Native American groups, sanctified a bundle of magical objects given to each individual by a guardian spirit drawn from the natural world.[3] Each person possessed a different bundle, and each bundle contained objects that helped to define the role of that individual in the larger society, as well as that person's relationships to the natural and spiritual worlds. A person who accepted the gifts of a spirit partner obtained certain privileged relationships to nature—being a skilled hunter, for example—and had obligations to behave in certain ways. To act irresponsibly was to violate one's duty to both community and nature.

Euro-Americans, too, understood their relationship to the world in terms of a sacred bundle, that of individual rights in property. Private property, as John Locke noted, was that mechanism by which individuals withdrew natural resources, among other things, from the commons so "that another can no longer have any right to it."[4] God had expressly sanctioned humans to take from the common share and to control nature. The bundle of property contained the different rights and privileges obtained by its holder. If the owners of those sacred bundles fashioned from their property useful products and profit, then according to Locke's vision, society would prosper.

Just as the Native American sacred bundle contained the tenets for the proper human relationship to both persons and nature, so did that of private property. Over the course of the nineteenth century, both versions of the sacred bundle coexisted on the Plateau at times and at times even overlapped at their margins. The early conflict between these two symbols set the stage for the treaties of the 1850s between Plateau societies and the United States. In those agreements, Euro-Americans forcibly imposed their own sacred bundle on Native peoples.

The *Wyakin*'s Gift

The earliest human Plateau inhabitants drew upon a wide variety of resources including and especially those of the region's rivers.[5] Over time, people

---

[3] See for example Clark Wissler, "Ceremonial Bundles of the Blackfoot Indians," American Museum of Natural History, *Anthropological Papers* 7, pt. 2 (1912): 71-104.

[4] John Locke, *The Second Treatise of Government*, 1690, Thomas P. Peardon, ed. (New York: Macmillan Publishing Company, 1952): 17.

[5] This early pattern was termed the "Northern Forest Culture" pattern, a living style that incorporated adaptations to sub-arctic, coastal, and desert areas, all of which are found in that region. E. S. Lohse and D. Sammons-Lohse, "Sedentism on the Columbia Plateau: A Matter of Degree Related to the Easy and Efficient Procurement of Resources," *Northwest Anthropological Research Notes (NwARN)*, v. 20 (Fall 1986): 115-136; Christopher Miller, *Prophetic Worlds, Indians and Whites on the Columbia Plateau* (New Brunswick, NJ: Rutgers University Press, 1985): 10; David Sanger, "Development of the Pacific Northwest Culture Area, Historical and Environmental Considerations," in *Contributions to Anthropology, Ecological Essays*, National Museum, Canada, Bulletin, 230 (Ottawa: Queen's Printer, 1969): 15-23.

adopted specialized subsistence patterns oriented to the different, major ecological areas: coastal, plateau, and desert. This diversification was complete by about 1300 A.D.[6] Within the emergent subcultures, groups further developed adaptations to the particular resources of their local homelands. That strategy necessitated inter-group sharing and trading of local produce and manufactured goods, as well as a highly mobile style of subsistence. When feral Spanish horses made their way northward in the early 1700s, people readily adopted them into their burgeoning trade network.[7] An individual could travel up to seventy miles per day on horseback; consequently, Plateau peoples developed extensive trade, resource sharing, and communication routes to Native groups on the coast and the Great Plains.[8]

Plateau peoples did not view land as divisible into individual, alienable entitlements, but these peoples did organize their territories and use of resources through distinct village- or family-based rights; a system we may term "possessive communitarianism."[9] Each village held "permanent vested rights of ownership regardless of temporary absence, use, or disuse" in its territory.[10] Other groups who wanted to use a village's root grounds or a family's fishing site would have to ask formal permission to obtain access. As long as resources remained plentiful, such permission was seldom refused. During the late nineteenth century, however, as Euro-American commercial fishing increasingly encroached on traditional Yakama fishing sites, for example, intra-tribal conflict over these inherited locations was not unusual.[11]

Although Plateau peoples generally recognized communal property in land and sometimes individual entitlements to specific resource sites, such rights apparently were not bartered or sold. Nor do people appear to have held equally well defined entitlements to every resource. While families may have controlled fishing at specific, inheritable sites such as particular rocks or cliffs

---

[6] Verne Ray, *Cultural Relations in the Plateau of Northwestern America*, Series Publications of the Frederick Webb Hodge Annual Publication Fund, v. 3 (Los Angeles: The South Western Museum, 1939): 3; Sanger, "Development of the Pacific Northwest Culture Area," 15-23.

[7] Francis Haines, "The Northward Spread of Horses Among the Plains Indians," *American Anthropologist* 40, n.s. (1938): 429-37.

[8] Angelo Anastasio, "The Southern Plateau: An Ecological Analysis of Intergroup Relations," *NwARN* 6 (1972): 127-28; Eugene S. Hunn, "Mobility as a Factor Limiting Resource Use in the Columbia Plateau of North America," in Nancy M. Williams and Hunn, eds., *Resource Managers: North American and Australian Hunter-Gatherers*, AAAS Selected Symposium 67 (Boulder, CO: Westview Press, 1982): 23-33.

[9] This term was suggested by Harry N. Scheiber, and is a play on the term "possessive individualism" used by C. B. Macpherson. See Macpherson, *The Political Theory of Possessive Individualism: Hobbes to Locke* (New York: Oxford University Press, 1962).

[10] Anastasio, "Southern Plateau," 189.

[11] Click Relander describes one ancient dispute over gear and location in *Drummers and Dreamers* (Caldwell, ID: The Caxton Printers, 1956): 25, 308. For intra-tribal disputes over inherited fishing locations during the 1920s, see Chapter 8 below.

along the rivers, rights to use other resources, such as soda springs and berry and root grounds, were held for common use by a village.[12] Because different village groups controlled specific regions and resource sites, Plateau peoples necessarily developed well defined arrangements for sharing resources among groups travelling over the Plateau during the course of their annual subsistence migration.

By the nineteenth century, Plateau peoples shared generally a subsistence pattern in which people wintered in centralized villages, usually located in river valleys, and spent the rest of the year travelling to collect subsistence resources.[13] Temperature, precipitation, and the unique characteristics of different ecosystems that make up the Plateau landscape all shaped the timing and yield of annual subsistence cycles. Consequently, no one group strictly repeated its pattern from year to year, nor would any two groups share exactly the same pattern. Winters were often harsh, and there were many hungry times in which people relied upon the hospitality of their neighbors and kin or starved. On the Plateau, flexibility and sharing were of key importance.[14]

The subsistence year generally began in early spring and included both plant and root gathering, fishing, and hunting. In mid-February, women

---

[12] On inherited fishing locations, see Agent Evan Estep to Commissioner of Indian Affairs (CIA), June 9, 1924, file 39001-24-115, Yakima Agency, Central Classified Files, General Records, 1907-39, Records of the Bureau of Indian Affairs, Record Group 75, National Archives, Washington, D.C. [hereafter cited as YA, CCF, GR, BIA, RG 75, NA-branch]. See also testimony of Moses Strong, in *U.S. v. Winans*, Transcript of Record, Testimony and Final Report of Examiner, enclosed in Attorney General to Clerk of the Supreme Court, Jan. 21, 1904, Appellate Case File no. 19213, Records of the Supreme Court, RG 267, NA, p. 112; testimony of Louis Simpson, ibid., 131, noting that "See-we-pam and Wisham [fisheries] are together and it belonged to me personally my father was chief"; testimony of Charley Colwash, ibid., 138; testimony of Bill Charley, ibid., 162; Deward E. Walker, Jr. "Mutual Cross-Utilization of Economic Resources in the Plateau: An Example from Aboriginal Nez Perce Fishing Practices," Washington State University, Laboratory of Anthropology, *Report of Investigations*, no. 41 (1967): 15-39; Schuster, "Yakima Indian Traditionalism," 85, noting Yakama held reciprocal rights to fish at the Wenatshapam fishery, owned by the Wenatchee band of Yakama. On communal sharing of springs, see Chapter 6; on sharing of root and berry grounds, see Chapter 9.

[13] Plateau peoples can be divided according to which of the area's two major linguistic groups they belonged. In general, Salish-speakers lived in the northern part of the Plateau, while the Sahaptin-speakers inhabited the southern part, but within each grouping smaller sub-groups took up their own dialects which often were unintelligible to the others. Two other language groups of lesser importance on the Plateau were Chinook and Cayuse speakers, whose language was a derivative of the Penutian stock. The linguistic boundary roughly coincided with distinctions in the material culture of Plateau Peoples: Salish-speakers tended to be coast-oriented, while Sahaptin-speakers were peoples of the interior plains. Ray, "Native Villages and Groupings," 107; Melville Jacobs, "A Sketch of Northern Sahaptin Grammar," in *University of Washington Publications in Anthropology* 4 (2) (1931): 93-6; Anastasio, "Southern Plateau," 112; Jacobs, "Historic Perspectives in Indian Languages of Oregon and Washington," *Pacific Northwest Quarterly* 28 (1937): 55-74.

[14] Anastasio, "Southern Plateau," 123; Hunn, "Mobility as a Factor," 23-36.

collected the first fresh plants, including several species of lomatium, or "Indian celery." Women used lomatium for its greens and fresh and dried roots. They also made it into insect repellents, fish stupefacient, and medicines.[15] Women added bitterroot, another storable plant, to their collection baskets by mid-April. In late summer and early fall, depending upon elevation, women also collected and dug many other plants, including balsamroot, yellowbells, onions, camas, carrots, and Indian potatoes.[16]

Native fishing on the Plateau was highly developed, and people utilized resident riverine species as well as anadromous salmon that appeared annually. Suckers arrived in the rivers in spring, before salmon, and they often provided badly needed food. Salmon fishing began as early as May, with the most intense fishing in July, as many families gathered at the Columbia and its tributaries to share in the harvest. At these camps, men fished while women processed and preserved the catch for the coming months. Summer fairs and sporting events also brought large numbers of people to such centralized locations on the Columbia River as The Dalles and Celilo Falls, for trading and socializing.[17]

By August, with the year's fish supplies laid in, families left river valleys for the uplands where women gathered several different varieties of berries and nuts, and men hunted game. From as early as June and through August or September, berries and other plants could be collected in the higher elevations of the Cascade berry fields. Those berries were eaten fresh or dried over slow-burning fires. Women also collected pine nuts, beargrass, white pine, and medicinal plants at this time.[18] While women collected, men hunted large game such as mountain goat, elk, deer, and bighorn sheep. Meat from those hunting expeditions was stored, while the skins provided the raw materials for blankets, clothing, gloves and moccasins, as well as other household and trade goods.[19] With the advent of winter, families returned to their winter villages.

In winter, people drew upon the stores of the previous year, and prepared the tools needed for the next year's harvests. Occasionally, men went on short hunting expeditions for small game such as rabbit, squirrel, beaver, muskrat,

---

[15] Morris L. Uebelacker, "Geographic Explorations in the Southern Cascades of Eastern Washington: Changing Land, People, and Resources" (Ph.D. diss., University of Oregon, 1986): 121; Eugene S. Hunn and D. H. French, "Lomatium: A Key Resource for Columbia Plateau Native Subsistence," *Northwest Science* 55 (1981): 87-94; Hunn, "Mobility," 27-29.

[16] Uebelacker, "Geographic Explorations," 121-3; Hunn, "Mobility as a Factor," 29; Anastasio, "Southern Plateau," 119-20.

[17] Anastasio, "Southern Plateau," 159; Walker, "Mutual Cross-utilization of Economic Resources," 17.

[18] Uebelacker, "Geographic Explorations," 126-27; Hunn, "Mobility as a Factor," 32-33.

[19] Uebelacker, "Geographic Explorations," 161. See also Eugene Hunn, "On the Relative Contribution of Men and Women to Subsistence Among Hunter-Gatherers of the Columbia Plateau: A Comparison with *Ethnographic Atlas* Summaries," *Journal of Ethnobiology* 1 (1981): 124-34.

fox, ruffled grouse, sage hen, geese, and duck; and they took some fish including steelhead trout, whitefish, sucker, and river mussels.[20] But winter hunting was unpredictable and often yielded little.

Winter provided the only time during which Plateau people allowed storytelling—one method by which children were educated and socialized into the culture.[21] Winter was also the time for the Winter Dance complex, a festival celebrating the acquisition of spirit partners by individual members of various groups.[22] Every Plateau group possessed some belief in guardian spirits, or spirit partners.[23] The spirit partner and its gifts to its human host functioned as powerful symbols through which people understood both their own place in the social network and their role in the larger natural and spirit world around them.

By the beginning of the early nineteenth century, long-term inter-group cooperation and sharing had resulted in a "task group" system, whereby different village groups jointly could organize resource use among their various territories.[24] The task group system allowed people from many village groups to organize and share subsistence and social tasks that required regional cooperation. Such tasks included fishing, berrying, trading, celebrating, gambling, participating in sporting events, and holding councils.[25]

---

[20] Uebelacker, "Geographic Explorations," 157-58.

[21] Jarold Ramsey, ed., *Coyote Was Going There: Indian Literature of the Oregon Country* (Seattle: University of Washington Press, 1977): xxv-xxvii, xxix; Leslie Spier and Edward Sapir, "Wishram Ethnography," *University of Washington Publications in Anthropology* 3 (1930): 257.

[22] Anastasio, "Southern Plateau," 138-39; H. G. Barnett, *The Yakima Indians in 1942*, Mimeograph (Eugene: OR, University of Oregon, 1942): 1-2; Uebelacker, "Geographic Explorations," 151-161; Ray, "Cultural Relations," 102-31.

[23] In some groups all men and some women had such powers (the Sanpoil, Nez Perce, Umatilla, and Kittitas, for example); sometimes only men (the Thompson River Indians); and sometimes only a select group (the Kwakiutl). Ruth F. Benedict, "The Concept of the Guardian Spirit in North America," American Anthropological Association *Memoirs* no. 29 (1923): 10-13; Verne F. Ray, "The Sanpoil and Nespelem: Salishan Peoples of Northeast Washington," *University of Washington Publications in Anthropology* 5 (1932): 182; Ray, "Cultural Relations," 68-75, describing the different styles of the Guardian Spirit concept, and 124, "Table 2. Areal Distribution of Typical Aspects of Plateau Religious Life."

[24] Walker, "Mutual Cross-Utilization," 39; Hunn, "Mobility as a Factor Limiting Resource Use," 33-34.

[25] Anastasio, "Southern Plateau," 139, 156-64ff; Walker, "Mutual Cross-Utilization," 13-14, 26, 39. The system was very flexible; groups coalesced according relationships individuals had formed through intermarriage, trade relationships, or travel. Participation in work sharing varied depending upon the activity involved and location, as well as the personal relationships among villagers in many groups. Peoples who participated in the task group system included Cayuse, Umatilla, Wayam, Wasco, Wishram, Klickitat, Yakama, Wallawalla, Nez Perce, Palouse, Kittitas, Columbia, Flathead, Coeur d'Alene, Wenatchi, Chelan, Spokane, Sanpoil, Methow, Nespelem, Kalispel, Sinkaietk, and Colville. Anastasio, "Southern Plateau," defines the shifting patterns of task grouping for various activities; Schuster, "Yakima Indian

The role each Plateau inhabitant took in the community's subsistence life, and the larger task group system was defined by trade and kinship relations, and also by the unique spiritual powers the individual possessed by virtue of his or her spirit partner. Power that flowed from the spirit partner relationship endowed each person with special skills and talents necessary for the group to function. A man might be a successful warrior, leader, hunter, fisher, or gambler; a woman might be an adept gatherer, basket weaver, or occasionally a fisher or warrior. Both men and women might have abilities for healing or telling stories. Individuals honed their skills through long practice and by taking care to observe the particular taboos and other rules surrounding the use of spirit power.[26]

The catalogue of spirit partners and their respective powers was as varied as the world in which Plateau peoples lived. Since all of nature, including humans, was infused with spiritual power, virtually anything might give spirit power. A grizzly bear, or buffalo bull, for example, endowed its recipient with strength in war; thunder or lightning gave "terrible potency in battle"; deer gave fleetness of foot; the wolf gave excellence in hunting and battle; a rock-wren gave powers to handle rattlesnakes; and a cloud gave the ability to bring rain. "The life in trees, in grass, might compose your power," as well, according to Yellow Wolf, a Nez Perce warrior.[27] A mallard duck gave the power to bring the Chinook wind, or warm spring wind, to a disabled girl, for example. Other powers included skill in midwifery, curing supernatural illnesses, and working in burial grounds.[28] A person might possess more than one spirit partner.

Yellow Wolf recounted his own early nineteenth century, experience with his spirit partner. As a child he was tutored by an older man in the skills of hunting and battle. At around the time of puberty, he went on a vision quest during which he fasted and prayed in solitude.[29] One had to stay focused on the object of the quest, and after a time the candidate fell "into a comatose state of mind." It was then that the guardian spirit, or *wyakin*, would reveal itself;

Traditionalism," 97-98. See also Alan G. Marshall, "Nez Perce Social Groups: An Ecological Interpretation" (Ph.D. diss., Washington State University, 1977).

[26] Anastasio, "Southern Plateau," 177-78; Helen Hersh Schuster, "Yakima Indian Traditionalism: A Study in Continuity and Change" (Ph.D. diss., University of Washington, 1975): 53-58.

[27] Benedict, "Guardian Spirit," at 11; Lucillus Virgil McWhorter, *Yellow Wolf: His Own Story* (Caldwell: ID, Caxton Press, 1940): 296-99; Ray, "Sanpoil and Nespelem," 183. The Nez Perce were a politically distinct Plateau group, but shared many cultural traits with other Plateau groups, including the Yakama.

[28] Ray, "Sanpoil and Nespelem," 184; Schuster, "Yakima Traditionalism," 114-15.

[29] Certain places had special spiritual significance for those seeking visions. Yakama boys and girls went to Saddle Mountain, for example. Charles "Click" Relander (Now Tow Look), *Drummers and Dreamers: The Story of Smohalla the Prophet and his Nephew Puck Hyah Toot...*, With a foreword by Frederick Webb Hodge (Caldwell, ID: The Caxton Printers, 1956): 40; Schuster, "Yakima Traditionalism," 156, describes Yakama guardian spirit shrines in the mountains.

"sometimes merely as a voice, or at other times as a recognizable apparition."[30] Yellow Wolf's *wyakin* was a wolf, who made him a "great hunter, a sure scout."

The *wyakin* gave its chosen individual a spirit song, and often one or more sacred objects that were known as "sacred bundles" because when not in use they were kept safely wrapped in a cloth or bag. Each song and bundle were unique. While two or more people might have an elk as their spirit partner, for example, they would have different relationships with their guardians. Yellow Wolf's wolf spirit, for example, instructed him in making a war club and war whistle that aided him in battle. In the Alsea legend of "The Magic Hazel Twig," the eyes, ears, nose, and sinews of an elk, given to a boy and stored in his quiver, became a powerful tool in helping him escape from a deserted island.[31]

Those who accepted the gifts of the *wyakin* had to take care to obey the conditions upon which the spirit power was given. One had the responsibility of exercising the power for good only; to use the power for evil would make one vulnerable to someone with stronger powers. One also could not use the power recklessly. In the Wasco legend, "The Elk, the Hunter, and His Greedy Father," a man is tricked by his father into using his hunting powers wastefully. After slaying five herds of elk, he falls into a dream in which the elk, his spirit partner, admonishes him and tells him he will leave him. When the spirit leaves, the man dies.[32] To disobey a spirit's instructions and misuse the power could cause illness or death. If a spirit had instructed a man not to let sacred feathers touch the ground and someone accidentally brushed them to the floor, the man would suffer. Additionally, in order for the power to be effective, one had to use it while consciously calling the spirit to mind.[33]

As practiced by some groups, including the Yakama, a person might not remember his or her *wyakin* until after he or she was mature. In other groups, the child would retain a complete memory of his or her *wyakin*.[34] The relationship between an individual and his or her *wyakin* evolved over time: A person might receive further spiritual guardians or the kinds of powers that a *wyakin* bestowed on an individual could change as the person became older.[35]

Among Southern Plateau peoples, including the Yakama, medicine men and women traditionally tended to control both curing and the guardian spirit complex, a pattern that did not change until Euro-American disease epidemics

---

[30] McWhorter, *Yellow Wolf*, 296-98.

[31] McWhorter, *Yellow Wolf*, 300-03; "The Magic Hazel Twig," in Ramsey, *Coyote Was Going There*, 153-56; Ray, "Cultural Relations," 187-88, describing special sticks made after securing a spirit partner; see also Wissler, "Ceremonial Bundles of the Blackfoot Indians."

[32] Ramsey, *Coyote Was Going There*, 64-5. See also Ray, "Sanpoil and Nespelem," 188.

[33] Ray, "Sanpoil and Nespelem," 188; McWhorter, *Yellow Wolf*, 297.

[34] Ray, "Cultural Relations," 68-75.

[35] Ray, "Sanpoil and Nespelem," 187-89; McWhorter, *Yellow Wolf*, 296-98; Schuster, "Yakima Traditionalism," 115-16.

of the mid-nineteenth century defied the curative abilities of Native medicine practices.³⁶ Medicine people played a crucial role in assisting children to determine what their spirit powers would be. Sometime after going on a vision quest, a child would become ill, a sign that the spirit was ready to manifest itself. The medicine person helped the child express the new power through spirit songs, special totems, dress, and dancing.³⁷

The *wyakin* taught prudence in human-nature relations. In the myth of "The Elk, the Hunter, and His Greedy Father," above, the elk spirit is angry over his human partner's violation of taboos against wasteful hunting. In the man's dream the elk chastises him, showing him "bears, deer, and elks without number, and they were all persons. Those that he had killed were there too, and they groaned." Eventually the man is drawn toward his spirit partner who asks:

> Why did you go beyond what I commanded? Do you see *your people on both sides*? These are they whom you have killed. You have inflicted many needless wounds on our people.... Now I shall leave you, and never be your guardian spirit again.³⁸

Clearly, human and non-human spirits sprang from the same source and would return there one day.

Plateau dwellers believed that the "earth was the mother of all life" and that humans should use the earth and its life as if they were gifts.³⁹ While people traded goods, they did not trade their lands; as Cayuse Chief Five Crows noted, "Goods and earth are not equal."⁴⁰ People traded to make diverse relationships and to enrich others—not for personal profit. Trade focused on the process of relationship building, not the accumulation of goods, a difference that set Plateau economies apart from later Euro-American market relations.

Additionally, the standard against which human use of the earth ultimately would be measured was not that of the individual, as the story of "The Elk, the Hunter, and His Greedy Father," makes clear: Human conduct would be measured by its fidelity to the greater spiritual ordering of the world, in which humans were not the most well informed or dominant players. Thus, the *wyakin*'s gift of the sacred bundle anchored each person in a sacred, unique, and evolving relationship with the natural and spiritual world where she or he lived.

---

³⁶ Schuster, "Yakima Indian Traditionalism," 57. On the development of new religions during the decline of traditional medicine people, see Chapter 3 below.

³⁷ Schuster, "Yakima Traditionalism," 115-17.

³⁸ Ramsey, *Coyote Was Going There*, 64-65 (emphasis added).

³⁹ Anastasio, "Southern Plateau," 175.

⁴⁰ Transcribed in Stevens, *Council Proceedings*, 57.

Significantly, spirit powers were gifts to the community and not the product of individual accomplishments.[41] Because each person possessed unique skills and talents, each had distinct roles within the family group and village. Villages had many designated individuals—sometimes called "chiefs"—to supervise different activities such as salmon fishing, root-digging, gambling, healing, and war. Usually these positions were inherited, but there were exceptions. These individuals supervised specific activities and ensured coordination among participants.[42]

In Plateau society, personal status was dynamic, and it could change relative to the particular needs of the group at any time and with the balance of spiritual power in the world. In a time of food shortage, a person with excellent hunting skills would be very important; at a social gathering, someone with talent at gambling might be favored; in a time of long winter a person who could bring the warm Chinook winds would be important.[43]

The Winter Dance Complex celebrated the confluence of spiritual powers that bound humans and nature together in "connecting webs, reaffirming the relative identities of all of the Plateau dwellers, human and nonhuman alike."[44] At these ceremonies, people joined together to publicly perform spirit songs and spirit dances, impersonate spirits, and sometimes to demonstrate spirit powers.[45] Such displays integrated individual spirituality and personal connections at the village and inter-village level, thereby stitching everyone into the larger spiritual, ecological, and social fabric of the Plateau.

A New Bundle

The arrival of Meriwether Lewis and William Clark in the Columbia Basin in 1805 marked the beginning of a sustained U.S. presence in the area.[46]

---

[41] Schuster, "Yakima Traditionalism," 119. Schuster notes that her informants said that acculturation is widely seen as the reason so few people possess guardian spirit today, ibid., 117. For a contemporary view of the Native American relationship to nature, see Sue Whalen, "The Nez Perces' Relationship to Their Land," *Indian Historian* 4 (1971): 30-33.

[42] Inheritance was governed by a bilateral kinship system according to which a chief was usually succeeded by his eldest son; occasionally by a brother; and less frequently a brother's or sister's son-in-law or son. A person had the right to refuse the office, and villagers could depose ineffective headmen. Occasionally, more than one group would act to choose a headman. Anastasio, "Southern Plateau," 180. There, is little information about such positions for women. Charles Relander notes a woman who was chief root digger for the Wapato Long House. Relander, *Drummers and Dreamers*, 176-77.

[43] Anastasio, "Southern Plateau," 178-85; Schuster, "Yakima Traditionalism," 119.

[44] Miller, *Prophetic Worlds*, 20; Ray, "Cultural Relations," 102-03, 111-23; Schuster, "Yakima Traditionalism," 156, 163-64.

[45] Ray, "Cultural Relations," 113-16; Schuster, "Yakima Traditionalism," 164.

[46] Lewis and Clark were not the first Euro-Americans to wander into the area; fur traders with the Hudson's Bay Co. had pushed into the plateau before them. French-Canadian explorers had also entered the area. See also the accounts of Alexander Ross, who chronicled his

Commissioned by President Thomas Jefferson, their expedition was instructed to explore possible routes for trade and commerce that would channel Pacific fur resources into eastern markets.[47] In September 1805, the pair, accompanied by Indian guides, found their way onto the vast "Prairie" of the Columbia Plateau on their way to the Pacific Ocean.[48]

The expedition glimpsed the fertile prairies of the Plateau that kept Indian horses sleek and fat despite the evident draught, noted great forests and an abundance of sea otter. Lewis believed that the region held great promise for settlement, commerce, and conquest:

> [T]his country would form an extensive settlement; the climate appears quite as mild as that of similar latitude on the Atlantic coast if not more so and it cannot be otherwise than healthy; it possesses a fine dry pure air. The grass and many plants are now upwards of knee high. I have no doubt but this tract of country if cultivated would produce in great abundance every article essentially necessary to the comfort and subsistence of civilized man.[49]

Lewis and Clark's reports, eventually published in 1814, provided information and an invitation to a variety of easterners who headed west to the Columbia until mid-century, including missionaries—both Catholic and Protestant—traders, land speculators, gold miners, and homesteaders.[50]

Yet before the first Euro-American missionaries arrived on the Plateau in the 1830s, scraps of Christian doctrine and ritual were carried into the area. Canadian fur traders were predominantly Catholic and took their beliefs with them to the Plateau in the early 1820s. Native groups, such as the Nez Perce, learned of the foreigners' practices through trading. Eastern tribes, such as the Iroquois, some of whom had been educated at outpost schools such as the Anglican and Catholic missions at Red River, near present-day Winnipeg, Manitoba, brought Christian practices to the Plateau as well.[51]

---

experiences in the region as a trapper for the Pacific Fur Company and the Hudson's Bay Company from 1810-1822: *Adventures of the First Settlers on the Oregon or Columbia River*, Milo Milton Quaife, ed., Lakeside Classics (Chicago: R. R. Donnely & Sons, Inc., 1923), and *The Fur Hunters of the Far West*, Quaife, ed., Lakeside Classics (Chicago: R. R. Donnely & Sons, Inc., 1924).

[47] Lewis, too, perceived the Pacific as a link in a larger commercial scheme, but envisioned the Pacific as the gateway through which the American fur trade could reach Cantonese buyers, who formed a major market. Donald W. Meinig, *The Great Columbia Plain, A Historical Geography, 1805-1910* (Seattle: University of Washington Press, 1968): 34.

[48] Reuben Gold Thwaites, ed., *Original Journals of the Lewis and Clark Expedition*, 1804-1806, v. III (New York, 1905): 73, quoted in Meinig, *Great Columbia Plain*, 26.

[49] Thwaites, ed., *Journals of Lewis and Clark*, v. V, 11, quoted in Meinig, *Great Columbia Plain*, 31. The entry was recorded on May 9, on the expedition's return to St. Louis.

[50] Meinig, *Great Columbia Plain*, 29-34.

[51] The Red River School was an Anglican school that had been set up as a tangent to the Hudson's Bay Company's fur trade operations following the insistent pressure of London's

Christianity interested Plateau peoples because its elements reinforced emergent Plateau religious beliefs. Beginning roughly in 1770, Plateau peoples began practicing the "Prophet Dance" religion. This new form developed from the knowledge that the earth mother, like other living beings, had only a limited lifespan and that her life would soon come to an end. At Yakima, the Prophet Dance gradually grew into the Washat, or Long House, religion, that has been practiced there ever since.[52] The Prophet Dance was separate from the earlier, *wyakin*-based system, although its teachings on the proper human relationship with nature were consistent with those symbolized by the sacred bundle.

The Prophet Dance evolved out of older, probably pre-contact, Plateau beliefs that included stories of the dead returning to visit the living, and the experiences of medicine people who visited the dead in order to work cures.[53] Plateau prophets promised death would be transcended, however. At the moment of the Earth mother's death she would be transformed, and would return to the world together with Coyote and the "Old Ones" to work many extraordinary events. Prophets who had been brought back from death brought continuing information of this coming "millennium" to Plateau peoples. People celebrated the expected coming by holding "Prophet Dances" in which participants joined hands and danced in a circle, hastening the coming millennium. Those who did not dance could not expect to join in the new life; they would be transformed into non-human natural objects when they died.[54]

Plateau peoples found that Christian doctrine confirmed their beliefs in the transformative power of death, and the coming of a new and better life.[55] Consequently, Christian-styled rituals began to enter the Prophet Dance complex. By 1830—four years before the first missionaries arrived on the Plateau—fur traders noted that they met groups who made the sign of the cross, observed the Sabbath, knew the Lord's Prayer, and, in the case of at least one Nez Perce group, possessed a calendar of annual Catholic feast and fast

---

Church Missionary Society for Africa and the East. Alvin M. Josephy, Jr., *The Nez Perce Indians and the Opening of the Northwest,* abridged ed. (Lincoln, NE: University of Nebraska Press, 1965): 75-81, 86-88; Clifford M. Drury, *Henry Harmon Spalding* (Caldwell, ID: Caxton Printers, Ltd. 1936): 72-86.

[52] Leslie Spier, *The Prophet Dance of the Northwest and its Derivations: The Source of the Ghost Dance,* General Series in Anthropology, no. 1 (Menasha, WI: George Banta Publishing Co., 1935): 13-15; Relander, *Drummers and Dreamers,* 96, 139, 156; Schuster, "Yakima Traditionalism," 156; 185ff.

[53] Spier, *Prophet Dance,* 13-15; Anastasio, "Southern Plateau," 175. Schuster reported that pre-contact Yakama peoples did not have a concept of the afterlife. See "Yakima Traditionalism," 149.

[54] Spier, *Prophet Dance,* 9-11, 24ff. For a discussion of the subsequent history of the Prophet Dance, see Chapter 3.

[55] Spier, *Prophet Dance,* 30-40.

days.[56] Yet these were no new converts to Christianity; people adopted its forms to substantiate their own beliefs, a fact that missionaries did not understand.[57]

Plateau peoples' desire for more knowledge of Christianity led some of them to seek out Catholic "black robes" and to welcome Protestant missionaries in the 1830s. Beginning in 1831, a series of small Nez Perce-Flathead delegations travelled to St. Louis allegedly to acquire "the book" of the whites, but more likely to convince Jesuits of St. Louis College to establish a mission in their area.[58] While Christians generally interpreted the delegations as heralding the "Indian Call from Macedonia," it seems more probable that the delegations were seeking further confirmation of their own beliefs.[59] Following years of efforts by both Catholic and Protestant missionaries to respond to this "Call," Plateau peoples continued to practice their own religion within the outwardly Christian forms missionaries preached.

Judeo-Christian tenets were only one component of the larger belief system that Euro-Americans brought to the Plateau. Religion converged with social and economic order in the newcomers' concept of private property, and it was this 'bundle" that they carried with them to the Plateau. Just as the Native Plateau peoples' sacred bundle gave coherence to human and human-nature relationships, so the bundle of rights inherent in the concept of property structured those relationships for Euro-Americans. Property makes a convenient lens through which we may examine not only attitudes about natural resources but also views of society and spirituality in the early period of Euro-American contact with Plateau peoples.

In a legal sense, private property is a "bundle of rights" which entitles the holder to do certain things with the object in which he or she holds an entitlement.[60] Such rights include the right to claim something—land or capital—as

---

[56] Spier, *Prophet Dance*, 32. The Nez Perce may have been directly influenced by Iroquois who were present in their territory during the period 1812-20 and who had adopted some Christian rituals, Spier, ibid., 30-31.

[57] Spier, *Prophet Dance*, 30-31, 35; Miller, *Prophetic Worlds*, 62.

[58] The delegates arrived in St. Louis probably first in 1831, and then in 1835, 1837 (this delegation never made it), 1839, and 1840, Spier, *The Prophet Dance*, 30. See also Miller, *Prophetic Worlds*, 57-62; Robert I. Burns, *The Jesuits and the Indian Wars of the Northwest*, Yale Western Americana Series (New Haven: Yale University Press, 1966): 17-18. No historian appears to agree on what this series of delegations were seeking. Clifford Drury maintained that the Indians went to St. Louis seeking a copy of the Bible which they had seen when an Indian at the Red River Settlement School passed through their territory, Drury, *Henry Harmon Spalding*, 85-6. Burns maintains that the idea that the delegates requested a book was a "fraud," ibid., 18.

[59] Spier, *Prophet Dance*, 30-31; Miller, *Prophetic Worlds*, 62.

[60] The term "bundle of rights" appears in Armen Alchian and Harold Demsetz, "The Property Rights Paradigm," 33 *Journal of Economic History* (March 1973): 17. See also Lawrence M. Friedman, *A History of American Law*, 2d ed. (New York: Touchstone Books, 1985): 234-37;

one's own; the right to use something; the right to change the object—by mining, flooding, or clear cutting land, for example; and the right to alienate one's entitlement in that property, subject to state regulatory powers. In those very tangible ways, property rights express socially sanctioned methods by which humans not only relate to nature, but may appropriate it for their own use to the exclusion of others.[61]

Private property, Locke said, was that which humans removed from the earth and made valuable through their efforts to change it. Simply using some bit of nature was not sufficient, however. Under the common law, a potential property holder was required to communicate in a particular way her ownership or intent to make property of something: The would-be owner had to demonstrate her claim in a set of symbols usually a written instrument such as a deed, accepted by the community.[62] Most Native American societies could not meet this common law burden because they had no written title to the land, nor did they utilize the land in ways seen or acknowledged by Euro-Americans.[63]

Although many Native peoples viewed private property as theft from the commons, to Euro-Americans such "theft" was divinely sanctioned and a necessary civil right.[64] According to U.S. Supreme Court Justice William Paterson, writing in 1795,

> [T]he right of acquiring and possessing property, and having it protected, is one of the natural, inherent, and unalienable rights of man. Men have a sense of property: Property is necessary to their subsistence, and correspondent to their natural wants and desires; its security was one of the objects, that induced them to unite in society. No man would become a member of a community in which he could not enjoy the fruits of his honest labor and industry.[65]

In the United States, Paterson believed, the special relationship between citizens and the government rising from the liberating fires of revolution had secured to property a special place: "The Constitution encircles, and renders it

---

Commonwealth v. Alger, 7 Cush. 53, 85 (1851); Edward S. Corwin, "The Basic Doctrine of American Constitutional Law," *Michigan Law Review* 12 (1914): 247.

[61] For the development of common law doctrines of property, see J. H. Baker, *An Introduction to English Legal History* (2d ed.) (London: Butterworths, 1979): 193-335. See also Locke, *Second Treatise*, 19-22.

[62] Carol M. Rose, "Possession as the Origin of Property," *University of Chicago Law Review* 52 (1985): 85. See also *Calder v. Bull*, 3 Dallas 386, 388, 394 (1798), for U.S. Supreme Court Justice Samuel Chase's discussion of property as structured by positive law.

[63] Rose, "Possession," 85-87.

[64] On property as theft in Euro-American culture, see Pierre Joseph Proudhon, *What is Property*, trans. Benjamin R. Tucker (New York: Dover Publications, Inc., 1970): 1.

[65] *Van Horne's Lessee v. Dorrance*, 2 Dallas (2 U.S.) 304, 310 (1795).

an holy thing."⁶⁶ The sacred right of citizens to hold private property could be abridged only by the government acting on behalf of the polity in special circumstances.⁶⁷

Property incorporates a particular view of the relationships among God, humans, and nature. In the mythical origins of the world, according to Judeo-Christian tradition—and not unlike Plateau beliefs, God created the earth for the benefit of humans.⁶⁸ Yet Euro-Americans interpreted God's act in very different ways than did their Plateau counterparts. In Puritan and Calvinist theology, the origin myth demonstrated the hierarchical arrangement of the universe: God above humans, and humans above the earth. Nature was a passive object, subject to the manipulations of humans. Natural objects drew their value from their use as property, and in this world everything might be transformed into a "good," and goods and earth were interchangeable.⁶⁹

The human relationship with non-human nature tended to be one of dominance and control that paralleled to a certain extent God's relationship to humans. As the Yale theologian Timothy Dwight put it in a sermon published posthumously in 1819, "the properties and the exertions, of matter, are derived from an extrinsic cause; and that cause is possessed of intelligence and power, to which no bounds can be assigned."⁷⁰ In that scheme, God had endowed only humans and *himself* with spiritual significance; nature had none.⁷¹

If God had endowed no aspect of nature with spiritual potential, humans were a different species altogether. The individual provided the central focus of both Judeo-Christian teachings and the capitalist framework within which

---

⁶⁶ 2 Dallas 304, 311.

⁶⁷ 2 Dallas 304, 311-13; Charles Grove Haines, "Judicial Review of Legislation in the United States and the Doctrines of Vested Rights and of Implied Limitations on Legislatures" [in three parts], *Texas Law Review* 2 (1924): 257-90, 387-421, *Texas Law Review* 3 (1925): 1-43. Haines discusses some of the limits on government imposed by the particularly American notion of individual rights vested in private property. See also discussion below.

⁶⁸ 1 Gen. 1:28-30, New American Bible.

⁶⁹ Locke, *Second Treatise*, 17-18.

⁷⁰ Dwight, *Theology, Explained and Defended, in a Series of Sermons...*, 5 vols. (Middletown, CT: Clark & Lyman for T. Dwight, 1818-19): 1: 10. On Dwight's role in the Second Awakening, see William McLoughlin, *Revivals, Awakenings, and Reform: An Essay on Religion and Social Change in America, 1607-1977* (Chicago: University of Chicago Press, 1978): 109-11.

⁷¹ Max Weber stated this development succinctly when he wrote that the development of Protestant religions from their Judeo-Christian roots secured "the elimination of magic from the world." Weber, *The Protestant Ethic and the Spirit of Capitalism*, trans. by Talcott Parsons, (Gloucester, MA: Peter Smith, 1988): 105, 95-128. See also Lynn White Jr., "The Roots of Our Current Ecological Crisis," *Science* 155 (1967): 1203-07. White's is not the only interpretation of the Judeo-Christian belief system. The Gnostic Gospels provide an alternative view, see Elaine Pagels, *The Gnostic Gospels*. See also J. Baird Callicott, "Genesis Revisited: Murian Musings on the Lynn White, Jr. Debate," *Environmental History* 14 (1990): 65-90.

Euro-Americans organized their economic relations.[72] Individuals might find divine salvation by adhering to God's plan. Humans would achieve their own betterment and that of society by developing their properties, or engaging in market relations. If everyone did this, according to the myth, individual gain would be maximized and society would progress. Property thus was the vehicle by which individual salvation and social progress would take place.

Property organized social relationships in several ways. An individual's property was a zone within which the person was relatively free of state and private interference. Therein, an individual could express creative energies by transforming his or her property in any way that did not interfere too much with the commensurate right of another person. Property also organized the distribution of individual rights, including who could vote and hold a public office. Restrictions on property owning served to regulate who had access to political and economic power and thereby defined membership within communities as well as individuals' roles within those communities.[73]

The notion of property as a bundle of rights structured the political realm as well as the economic sphere. As members of the polity, people held individual rights vested in property. That is, by virtue of the fact that they owned property, they also acquired the right to participate in the political process. Although political participation and property ownership generally occurred in the same place, Euro-Americans often lacked a collective consciousness of place because ultimately all property was alienable and convertible into cash—either by the individual owner's will or that of the community. To Euro-Americans on the frontier, land and natural resources were plentiful and cheap, human resources were scarce.[74]

---

[72] This is a fundamental tenet of liberalism. See L. Hobhouse, *Liberalism* (London: Oxford University Press, 1964); Roberto Mangabeira Unger, *Knowledge and Politics* (New York: Free Press, 1975): 81-83, 155-56; Macpherson, *Political Theory of Possessive Individualism*.

[73] On the centrality of property to the organization of American political life, see Charles Reich, "The New Property," *Yale Law Journal* 73 (1964): 733-87. On the historical disenfranchisement of American Blacks, see Edmund S. Morgan, *American Slavery, American Freedom: the Ordeal of Colonial Virginia* (New York: W. W. Norton & Co., 1975): esp. 380-87; Eric Foner, *Reconstruction, America's Unfinished Revolution, 1863-1877* (New York: Harper & Row, Publishers, 1988): 446-49; and Derek Bell, *And We Are Not Saved: The Elusive Quest for Racial Justice* (New York: Basic Books, 1987). On Native Americans, see Russel Lawrence Barsh and James Youngblood Henderson, *The Road: Indian Tribes and Political Liberty* (Berkeley: University of California Press, 1980): 85-95. See generally Friedman, *History of American Law*, 202-229. See also Catherine A. MacKinnon, *Feminism Unmodified: Discourses on Life and Law* (Cambridge, MA: Harvard University Press, 1987): esp. 206-13.

[74] On the mobility of Euro-Americans during the nineteenth century in relation to plentiful land, see Daniel J. Boorstin, *The Americans, The Colonial Experience* (New York: Vintage Books, Random House, 1958): 193-94.

Property rights, however, could never be absolute.[75] Just as individual Yakama held entitlements to use certain resources subject to community values, Euro-Americans held their property rights on the condition that they used them in a way consistent with community norms. Government regulation of property rights, through the three broad powers of taxation, eminent domain, and the police power historically served to hold individuals accountable to community values in the exercise of their rights.[76] Over the course of the nineteenth century, as state officials perceived community interests, first in developing the nation's resources and then in conserving them, government-sanctioned interference with individual property rights increased.[77]

As state and federal legislation increasingly reached into the private realm, much controversy focused on how to strike a balance between individual and community interests that protected fundamental private rights while acknowledging that the public had a stake in how individuals used resources.[78] State or federal land grants, state-granted water rights, state fishing licenses, and federal grazing permits were just a few of the means by which governments came to regulate private use of resources for public benefit. Just how Indians and Indian-owned resources would factor into the calculus of the public good remained, however, and largely remains, an unanswered question.[79]

---

[75] See, for example Chief Justice Shaw's opinion in the Massachusetts Supreme Court case of *Commonwealth v. Alger*, 7 Cush. 53 (1851): "All property ... is derived directly or indirectly from the government, and held subject to those general regulations, which are necessary to the common good and the general welfare," ibid., p. 85.

[76] Harry N. Scheiber, "Property Law, Expropriation, and Resource Allocation by Government, 1789-1910," *Journal of Economic History* 33 (1973): 232-51; Scheiber, "The Road to Munn: Eminent Domain and the Concept of Public Purpose in the State Courts," *Perspectives in American History* 5 (1971): 287-328; Molly Selvin, "The Public Trust Doctrine in American Law and Economic Policy, 1789-1920," *Wisconsin Law Review* (1980): 1403-42; Charles W. McCurdy, "Stephen J. Field and Public Land Law Development in California, 1850-1866: Case Study of Judicial Resource Allocation in Nineteenth Century America," *Law and Society Review* 10 (1976): 235-66; James Willard Hurst, *Law and the Conditions of Freedom in Nineteenth United States History* (Madison: University of Wisconsin Press, 1956).

[77] Harry N. Scheiber, "Public Rights and the Rule of Law in American Legal History," *California Law Review* 72 (1984): 217-51; Scheiber, "Property Law, Expropriation, and Resource Allocation by Government"; Scheiber, "The Road to Munn"; Selvin, "Public Trust Doctrine." For a contemporary legal analysis of these historic doctrines, see Joseph Sax, "The Public Trust Doctrine in Natural Resource Law: Effective Judicial Intervention," *Michigan Law Review* 68 (1970): 471-566; Sax, "Takings and the Police Power," *Yale Law Journal* 74 (1964): 36-75.

[78] Lawrence Friedman, *A History of American Law*, 2d ed. (New York: Simon & Schuster, 1985): 178-79ff; Haines, "Judicial Review of Legislation," *Texas Law Review* 2: 405-18, esp. 417-18.

[79] For a general discussion of the degree to which there was consensus or conflict over policies promoted under the banner of the public good, see Harry N. Scheiber, "Public Economic Policy and the American Legal System: Historical Perspectives," *Wisconsin Law Review*

A Great Awakening

Just as the concept of property justified and structured Euro-American relationships to land, it also guided Euro-American conquest of Native Americans. By virtue of the British colonial experience in Ireland beginning in 1565, common law rules governing the occupation of foreign lands were well developed by the time Europeans arrived on American shores.[80] The English common law recognized a right to legal title of lands by conquest, by discovery, and by divine entitlement.[81]

Equally important to the conquest ideology was the belief that Christianity and civilization were distinct categories, and while one could be civilized without being Christian, one could not be made Christian without first becoming civilized. In this myth, Europeans had a divine duty to deliver others, not so fortunately endowed, from the clutches of barbarism.[82] British colonizers relied on the myth to justify their conquest of Irish peoples, and transplanted to American shores, that doctrine provided the foundation for modern federal Indian law.[83] Together, those legal and moral assertions provided a highly effective law and policy of colonialism. For Native Americans, law increasingly became the language through which they were forced to articulate their claims.

During the nineteenth century, Euro-Americans blended Christian teachings and law to form a peculiarly dynamic westward vision. "When we look

---

(1980): 1166-68; Louis Hartz, *Economic Policy and Democratic Thought: Pennsylvania 1776-1860*, with a foreword by Benjamin F. Wright (Chicago: Quadrangle Books, 1968): 9-33ff; Paul W. Gates, "The Homestead Law in an Incongruous Land System," *American Historical Review* 41 (1936): 67-78; Gates, *Fifty Million Acres: Conflicts over Kansas Land Policy, 1854-1890* (New York: 1954).

[80] Nicholas P. Canny, "The Ideology of English Colonization: From Ireland to America," in Stanley N. Katz and John M. Murrin, *Colonial America, Essays in Politics and Social Development* (3d ed.) (New York: Alfred A. Knopf, Inc., 1983): 47-68.

[81] Canny, "Ideology of Colonization," 51-2; Robert A. Williams, Jr., "The Algebra of Federal Indian Law: The Hard Trail of Decolonizing and Americanizing the White Man's Indian Jurisprudence," *Wisconsin Law Review* (1986): 224-25, 229-235ff; Arrell Morgan Gibson, "Philosophical, Legal, and Social Rationales for Appropriating the Tribal Estate, 1607-1980," *American Indian Law Review* 12 (1984): 3-37; see also Chief Justice John Marshall's opinion in *Johnson v. M'Intosh*, 21 U.S. (8 Wheat.) 543, 573-4 (1823).

[82] Canny, "Ideology of Colonization," 65-68, Canny notes that the Spanish were developing parallel doctrines to justify their own settlement patterns, ibid., 63-4; Williams, "Algebra of Federal Indian Law," 229-46.

[83] The best current discussions of the roots of federal Indian law are Robert A. Williams, Jr., "Documents of Barbarism: The Contemporary Legacy of European Racism and Colonialism in the Narrative Traditions of Federal Indian Law," *Arizona Law Review* 31 (1989): 237-78; Williams, The *American Indian in Western Legal Thought: The Discourses of Conquest* (Oxford: Oxford University Press, 1990). See also Rennard Strickland, "Genocide-at-law: An Historic and Contemporary View of the Native American Experience," *University of Kansas Law Review* 34 (1986): 713-55.

round about us with an attentive eye," began Philip Doddridge in his 1849 treatise, "Rise and Progress of Christianity in the Soul,"

> and consider the characters and pursuits of men, we plainly see, that though, in the original constitution of their natures, they only, of all the creatures that dwell on the face of the earth, be capable of religion, yet many of them shamefully neglect it.[84]

There follows Doddridge's scheme for Christian conversion, parsed in the metaphor of the arraignment, conviction, "pleas," sentencing, "condemnation," and eventual salvation of the guilty sinner.[85]

The metaphor is a useful one because it points to the parallel understandings of law and theology as systems of social ordering exactly as the laws of science provided the way for humans to understand non-human nature. Indeed, Dwight employed the term "Theological Science" to describe the rigor and precision with which humans could discern Divine law, exactly as they could determine the laws of nature by following the rules of scientific inquiry.[86] Both religion and science in that Enlightenment scheme proceeded from the assumption that causation was determinative and that humans gained knowledge of the world through direct observation expressed in mathematical formulae.[87]

At the turn of the eighteenth century, American Calvinist ideals of religion were rapidly giving way to new Protestant interpretations of the human relationship with God fueled by Enlightenment rationalism.[88] Key to understanding those innovations was a changing view of the role of America and Americans in world history. Americans had won their independence from Britain and impatiently were pushing back the boundaries of the western frontier. It was their divine right to people the land and appropriate its resources for their own benefit.

Yet there was widespread disagreement over how next to proceed.[89] Many felt that at the least Calvinisim's morosivity, not to mention its strict belief in

---

[84] Doddridge, "Rise and Progress of Religion in the Soul," (1744), in *Select Christian Authors*, 2 vols. (New York: Robert Carter & Brothers, 1849): 2:57.

[85] Doddridge, "Rise and Progress," 2:57-175; Dwight, *Theology*, 5:577-79.

[86] Dwight, *Theology*, 5:572-5; Carolyn Merchant, *The Death of Nature: Women, Ecology, and the Scientific Revolution* (San Francisco: Harper & Row, 1980): 192-215.

[87] Dwight, *Theology*, 1:4-8; William McLoughlin, The *American Evangelicals, 1800-1900: An Anthology* (Gloucester, MA: Peter Smith, 1976): 6-8, 11-12; Marvin Harris, *Cultural Materialism: The Struggle for a Science of Culture* (New York: Random House, 1979): 5-18; Merchant, *Death of Nature*, 164-191ff; Weber, *Protestant Ethic*, 24.

[88] McLoughlin, *American Evangelicals*, 1-27; Weber, *Protestant Ethic*, 139-154.

[89] McLoughlin, *Revivals, Awakenings, and Reform*, 98-106; Sandra Sizer, *Gospel Hymns and Social Religion: The Rhetoric of Nineteenth Century Revivalism* (Philadelphia, PA: Temple University Press, 1978): 50-82. See also Paul E. Johnson, *A Shopkeeper's Millennium: So-*

predestination and an unsympathetic god, failed to make sense in light of a growing pride in the nation's past and optimism over its future.[90] The range of religious beliefs that emerged in the ensuing "Second Great Awakening" drew upon Enlightenment views of nature and humans, and stressed the orderliness of the universe, God's benevolence, and human free will. Although Calvinism did not disappear, many people took up more optimistic religions.[91]

The "Second Great Awakening" became the process through which Americans redefined their understanding of the future: Theirs would be a nation fueled by individual creative energies working for both economic progress and spiritual salvation, and peopled by a special race of white, Anglo-Saxon Protestants "chosen by God to perfect the world."[92] Thus, the work at hand was to transplant the bundle of property throughout the continent, making way for new settlement and, to a lesser extent, teaching Native peoples to take up white ways to ensure that they did not get in the way of this grand progress.

At its most extreme, the notion of Americans as God's chosen stood for the belief—widely shared among Protestants—that if Americans worked together they would personally host Christ's Second Coming.[93] One logistical defect in the plan, however, was that although Protestants envisioned themselves united at least against Catholics and heathens in that cause, among themselves Protestants splintered into rival factions who more often imagined themselves competing for a hand in the millennium than in cooperating to bring it about.[94] In its secular form, the "Manifest Destiny" ideal held that the continent belonged to the Euro-American People for their own growth and development, a view which is still alive.[95]

---

ciety and Revivals in Rochester, New York, 1815-1837 (New York: Hill and Wang, 1978); Perry Miller, The Life of the Mind in America (New York: Harcourt, Brace, 1965).

[90] On Calvinist beliefs, see Weber, Protestant Ethic, 102-105; Robert Middlekauff, The Mathers, Three Generations of Puritan Intellectuals, 1596-1728 (London: Oxford University Press, 1971): esp. 6-9; and McLoughlin, Revivals, Awakenings, and Reform, 101-102.

[91] McLoughlin, Revivals, Awakenings, and Reform, 100-101, 108-111, discussing conflicts between Calvinist and Deist beliefs.

[92] McLoughlin, Revivals, Awakenings, and Reform, 105; Weber, Protestant Ethic, 105.

[93] McLoughlin, Revivals, Awakenings, and Reform, 98; Michael C. Coleman, Presbyterian Missionary Attitudes Toward American Indians, 1837-1893 (Jackson, MS: University Press of Mississippi, 1985): 10.

[94] On schisms among Protestant sects, see McLoughlin, Revivals, Awakenings, and Reform; Coleman, Presbyterian Attitudes, 10, 11-12. On rivalry between Protestants and Catholics in the Pacific Northwest, see Coleman, ibid., 114; Josephy, Nez Perce Indians, 195-98, 237-40.

[95] Henry Nash Smith, Virgin Land: The American West as Symbol and Myth (Cambridge, MA: Harvard University Press, 1950): esp. 3-48; Roderick Nash, Wilderness and the American Mind, 3d ed. (New Haven, CT: Yale University Press, 1982): 40-43; Frederick Jackson Turner, "The Significance of the Frontier in American History," in Turner, The Frontier in American History (New York: Holt, Rinehart, and Winston, 1947; reprinted with a foreword by Wilbur R. Jacobs, Tucson: The University Press of Arizona, 1986): 1-38; Barbara Novak, Nature and Culture. American Landscape and Painting, 1825-1875 (New York: Oxford

In both its religious and secular expressions, Manifest Destiny contained the assumption that Native Americans were part of the wilderness for whites to conquer and civilize much as was the land.[96] Euro-Americans wanted Native peoples' land and resources, but they had to make them into property before they could take them away. If Native peoples would not willingly participate in that process, Euro-Americans were prepared—and felt themselves entitled—to take what they wanted by force.

University Press, 1980): see esp. paintings and text in Chapter VIII, "Man's Traces: Axe, Train, Figure," 157-200. For a modern expression of the Manifest Destiny idea, see Francis Fukuyama, deputy director policy planning staff, State Department, "Witnessing the End of Political History," *San Francisco Chronicle*, Aug. 9, 1989, z-6, 1.

[96] Nash, *Wilderness and the American Mind*, 24, 28, 36-7; Gary B. Nash, "The Image of the Indian in the Southern Colonial Mind," *William & Mary Quarterly* 3d ser., 29 (1972): 197-230; William S. Simmons, "Cultural Bias in the New England Puritans' Perception of Indians," *William & Mary Quarterly* 3d Ser., 38 (1981): 56-72. See also Patricia Nelson Limerick, *The Legacy of Conquest, The Unbroken Past of the American West* (New York: W.W. Norton & Co. 1987).

3

GOODS AND THE EARTH

> We believe that redeeming [is] to be the means of civilization & a permanent subsistence: & therefore while we point them [the Indians] with one hand to the Lamb of God which taketh away the sins of the world, we believe it to be equally our duty to point with the other to the hoe, as the means of saving their famishing bodies from an untimely grave & furnishing the means of subsistence to future generations.
> —Henry Harmon Spalding and Marcus Whitman, 1838[1]

The ideological differences between Plateau peoples and Euro-American settlers soon precipitated open warfare as non-Indians increasingly encroached upon the homelands of peoples throughout the Plateau and the Pacific Northwest. For Euro-Americans, the nineteenth century dawned with the bright promise of unexplored western lands upon which they hung not only hopes for personal fortunes and freedom, but the conviction that theirs would be the generation to make God's kingdom on earth a reality.[2] The combination of unopened lands newly wrested from British occupation after 1846 and the possibilities for progress through industry, made a volatile fuel for western settlement and resource exploitation.[3]

Until 1846, when the U.S.-Canadian boundary was settled, both Britain and the United States shared legal control of the Columbia Plateau under the Joint Occupation Agreement of 1812. British-Canadian and U.S. interests in the region were quite different. British-Canadians were predominantly male "voyageurs": adventurers, trappers, and Indian traders who tended to see

---

[1] Spalding and Whitman to Daniel Greene, April 21, 1838 [Spalding Letter no. 21], quoted in Clifford Drury, *Henry Harmon Spalding* (Caldwell, ID: Caxton Printers, Ltd., 1936): 182.

[2] William McLoughlin, *Revivals, Awakenings, and Reform: An Essay on Religion and Social Change in America, 1607-1977* (Chicago: University of Chicago Press, 1978): 98-99; McLoughlin, *The American Evangelicals, 1800-1900, An Anthology* (Gloucester, MA: Peter Smith, 1976): 10-13.

[3] The United States and Britain entered a joint occupation agreement for the Pacific Northwest in 1818, and by an agreement of June 1846, the two nations decreed the 49th parallel as their mutual boundary. According to the terms of the 1818 agreement, neither nation could establish a permanent government in the region. On what "fueled" individuals during the century, see J. Willard Hurst, *Law and the Conditions of Freedom in the Nineteenth Century United States* (Madison: University of Wisconsin Press, 1956); cf. Morton J. Horwitz, *The Transformation of American Law, 1780-1860* (Cambridge, MA: Harvard University Press, 1977). See also Paul W. Gates, *History of Public Land Law Development*, The Management of Public Lands in the United States Series (New York: Arno Press, 1979).

the Pacific Northwest as a commercial outpost whose purpose was to extract wealth and channel it into their own pockets or Canadian coffers.[4]

Americans certainly had no qualms about mining natural resources for personal and national economic gain, but they were equally interested in the west for its potential to house scores of farmer-homesteaders, "whose tools were to be wagons and plows as well as traps and rifles."[5] Americans came with families, farm animals, bags of seed, and dreams of building permanent homes in the west. Consequently, Americans—much more than Canadians—saw Indian occupation of western lands as an obstacle to their plans.

French traders tended to see Native peoples as partners and peoples engaged in mutually beneficial business transactions. American settlers, however, generally perceived themselves as superior to Native peoples, a view which precluded respect for their racial, cultural, and social differences. By turns, Native Americans were a part of the wilderness to be conquered, savage and untutored minds to be converted to God and civilization, and the owners of lands that non-Indians would colonize.

Yet long before Euro-American feet walked the Plateau, European pathogens—smallpox, bubonic plague, influenza, and a host of others—crossed the Rocky Mountains and killed thousands of Native Americans. The survivors of these disease epidemics became the "miserable remnants" scorned and pitied by Euro-American missionaries and treatymakers who followed in the wake of these vanguards of settlement. The death toll from these diseases was staggering: fifty to ninety-five—sometimes even one hundred percent of a population. Those who survived watched not only the deaths of their kin, but the wrenching apart of entire social and cultural systems of organizing the world. Into this ideological chaos, missionaries and other foreigners arrived, determined to interject their own world views into the seeming void. What emerged was not the "Christianization" or "civilization" of Native peoples, but rather the amalgamation of bits of both worlds in the hearts and minds of Plateau survivors.

The Plateau's earliest missionaries established a policy that later found expression in federal Indian law: Indians could become civilized if they took up the Bible and the plow, both symbols that drew their power directly from the divinely ordained place of property in Euro-American life. U.S. federal policy at first was to relocate Indians in a western "Indian Country," spanning the west to the Pacific Ocean, but this quickly gave way to the clamor of settlers for

---

[4] On Canadian fur trade operations in the Pacific Northwest, see Donald W. Meinig, *The Great Columbia Plain: A Historical Geography, 1805-1910*, The Emil and Kathleen Sick Lecture-Book Series in Western History and Biography (Seattle: University of Washington Press, 1968): 66-95; Alvin M. Josephy, Jr., *The Nez Perce Indians and the Opening of the Northwest*, abridged ed. (Lincoln, NE: University of Nebraska Press, 1965): 37-68ff.

[5] Meinig, *Great Columbia Plain*, 101.

Indian lands and a new policy to resettle Indians on special reserves.[6] Marcus Whitman, a missionary to the Cayuses, commented in 1844,

> it cannot be hoped that time will be allowed to mature either the work of Christianization or civilization before the white settlers will demand the soil and seek the removal of both the Indians and the Mission. What Americans desire of this kind they always effect, and it is equally useless to oppose or desire it to be otherwise.[7]

Just as Protestant conquest of the land was divinely sanctioned, Native peoples would either die out from disease and moral failure or take up Euro-American ways.

In the world made by non-Indians, the Euro-American sacred bundle of individual property ownership in land replaced the *wyakin*'s bundle as the dominant symbol of human-nature relations on the Plateau. Federal treaties negotiated with many of the Pacific Northwest bands during the 1850s wrote the white conception of property into the futures of Native peoples. Many Plateau groups lashed out against the treaties, and war engulfed the region until the 1860s. When federal troops crushed the last of the Indians' resistance and interned many Native groups on reservations that were mere fractions of their homelands, another government campaign began to sever forcibly the cultural and social ties that bound Native peoples to their lands.

"Widowing the Land"

The largest destructive force to Plateau Indian social organization and religious beliefs during the late eighteenth and early nineteenth centuries was the collection of European diseases that repeatedly swept across this world. The anthropologist Helen Schuster noted that of an estimated pre-contact Yakama population of 7000 individuals, 2000—or only, about 29 percent— survived the epidemics that raged across their homelands between 1800 and 1853.[8]

The attack on the Plateau came relatively late in the history of Euro-American diseases epidemics on the North American continent; many diseases struck first on the east coast, where contact was earliest, and then moved west. The death tolls from these successive attacks was so high that missionaries who arrived in the region in the early 1840s believed that the demise of

---

[6] Felix Cohen, *Handbook of Federal Indian Law*, 1982 ed. (Charlottesville, VA: The Michie Company, 1982): 78-98; Frederick E. Hoxie, *A Final Promise: The Campaign to Assimilate the Indians, 1880-1920* (Lincoln, NE: University of Nebraska Press, 1984): 147-87.

[7] Marcus Whitman to Stephen Prentiss, May 16, 1844, reprinted in Narcissa Whitman, "Mrs. Whitman's Letters," in Oregon Pioneer Association, *Transactions of the 21st Annual Reunion* (Portland, OR, George H. Himes & Co. Printers, 1894): 64.

[8] Helen Hersh Schuster, "Yakima Indian Traditionalism: A Study in Continuity and Change" (Ph.D. diss., University of Washington, 1975): 13-94.

Indians as a race was near at hand. Dr. Marcus Whitman, of the American Board of Commissioners for Foreign Missions, who ministered to 72 disease-plagued Cayuse peoples at his mission at Waiilatpu, on the Walla Walla River, noted in 1844 that "it does not concern me so much what is to become of any particular set of Indians, as to give them the offer of salvation through the gospel and the opportunity of civilization."[9] The demise of Indians would make European settlement of the continent significantly easier.

As non-Indian settlers pushed the nation's frontier westward, they brought with them many new diseases to which Native Americans carried no natural immunities. People could catch a disease from direct physical contact with a carrier or from shared trade goods or living spaces. While disease outbreaks often occurred only after non-Indians made contact with a particular population, it was not unusual for disease to precede their arrival simply through Indians' relations with other Native peoples who had made previous encounters. Rather than beginning anew in a "virgin" land, then, European colonists triggered a massive Native American depopulation by disease that enabled Europeans to establish themselves in a "widowed" land.

Early estimates of Native American populations set the pre-contact population of North America at about one million, with about eight to fourteen million for the entire western hemisphere at the same time.[10] Recent scholarship on Native American demography has challenged those figures and made obsolete the idea that European settlers to the new world were peopling a "virgin land." Although there is yet much disagreement among revisionist scholars, recent studies that take into account the impact of diseases on Native

---

[9] Marcus Whitman to Stephen Prentiss, May 16, 1844, reprinted in Narcissa Whitman, "Letters," 64.

[10] Wilbur R. Jacobs, "The Tip of an Iceberg: Pre-Columbian Indian Demography and Some Implications for Revisionism," *William and Mary Quarterly*, 3d ser., 21 (1974): 123; Henry F. Dobyns, "Estimating Aboriginal American Population, An Appraisal of Techniques with a New Hemispheric Estimate," *Current Anthropology* 7 (1966): 397-409, summarizes earlier methods and estimates. For discussions of the virgin land idea in contemporary thought, see Henry Nash Smith, *Virgin Land, The American West as Symbol and Myth* (Cambridge, MA: Harvard University Press, 1950; reissued, 1970); Roderick Nash, *Wilderness and the American Mind*, 3d ed. (New Haven, CT: Yale University Press, 1982): 23-43; Walter Prescott Webb, "Ended: 400 Year Boom: Reflections on the Age of the Frontier," *Harper's Magazine* (October 1951): 27.

Low estimates of Native populations may have been motivated in some part by racist attitudes. Dobyns noted that Kroeber may not have wanted to admit that Spanish slave labor brutality contributed to Native Americans' high mortality rates. See Jacobs, "Tip of an Iceberg," 128 n. 14; Dobyns, "Estimating Aboriginal Population," 397. Dobyns himself later backed away from placing a value judgment on the role of colonial brutality in the decrease of Indian populations, Henry F. Dobyns, *Their Number Become Thinned: Native American Population Dynamics in Eastern North America* (Knoxville, TN: University of Tennessee Press in cooperation with the Newberry Library Center for the History of the American Indian, 1983): 24.

American communities set the pre-contact Native population much higher.[11] One study, using a rate of death from disease to survival of 20:1 set this figure at nearly ten million for the North American continent alone.[12]

Such high Native American mortality as a result of European disease epidemics resulted from several factors. First, Native Americans constituted a "virgin population," that is, because they had never been exposed to European diseases, Native American communities possessed no natural immunities to European pathogens. Before contact, Native Americans suffered from various forms of intestinal parasites also common to European populations, as well as more serious diseases including encephalitis, polio, infectious hepatitis, and perhaps some form of syphilis.[13] European pathogens, however, were foreign, and when introduced, spread rapidly among both adults and children and killed high numbers. High mortality rates among young adults, especially—between fifteen and forty—would have had a tremendous impact upon a

---

[11] Crosby, "Virgin Soil Epidemics as a Factor in the Aboriginal Depopulation in America," *William and Mary Quarterly*, 3d ser., 33 (1976): 289-91; Douglas H. Ubelaker, "Prehistoric New World Population Size: Historical Review and Current Appraisal of North American Estimates," *American Journal of Physical Anthropology*, XLV (1976): 661-66; Dobyns, "Estimating Aboriginal American Population," 395-416; Jacobs, "Tip of an Iceberg," 123-32; Dobyns, "Brief Perspective on a Scholarly Transformation: Widowing the 'Virgin' Land," *Ethnohistory* 23 (1976): 95-104. See also William McNeill, *Plagues and Peoples: A Natural History of Human Infections* (Garden City, NY: Anchor/Doubleday, 1976).

[12] Dobyns, "Estimating Aboriginal, American Population," 415. To reach that figure, Dobyns multiplied the Native American population nadir for which census data exists (490,000 in 1930) by the ratio of deaths to survivors resulting from disease epidemics and other factors among Native Americans following contact, which has been estimated at between 20 to one and 25 to one. Using the 25:1 ratio, Dobyns calculated a population of 12,250,000 for North America. Dobyns estimated Native populations of 90,043,000 (at 20:1) to 112,553,750 (at 25:1) for all of the Americas. On Dobyn's methods, see Jacobs, "Tip of an Iceberg," 125.

Dobyns calculated even higher pre-contact population estimates in his controversial book, *Their Number Become Thinned*, 42, where he suggested 18 million as the North American continental estimate. Cf. Daniel K. Richter, Review of *Their Number Become Thinned*, In *William and Mary Quarterly* XLI, 3d Ser., (1984): 649-53; William C. Sturtevant, Review of *Their Number Become Thinned*, In *American Historical Review* 89 (1984): 1380-81.

[13] Lucile E. St. Hoyme, "On the Origins of New World Paleopathology," *American Journal of Physical Anthropology* XXXI (1969): 295-302; Dobyns, *Their Number Become Thinned*, 34-35; Crosby, *Ecological Imperialism: The Biological Expansion of Europe, 900-1900* (Cambridge: Cambridge University Press, 1986): 215-16. Dobyns and Crosby discuss only a few "New World" pathogens that affected European colonists: Verruga, a disfiguring and lethal disease spread by sandflies and present only in some high altitude Andean valleys, and some forms of veneral disease (syphilis). Verruga would have been a problem only for colonists to the Andes, since the sandfly did not survive transplantation to Europe aboard sailing ships (as did the anopheles and Aedes Aegypti mosquitoes that were transplanted from the Old World to the New, carrying with them malaria and yellow fever). And, as Crosby notes, "Veneral syphilis may be the New World's only important disease export, and it has, for all its notoriety, never stopped population growth in the Old World."

group's ability to secure food, take care of the very young and very old, and reproduce biologically.[14]

Very young children were also at high risk, since they would not receive immunity to disease from their mothers either before birth or afterward through mothers' milk. Additionally, since Indian children usually were two or more years old before they were weaned, the deaths of nursing mothers during an epidemic would have killed their children as well.[15] Narcissa Prentiss Whitman, a missionary herself and wife of Dr. Whitman, noted in a letter to her parents in March 1838 that many Cayuse babies died "because their mothers have not milk for them, and they know not how to prepare food to feed them or have no means to do it. They usually nurse them until they are three or more years old."[16]

A second reason for the extraordinary destructiveness of European pathogens was the patterns by which they swept through Native villages. Disease epidemics came in distinct attacks that were either successive or simultaneous. That is, a particular group might be infected with small pox one year, measles the next, and malaria after that; or worse, all of them together. Any individual who happened to survive the first round carried no immunity to the second, and so on. An individual who might have been capable of fighting off one infection would stand less of a chance if several different pathogens struck together. Contemporary observers usually noted only the major symptoms; many people may have died of secondary infections such as the measle epidemic complicated by dysentery reported at the Dr. Whitman's mission in 1847-1848. At the height of the infection three to five Indians died per day.[17]

In the region west of the Rocky Mountains, disease epidemics decimated Native populations in roughly the following order: influenza as early as 1761; smallpox as early as 1782, throughout the region; malaria in 1830-1833; smallpox again in 1836-40; measles and dysentery in 1843-47; smallpox in 1846, and 1852-1853, and 1862; influenza in 1889-1890 and 1902; smallpox in

---

[14] Crosby, "Virgin Soil Epidemics," 293-94.

[15] Crosby, "Virgin Soil Epidemics," 294.

[16] Whitman to her parents, March 14, 1838, reprinted in Narcissa Whitman, "N. Y. Letters," 100.

[17] Spaulding to Mr. and Mrs. Prentiss, April 6, 1848, reprinted in "N. Y. Letters," 97; Josiah Osborn to Brother and Sister, April 7, 1848, reprinted in Hulbert and Hulbert, *Marcus Whitman*, 3:257, 260. See also testimony of Moses Strong, and testimony of Michelle Martineau, both in *U.S. v. Winans*, Transcript of Record, Testimony and Final Report of Examiner, enclosed in Attorney General to Clerk of the Supreme Court, Jan. 21, 1904, Appellate Case File no. 19213, Records of the Supreme Court, Record Group 267, National Archives, Washington, D.C., 113, 227 [hereafter cited as *U.S. v. Winans*, transcript of record]. The transcript has several sets of page numbers. I have used the handwritten page numbers that have not been crossed out. I have also indicated the use of interpreters where Yakama witnesses were not speaking in English.

1901; smallpox and measles in 1903; and influenza again in 1918.[18] Scarlet fever, diphtheria, bubonic plague, typhus, cholera, tuberculosis, whooping cough, and bronchopneumonia also proved fatal to Native Americans.[19]

A third factor in the lethal effects of disease epidemics was that Native American knowledge of medicines and healing had no effective remedies against these diseases. Traditional methods of curing illness usually were ineffective against the new sicknesses—and often heightened their effects. The Reverend Samuel Parker, also a missionary with the American Board, noted of a malaria epidemic among the Indians of the Lower Columbia River below Celilo in 1829:

> The malignancy of this disease may have been increased by predisposing causes, such as [?] intemperance and the influence of intercourse with sailors. But a more direct cause of the great mortality was their mode of treatment. In the burning stage of the fever, they plunged into some lake or river and continued in the water until the heat was allayed, and rarely survived the cold stage which followed. The shores were strewn with the unburied dead. Whole and large villages were depopulated; and some entire villages have disappeared.[20]

Narcissa Whitman often mentioned the inefficacy of Indian "jugglers" in curing the sick. "They are anxious to take medicine, but they do not feel satisfied with this alone—they must have their jugglers playing over them or they will surely die. We have two or three instances where some have died

---

[18] The list of diseases was compiled from the following sources: S. F. Cook, "The Epidemic of 1830-33 in California and Oregon," University of California, *Publications in American Archaeology and Ethnography*, 43 (no. 3) (1955): 303-25; Daniel R. Hopkins, *Princes and Peasants: Smallpox in History* (Chicago: University of Chicago Press, 1983): 270-74; Henry H. Spaulding to Mr. and Mrs. Stephen Prentiss, April 6, 1848, reprinted in Narcissa Whitman, "N. Y. Letters," 97; Marcus Whitman, Report to American Board of Commissioners for the Foreign Missions, July 6, 1840, reprinted in Hulbert and Hulbert, *Marcus Whitman*, 2: 179; Narcissa Whitman to Rev. Leverette and Mrs. Hull, Oct. 25, 1836, and Narcissa Whitman to Parents, brothers, and sisters, March 30, 1837, both reprinted in Hulbert and Hulbert, *Marcus Whitman*, 1: 245, 272; CIA-AR, 1901, 394-5, describing vaccination of children in reservation school against smallpox; CIA-AR, 1903, 342.

[19] Burns notes an outbreak of cholera among the Flathead Indians in 1854-55, the deadly "cholera year" of 1853 on the Great Plains in which thousands of Sioux died, and a measles outbreak among the Crow Indians in 1856. Burns, *Jesuits and Indian Wars*, 92, 121; see also Crosby, "Virgin Soil Epidemics," 294-95. Ruby and Brown note smallpox on Upper Skagit River up to 1889, *Indians of the Pacific Northwest*, 171; smallpox among Salish (contracted from Gros Ventures) in 1869-70, Ruby. and Brown, ibid., 188; smallpox among the Makahs and every Puget Sound tribe, and the Wishrams in 1853, Ruby and Brown, ibid., 171, 188, 127-28; Dobyns, *Their Number Become Thinned*, 8-32, adding, 23-24, that the high incidence of diabetes among Native Americans through to the present would indicate that they have had frequent viral infections.

[20] Parker, *Journal*, 191, quoted in Leslie M. Scott, "Indian Diseases as Aids to Pacific Northwet Settlement," *Oregon Historical Quarterly* 29 (1928): 153.

without being played over. They are such miserable nurses that they die by their own neglect."[21] Pre-contact Native Americans did not have germ theories and consequently had no concept of quarantine for the infected."[22]

Because of the suddenness and virulence of most epidemics there was no time to develop an effective response to the invasions; in a matter of days an entire tribe might be dead.[23] If everyone within the group became sick simultaneously, no one remained to care for the ill. Narcissa Whitman's "miserable nurses" very likely were ill themselves or just recovering from a disease. Although Catholic priests, some protestant missionaries, and a few sympathetic settlers attempted to vaccinate Indians against smallpox and cholera, those efforts were sporadic and often met with suspicion and fear.[24]

The decline in Indian populations, especially from disease epidemics, had direct and significant social consequences for the political and economic organization of Native groups over time. Social responses to massive depopulation following disease epidemics included abandoning settlements in marginally productive areas, regrouping of survivors into fewer new bands, and adopting new subsistence and cultural practices as a result of relocation and social amalgamation.[25] Yakama social life in the pre-treaty time when "all of these people died," necessarily was reshaped even before Euro-Americans arrived.[26]

---

[21] Narcissa Whitman to her father, April 30, 1840, reprinted in Narcissa Whitman, "N.Y. Letters," 130.

[22] Crosby, "Virgin Soil Epidemics," 296-297.

[23] Scott, "Indian Diseases as Aids to Settlement, 153.

[24] Indians feared that evil spirits would enter their bodies through vaccinations. Ruby and Brown, *Indians of the Pacific Northwest*, 127-28; Burns, *Jesuits and Indian Wars*, 50. Beginning in 1837, federal officials began including provisions for health care in Indian treaties. Between 1873 and 1877, the Office of Indian Affairs ran a medical and educational division that had responsibility for repressing liquor sales and overseeing reservation health and sanitation. Services were inadequate; in 1880 seventy-seven physicians and four hospitals were responsible for serving all U.S. Indians. In 1908 the OIA created a chief medical supervisor position to coordinate its health care services. Congress, however, first funded the new program in 1910. The Snyder Act of 1921 authorized federal funding for Indian health care services. In 1934, the Johnson-O'Malley Act authorized the BIA to contract with state and local governments and private care providers to provide health services. Cohen, *Handbook of Federal Indian Law*, 696-98; U.S. Public Health Service, *The Indian Health Program of the United States Public Health Service* (Washington, D.C.: Government Printing Office, 1969): 17-18; Snyder Act, Ch. 115, 42 Stat. 208 (codified as amended at 25 U.S.C. § 13); Johnson-O'Malley Act, Ch. 147, § 1, 48 Stat. 596 (codified as amended at 25 U.S.C. § 452).

[25] Dobyns, *Their Numbers Become Thinned*, 311.

[26] Testimony of Moses Strong, describing deaths of inhabitants at Columbia River fishing villages, in *U.S. v. Winans* transcript of record, 13; testimony of Michelle Martineau, ibid., 227; Cook, "Epidemic of 1830-1833," 303-25.

With the rapid loss of such a large portion of their populations, Indian groups also must have lost a great deal of collective knowledge about their environments and traditions, and individuals surely must have experienced severe psychological stress. Some contemporary observers noted that in the face of an incurable disease epidemic, entire villages committed mass suicide rather than suffer the course of a fatal disease.[27] Others, no doubt, saw the end of their world approaching and consoled, themselves in the various apocalyptic Plateau religions which sprung up during the nineteenth century. These religions all promised a renewed world of abundant resources and peace following the cataclysmic destruction of the old world.[28]

Native Americans left us no written records of what life was like following an epidemic; we have only observations recorded by non-Indians who were largely removed from what they reported. We can only imagine, for example, what the Plateau might have looked like through the eyes of a [Clatsop?] Indian woman encountered by William Clark near the mouth of the Willamette River in 1806. Her "face was badly marked with smallpox," he wrote, and she told him that she had nearly died from the disease when she was a girl some thirty years before when "this disorder raged in their towns and destroyed their nation."[29] The questions remain: How did she live through the disease? Which family members survived with her? How did the survivors such as she carry out their annual subsistence work? Who remained alive to teach her the stories of her ancestors?

Into the resulting social and cultural disorder, Native peoples looked for new ideas to patch their now-fragmented system of ordering the world. The ideas and symbols carried by Euro-Americans, who not only did not succumb to the epidemics but also sometimes brought cures for them, proved particularly appealing.

Euro-Americans carried natural immunities to the pathogens unleashed during the "virgin soil epidemics." Indeed, many eastern emigrants sought out western lands especially for their healthful climates.[30] Missionaries generally interpreted what they saw upon their arrival—the sickness and brokenness of Native communities—as proof of the contrast between Native and "civilized" life that they constantly projected onto the world around them.

To the Whitmans, and other Protestant missionaries in particular, Indian mortality stemmed from the refusal to obey God's command to "multiply and replenish" the earth. Thus, the future of Indian peoples would only be in

---

[27] See accounts in Crosby, "Virgin Soil Epidemics," 298-99.

[28] See the discussion of the Smohalla Religion in the following section.

[29] Meriwether Lewis and William Clark, *Original Journals of the Lewis and Clark Expedition, 1804-1806*, Reuben Gold Thwaites, ed. (New York: Dodd, Mead & Co., 1904-1906): 4: 241.

[30] See for example Hubert Howe Bancroft, *The Works of Hubert Howe Bancroft*, vol. XXXI: *History of Washington, Idaho, and Montana, 1845-1889* (San Francisco: The History Co., 1890): 539-40.

heaven, leaving the land free for those who would comply with God's command. In that view, missionary work was merely a stepping stone to the larger mission of ensuring white Christian settlement of the west. The idea that Indians were not long for this world colored both missionary efforts as well as federal Indian policy well into the twentieth century.[31]

Confusion in the Ranks

Euro-Americans arrived on the Plateau only after European disease epidemics already had killed large numbers of Plateau inhabitants. Trappers and traders affiliated with the British-run Hudson's Bay Company were the first Euro-Americans to maintain a sustained presence on the Plateau, beginning in 1821, when Hudson's Bay Company merged with the North West Company.[32] Unlike the missionaries and American settlers who followed them, fur traders did not have much interest in or motivation for trying to "civilize" Plateau peoples. Their interests lay in developing favorable alliances with friendly Plateau groups, fostering dependable trade relationships, and establishing control over a constant supply of furbearing animals.[33]

Many of the traders were French Catholics, and soon were followed by priests who came both to minister to whites and to bring the Gospels to Native peoples. Indians tended to like those priests not only for their teachings, but because, like the *voyageurs*, they viewed Plateau peoples with more egalitarian eyes than did their Protestant counterparts. Fur trappers and priests, Indians often noted, paid for what they used. Protestant missionaries, and certainly homesteaders, largely took what they wanted.[34]

Native groups on the Plateau participated in the fur trade to varying degrees. Those who lived along major communication and travel routes, along the Columbia River, for example, necessarily had more regular contact with foreigners. Groups such as the Chinook and Nez Perce, who were premier traders in the area also developed more ties to non-Indians. Peoples in the Yakima Basin, on the other hand, lived farther from the popular travel routes and consequently had only irregular contact with non-Indians. Natives typically traded horses for metal products and later muskets and guns.[35]

---

[31] Dobyns, *Their Number Become Thinned*, 3-4.

[32] For a general discussion of the Hudson's Bay Company's presence on the Plateau, see Meinig, *Great Columbia Plain*, 66-95. See also Edwin Ernest Rich, *History of the Hudson's Bay Co., 1670-1870*, with a foreword by Winston Churchill, 2 vols., Publications of the Hudson's Bay Record Society nos. 21-22 (London: Hudson's Bay Record Society, 1958-59): 2: 563-748.

[33] Josephy, *Nez Perce Indians*, 74-75ff; Meinig, *Great Columbia Plain*, 66-95, 101.

[34] Sometimes settlers negotiated sales of small parcels of land from Indians. See Josephy, *Nez Perce Indians*, 159; Coleman, *Presbyterian Attitudes*, 120.

[35] Angelo Anastasio, "The Southern Plateau: An Ecological Analysis of Intergroup Relations," *Northwest Anthropological Research Notes (NwARN)* 6 (1972): 186; Meinig, *Great Colum-*

Both Euro-Americans and Native Americans perceived ways to benefit from those trade relationships in relatively equal ways. Fur traders needed Indian permission and occasionally protection in order to trap or travel in the region; additionally they came to rely on Indian trade to secure horses—for both travel and meat—and foods, such as dried salmon. Those Euro-Americans were used to a meat-based diet year round: The normal Canadian ration was eight pounds per day. Since those men generally disliked fish and possessed poor fishing skills anyway, and because bison and other game were only seasonally available or locally unavailable, they relied on Indian horses for their main protein source.[36]

That circumstance proved lucrative to Indians, and they regularly exchanged numbers of their plentiful horses for eastern trade goods. This trade required only slight modification of pre-existing inter-Plateau trade networks, and fit well within the pre-existing task group organization. Thus unlike Indian-white relations in the east, Plateau peoples were not losers in this balance of trade and they never came to depend upon Euro-American trade goods as much as Euro-Americans depended on what they got in exchange. It was only after 1850 that Euro-Americans forcibly shifted this balance in the west.[37]

Unlike traders and explorers, missionaries, settlers, and treaty makers wanted to physically transplant their bundle, or property concepts, to the Plateau and encourage or force others to accept it. Missionaries, especially, embodied the most conscious expression of the Euro-American bundle. They came to teach both the Gospel and civilization to Plateau peoples, two lessons that reached their fullest expression in the ideal of transforming Indians into individual, property-holding farmers.[38] And while Christians were united in educating Natives in the tenets of Christian brother- and sisterhood, often they were hard-pressed to view one another with such kind eyes.

One major schism was the rivalry between Catholics and Protestants. Protestants labored under the twin burdens of expediting the anticipated millennium and developing the American continent. Catholics, like their Protestant counterparts, saw their mission as rescuing Indians from barbarism

---

bia Plain, 59-61; Josephy, *The Nez Pence Indians*, 104-05ff; Lester A. Ross, "Early Nineteenth Century Euroamerican Technology Within the Columbia River Drainage System," *NwARN* 9 (no. 1) (Spring 1975): 32-50. On Indian participation in the Canadian and eastern U.S. fur trade, see Calvin Martin, *Keepers of the Game: Indian-Animal Relationships and the Fur Trade* (Berkeley: University of California Press, 1978); Shepard Krech III, ed., *Indians, Animals, and the Fur Trade: A Critique of Calvin Martin's Keepers of the Game* (Athens: University of Georgia Press, 1981); Daniel Francis and Toby Morantz, *Partners in Furs: A History of the Fur Trade in Eastern James Bay, 1600-1870* (Kingston and Montreal: McGill-Queen's University Press, 1983); Theodore J. Karamanski, *Fur Trade and Exploration, Opening the Far Northwest, 1821-1852* (Norman: University of Oklahoma Press, 1983).

[36] Meinig, *Great Columbia Plain*, 59.

[37] Meinig, *Great Columbia Plain*, 59-60.

[38] Later expressed in the Dawes Allotment Act of 1887, see Chapter 6 below.

as well as providing guidance for their own flocks in the wild.[39] The two sects constantly battled one another over access to potential converts.

Catholics priests had several advantages over their Protestant counterparts, however. They were single men without families to maintain and they found ready congregations among the French-Canadian trappers. Indians generally favored them too because they were intrigued by the church's rituals and priests sometimes treated Indians with less arrogance than did Protestant missionaries.

Catholic theology portrayed the individual as rooted in a shared community that was framed and infused with meaning by liturgical ritual. The community ideal structured Catholic plans for converting and "civilizing' Indians. Catholics, to a much larger extent than Protestants, tolerated Plateau peoples' continuing pursuit of subsistence lifeways. They also invited Indian participation in ritual from the very start of their missionary activities, and baptized people of all ages without requiring the initiates to attain some preconceived ideal of parochial achievement.[40]

The typical Catholic mission, or "reduction," had several stages. First, missionaries would cultivate interest among a particular group of Indians, a process that could take several years. Once Indians appeared suitably interested, priests organized the construction of mission facilities using Indian labor. After the buildings were up, the priests tried to encourage Indians to live there year-round, filling their days with labor, prayer, and organized play in such a way to "deprogram" Indian lifeways and substitute their own. The policy was never fully implemented in the Oregon missions because a chronic shortage of funds made it impossible to establish facilities big enough to house large numbers of Indians, and Indian interests lay in using Catholicism for their own purposes, not in converting and adopting Euro-American lifestyles.[41]

---

[39] Robert I. Burns, *The Jesuits and Indian Wars of the Far Northwest,* Yale Western Americana Series (New Haven: Yale University Press, 1966): 36-42; Drury, *Henry Harmon Spalding,* 329. See also Daniel Fogel, *Junipero Serra, the Vatican, and Enslavement Theology* (San Francisco: ISM Press, 1988).

[40] Michael C. Coleman, *Presbyterian Missionary Attitudes toward American Indians, 1837-1893* (Jackson: University Press of Mississippi, 1985): 120, 122; Robert H. Ruby and John A. Brown, *Indians of the Pacific Northwest,* The Civilization of the American Indian Series (Norman: University of Oklahoma Press, 1981): 86-87.

[41] Burns, *Jesuits and Indian Wars,* 48-55. See also Fogel, *Junipero Serra,* 114-64, for a description of the effect of mission life on Indians. Catholics by 1845 had established missions among the Flathead, Coeur d'Alene, Kalispel, Kutenai, San Poil, Spokane, Okanagan, and the Crees. Additional missions served Kettle Falls, and the Willamette and Cowlitz valleys, Fort Vancouver, Whidbey Island, and New Caledonia [British Columbia]. Before 1848 priests had also begun work with the Yakama and Cayuse, the Shoshone, Bannock, and Blackfeet. See Burns, *Jesuits and Indian Wars,* 44-48; Francis N. Blanchet, *Historical Sketches of the Catholic Church in Oregon During the Past Forty Years* (Portland, OR: Catholic Centennial Press, 1878).

Protestants differed from their Catholic counterparts in many respects. Most notably, their ranks included women and family groups who went west as much to homestead as to bring the Word to Native peoples. Setting up a homestead and feeding a family was hard work that kept many of these missionaries from devoting their concentrated energies on their intended pupils.

One such missionary was Narcissa Prentiss. A New York native, Prentiss traced her conversion experience to a revival she had attended at the age of eleven.[42] In 1835, she wrote to the American Board, regarding a post where she could employ her "particular interest for the salvation of the heathen."[43] While the Board viewed with favor her intention to "consecrate myself without reserve to the Missionary work," the organization was unwilling to send a single woman over the Rocky Mountains alone.[44] The American Board turned prudent matchmaker and introduced Prentiss to Dr. Marcus Whitman, an eligible physician-minister, also seeking to join the American Board's cause. The pair was well suited. They married and in 1836, accompanied by three other missionaries, three Nez Perce boys, and two drifters, left for Oregon country. There they eventually established three missions among the Cayuse and Nez Perce and, despite their deaths in an attack of the mission in 1848, set the stage for other missionaries who followed.[45]

Protestants did not have an easy time establishing themselves in the west, which in part strengthened their conviction that God intended them to work

---

[42] Prentiss to David Greene, Feb. 23, 1835, reprinted in Archer Butler Hulbert and Dorothy Printup Hulbert, *Marcus Whitman Crusader: 1802-1839*, 3 vols. (Colorado Springs and Denver: The Stewart Commission of Colorado College and the Denver Public Library, 1936): 1:139-40.

[43] Narcissa Prentiss to David Greene, Feb. 23, 1835, reprinted in Hulbert and Hulbert, *Marcus Whitman Crusader*, 1:139-140. The Whitmans are probably the best known of the Oregon Country missionaries and their correspondence and other writings provide a good view into their work with and attitudes toward Indians. Hulbert and Hulbert's work contains an almost complete collection of the letters written by Narcissa's husband Marcus Whitman from their Oregon mission to the Cayuse between about 1835 and 1847. Hulbert and Hulbert include a few of Narcissa's letters in their work, but the bulk of her personal correspondence and her journal documenting their overland journey to the Oregon country have been published in Narcissa Prentiss Whitman, "A Journey Across the Plains in 1836," and "Letters Written by Mrs. Whitman from Oregon to her Relatives in New York," [hereafter cited as "N. Y. Letters"], Oregon Pioneer Ass'n, *Transactions of the 19th Annual Reunion, 1891* (Portland, OR, A. Anderson & Co. Printers and Lithographers, 1893):40-68 and 79-179; and "Mrs. Whitman's Letters," 53-219.

[44] Prentiss to Greene, Feb. 23, 1835, reprinted in Hulbert and Hulbert, *Marcus Whitman* 1:139-140.

[45] The three missionaries were the couple Henry and Eliza Spaulding, and William Gray. Drury, *Henry Harmon Spalding*, 132. [Spaulding's legal last name is spelled with an "au," although he himself always omitted the "u".] The attack of the mission became known as the "Whitman Massacre," which was followed by the Cayuse War, discussed below.

there.[46] Unlike the priests, Protestants had no ready congregations because up to the early 1840s most non-Indians on the Plateau were French-Canadian Catholics. Even where they encountered fellow Protestants, they were not always greeted joyfully. Marcus Whitman recounted that his guides on the overland passage—American Fur Company personnel—contemptuously pelted him with rotten eggs.[47]

Protestant sects tended to view themselves as competing for Indian converts, not working for a single cause. The American Board, for example, was a coalition of Congregationalist, Presbyterian, and Dutch Reformed groups; a volatile mix according to Marcus Whitman who complained that "We cannot keep the mission together at our General meetings long enough to settle upon any principle of action. It has always been the case that we must break up our meetings before any of the work necessary for harmonizing the Mission was entered upon."[48] Other sects, such as Methodists, Anglicans, and, later, Presbyterians ran their own missionary societies as well.

From 1834 to 1847, when the Oregon Provisional Government ordered all missionaries out of the Pacific Northwest with the outbreak of the Cayuse War, Protestant missionaries battled one another and collectively battled Catholic missions for control over the bodies and spirits of the Native Plateau peoples.[49] The issue was which one of two interpretations of the Euro-American bundle would be imposed on the Plateau peoples. While Catholics and Protestants shared key concepts of the bundle, they also differed. Both perceived a radical separation between humans and God and between humans and nature, but

---

[46] In 1834 and 1836 Methodist missionaries had been sent into the Willamette Valley, although these missions initially did not include women among their personnel. For a history of the ABCFM see Clifton J. Philips, *Protestant America and the Pagan World: The First Half Century of the American Board of Commissioners for Foreign Missions, 1819-1860* (East Asian Research Center, Cambridge MA: Harvard University Press, 1969). Drury asserts that Narcissa Whitman and Eliza Spaulding were the first white women to cross the Rocky Mountains. He speculated that had the War Department—whose permission had to be secured to station whites in Indian Country—been informed of the ABCFM plan to send the women, the missionaries might not have received permission to settle. Drury, *Henry Harmon Spalding*, 124.

[47] Josephy, *Nez Perce Indians*, 125-26. The American Fur Company people also tried to scare the two missionaries by pretending that they were plotting to kill the pair as soon as their overland caravan reached the Plains. The table was turned, however, Josephy reports, when cholera broke out among the group and they had to rely on Whitman's medical skills.

[48] Marcus Whitman to Daniel Greene, Oct. 29, 1840, reprinted in Hulbert and Hulbert, *Marcus Whitman, Crusader*, 2: 199-200.

[49] The November 1847 "Whitman Massacre" followed an outbreak of measles which affected native peoples more virulently than the Whitman's Wailaptu mission staff. A small group of Cayuse led the attack, killing both Marcus and Narcissa, along with twelve other mission personnel. See Josephy, *Nez Perce Indians*, 256-72. Only the ABCFM missionaries followed the directive to leave, however. Catholic missionaries remained in the interior and continued to expand their activities. Burns, *Jesuits and Indian Wars*, 24-25, 117-18. Burns describes some incidents of cooperation among the competing sects, ibid. 35.

they disagreed about the importance of the individual. Catholics, as we have already seen, tended to focus on the individual's role within the community. Protestants focused primarily on the individual as an independent entity.

Protestants stressed the individual's role in discerning God for oneself and wedded that idea to the image of the yeoman farmer whom they believed would ultimately conquer the frontier by God's will and for the nation's benefit. Such rampant individualism tended to reduce the effectiveness of the work at hand.[50] Marcus Whitman, surveying "the increase of [the American Board's] stations" to four in 1840, lamented: "why all must grow grain for themselves is more than I can say. But I do know that no minister would receive his support from any one else in the Mission.... For every one to be his own farmer, house builder &c, is too much work. For one to be alone is to limit his time so much to the care of his family that little can be done for the Indians."[51]

Yet Protestants, powered by a "Theological Science," maintained that they embodied both reason and God's law. To them, Catholics were creatures of ritual, helpless puppets of Rome. To missionaries such as the Whitmans, the Indians' ready adoption of Catholic ritual strengthened their own conviction that Catholicism was an evil collection of "heartless forms and ceremonies" favored by the Indians because it appealed to their heathen, senseless "instincts."[52]

Protestant missionaries generally believed that Catholics were out to undermine their efforts. Daniel Greene, advising the Whitmans about how to suffer the Catholic Plateau presence, told them "it is probably the policy of that [Catholic] church to meet Protestants every where on heathen ground ... & do what can be done to hinder their efforts."[53] Henry Spalding was shocked to discover that Catholic priests had begun teaching doctrine by using small printed charts "on which the Road to Heaven is exhibited & from which Luther is represented as branching off in a road that leads to hell." To combat this

---

[50] The Presbyterian Board of Foreign Missions established an Oregon mission on its own in 1871. See Coleman, *Presbyterian Attitudes*, 69-71. On rivalry between the ABCFM mission and the Methodist mission, see Greene to Whitman, Aug. 3, 1840 and Whitman to Greene, Oct. 29, 1840, reprinted in Hulbert and Hulbert, *Marcus Whitman*, 2: 180-200. Drury, in *Henry Harmon Spalding*, notes that the Methodists experienced many problems with factionalism in their own mission in the early 1840s, ibid., 275-84. On problems between the ABCFM and the Whitman-Spalding mission, see Greene to Whitman, Sept. 6, 1839, and Greene to Whitman and Spalding, March 21, 1839, reprinted in Hulbert and Hulbert, *Marcus Whitman*, 2: 133, 149-52.

[51] Whitman to Greene, Oct. 29, 1840, reprinted in Hulbert and Hulbert, *Marcus Whitman*, 2:200.

[52] Eliza Spaulding, *Diary*, March 31, 1836, quoted in Drury, *Henry Harmon Spalding*, 124-25; Hulbert and Hulbert, *Marcus Whitman*, 3: 53-55.

[53] Greene to Whitman, Aug. 3, 1840, reprinted in Hulbert and Hulbert; *Marcus Whitman*, 2: 182.

"attack," he wrote, "I have planned and Mrs. S. has drawn and painted a chart about 6 feet long and 2 wide containing two ways one narrow & one broad.... Luther is represented as leaving the broad road & returning to the narrow way."[54]

Such timelines may have been inspired initially by the Plateau people's own method of depicting history on long lines of knotted string or notched sticks. Plateau missionaries of all persuasions appear to have used such charts widely, attracted by their portability and easy portrayal of the "right way" to Indians who were constantly moving and did not stay near any one mission for very long. Importantly, the possession of one of the Catholic charts, according to Narcissa Whitman, "binds him [the Indian] not to hear any more the instructions of the Protestants, so far as my observations can prove."[55] Perhaps exasperated Plateau dwellers took to carrying the charts simply to avoid further harassment from zealous missionaries.

The influx of missionaries of all sorts rapidly threatened "to bewilder our poor Indians already perplexed beyond measure by the number and variety of their instructors," lamented John McLoughlin, chief factor of the Hudson's Bay Company.[56] Rather than being bewildered, however, most Plateau peoples seem to have taken what they wanted of missionary teachings and proceeded as they pleased. Prophet Dance adherents sought out Christians to confirm their own religious ideals.[57] Further, many of them welcomed the coming of both Catholic and Protestant personnel because they perceived an opportunity to exploit interfaith rivalry to their own benefit.[58]

Some people no doubt gave up their pre-contact lifestyles and converted wholeheartedly to both Christianity and Euro-American ways. Missionaries occasionally recounted tales of young women who had come to adore the Virgin Mary so passionately that they sickened and died rather than entered marriages with Indian men arranged by their families.[59] Even if we take those

---

[54] Spalding to Greene, Feb. 12, 1846, excerpted in Drury, *Henry Harmon Spalding*, 330. Narcissa Whitman, too, noted the use of a similar chart hanging in the office of D. F. McLoughlin, Chief Factor of the Hudson's Bay Co. in Vancouver, "which represents all Protestants as the withered ends of the several branches of the papacy falling off down into infernal society and flames, as represented at the bottom." Narcissa Whitman, "N. Y. Letters," 150. See generally, on origins and uses, Ruby and Brown, *Indians of the Pacific Northwest*, 87.

[55] Narcissa Whitman to her parents, Oct. 6, 1841, reprinted in "N. Y. Letters," 150-51.

[56] Quoted in Ruby and Brown, *Indians of the Pacific Northwest*, 81.

[57] Spier, *Prophet Dance*, 35, 44.

[58] See for example Green to Whitman and Spaulding, March 21, 1839, reprinted in Hulbert and Hulbert, *Marcus Whitman*, 2:133, 136-37, noting that the ABCFM has chosen not to increase the number of missionaries at the Cayuse and Nez Perce outposts because of "The jealousy & opposition of the traders" and "suspicions of your designs might be excited in the bosoms of the Indians." See also Hulbert and Hulbert, Introduction, *Marcus Whitman*, 3:51.

[59] Victor Garrand, *Augustine Laure, S.J.: Missionary to the Yakimas*, trans. Michael M. O'Malley (Fairfield, WA: Ye Galleon Press, 1977): 26-27. It is impossible to know whether

stories at face value—overlooking the greater potential that these women contracted a European disease from which they died, or that the stories were wholly make believe—many Plateau peoples did not accept missionary teachings. One Cayuse told Narcissa Whitman, "Your instruction is good; the wise and discreet appreciate it; for the mass of us, we hear it, but it falls powerless upon our hearts, and we remain still."[60]

Still others expressed confusion at the new order held out by whites and adopted an attitude of waiting. When, in 1836, a delegation of Indians from the Dalles, probably Upper Chinook, visited the missionary Samuel Parker at Fort Vancouver, their Chief said: "He had prayed much to the Great Spirit, and found his heart was no better, but worse."[61]

Both Protestants and Catholics believed that those Indians who survived the toll of disease and lived through white settlement of their homelands needed to have alternative methods of subsistence in order to survive. Farming, especially because it captured and made tangible so many elements of the Euro-American bundle—individual ownership of property, cultivation of land, participation in a market economy—was the missionaries' perfect alternative.[62] Catholics seem to have been more willing than Protestants to tolerate the Indian practice of combining small scale farming with pre-contact subsistence patterns, but both camps proved unable to break Indian subsistence lifeways.

Teaching farms were an important part of all the missions, and Indians observed and participated in those farms to a certain extent. The Whitmans may have established the first irrigated farm on the Plateau. Here, by 1838, they grew "six acres of potatoes two & half of wheat & peas oats & corn enough to make forty acres probably[.]"[63] Other missionaries followed their practice. Francoise Blanchet and Eugene Chirouse helped Indians establish "garden patches" at the Ahtanum Creek Catholic mission in 1847. By the 1860s they had established a "field and meadow and orchard" watered by a gravity flow ditch.[64] Additionally, missionaries encouraged Indians to raise sheep and cattle, to supplement their own horses.

Plateau peoples who survived disease epidemics responded with new ideologies embodying the conviction that they would eventually overcome the terrible destruction of diseases and increasing non-Indian settlement. By the

---

other factors such as disease or depression played a role in their deaths. Depression was widespread among Indians who lived at mission reductions full time.

[60] Narcissa Whitman to Mr. and Mrs. Allen, Aug. 23, 1842, reprinted in "Letters," 152-53.

[61] Spier, *Prophet Dance*, 20.

[62] See, for example, Marcus Whitman to David Greene, May 8, 1838, reprinted in Hulbert and Hulbert, *Marcus Whitman*, 1: 314-15.

[63] Marcus Whitman to Greene, May 8, 1838, reprinted in Hulbert and Hulbert, *Marcus Whitman*, 1: 315.

[64] *The Yakima Valley Catholic Centennial, 1847-1947* (Yakima, WA: n.p., 1947); Burns, *Jesuits and Indian Wars*, 48-55, for a description of a Catholic mission "reduction."

1850s, the Prophet Dance religion had grown into a complex, apocalyptic belief system, in which the idea of a coming millenium was joined to the anticipated genocide of Euro-Americans. This new Smohalla religion, named after the hunchbacked, Wanapum prophet who founded it, promised that if people retained pre-contact modes of dress and life, they would hasten the destruction of Euro-Americans.[65]

Apocalyptic religions historically have arisen in cultures that feel the impending destruction of their world or way of life. The appearance of such beliefs on the Plateau during this time indicates the desperation people must have felt about a world whose patterns could no longer be reliably predicted based on former belief systems. One scholar who studied the apocalyptic tradition among Americans in the post-nuclear age, suggested that

> [The apocalyptic perspective] resists the extremes of passivity and panic by speaking of continuity, by offering direction to a people overwhelmed by sheer process. It resists the crisis of change by inculcating change into its very vocabulary. It speaks most eloquently and most directly to a community of the frightened, the despairing, the uncertain and assures it that the apparent disorder of history will finally affirm order, will finally give heart.[66]

Smohalla and other Plateau prophets of the time used the Prophet Dance to bridge the chaotic present and the customs of the past, and taught people that they had the power to turn back the Euro-American tide, if not in this world, then the next.

Smohalla and other prophet cults challenged the Euro-American notion of property, teaching that all human attempts to survey, fence, farm, or mine the earth would violate the earth mother. These prophets amplified existing notions of the proper relationship between humans and the earth: Dividing land into individual property holdings was wrong, as was any action that would break the earth mother's skin.[67] Significantly, the Smohalla religion was the impetus to later important healing faiths including Shakerism, Pom-pom

---

[65] Spier, *Prophet Dance*, 21-24, 40-41.

[66] Joseph Dewey, *In a Dark Time the Apocalyptic Temper in the American Novel of the Nuclear Age* (West Lafayette, IN: Purdue University Press, 1990): 11. See also Zbigniew Lewicki, *The Bang and the Whimper: Apocalypse and Entropy in American Literature*, Contributions in American Studies, no. 71 (Westport, CT: Greenwood Press, 1984): 3-19.

[67] Spier, *Prophet Dance*, 40-54; *CIA-AR*, 1895-96, 321; E.L. Higgins, "Smohalla, the Prophet of Priest Rapids," *Overland Monthly*, ser. 2, 17 (1891): 208-15; Deward E. Walker, Jr., "New Light on the Prophet Dance Controversy," *Ethnohistory* 16 (1969): 245-55; Charles Relander (Now Tow Look), *Drummers and Dreamers: The Story of Smohalla the Prophet and his Nephew Puck Hyah Toot...*, with a foreword by Frederick Webb Hodge (Caldwell, ID: The Caxton Printers, 1956): 96, 139ff.

religion, and the Yakama's Longhouse or Washat religion, still practiced today.[68]

Yakama practiced their own religion despite adopting the outward trappings of Judeo-Christian beliefs. In 1939, Yakima Agent C. R. Whitlock noted that "[p]ractically all of the older Indians participate in the 'Pom-pom' Indian ceremony even though they belong to one of the other denominations."[69] One informant told anthropologist Helen Schuster in the 1960s that her father taught Washat to children every Sunday, after which they went to a Methodist church; their father remained a medicine man even after he too began attending the church.[70]

Plateau peoples did not view themselves as mere elements within Euro-American schemes for the west. Throughout the nineteenth century, Indians continued to pursue their own religious practices, methods of social organization, and subsistence schedules, despite hostile white settlers and the often harsh missionary policies and warnings that "[the Indians] are all of them in the broad road to destruction; and their worshipping will not save them."[71]

Such warnings succeeded in angering Indians who in one case "threatened to whip [Whitman] & burn the crops" and who then sent cattle out "to trample the potato field nightly." Other antagonized groups broke into missionary stations, and threatened to charge mission personnel rent for building on Indian lands, and occasionally they raided settlers's encampments.[72] Intercultural violence was hardly limited to the missions: From the late 1840s

---

[68] Spier, *Prophet Dance*, 49-54; Schuster, "Yakima Traditionalism," 57, 246-47, 339-81. Shakerism was a healing cult, that, together with the Feather Cult (also a healing faith), spread throughout the Plateau in the 1880s and 1890s; Washat is not a healing faith. See also Rev. George Waters to Thomas Priestly, Yakima Indian Agent, Jan. 20, 1889, noting Pom-Pom religion and urging that the police and justice of the peace be enlisted to prevent Indians from by-passing church in order to "go dancing" and "idol worshiping," in filebox 115, folder 22 [hereafter cited as box:folder, CRP], Click Relander Papers, Yakima Valley Regional Library, Yakima, Washington; "Letters, Some Reminiscences of Experiences as Yakima Preacher," Bancroft Library, Univeristy of California, Berkeley. See also Ray Harmon, "Indian Shaker Church, The Dalles," *Oregon Historical Quarterly*, 72 (1971): 148-58; Cora Alice Du Bois, *The Feather Cult of the Middle Columbia*, General Series in Anthropology, ed. Leslie Spier, no. 7 (Menasha, WI: George Banta Publishing Co., 1938).

[69] C. R. Whitlock to H. D. Guie, Sept. 21, 1936, Folder 816:1, YA, Decimal Subject File, 803-826, Record Group 75, Records of the Bureau of Indian Affairs, NA-Seattle.

[70] Schuster "Yakima Traditionalism," 339.

[71] ABCFM missionaries sometimes whipped Indians who did not conform to their ideals. See for example Drury, *Henry Harmon Spalding*, 181-2, noting that Spalding, because of his quick temper, often took out his frustrations on Indians; Narcissa Whitman to Stephen Prentiss, Oct. 10, 1840, in "N. Y. Letters," 131. See also Fogel, *Junipero Serra*, with a discussion of Catholic missionary practices mostly with California Indians.

[72] Narcissa Whitman to Prentiss, Oct. 10, 1840, "N. Y. Letters," 131; Narcissa Whitman to Greene, ca. Nov. 18, 1841; N. Whitman to Marcus Whitman, Oct. 7, 1842 and N. Whitman to Stephen Prentiss, Feb. 7, 1843, ibid., 154-172. See also Drury, *Henry Harmon Spalding*, 231 (referring to 1847 incidents).

to the end of the century, Native Americans and Euro-Americans fought over the right to live free of interference on the Plateau. Those battles ranged from stock raids to massacres of Indians and settlers alike.[73] The history of the Plateau during this period cannot be separated from this ongoing warfare.

"You Have Spoken in a Manner Partly Tending To Evil"

In May 1840, Narcissa Whitman wrote to her mother, "A tide of immigration appears to be moving this way rapidly. What a few years will bring forth we know not."[74] Beginning in 1840, increasing numbers of non-Indian immigrants began moving to the Oregon country. Those peoples were attracted by reports sent east by Oregon missionaries and other publications emphasizing the Oregon Country's desirability as a place for settlement.[75]

By the end of the decade, 12,000 Americans had settled there, first in the Willamette Valley and then spreading northward. Under such laws as the Oregon Donation Land Act of 1850 settlers simply stole 2.5 million acres of Indian lands.[76] Settlers wanted large areas of unoccupied lands for farms, stock, grazing and resource mining; all uses that were compatible with the Euro-American bundle of property. Yet missionaries had only imperfectly introduced that bundle to the Plateau. As non-Indian settlement increasingly encroached on Plateau peoples, so did friction between those two societies, eventually breaking out in the Cayuse War of 1847, prompted by the massacre at the Whitman's mission; and continuing in various armed confrontations through 1858.[77]

---

[73] Besides the missions, there were many other sources of intercultural tensions on the Plateau. Non-Indians rushed across tribal lands in order to get to newly discovered gold fields; others simply appropriated Indian lands for their homesteads; settlers built roads across Indian lands, as they did on Yakama lands in 1853; white trappers depleted game populations; Indians stole settlers' stock; and Indians raided immigrant wagon trains moving west, taking goods, killing people sometimes, and kidnapping people as hostages or slaves. Ruby and Brown, *Indians of the Pacific Northwest*; Robert M. Utley, *The Indian Frontier of the American West 1846-1890* (Albuquerque: University of New Mexico Press, 1984).

[74] Narcissa Whitman to Mrs. Prentiss, May 2, 1840, reprinted in Narcissa Whitman, "N.Y. Letters," 134.

[75] Meinig, *Great Columbia Plain*, 152-200.

[76] Donation Land Act, ch. 69, 9 Stat. 496 (1853); Josephy, *Nez Perce Indians*, 278-79, noting that the Donation Land Act provided for appropriation from the public domain, but because there was no public land yet, Congress passed an Indian Treaty Act that authorized the purchase of Indian land and the removal of the tribes to undesirable lands. Under the terms of the Donation Act, male settlers over the age of 18 could get land grants to half sections if they had occupied and cultivated their lands for 4 consecutive years prior to December 1851. If married by December 1851, their wives could get a half section as well. White males, over the age of 21, and their wives could get 160 acre sections if they settled between December 1, 1850 and December 1, 1853.

[77] Josephy, *Nez Perce Indians*, 255-76. Drury, *Henry Harmon Spalding*, 231; Spalding to Mr. and Mrs. Prentiss, April 6, 1848, letter reprinted in Narcissa Whitman, "Letters," 93-97.

Plateau peoples were not united in their position on non-Indian settlement of their homelands and that splintering hampered a concerted effort to stave off white conquest. Some welcomed increased opportunities for trade and increased contact with non-Indians. Others, putting their stakes in the Prophet Cult and Indian solidarity saw whites as an increasing threat to both their lands and lives that could be met only by force. Still others believed that their only course was to accept whatever compensation they could get for their lands and move out of the way of non-Indian settlers.

Thus, by the 1850s both Native American and Euro-American bundles were operative and in direct competition on the Plateau. The American presence on the Plateau, however, was no longer an uncertain prospect and non-Indian settlers eagerly sought and secured federal backing for their own interests.

Several legal developments were key to entrenching American interests in the Pacific Northwest. In 1848, Oregon became a territory, followed by Washington in 1853, which entitled settlers to both a government and to federal troops recruited from the Mexican war to help put down the festering Indian war. With territorial status came formal organization of federal Indian affairs for Washington and Oregon. According to the act creating the Washington Territory, for example the federal government reserved control over the Indians and designated the territorial governor to be superintendent of Indian Affairs. Indians, by the terms of the act, retained all the rights that they had before the territory was created.[78]

In addition to territorial laws, federal land laws made available large areas of Indian lands for settlement.[79] As Indian policy moved toward a reservation system, federal officials decided to create a few reserves east of the Cascades, where all Native peoples of the new Washington Territory—from the coast to the interior—would be relocated.[80]

The most important purpose served by the reservation policy was to secure to the United States title to Indian lands and establish the legal basis for the subjugation of those peoples. Euro-American interest in getting the treaties negotiated rapidly increased with discoveries of gold in the Rogue Valley in 1851, and national fervor to build the transcontinental railroad.[81] Federal efforts to conclude treaties with the Washington tribes culminated in 1855-56

---

[78] An Act to Establish the Territorial Government of Washington, Mar. 2, 1853, 10 Stats. L., 172; C. F. Coan, "The Adoption of the Reservation Policy in the Pacific Northwest, 1853-55," *Oregon Historical Quarterly* 23 (March 1922): 11.

[79] On military volunteers, see Josephy, *Nez Perce Indians*, 255-56; see also Utley, *Indian Frontier*, 52-55.

[80] Coan, "Adoption of the Reservation Policy," 13-38; Utley, *Indian Frontier*, 52-53; Richard D. Scheuerman, "Territorial Indian Policy and Tribal Relations, 1850-1856," in Clifford Trafzer, ed., *Indians, Superintendents, and Councils: Northwestern Indian Policy, 1850-1855* (Lanham, MO: University Press of America, 1986): 7-18.

[81] Josephy, *Nez Perce Indians*, 279-80ff.

in a series of agreements negotiated between Native groups and Isaac Ingalls Stevens, newly appointed governor of the Washington Territory, though it would take another couple years to officially quell outbreaks of war.

Stevens was first in his graduating class at West Point in 1839, and had gone west that year as second in command of the U.S. Pacific Coast Survey. He viewed the Pacific Northwest as an area suitable for agriculture, business, and international trade; as a Jacksonian democrat he carried the ideal of America's Manifest Destiny near to his heart. He apparently was little interested in the peoples with whom he treated. As one historian has noted,

> In Stevens' plan for setting up reservations east of the Cascades, he seemed to ignore basic linguistic and cultural differences between various tribal groups. He submitted reservation boundaries at the outset of negotiations, apparently without considering the extensive seasonal rounds followed by the Plateau Indians."[82]

Stevens, like the settlers and their congressional representatives, wanted fast negotiations that would allow the area to be opened to immediate non-Indian settlement.[83]

At the least, a discussion of the impact of disease on Native American populations raises the question of who remained alive on the Plateau for the United States to treat with and how representative and able to "negotiate" those Indians could have been. Contemporary observers note that in the late 1840s and continuing through the 1860s, Plateau tribes suffered several bouts of measles and smallpox. In 1853, Joel Palmer, superintendent of Indian Affairs for Oregon Territory, reported "miserable remnants" of tribes whose dead kin, victims of a smallpox epidemic, lay strewn along the Puget sound and the mid-Columbia.[84] The visible effects of disease epidemics among the Plateau and coastal tribes strengthened treaty makers' beliefs that their agreements were made with "feeble" races whose members could provide no long-term challenge to Euro-American settlement.[85]

Plateau peoples knew of U.S. plans to create reservations because of several federal officials that had travelled in the area before the Stevens' treaty party arrived.[86] The news spread rapidly through the Plateau and beyond, and many groups agreed to resist Stevens's offer. Coastal tribes had no desire to be relocated, and peoples east of the Cascades, such as the Yakama, did not want

---

[82] Scheuerman, "Territorial Indian Policy," 9.

[83] The area had been officially closed to settlement since the Whitman massacre, by order of General John E. Wool, commander of the U.S. Army's Department of the Pacific.

[84] Joel Palmer, Annual Report to Commissioner of Indian Affairs, Oct. 8, 1853, reprinted in Coan, "Adoption of the Reservation Policy," 31.

[85] Palmer, "Annual Report," in Coan, "Adoption of the Reservation Policy," 31.

[86] Dart had been authorized to conclude treaties with the Oregon tribes, but the Senate did not ratify them, leading to Dart's resignation in 1853. Joel Palmer was appointed to replace him that same year. Coan, "Adoption of Reservation Policy," 1.

to give up their lands and feared that the influx of western tribes would disrupt their economies or perhaps even destroy their entire way of life.[87]

In 1855, Palmer and Stevens travelled around the Plateau negotiating, although more often imposing, treaties on "the miserable bands and remnants of tribes in the region."[88] They concluded a dozen treaties, often coercively. Stevens's position was that resistance was futile: If Indians refused the federal government would take their lands by force. Large-scale organization for resistance was impossible because so many of the bands in the Plateau region were now decimated.[89]

The treaty proceedings make clear that some aspects of the Europeans' sacred bundle of property had already been incorporated—albeit unevenly—into the Plateau world view. Cayuse Chief Five Crows summed up the ambivalent feelings of many Plateau peoples gathered at the 1855 treaty council at Walla Walla upon hearing Stevens's plans, "You have spoken in a manner partly tending to Evil.... I should feel very much ashamed if the Americans should do anything wrong."[90]

Participants at the Walla Walla Council expressed mixture of attitudes in their discussion of Stevens's proposed land purchase. Some individuals, such as Cayuse Chief Steachus argued that the groups could accept no treaty: "If your mothers were here in this country who gave you birth and suckled you, and while you were sucking some person came and took away your mother and left you alone and sold your mother, how would you feel then? This is our mother, this country, as if we drew our living from her."[91] As Chief Five Crows put it, "Goods and earth are not equal"; Stevens's proposal made no sense because one could not sell what one did not own.[92]

Yakama Chief Owhi asked, "God named this land to us that is the reason I am afraid to say anything about this land.... Shall I steal this land and sell it?.... What shall I do? Shall I give the lands that are a part of my body and leave myself poor and destitute?"[93] The *wyakin*'s gift to humans depended upon a permanent and spiritual connection between humans and the earth, that necessarily was severed in the Euro-Americans bundle of property. People would be "poor" if they violated the connection, much as when a *wyakin*

---

[87] Josephy, *Nez Perce Indians*, 279; Scheuerman, "Territorial Indian Policy," 10, 13-16ff. See generally the essays in Trafzer, *Indians, Superintendents, and Councils*, for a discussion of Indian responses to treaty makers' demands in other Pacific Northwest treaty negotiations.

[88] Palmer, *Annual Report*, in Coan, "Adoption of the Reservation Policy," 31.

[89] Chief Lawyer, quoted in Stevens, *Council Proceedings*, 58; Chief Peopeo Moxmox, quoted in Stevens, ibid., 60. See also Scheuerman, "Territorial Indian Policy," 77.

[90] Stevens, *Council Proceedings*, 57.

[91] Stevens, *Council Proceedings*, 72.

[92] Five Crows, quoted in Stevens, *Council Proceedings*, 57; see also How-lish-wam-pum, quoted in ibid., 86.

[93] Quoted in Stevens *Council Proceedings*, 81-82.

withdrew from a human partnership. Many shared Owhi's fears and wished to postpone the negotiations until they could ponder further the terms of Stevens's offer and confer with their people.[94]

Other individuals, however, attempted to blend the old Plateau concept of land with a newer understanding of land as property. Young Chief of the Cayuse told Stevens:

> The reason that I do not know anything about this ground is I do not see the offer you have made as yet. If I had the money in my hand then I would see. The country is very large is the reason this land is afraid. I wonder if this ground has any thing to say. I wonder if the ground is listening to what is said. I wonder if the ground would come to life and what is on it.... God said, You Indians who take care of a certain portion of the country should not trade it off unless you get a fair price.[95]

Here, humans and the earth still were divinely connected, but God had also given humans the choice to alter that relationship if they received a "fair price." Yakama Chief Skloom told Stevens, "My friends, I have understood what you have said. When you give me what is just for my land you shall have it."[96]

The sentiments of most Plateau peoples at the treaty council went against Stevens and his proposals more strongly as the proceedings progressed. With the exception of Nez Perce Chief The Lawyer, and some participants whose lands were not affected by Stevens's plans, all other participants were against Stevens. Stevens had originally proposed the creation of two reserves, one in Nez Perce country and one in Yakama country. Here he expected to collect all the Plateau peoples. He added a third reservation in the Umatilla Valley as a result of Cayuse, Umatilla, and Walla Walla opposition to being forced to move to the Nez Perce reservation.

Although it is possible some of the participants were able to convince Stevens to include important lands within the reservation system, the Council clearly did not work to the advantage of any Indian group. First, many bands later held to the treaty were not present at the Council. Second, the reservations fell grossly short of protecting the boundaries of each band's homelands. Some of the Plateau groups had planned before the Council to divide the entire Plateau region among themselves along the lines of their territories and request that Stevens recognize those boundaries. That plan ultimately failed because the tenuous alliances among the tribes did not withstand the pressure of the negotiations.

Many chiefs present were silent or accepted Stevens's terms with bitterness, but the Nez Perce War Chief Looking Glass, who arrived only at the end

---

[94] Peopeo Moxmox, quoted in Stevens *Council Proceedings*, 79; Owhi, quoted in ibid., 80-81.

[95] Stevens, *Council Proceedings*, 77. Young Chief includes a long section detailing what the earth, fish, grass, and water speaks to the Indians.

[96] Quoted in Stevens, *Council Proceedings*, 95.

of the Council, admonished the Indians, "My people, what have you done? While I was gone, you have sold my country. I have come home, and there is not left me a place on which to pitch my lodge. Go home to your lodges. I will talk to you." Looking Glass, too, eventually signed.[97] Kamiakin, Yakama chief, also eventually signed, although only after Stevens told him that he "would walk in blood knee deep" if he refused.[98] Thus Stevens's successful conclusion of the Walla Walla Council came at the expense of the Plateau peoples.

Conclusion: The 1855 Treaty

The most readily identifiable effect of the treaty was to convey title of Indian lands to the United States in exchange for small reservations for the peoples who were party to the treaties. The treaties provided written and public notice of the federal government's extinguishment of "all their [Indians'] right, title, and interest in and to the lands and country occupied and claimed by them...."[99] Thereafter, to be heard, Indians had to express their claims in the language of their colonizers: Now the legal imposition of the Euro-American property bundle was fully manifest.

The Nez Perce succeeded in retaining much of their homelands but others were less fortunate. Yakama lost their lands north of Ahtanum Creek, including in the Naches, Wenas, and upper Yakima river valleys. Several other groups retained none of their ancestral lands and were to move onto the Yakamas' reservation. Those groups included peoples in the Grand Coulee and Moses Lake areas (who were not at the Council), Palouse groups who lost their grazing and fishing grounds east of the Columbia, and the Wallawallas.[100]

Fourteen head men signed the treaty establishing the Yakamas' reserve. Those men represented the Yakama, Kittitas, Palouse, Wenatchi, Klickitat, Columbia, Chelan, and Wishram groups.[101] The Yakama "tribe" as it has come to be known, is a product of the treaty; not of any prior alliance among Plateau peoples. Euro-Americans who were eager to set Indians into familiar structures, designated Kamiakin, a Yakama chief, as chief of the entire collection of peoples to be relocated on the reserve.

---

[97] Looking Glass, quoted in Josephy, *Nez Perce Indians*, 319. Josephy argued that Looking Glass signed because his authority was subordinate to that of Lawyer, who had already signed, ibid., 322.

[98] Quoted in Andrew Dominique Pambrun, *Sixty Years on the Frontier in the Pacific Northwest* (Fairfield, WA: Ye Galleon Press, 1978): 95.

[99] Treaty with the Yakima, art. 1.

[100] Josephy, *Nez Perce Indians*, 326.

[101] Fourteen tribes were supposed to have been assigned to the reservation, but some of those tribes never existed or were actually conglomerations of diverse tribes. Treaty with the Yakima, 12 Stat. 951 (1855); Schuster, "Yakima Traditionalism," 44, 242; Scheuerman, "Territorial Indian Policy," 77.

The treaty provided that the Yakama would give up about ten million acres for $200,000, a 1.25 million acre reservation, and an adjacent fishery on the Wenatshapam River. The $200,000 compensation was payable over a twenty-year period and disbursed according to the President's determination "upon what beneficial objects to expend the same [monies] for them."[102]

According to the treaty, the Yakama reservation boundaries were Ahtanum Creek on the north; the Yakima River on the east; the ridge of the Cascade Mountains on the west; and on Satass Creek to the south.[103] The treaty provided that the people could continue to subsist in pre-contact ways, but also that the federal government would ensure that the tribe received the proper introduction to Euro-American culture.

Stevens had been authorized to allow the Indians to retain some fishing rights and all of the Stevens treaties contained similar clauses that guaranteed to the Indians rights to their traditional fisheries. Article Three of the Treaty with the Yakima stated:

> The exclusive right of taking fish in all the streams, where running through or bordering said reservation, is further secured to said confederated tribes and bands of Indians, as also the right of taking fish at all usual and accustomed places, in common with the citizens of the Territory, and of erecting temporary buildings for curing them; together with the privilege of hunting, gathering roots and berries, and pasturing their horses and cattle upon open and unclaimed land.[104]

Article Ten of the treaty also secured for the Indians a six-mile square tract of land between the forks of the Wenatshapam River, known as a valuable fishery.[105] In the 1850s, such reserved subsistence rights did not appear to encroach upon the Euro-American interests too much. In any event, policy-makers fully expected Indians to die out or adopt white ways of life in the near future.

The Yakamas' treaty contains only two clauses that pertain to subsistence. Much more important to Stevens and federal policymakers was how Indians were to use their lands. The other clauses outline a plan for this anticipated land use. Article Two states that the land of the reserve is to be used for the "use and benefit" of the tribe but allows white people to move to the reserve with the permission of the Indian agent and the tribe. The purpose of that provision was to enable white farmers and others to live in the reserves as examples to the Indians of the civilized way of life.[106] Article Four, further, details the pattern that Indian settlement should follow: The first compen-

---

[102] Treaty with the Yakima, art. 4.

[103] Treaty with the Yakima, art. 2.

[104] Treaty with the Yakima, art. 3.

[105] Treaty with the Yakima, art. 10.

[106] *CIA-AR*, 1909-10, in *Reports of the Department of the Interior* (1910): 5-7.

sation payment of $60,000 would go to "breaking up and fencing farms, building houses for [the Indians], supplying them with provisions and a suitable outfit...."[107]

In addition, the federal government would establish on the reserve two schools, two blacksmith's shops, a wagon and plough maker's shop, a saw mill, a flour mill, and a hospital, and would employ the personnel necessary to staff them for the purpose of instructing the Indians.[108] Finally, Article Six provided that the reserve could be surveyed into lots at the President's discretion and that those lots would be made available to individual members of the tribe.[109] Article Six became very important during the 1870s, with the adoption of federal allotment policies by which the federal government divided Indian lands into individual allotments and made the remaining "surplus" of allotted lands available to white settlers.

Congress did not ratify the Stevens treaties until 1859, and during the four years between the Council and ratification, many of the bands made party to the treaty engaged settlers and federal troops in a bloody war that Indians eventually lost. Stevens placed a newspaper ad in the *Oregon Weekly Times* twelve days after the Walla Walla treaties had been signed, stating that land east of the Cascades was now open to settlement. The resulting infestation of white settlers and land grabbers angered and frightened many of the people who believed that their homelands would remain closed to white entry until ratification. Moreover, as gold seekers poured into the region with news of gold strikes in Colville and elsewhere, Indians increasingly saw the treaties as meaningless: Many of the these migrating non-Indians tramped across Indian lands telling the residents that they no longer had any right to the land.[110] The war on the Plateau ended in late 1858—thanks in large part to the howitzers and long-range rifles of U.S. troops—with the defeat and execution of many Indian leaders.[111]

By 1857, J. W. Nesmith, the U.S. Superintendent of Indian Affairs for Oregon and Washington territories reported, "They [the Yakama] have been reduced by war, pestilence, and famine, to a small band consisting principally of old squaws and young children...."[112] Elsewhere in the territory, agents reported that the Rogue River Indians had lost half their population from disease since their treaty of 1853, and Indians along the Siletz River "are constantly telling the agent that they lost more by sickness last winter than they did in all of the preceding ten months' war, and frequently say '*it is your peace that is*

---

[107] Treaty with the Yakima, art. 4.

[108] Treaty with the Yakima, art. 4.

[109] Treaty with the Yakima, art. 6.

[110] Josephy, *Nez Perce Indians*, 326-28.

[111] Josephy, *Nez Perce Indians*, 324-76; Utely, *Indian Frontier*, 53-55.

[112] *CIA-AR*, 1857, 333.

killing us.'"[113] Nesmith concluded, "The sources from which they [Indians] are expected to receive those blessings [of civilization] contain the elements of their destruction ... while the last fifteen years has witnessed the most frightful diminution in their numbers, their deterioration morally, physically, and intellectually, has been equally rapid. Starvation, disease and bad whiskey combined is rapidly decimating their numbers, and will soon relieve the government of their charge."[114]

It was up to Indian peoples to see to it that the seeds destruction contained in their Euro-American way of life in general, and the treaties in particular, did not bear fruit. The treaties provided the framework for all subsequent dealings between the tribes and the federal government: They served as the means by which Indians actively claimed entitlements and reserved rights, but they were also tools which Congress could manipulate and completely redefine. Because the treaties were legal expressions of the Indians' entitlements, Indians at least had to learn to speak in the language of the Euro-American bundle. The new Yakama Nation took up both that challenge and burden.

---

[113] *CIA-AR*, 1857, 316, 318-19 (emphasis in original).

[114] *CIA-AR*, 1857, 319.

4

"SHALL I TEAR MY MOTHER'S BOSOM?"

> You ask me to plow the ground? Shall I take a knife and tear my mother's bosom? Then when I die, she will not take me to her bosom to rest. You ask me to dig for stone. Shall I dig under her skin for her bones? Then when I die I cannot enter her body to be born again. You ask me to cut grass and make hay and sell it and be rich like white man, but how dare I cut off my Mother's hair? It is bad law and my people cannot obey it."
> —Smohalla (ca. 1860)[1]

The goal of federal Indian policy between the 1860s and 1887 gradually shifted from one of seeking to remove tribes to isolated reserves where they would continue some of their traditional ways of life to one advocating instead the total destruction of Indian culture and replacing it with Euro-American institutions, practices—and ultimately, values. Such cultural arrogance had its roots in European colonial policies and subsequently in the notion of an American "Manifest Destiny." Native American mortality in the face of Euro-American diseases fueled convictions that Indians were an inferior race that must either assimilate or die.

Indians' place in Euro-American society became known commonly as "The Indian Problem." Proposed solutions to the "Problem" provided a topic of debate for religious reformers, military strategists, and federal policymakers.[2]

---

[1] Quoted in Click Relander (Now Tow Look), *Drummers and Dreamers: The Story of Smohalla the Prophet and his Nephew Puck Hyah Toot...*, with a foreword by Frederick Webb Hodge (Caldwell, ID: Caxton Printers, 1956): 139.

[2] Excerpt from *Annual Report of the Secretary of Interior*, reprinted in U.S. Commissioner of Indian Affairs, *Annual Report to the Secretary of the Interior*, 1865 (Washington, D.C.: Government Printing Office, 1866) [hereafter cited as *CIA-AR*, year]: iii-iv, discussing the merits of a policy promoting Native American genocide and deciding against it on the grounds of, in order of significance, (1) prohibitive expense in money and white lives; (2) [Christian] morality; Carl Schurz, "Present Aspects of the Indian Problem," *North American Review* 133 (July 1881): 12.

For a discussion of Indian policy during the post-Civil War period, see Francis Prucha, *American Indian Policy in Crisis: Christian Reformers and the Indians, 1865-1900* (Lincoln: University of Nebraska Press, 1976); Prucha, *The Great Father: The U.S. Government and the American Indians* 2 vols. (Lincoln: University of Nebraska Press, 1984): 1:462-581; Frederick E. Hoxie, *A Final Promise: The Campaign to Assimilate the Indians, 1880-1920* (Lincoln: University of Nebraska Press, 1984).

For a discussion of Indian law during the period, see Felix S. Cohen, *Handbook of Federal Indian Law* 1982 ed. (Charlottesville, VA: The Mitchie Company, 1982): 121-43; Russel Lawrence Barsh and James Youngblood Henderson, *The Road, Indian Tribes and Political Liberty* (Berkeley: University of California Press, 1980): 75-95; cf. Charles F. Wilkinson,

Reformers envisioned a world in which Native Americans would be transformed from tribally-based societies into individual capitalists by virtue of the American melting pot.³

Although reformers tended to see Native Americans as passive—or at most, recalcitrant—objects for their programs, such characterization can easily distort our understanding of Indian history during that period. While federal officials contemplated the transformation of Indian society on all levels, some Indians clung tenaciously to old ways of life and perceptions of the world. The followers of Smohalla despised the white way of life and its implications for nature. For them, the question of learning to farm could not be separated from asking "Shall I tear my mother's bosom?"⁴ These "Wild Yakimas," said Agent L. T. Erwin in 1895, claim that "when they were born they lived upon their mothers' breasts until they reached a certain age, then they lived off the things that come from mother earth, therefore it became their mother. They hold her sacred and declare her bosom should not be scarred with section lines and subdivisions.⁵

Other Yakama saw their future in Euro-American society. They actively requested the assistance of federal officials in teaching them farming and other skills. Members of the Yakima Tribal Council at White Swan (whose motto became "ON THE WARPATH FOR PROGRESS AND JUSTICE") petitioned for reclamation projects that would bring water to their lands.⁶

These opposing viewpoints sprang from at least three sources. Plateau society historically had fostered a strongly individualistic mentality. It was an individual's prerogative to perceive the world for him or herself, as evidenced by vision questing and an individual's relationship with his or her spirit partner. Additionally, the cumulative effects of Euro-American disease epidemics upon Plateau societies had resulted in widespread depopulation; the social demoralization that must have followed may have led some to abandon

---

American Indians, Time, and the Law: Native Societies in a Modern Constitutional Democracy (New Haven: Yale University Press, 1987): 14-28, discussing tension in federal Indian law between separatism and assimilation.

³ See Franics A. Walker, *The Indian Question* (Boston: Rand, Avery & Co., 1874); George Manypenny, *Our Indian Wards* (Cincinnati: R. Clarke & Co., 1880); and Francis Leupp, *The Indian and his Problem* (New York: Charles Scribner's Sons, 1910). See also Helen Hunt Jackson, *A Century of Dishonor: A Sketch of the United States Government's Dealings with Some of the Indian Tribes* (Boston: Roberts Bros., 1889); and William Barrows, *The Indian Side of the Indian Question* (Boston: D. Lothrop Co., 1887).

⁴ Relander, *Drummers and Dreamers*, 139; Leslie Spier, "The Prophet Dance of the Northwest and Its Derivations: The Source of the Ghost Dance," General Series in Anthropology (no. 1), (George Banta Publishing Co., Menasha, WI, 1935): 11ff.

⁵ *CIA-AR*, 1895, 321.

⁶ Petition of David Miller and Hackett Wesley to W. S. Post, director of Indian reclamation, Aug. 29, 1931, file 51656-20-341, part 5, Yakima Agency, Central Classified Files, General Records, 1907-39, Records of the Bureau of Indian Affairs, Record Group 75, National Archives, Washington, D.C. [hereafter cited as YA, CCF, GR, BIA, RG 75, NA-branch].

Yakima Indian Agent Captain Thomas Priestley along with government employees at Fort Simcoe, Washington, 1889

University of Washington Libraries, Special Collections,
Negative # NA 4114, used by permission

traditional ways as no longer viable. Finally, many who came to live on the Yakama Reservation had been removed from their homelands. These displaced peoples tended to have fewer localized ties to the land than did those whose ancestral lands had been enclosedwithin reservation boundaries.

The Yakamas' treaty and subsequent federal law regulating tribal economic relations ostensibly existed to induce Indians to become independent yeoman farmers after the American ideal. The Office of Indian Affairs (later the Bureau of Indian Affairs) gradually abandoned that policy as unworkable and settled for a program of partial assimilation that did not challenge the white settlers desires to acquire Indian lands and resources. In this new reformulation, as the historian Frederick Hoxie wrote, the idea of Indians entering society on an equal footing gave way to assimilation without equality.[7]

Although some Yakama came to live out the ideal of the independent farmer—such as the Olney family, who grazed large herds on reservation lands with the same entrepreneurial spirit as their non-Indian counterparts—the majority did not. The overwhelming impact of assimilationist policies was to create a supply of wage laborers for American agriculture and industry and to channel Indian lands and resources into American markets.

Relocation Within Uncertain Boundaries

In 1859, the Senate finally ratified the Stevens treaties.[8] According to the terms of the Yakamas' treaty, members of the individual bands that made up the Yakama confederation had one year following ratification of the treaty to move to the reserve. Some peoples were fortunate to have had their homelands included within the reservation boundaries. Groups historically living north of Ahtanum Creek and the Columbia River peoples, however, lost their lands. Undoubtedly, some voluntarily moved to the reservation; others would not willingly leave their homelands—in any case removal involved great personal cost to all.[9]

In theory, the federal government was to compensate individuals for expenses incurred in relocation as well as to pay people for the value of any

---

[7] Hoxie, *A Final Promise*, 152ff.

[8] *CIA-AR*, 1858, 222; *CIA-AR*, 1859, 382-83; Robert M. Utley, *The Indian Frontier of the American West 1846-1890* (Albuquerque: University of New Mexico Press, 1984): 54. See also "Indian Depredation Claims Involving Yakima Tribe," claims arising from the 1855 war, Records of the U.S. Court of Claims, RG 123, NA.

[9] In 1857, a band of Indians led by Tieas, a Yakama chief, requested that Stevens assist them in moving to a reservation on Puget Sound until hostilities on the Plateau ceased. Stevens Report, May 31, 1856, *CIA-AR*, 1856, 187; Lansdale report, *CIA-AR*, 1860, 206-207 (removal of Lewis River Band of Klickitats); Sarah Winnemucca Hopkins, *Life Among the Piuates: Their Wrongs and Claims* (New York: Putnam, 1883; reprint ed., Bishop, CA: Chalfant Press, 1969): 203-48, removal of Paiutes to Yakama Reservation; Martha C. Knack and Omer C. Stewart, *As Long as the River Shall Run: An Ethnohistory of Pyramid Lake Indian Reservation* (Berkeley: University of California Press, 1984): 75.

improvements left behind. The treaty promised that no one would leave houses or cultivated lands "until their value in money, or improvements of an equal value shall be furnished him as aforesaid."[10] In practice, however removal did not work that way.

The example of the removal of the Lewis River Band of Klickitats to the Yakama Reservation in 1860 is one example of how relocation worked in practice. R. H. Lansdale, Indian Agent for Washington Territory (who served from 1858-1961), reported in 1860:

> Forty-three have undertaken to remove their horses, their cattle, and themselves, over the Cascade mountains to Yakima reservation, and the remainder the agent has not yet succeeded in inducing to leave willingly their old hunting and fishing lands, though he yet hopes to accomplish so necessary an undertaking, as soon as possible.[11]

The Lewis River Band was not included in the treaty proceedings of 1855, yet federal officials treated them as if their land claims had been extinguished by the Yakamas' treaty. Lansdale wrote that the tribe had never received compensation or funds for relocating on the Yakama Reservation. As a result, "because of the threatening aspect of relations between those Indians and the white settlers," Lansdale took their removal into his own hands:

> These Indians have been badly treated by the whites; driven without compensation from their own lands; their houses burned and otherwise destroyed; the graves of their people inclosed in the white man's fields. They unwillingly consent to remove to please the government agent, hoping and trusting that their great father will yet provide some compensation for their lands in the form of annuities for beneficial objects, apart from the other bands treated with and settled on the Yakima reservation.[12]

Landsdale, "with the aid of head chief and interpreter, without the expensive interposition of superintendent of removal, conductors, &c., &c," assisted thirty-seven of the one hundred individuals onto a steamer from the Lewis River to Rockland, Washington Territory. Once in Rockland, they continued their journey to Fort Simcoe overland. Lansdale hoped that the Lewis River Band would obtain some compensation for what they had lost.

The actual process of identifying and policing the boundaries of the reservation also proved to be a far messier process than the treaty indicated.[13]

---

[10] Treaty with the Yakima, art. 2.

[11] *CIA-AR*, 1860, 206.

[12] *CIA-AR*, 1860, 206-07.

[13] Some of the tribes whose land was ceded to the United States by the Yakama's treaty had not been present at the Walla Walla council, including the Lewis River Band of Klickitats, *CIA-AR*, 1860, 206. While Stevens and his aides did consult during the council with some individual Indians about the location of reservation boundaries, the question of boundaries

Article 2 of the treaty stated that the tribes had reserved from the areas ceded

> the tract of land ... on the Yakama River, at the mouth of the Attah-nam River; thence westerly along said Attah-nam River to the forks; thence along the southern tributary to the Cascade Mountains; thence southerly along the main ridge of said mountains, passing south and east of Mount Adams, to the spur whence flows the waters of the Klickatat and Pisco Rivers; thence down said spur to the divide between the waters of said rivers; thence along said divide to the divide separating the waters of the Satass River from those flowing into the Columbia River; thence along said divide to the main Yakama, eight miles below the mouth of the Satass River; and thence up the Yakama River to the place of beginning.[14]

Article 2 further specified that the reservation was to be used for the "exclusive use and benefit" of the Yakama Indians. Employees of the Indian Bureau could enter the reservation; all others would require the permission of the tribe and U.S. agent.

As settlers, followed by federal surveyors, streamed across Yakama lands, nothing was beyond appropriation. The treaty itself promoted this land grab by "Guaranteeing ... the right to all citizens of the United States to enter upon and occupy as settlers any lands not actually occupied and cultivated by said Indians at this time, and not included in the reservation above named."[15] Because Stevens and Palmer added this provision to the treaty without telling the Indian council and then promoted it immediately after they concluded the treaty, thousands of settlers and others flocked to the area in the three years prior to ratification of the treaty.[16] The actual location of reservation boundaries provided an issue for litigation until the 1960s.[17]

The treaty-established reservation boundary usurped tribal authority over the use of natural resources on the reservation. Federal wardship of the tribe

---

was never put to the entire council for decision. Further, Indians who participated in the treaty council did not agree among themselves, much less with Stevens, about the effect of the treaty. Some, for example, believed the treaty to be a promise of further negotiation, while others saw it as binding only if both sides carried out their obligations under the terms, see Chapter 3.

[14] Treaty with the Yakima, art. 2.

[15] Treaty with the Yakima, art. 2.

[16] Isaac I. Stevens and Joel Palmer, article, *Oregon Weekly Times*, June 23, 1855, the article was reprinted in California newspapers. *CIA-AR*, 1857, 317-318; *CIA-AR*, 1858, 276.

[17] *Yakima Tribe v. United States*, 4 U.S. Indian Claims Commission *Decisions* 294 (June 5, 1956) (holding tribe entitled to compensation at $3.00 per acre of 27,000 acres of Wenatshapam fishery); *Yakima Tribe v. United States*, 5 U.S. Indian Claims Commission *Decisions* 661 (Nov. 29, 1957) (settling boundary and compensation for 27,647.71 acres of Cedar Valley lands at $2.50 per acre); "Yakimas to get 2-1/4 Million Cash," newspaper article, n.d., file—"Indians-Yakima-Government," Yakima Valley Museum, Yakima, WA [hereafter cited as YVM].

took away the tribe's ability to define themselves and their land base. Instead of assimilating Yakama peoples into Euro-American social and economic life, federal wardship barred Indians from meaningful participation within the dominant society at the same time it denied them the right to continue to maintain their own cultures.

Federal Indian Farm Policy

Prior to their treaty of 1855, the Yakama were primarily a gathering-fishing-hunting people who had limited experience with farming or the market. Some cultivated small riparian gardens along tiny streams. Kamiakin purportedly left the treaty proceedings in 1855 to tend to his garden on the Ahtanum, and others also kept small gardens in the Medicine Valley, White Swan, and Toppenish creek areas to supplement food collected during the annual subsistence trek.[18] Missionaries to the area, such as the Whitmans and Spauldings, had constructed small irrigation works for mission fields where they grew wheat, hay, and vegetables. Catholic missions also included artificially irrigated fields.[19] Yakama women in the post-treaty period continued to keep small riparian gardens near their homes, and that may have been an expression of the earlier farming practice.[20]

Although some farmed, the Yakama were not primarily an agricultural people. Annual subsistence work precluded labor-intensive, long-term tending. Additionally, the best farmlands were flood-irrigated creek bottomlands, and there was not enough to provide everyone with farmland.[21] "It is evident to me

---

[18] Testimony of Joe Ko-lock-en, in *U.S. v. Winans*, Transcript of Record, Testimony and Final Report of Examiner, enclosed in Attorney General to Clerk of the Supreme Court, Jan. 21, 1904, Appellate Case File no. 19213, Records of the Supreme Court, RG 267, NA, [Hereafter cited as *U.S. v. Winans*, transcript of record]: 152, stating that Colwash Indians had small gardens above the Wisham fishery and below the Se-we-pam fishery where they raised crops not including wheat; testimony of Bill Se-hi-am, ibid., 162, stating that "the old men" had gardens. The transcript has several sets of page numbers. I have used the handwritten page numbers that have not been crossed out. I have also indicated the use of interpreters where Yakama were not speaking in English.

See also A.C. Fairchild, superintendent of instruction at Yakima, June 1868, reprinted in "A Few References to the Earlier Practice of Agriculture and Irrigation on Yakima Indian Reservation from Reports on Indian Affairs, [n.d.], Special Case 190, BIA, RG 75, NA, noting that "many small fields and patches of ground were plowed and put in crops for the Indians at White Salmon, on the Klickitat river, at Cammash Lake, and on Columbia river, previous to its being known that the treaty was ratified. Some fifty acres were thus put in and turned over to those for whom the fields were made, and which will inure to their benefit." Fairchild's report implies that fields were made for the Indians, but it is not clear what role Indians played in creating or maintaining those fields.

[19] See Chapter 3.

[20] Dr. Emily C. Miller, Yakima Agency field matron, report, *CIA-AR*, 1891, 510 [hereafter cited as Miller's Report].

[21] Morris L. Uebelacker, "Geographic Explorations in the Southern Cascades of Eastern Washington: Changing Land, People, and Resources," (Ph.D. diss., University of Oregon,

that both the soil and the habits of life of these Indians favor pastoral rather than agricultural pursuits," noted Agent Lansdale in 1858. He believed it wise to encourage the Yakama to become cattle ranchers rather than farmers.[22] Yet other agents believed that the Yakama could become farmers, a belief that intensified as federal reclamation programs made large-scale agriculture at Yakima and elsewhere in the Columbia basin a reality.[23]

W. B. Gosnell (who served from Jan. 1861 to July 1861), Lansdale's immediate successor, was the first of many agents entrusted with the task of supervising the Yakamas' road to agriculture. He sent a team, plow, and two men—one white and one Indian—to go to nearby villages to plow all the available land, but those who lived farther away received only tools and seeds and no further assistance in getting started.[24] J. H. Wilbur, likewise,

> hired two [Indians] from among those who were capable of managing the oxen and holding the plough for each team, provided them with camping equipage and rations; they went to the different settlements, made their camps and prosecuted their work with a manliness that would do credit to white men. The Indians, where they have been ploughing have worked in assisting in herding the oxen, and doing such other work as their limited education would permit.[25]

Once the land had been broken, some Indians brought their own horses and used ploughs and harnesses supplied by the Bureau to make "fruitful fields." By 1866, reservation farmers at the agency had 1500 acres under cultivation.[26]

The objectives of federal Indian farming policy were threefold. First, policymakers saw farming as a desirable goal for Indians because it would speed their progress toward civilization; indeed, farming and civilization were often used as interchangeable terms. "With a fixed home, and with an individual right in the soil from which they will be instructed to derive their subsistence," argued Lansdale, "they will be stimulated to ... create an adaptation to civilized

---

1986): 12-80; William H. Redman, supervisor of ditches, "Yakima Reservation Classification of Land," 116: 10, CRP.

[22] *CIA-AR*, 1858, 275.

[23] See for example, report of school farm production, in *CIA-AR*, 1867, 47-48; Wilbur's reports in: *CIA-AR*, 1871, 284-85; *CIA-AR*, 1876, 145; *CIA-AR*, 1877, 201; *CIA-AR*, 1878, 139-41. For more information about the development of artificial irrigation and Washington agriculture, see John Fahey *The Inland Empire: Unfolding Years, 1879-1929* (Seattle: University of Washington Press, 1986): 87-109; A. C. McGreger, "Agricultural Development of the Columbia Plateau, McGreger Land and Livestock Co.: A Case History," 2 parts (Ph.D. diss., University of Washington, 1977).

[24] Gosnell's report, quoted in "A Few References to Earlier Practice of Agriculture and Irrigation...." Special case file 190, CCF, GR, BIA, RG 75, NA.

[25] *CIA-AR*, 1867, 46.

[26] *CIA-AR*, 1867, 45-6.

pursuits never to be acquired while the nomadic character is retained."[27] Indians, he believed, required "domestication," much as did cattle and other livestock, in order to "fix them to the soil, as such domestication must always underlie any permanent progress in civilization."[28] His ideas mirrored general federal policy on Indian agriculture until well into the twentieth century.[29]

When Lansdale purported to "fix [Indians] to the soil," he really meant to wed them to the notion of private property. When they became civilized they would stop roving over everyone else's property and stay on their own individual parcels. In that scheme there could be no collective subsistence sharing because all were to tend their own farms. Moreover, the human relationship to land turned upon the market. Land's primary worth came from its exchange value in an economy which encouraged the transfer of resources from those who would not develop them to those who would.

A second federal purpose in promoting agriculture was to enable Indians to become self-supporting and thereby decrease their reliance on government funds and supplies. Finally, Indian farm policy increasingly evolved into an extension of federal public land policies that sought to transfer "unproductive" lands to those who could develop them. Thus, any land that Indians could or would not put in production became open to lease or purchase by non-Indians as "surplus" reservation lands.[30]

The legislative cornerstone of federal Indian farm policy—and the vehicle through which officials promoted all three of the above goals—was the Dawes General Allotment Act of 1887, under whose terms reservation lands were divided among individuals for farming and grazing purposes.

The seeds of this policy were sown in many treaties pre-dating the Dawes Act. Article Six of the Yakamas' treaty of 1855, for example, contained the provision that:

> The President may ... cause the whole or such portions of such reservation ... to be surveyed into lots, and assign the same to such individuals or families ... as are willing to avail themselves

---

[27] *CIA-AR*, 1859, 384; *CIA-AR*, 1858, 275.

[28] *CIA-AR*, 1858, 275.

[29] Hoxie, *A Final Promise*; R. Douglas Hurt, *Indian Agriculture in America, Prehistory to the Present* (Lawrence: University of Kansas Press, 1987): 136-37; Thomas R. Wessel, "Agriculture, Indians, and American History," *Agricultural History* 50 (Jan. 1976): 9-20; Wilcomb E. Washburn, *The Assault on Indian Tribalism: The General Allotment Law (Dawes Act) of 1887* (Philadelphia: J. B. Lippincott Company, 1975); William T. Hagan, "Private Property: The Indian's Door to Civilization," *Ethnohistory* 3 (Spring 1956): 126-137.

[30] Leasing provisions are set out in Act of Feb. 28, 1891, ch. 383, § 3, 26 Stat. 794, 795 (codified at 25 U.S.C. § 397), Act of Aug. 15, 1894, ch. 290, § 1, 28 Stat. 286, 305 (codified at 25 U.S.C. § 402); ch. 787, 44 Stat. 894 (codified at 25 U.S.C. § 402a). See also Reid Peyton Chambers and Monroe E. Price, "Regulating Sovereignty: Secretarial Discretion and the Leasing of Indian Lands," *Stanford Law Review* 26 (1974): 1062, 1068-74.

of the privilege, and will locate on the same as a permanent home....[31]

Under this provision Yakama individuals and families obtained allotments of up to 200 acres. Many of those allotments were of riparian lands used for both livestock ranching and farming, and some Yakama families were able to retain some control over ancestral lands by making their claims at this point.[32] Early allotment progressed at the agent's discretion, and without rules for acreage limitations. By 1892, under that system, some "crafty and selfish" individuals were able to control "large bodies of rich pasturage under fence."[33] Whether such people were land grabbers or, rather, were families attempting to retain control over their previous territory, we do not know.

Under the terms of the Dawes Act, however, people no longer had the option of declining to avail themselves of individual property ownership; all Indians compulsorily received allotments. Although the Bureau sent commissioners to the various reservations to obtain approval for the survey and allotment of lands, such approval was a mere formality. Indians who refused to select their own allotments were assigned parcels of land chosen by the agent. Tribal lands that remained unallotted were deemed "surplus" and were available for homestead or other entries by settlers.[34]

Each head of an Indian family received a quarter section (160 acres), while each single person over eighteen and each orphan under eighteen received a one-eighth section. Others, including children born between 1887 and the date of a particular executive order allotting a given reservation, received a one-sixteenth section.[35] The federal government held the land in

---

[31] Treaty with the Yakima, 123 Stat. 951, art. 6.

[32] This is a very important topic for further research. It would be helpful to know who these families were, the nature of their prior connection to an area (e.g., a winter village), and how much land was allocated this way. Schuster notes that Felix Reville Brunot, president of the first board of Indian Commissioners, visited the Yakama Reservation in 1871 and recommended that patents be issued to families who were cultivating 3000 acres. Helen Hersh Schuster, "Yakima Indian Traditionalism: A Study in Continuity and Change" (Ph.D. diss., University of Washington, 1975): 251.

[33] Thomas J. Morgan, Commissioner of Indian Affairs, to John K. Rankin, OIA special allotting agent, April 14, 1892, 115: 24, CRP. For a general discussion of pre-Dawes allotment attempts, see Paul Gates, "Indian Allotments Preceding the Dawes Act," in J. Clark, ed., *The Frontier Challenge* (Lawrence: University Press of Kansas, 1971): 141-70; Cohen, *Handbook of Federal Indian Law*, 129-30.

[34] Act of Feb. 8, 1887, Ch. 119, 24 Stat. 389 (1887) (codified as amended at 25 U.S.C. §§ 331-334, 339, 341, 342, 348, 349, 354, 381). The following discussion is based on the act and its amendments.

[35] Originally, the Dawes Act contemplated allotment of 40 acres only to male heads of families, with married women receiving no separate allotment. Following protest, the act was modified to equalize allotments to men and women of 160 acres of grazing land or 80 acres of agricultural land. Act of Feb. 28, 1891, ch. 383, §§ 1-2, 26 Stat. 794 (codified as amended at 25 U.S.C. § 331). See also Cohen, *Handbook of Federal Indian Law*, 132-36.

trust for Indian allottees for a specified period of time, usually twenty-five years, during which the property was exempt from state taxation and the Indian allottee was supposed to develop the land into a profitable farm or range. At the end of the trust period, the federal government determined the legal "competency" of the allottee and issued a patent in fee simple based on this finding. Patent in hand, the new owner received all of the rights and burdens of U.S. citizenship, including the responsibility to pay taxes, and was to relinquish all tribal ties.[36]

Under subsequent acts, the federal government reserved reservation timber and mineral lands from individual allotment, to be sold for tribal "benefit." A 1904 act set aside almost 150,000 acres for tribal grazing and timber lands on the Yakama Reservation, for example. The same act empowered the Secretary of the Interior to set aside reservation lands potentially useful for reclamation projects.[37]

Allotment and the accompanying process of classifying reservation land into agricultural, irrigable, grazing, timber, mineral, and "surplus" lands provided a primary means by which the federal government sought to eliminate Yakama control over their land and resources. Land classification determined whether Indians had any authority over the use of resources on the land; whether the land could be held in trust, leased, or sold; and whether and how much acreage an individual could acquire in a particular class of land. At Yakima, for example, the Bureau reserved timbered areas from entry by Indians, and planned to sell the timber thereon for tribal benefit. The tribe did not negotiate its first own timber sale until 1944, although federal officials had authorized sales of timber on tribal lands as early as the 1880s.[38]

---

[36] 24 Stat. 389; 34 Stat. 182-183, Act of May 8, 1906, Ch. 2348.

[37] Act of Dec. 21, 1904, ch. 22, 33 Stat. 595, 596, 598.

[38] Click Relander, ed. *Treaty Centennial, 1855-1955, The Yakimas*, 1st ed. Washington State Historical Society and Oregon State Historical Society, published by authorization of the Yakima Tribal Council (Yakima, WA, Republic Press, 1955): 53. According to 33 Stat 597, timber on federally classed reservation timberlands was to be cut and sold in accord with rules determined by the Secretary of Interior. Cutting dead wood on reservations was authorized by the Act of Feb. 16, 1889, ch. 172, 25 Stat. 673 (codified at 25 U.S.C. § 196). For a discussion of federal Indian policy on tribal timber land and timber sales, see Cohen, *Handbook of Federal Indian Law*, 539-542 and accompanying notes. Under these provision and others, federal officials could enter into contracts to take dead wood out of timbered areas on the reservation, but once granted, contract holders often cut green timber.

See Louis Mann to Miles Poindexter, Feb 2, 1916; box 76, folder 12, Accession no. 3828, Miles C. Poindexter Papers, University of Washington Libraries Manuscript Collection, Seattle, Wash. [hereafter cited as box:folder, MCPP]; Mann to Poindexter, Feb. 7, 1916, ibid.; and James B. Saxton, Deputy Supervisor of Forests, Yakima Reservation, to Don M. Carr, Feb 23, 1916, ibid. See also Evan Estep, Yakima superintendent, to CIA, Aug. 20, 1926, noting that Washington State was granting permits to cut timber on reservation land, file 99347-07-308.1, Decimal Subject Files [hereafter DSF], YA, BIA, RG 75, NA; and Estep to CIA, March 16, 1926, with enclosed clippings, file 99347-07-308.1, DSJ, YA, BIA, RG 75, NA.

Yakama tepee on shore of the Yakima River
near Prosser, Washington, ca. 1898

Northwest Museum of Arts & Culture/Eastern Washington State Historical Society,
Spokane Washington, American Indians of the Pacific Northwest Images Digital Collection,
Negative # L93-72.4, photographer E. E. James, used by permission

The federal government also asserted authority to grant rights of way across reservations for telephone, telegraph, and railroad lines and offices.[39] The Northern Pacific Railroad obtained land grants parallelling the Yakima River for 130 miles, much of it on the Yakamas' riparian lands along the river.[40] The Northern Pacific systematically contested the claims of Indian homesteaders within its land grant area, succeeding in driving many away. Subsequently, the company developed a large reclamation project that competed with reservation farmers for Yakima River water.[41]

Indians had little say in the allotment process. In 1887, according to the minutes of a tribal council meeting, "Agent [Thomas] Priestly explained to Indians the law in regard to 'Indians taking land in severalty.'" When asked to comment, "many came forward for a talk with agent, & all expressed themselves as decidedly against a 'survey' of their lands."[42] Indians protested the work of the special allotting agent, stating that they "have never received any notice of the allotting by the government, except prior to the time the allotting was begun, [there] was a meeting of a few Indians with the agent and only four signed their names to an agreement to have their lands allotted."[43]

Yakama, who assumed that what little remained of their homelands would be left intact, were now bewildered to discover that more lands would be taken away.[44] Everywhere non-Indians were pushing against reservation boundaries. "You see at Yakima and Goldendale," said Chief White Swan in 1897, "there is a city over there at both sides and the whites is pushing us on each side ... they are hurting us on both sides...." "We are afraid of them [whites]," concurred Chief Louis Simpson. To open reservation boundaries was

---

[39] Appropriations Act of March 3, 1901, ch. 832, § 3, 31 Stat. 1015, 1018 (codified at 25 U.S.C. §§ 319, 357), authorizing granting of telegraph and telephone rights of way; Appropriations Act of March 3, 1909, ch. 263, 35 Stat. 781 (codified as amended at 25 U.S.C. § 320), authorizing land grants to railroads.

[40] Donald W. Meinig, *The Great Columbia Plain, A Historical Geography, 1805-1910*, The Emil and Kathleen Sick Lecture-Book Series in Western History and Biography (Seattle: University of Washington Press, 1968): 261, 340. The Company was also involved in a reservation boundary dispute case.

[41] *CIA-AR*, 1896, 29. On the Company's reclamation work, see Chapter 6.

[42] Minutes of Yakima Tribal Council meeting, White Swan [hereafter YTC-WS], Feb. 15, 1887, 115:18, CRP.

[43] Charles Ike to U.S. President, enclosing petition, quoted in Acting CIA to Jay Lynch, May 27, 1893, file—"Ahtanum Letters, 1881-1899," Letters received regarding irrigation matters, 1903-08, YA, RG 75, BIA, NA-Seattle.

[44] For an excellent first hand account of allotment on the Nez Perce Reservation from the perspective of a canny Euro-American woman, see E. Jane Gay, *With the Nez Perces, Alice Fletcher in the Field, 1889-92*, Frederick E. Hoxie and Joan T. Mark, eds. (Lincoln: University of Nebraska Press, 1981).

to lose a crucial protective barrier against non-Indians and their world.[45] The Dawes Act, with its provisions for mandatory allotment, however, made inevitable the alienation of Indian lands.[46]

The Dawes Act imposed acreage limitations on Indian allotments of 80 acres of farm land or 160 acres of grazing land. The first allotments at Yakima were made in 1892 by John Rankin, a special allotting agent for the Bureau. Rankin was to promote allotment on the reservation in addition to assisting heads of families to select land for themselves and their children. All allotments were to be made "with reference to the best interests of the Indians, the choice portions of the reservation being given them."[47]

Individuals who already had built on or cultivated lands were allowed to incorporate those improvements in their selections for allotments so far as they did not conflict with one another. All allotment boundaries were clearly marked, and that each allottee "of sufficient age should be personally shown the boundaries of the allotment selected by him, so that he will understand exactly where the land selected by him lies, and every possible means should be taken to familiarize him with his boundary lines."[48]

People obtained allotments on the Yakama Reservation if they were enrolled members of the tribe. Agent Lynch formed a committee of representatives of Yakama bands to determine who should be allotted.[49] Even with the assistance of that group, or perhaps because of it, Yakama allotment policy was widely perceived as a very permissive one. Agent Lynch noted in 1908 that "a very liberal policy was pursued in giving Indians allotments; so much so that this office was flooded with letters from mixed bloods all over the United States stating that they had been informed that the Yakima Reservation was to

---

[45] Statements of White Swan and Louis Simpson, in "Report of Council with Indians at Yakima Reservation by Commissioners Barge and Goodwin, Fort Simcoe, Feb. 20, 1897, folder "Yakima Council 1898," Tribal Records, 1897-1952, YA, BIA, RG 75, NA-Seattle. Many Indians expressed fear of whites throughout the period.

[46] The Dawes Act also provided that state law regarding descent and partition of real estate would apply to heirship of allotments, 24 Stat. 389, §5.

[47] Morgan to Rankin, April 14, 1892, 115:24, CRP.

[48] Morgan to Rankin, April 14, 1892, 115:24, CRP. Where two or more allottees had made improvements on the same piece of land, the General Allotment Act provided that the land should be divided among them or given to one of them provided that all parties agreed, Act of Feb. 8, 1887, ch. 119, § 2, 24 Stat. 388. See Gay, *With the Nez Perce*, for a detailed account of how difficult such allotting instructions were to implement.

[49] According to the Dawes Act "any Indian located thereon [reservation]" and "belonging thereon [reservation]" is entitled to an allotment, Ch. 119, § 1, 24 Stat. 388. For implementation of allotment at Yakima, see *CIA-AR*, 1893, 304-05.

be allotted to any and all Indians who had not already received an allotment...."[50]

Before the mid-1890s, however, there was little incentive for Yakama to take reservation allotments, aside from government pressure, and "Quite a number of Indians ... refused to have lands allotted to them," Agent Lynch reported after Rankin arrived.[51] Many Yakama, perhaps strengthened by the Smohalla faith, simply did not believe farming was a legitimate activity. These "Wild Yakimas" refused to take allotments on the reservation because of they despised all Euro-American practices.[52] In 1895 an estimated one-tenth—or about 400 individuals fell into this category, and these people declared that the earth was their mother and "her bosom should not be scarred with section lines and subdivisions."[53]

Another group took up homesteads on public lands bordering the reservation under the provisions of the Indian Homestead Act of 1875. By 1891 there were more than 100 such entries in Klickitat County.[54] Settlers saw these Indians as competitors for land and they engaged in a continuing battle to push Indians back on the reservation. A group of Rock Creek settlers petitioned the federal government to remove "roving Indians" at Klickitat, Rock Creek, Chapman Creek, Alder Creek, Pine Creek, the Columbia "and elsewhere in our county," because Indians "are themselves in many ways detrimental to the interests of the settler, and would be better off were they to live on the reservations.[55] Bureau officials periodically attempted to round up off-reservation Yakama and force them onto the reservation, but were generally unsuccessful.[56]

---

[50] Lynch to CIA, July 23, 1908, file 41246-08-313, YA, DSJ, BIA, RG 75, NA; *CIA-AR*, 1893, 338, reporting YTC-WS invitation to full-blooded Indians of any heritage to take allotments on Yakima.

[51] *CIA-AR*, 1898 304.

[52] *CIA-AR*, 1881, 174. It is not clear if these people took homesteads off the reservation. According to the Yakima Agent's report in 1894, a group of about 100 people who refused to take allotments were in the mountains, but since the report was written in August, we do not know if they were living in the mountains, or simply there to pick berries, see *CIA-AR*, 1894, 327.

[53] *CIA-AR*, 1895, 321. See also Schuster, "Yakima Traditionalism," 253-54.

[54] Act of March 3, 1875, 18 Stat. 420, §15; Act of July 4, 1884, 23 Stats 96; Schuster, "Yakima Traditionalism," 246. By the Appropriations Act of March 3, 1893, 27 Stat. 612, OIA established a $5000 fund to help pay for legal costs of defending allottees' claims, entries, and filings from challenges by non-Indians.

[55] Petition, March 1886, 115:17, CRP.

[56] Clay Wood, U.S. special agent, colonel U.S. Army, to James Wilbur, May 4, 1880, 114:23, CRP, stating that the Secretary of Interior has instructed him to travel up the Columbia to Spokane Falls and talk with "any roving bands of Indians" he could locate and "induce them to repair to" Yakima, Colville or Columbia (Modoc's) reservations for a "permanent location and house." Wood sought Wilbur's assistance in notifying him of the locations of any off-

For many Yakama, farming on the reservation meant being under the control—or at least legal authority—of the agent. In any case, farming was not sufficiently productive or culturally satisfying enough to replace subsistence,[57] and many who farmed did so to augment more traditional diets. Fishing remained a central subsistence activity and a central component to Yakama subsistence. As long as Yakama could subsist from the proceeds of fishing-gathering-hunting, they had no need for agriculture.

"Many of [the Indians] had changed their minds and wanted land," wrote Agent Lynch in 1896. "Many of the outside Indians, who belonged here, expressed their willingness to come to this reservation and take land in severalty."[58] Relentless Euro-American pressure on Indians living on public lands drove many to the reservation, especially with the rapid growth of the railroad towns of Toppenish, Simcoe, and later Wapato, along the Northern Pacific line.[59]

Moreover, as salmon runs declined noticeably toward the end of the 1880s, and the scarcity of game and the fences of non-Indian property owners made a hunting-gathering lifestyle increasingly difficult, more people saw an allotment of their own as a benefit. Sales of Yakama horses—a source of money in previous years—declined in the early 1890s, and this may have pressured people onto the reserve where they could set up farms, or more likely, receive annuity payments.[60] By 1912, the Bureau recorded 3,160 allotments, and by 1914, when the allotment rolls for Yakima closed, 440,000 acres had been granted to 4,506 individuals.[61]

Allotment affected individuals differently depending upon their family ties, familiarity with the system, and their pre-allotment status. By arranging their allotments carefully, for example, some families retained control over

---

reservation Indians. See also Report of Webster Stabler, Yakima Agent, in U.S. Department of the Interior, Census Office, *Report on Indians Taxed and Not Taxed: 1890*, 606, noting with some exasperation, that "The Yakimas are not on a reservation. The tribes of the agency have lived in this section of the country as long as there is any history of them. Some are living along the Columbia River, some on reservations, and some have become citizens." See also letters from U.S. Land Office receivers reporting numbers of Indian homesteads in 1912, file— "Homesteads and Allotments, Indian, 1902-12," General Correspondence, 1908-27, YA, BIA, RG 75, NA-Seattle.

[57] *CIA-AR*, 1884, 172.

[58] Lynch report, in *CIA-AR*, 1898, 304.

[59] Schuster, "Yakima Indian Traditionalism," 245, 248. Schuster noted that before the railroad began regular operations in 1883, most people remained within their old villages without much disturbance from whites.

[60] *CIA-AR*, 1884, 172; *CIA-AR*, 1894, 326.

[61] Relander, *Treaty Centennial*, 37; H. G. Barnett, The *Yakima Indians in 1942* (Eugene, OR: University of Oregon, mimeo., 1942): 6-7.

large blocks of land.⁶² Others used different names to capitalize on family connections and obtained multiple allotments at Yakima or other reservations.⁶³ Individuals without families, however did not fare as well because their holdings were limited to 160 acres.⁶⁴ Indians who were deemed legally incompetent were given allotments chosen for them by the agent, irrespective of their wishes. Those who challenged the allotment of their lands reported in 1893 that "the only heed paid to their protest was to be arrested by the agent, Mr. Lynch, and carried from one jail to another."⁶⁵ The Bureau demanded an immediate report from Lynch, informing him that "No coercive measures ... are permissible."⁶⁶ Indians had four years in which to select land for allotments and those who failed to choose in that time were assigned land by the agent; indeed, the allotment system itself was coercive.

Alienation: Earth into Goods

Once allotment was complete, federal officials hoped Indians would naturally and peaceably come to adopt farmers' ways. But many unanticipated problems cropped up: individuals could not remember or did not know the boundaries of their assigned allotments; others did not remember the English names under which they were to receive their trust patents. Still others died before the allotment process was complete or were born after a reservation had

---

⁶² "Report on the Conditions of Yakima, Washington," file 120334-12-341, YA, Correspondence File 1907-39, CCF, GR, BIA, RG 75, NA, 25, noting that many Yakama families succeeded in having their lands allotted "in one compact body." See also the case of William Charley, who attempted to exchange his allotment or buy an inherited allotment so that he could be close to a relative "so I can look after them and farms." Charley to CIA [?], April 8, 1910, file 30369-10-313, DSJ, YA, BIA, RG 75, NA.

⁶³ John A. Bower, "The Hydrogeography of Yakima Indian Nation Resource Use" (Ph.D. diss., University of Washington-Seattle, 1990): 272-73. Extensive family ties would have been useful here as well. Throughout the period federal officials were busy trying to determine who really was an enrolled member of the tribe and therefore entitled to an allotment on the Yakama reserve. E.g., case of Mrs. David Black/Adaline Black, who unsuccessfully—and with the aid of an attorney—attempted to secure an allotment on the Yakama Reservation although she was not an enrolled member of the tribe. Jay Lynch, Superintendent, to Commissioner of Indian Affairs, July 23, 1908, file 41246-08-313, DSJ, YA, BIA, RG 75, NA; Lynch to Commissioner of Indian Affairs, July 23, 1908, file 41246-08-313, DSJ, YA, BIA, RG 75, NA.

⁶⁴ Thomas J. Morgan to Rankin, April 14, 1892, 115:24, CRP.

⁶⁵ Charles Ike to U.S. President enclosing petition, quoted in Acting Commissioner of Indian Affairs to Jay Lunch, May 27, 1893, file—"Ahtanum Letters, 1881-1899," Letters Received regarding irrigation matters, 1903-08, YA, BIA, RG 75, NA-Seattle.

⁶⁶ Charles Ike to U.S. President, enclosing petition, quoted in Acting Commissioner of Indian Affairs to Jay Lynch, May 27, 1893, file—"Ahtanum Letters, 1881-1899," Letters Received regarding irrigation matters, 1903-08, YA, BIA, RG 75, NA-Seattle.

been allotted, vastly complicating an administrative system that barely could keep track of its living, and highly mobile, charges.[67]

Some Yakama chose favorable allotments and saw a way to meet Euro-Americans on their own terms. Such individuals peopled the Yakima Indian Commercial Club, ran successful livestock operations, and farmed. Nealy Olney, who acted as the secretary of the Yakima Indian Commercial Club and who ran a sheep ranch, is one example.[68] "I took heed to the agent's advice," Charley Olney recalled, "when he advised me, when I was grown to a pretty big boy. You want to learn to raise property and own property, thereby you will never learn to be a thief, to steal."[69] Yakama families who had ties to white homesteaders, ranchers, and speculators by marriage generally had closer ties to the market as well.[70] The Olneys, however, were the exception, not the rule, and those who prospered did so despite the Bureau's "assistance."[71]

Successful farming depended upon far more than merely an individual's ability and inclination to take up Euro-American practices. Land quality, access to water, cash for tools, seeds, and water charges for lands within reclamation projects all affected the productivity of a particular allotment. The cost of clearing, leveling, fencing, and irrigating sagebrush lands represented a $10.00 investment before the farmer received any returns. Many allottees simply abandoned their allotments and fished for food and cash.[72]

Productive claims were not the rule. Many people received allotments of land in the arid, sagebrush-covered hills above the valley floor. No suitable land remained from which to choose allotments by 1901. By that time, "all the lands that [were] considered of any value and where there was any possible

---

[67] See for example, *CIA-AR*, 1898, CLX (Instructions to agents in regard to family names, March 19, 1890), 305; *CIA-AR*, 1899, 363; case of Calvin Hale, whose son died with only 20 acres having been allotted him, and referring to a man who lived in his household who had received no allotment by 1898, "Report of Council of Commissioners and Yakima Tribe of Indians," n.d., folder "Yakima Council, 1898," Tribal Records, 1897-1952, YA, RG 75, BIA, NA-Seattle. See also Gay, *With the Nez Perces*.

[68] Olney to Miles Poindexter, Jan. 5, 1915, 78:5, MCPP. See Tables I:1-5, Appendix I, "Crop Yields and Land Holding Statistics, Yakima Reservation, 1898-1935." Crop census reports can give only a general idea of the area of Indian farming relative to non-Indian farming, however, because they list amounts of crops, but do not specify how many Indians are farming.

[69] Statement in Council Proceedings of Yakima Indians, Fort Simcoe, Wash., June 2, 1913, folder "Councils and Meetings (Tribal) 1913-25," Tribal Records, 1897-1952, YA, BIA, RG 75, NA-Seattle.

[70] We will simply never know personal motivations from existing records. Two Yakama, Frank Meacham and Josephine Lillie, established the townsites of Toppenish and Wapato, Bower, "Hydrogeography," 282. Additionally, Yakama who married whites, according to Agent Lynch, were among those who had exploited the allotment process to secure as much land as possible at Yakama and on other reserves, Bower, ibid., 272.

[71] Hurt, *Indian Agriculture in America*, 105-06.

[72] *CIA-AR*, 1902, 368-69.

chance to obtain water is allotted...."[73] Some, like one unfortunate allottee whose land "was undesirable on account of its being a high mountainous peak," sought to obtain in lieu lands in exchange for their original allotments.[74] After about 1900, however, the quality of unallotted lands was generally too poor to upgrade an allotment through such an exchange. Such land would yield nothing without the addition of water on a large scale.[75] Lynch believed federal reclamation works would bring these lands to fruition, but such projects were little more than promises for most would-be Yakama farmers.[76]

Non-riparian allottees found themselves in the unenviable position of holding lands that could be neither farmed nor grazed until federal projects brought water onto the reservation and only then possibly to their particular holdings. Lynch reported in 1898:

> The few Indians who have water for irrigating are improving a portion of their allotments and are raising some grain, hay, and vegetables. But a large majority have lands that are without water and are very poor—no teams, no wagons, no plows, no harness, no lumber, and no money—and how many of them live, is a mystery even to those who are most acquainted with them.[77]

As most Yakama soon learned, allotment merely provided the façade behind which the Bureau relegated Indians to economic dependence. As long as individual Indians were made to pay their own way, few could farm successfully, much less compete successfully with their non-Indian neighbors.[78]

Individuals with poor quality lands had few choices to support themselves. They could rely on meager federal assistance in the form of cash or goods; they could lease their allotments beginning in 1904; or they could sell their land. For various reasons, none of those alternatives provided sufficient means for an individual to support herself or himself. Therefore most people came to rely on an unsustainable combination of older subsistence ways supplemented by cash income from annuity payments, land sales or leases,

---

[73] Lynch to CIA, Aug. 30, 1901, file 41246-08-313, YA, Decimal Subject Files [hereafter DSF], BIA, RG 75, NA.

[74] S. A. M. Young, Yakima superintendent, to CIA, Oct. 30, 1911, file 94477-11-313, DSJ, YA, BIA, RG 75, NA; and C. F. Hauke, assistant CIA to Young, Dec. 5, 1911, ibid. See also case of Alice Estabrook, 10496-07-313, DSJ, YA, BIA, RG 75, NA. Estabrook hired an attorney to represent her request to the CIA that she be allowed to change an allotment in 1908. Her request was denied because there was no land more valuable to exchange in lieu of her original allotment. Congress enacted several laws to provide remedies to Indians denied allotments, see Cohen, *Handbook of Federal Indian Law*, 133 nn. 61-62.

[75] See Chapters 6 and 7.

[76] See Chapter 7.

[77] *CIA-AR*, 1899, 364.

[78] On Yakama members who held allotments but did not farm them, see testimony of Jo-Ko-Lock-en, *U.S.v. Winans*, transcript of record, 153; testimony of Mary Speedis, ibid., 202-203.

and the wages they earned as seasonal hired hands. The result was far short of the yeoman farmer ideal—still less an economically independent Indian population—promised by policymakers.

Traditionally, Yakima Indian agents, and more generally the Bureau, discouraged the disbursement of benefits to Indians. Indians would grow accustomed to "living in idleness" and never learn to work to support themselves, officials feared.[79] At Yakima, there had never been "a regular issue, nor annuity payments at this Agency," and only the very aged and sick ever received assistance.[80] Sometimes the Bureau issued livestock to Indians, but this apparently was not common at Yakima.[81]

Yakama and other Indians could not make ends meet with the cash available from federal payments. Luce Matk, a woman allotted on the Colville reservation, for example had about $500 in tribal funds out of which she received a monthly allowance of $15. If she needed extra money, she had to petition the agent. Matk was about 100 years old in 1914, and at that time a friend found her "nearly blind," "old, dirty and louse, and without sufficient clothes for changes, her head [?] is in the same condition."[82] The Bureau offered assistance only until an individual's share of federal payments to the tribe lasted; once the government had recompensed tribes for their land cessions and the payments discontinued, people were on their own.[83] If some people like Matk lived in poverty, at least the Bureau could rest assured that they were not living federally funded lives of luxury and indolence.

---

[79] *CIA-AR*, 1878, 141; *CIA-AR*, 1885, 201 (referring to "costly savages"); *CIA-AR*, 1901, 1-7 (noting that Indians have been "supplied lavishly"). OIA received general funds from the federal government to provide social services consisting of grants of food, cash, or farming tools in the nineteenth and early twentieth centuries. Under the Snyder Act of 1921, the BIA was authorized to provide for Indian welfare, but the BIA did not begin a general assistance or cash payment program until 1944. Snyder Act, ch. 115, 42 Stat. 208 (codified as amended at 25 U.S.C. § 13). See Cohen, *Handbook of Federal Indian Law*, 702-03 and accompanying notes. On a Lakota Indian perspective of these "lavish" federal goods, see Mary Crow Dog and Richard Erdoes, *Lakota Woman* (New York: Grove and Weidenfeld, 1990): 17, describing life on the Rosebud Sioux Reservation, South Dakota, growing up in the 1950s.

[80] Lynch to CIA, July 23, 1908, file 41246-08-313, DSJ, YA, BIA, RG 75, NA; *CIA-AR*, 1875, 368.

[81] *CIA-AR*, 1888, 230-31, noting issuance of 1717 head of cattle. See Crow Dog and Erdoes, *Lakota Woman*, 17 for a Lakota view: "Sometimes there was a beef issue of living cattle, the stringiest, skinniest beasts imaginable. This meat-on-the hoof was driven into a huge corral and then our men were allowed to play buffalo hunters for a couple of hours and ride after them and shoot down those poor refugees from the glue factory and butcher them."

[82] L. R. Phillips to Miles Poindexter, July 7, 1914, 77:12, MCPP.

[83] E. B. Meritt, assistant CIA, to Poindexter, July 30, 1914, 77:12, MCPP, noting that the department investigated Matk's claim, and while Meritt was unwilling to believe the allegations, he wrote "It is apparent now, however, that since Luce-Matk's (Margaret) money was not available until May 16, the Superintendent could not draw upon her funds for relief. The Office is, therefore, willing to admit that there may have been some inconvenience [sic] and perhaps hardship until her Colville payment became available."

Just as Congress and Bureau officials were reluctant to provide subsistence support to Indians, after 1913 the Bureau stopped supplying seeds, tools, and other farming supplies to Indian farmers in exchange for labor. In the new system, reservation farmers paid cash for their tools and materials, and replaced seed used after the harvest. The Bureau took money from tribal accounts to establish a $600 annual fund for each Indian farmer. From the fund, an individual drew cash, with the agent's approval, for livestock, seeds, tools, and other equipment. Five years after federal law made all Indians citizens in 1924, John Wyneco complained to the Secretary of Interior that he still required the agent's approval before he could buy a wagon and harness: "The law has made me a citizen of the United States and I certainly feel that I can take care of my rent money.[84] Citizens or not, many Yakama continued to have their land held in trust, and continued to be wards of the federal government.[85]

Additionally, an annual fund of $600 was not sufficient to support a viable farm, much less allow Indians to compete agriculturally with their better capitalized white counterparts.[86] Luce Matk used up $75 of her fund to purchase a cow in the summer of 1914.[87] If clearing and irrigating land cost $10 per acre, merely preparing an 80-acre farm was beyond the financial capabilities of Indians.

Allotment had not turned Indians into farmers, a situation that federal officials saw clearly as early as the 1890s. Much allotted land remained unfarmed, and white farmers and ranchers increasingly pressured Congress to open Indian lands. Leasing would benefit Indians with rental income, it now seemed, since they were too poor to farm themselves.[88]

---

[84] John Wyneco to Secretary of Interior, Nov. 11, 1929, box 1, folder "General Correspondence, re: Indian Matters," Henry J. Snively Papers, Accession no. 3095, University of Washington Libraries, Manuscript Collection, Seattle, Washington [hereafter cited as box:folder, HJSP].

[85] On Indian citizenship, see Michael T. Smith, "The History of Indian Citizenship," in Roger L. Nichols, ed., The *American Indian: Past and Present*, 3d ed. (New York: Knopf, distributed by Random House, 1986): 232-41.

[86] Hurt, *Indian Agriculture in America*, 157.

[87] Meritt to Poindexter, July 30, 1914, 77:12, MCPP.

[88] *CIA-AR*, 1893, 339 (Lynch recommends leasing); *CIA-AR*, 1898, 304-05; *CIA-AR*, 1901, 394 (classification of leased lands on reservation); *CIA-AR*, 1902, 369 (noting that lessees would make permanent improvements); *CIA-AR*, 1909, 7 (stating that lessees would model a "progressive spirit" for Indians). See Hoxie, *Final Promise*, 158-59. See also Department of the Interior, General Land Office, "Indian Reservations to be Opened" (Washington, D.C., January 21, 1908), describing lands "to be opened as fast as they are ready" to entry by whites, file [no number]-08-308.1 [box 08-308.1/10198-18-308.3], DSF, YA, BIA, RG 75, NA; Nealy N. Olney, Secretary Yakima Indian Commercial Club, to Franklin K. Lane, Secretary of the Interior, April 16, 1917, file 40795-17-308.1, DSJ, YA, BIA, RG 75, NA, noting pressure to open Yakama reservation land. Hurt, *Indian Agriculture in America*, 141-42; Cohen, *Handbook of Federal Indian Law*, 134-36.

In 1891, Congress authorized leasing of Indian allotments "[w]henever it shall be made to appear to the Secretary of the Interior that, by reasons of age or other disability, any allottee under the provisions of said act, or any other act of treaty can not personally and with benefit to himself, occupy or improve his allotment or any part thereof the same may be leased...."[89] Leases would be for three year terms on land utilized for farming and grazing, and for ten year terms on lands used for mining.[90]

These leasing provisions, however, did not attract many lessees, perhaps because the lease terms were too short. Congress extended the leasing period in 1894, to allow leases of farmland for five years. The number of leases consequently did increase. Still, Congress could not decide on a firm policy for leasing, and restricted leasing provisions in 1897, then loosened them again in 1900 and 1910. In 1919, Congress also authorized twenty-five year leases of tribal lands for mining in nine western states, including Washington. Leasing required no consent of the tribes, and lessees had a preferential and unlimited right to renew for ten-year periods.[91] Yakama regularly petitioned against the leasing of their lands to non-Indians without their permission, especially where non-Indian grazing practices impinged upon their subsistence practices and their own grazing needs.[92]

The 1891 Act, and subsequent relaxations of restrictions on leasing, departed from previous policy against leasing—most notably the Dawes Act—for the reason that Indians could not learn farming if someone else worked their lands. The rationale by 1891, however, was that if Indians had a supplemental source of income from leases, they could buy the tools necessary to develop their lands.[93] Further, if non-Indian farmers or ranchers made initial improvements in the land, Indians would be more likely to be successful farmers, both because the land would have been broken and white farmers would provide an example to Indians. White farmers on the land also meant that the land surely would be productive.[94]

On the Yakama Reservation, the number of leases went from "a few" in 1898 to more than 1,252 covering almost 87,000 acres by 1920. By 1928, the number of leases had risen to 1300.[95] The lands were leased primarily by non-

---

[89] 26 Stat. L. 795, § 3 (1891).

[90] Under the same act, lands purchased by individuals which were not needed for farming or grazing, and were not used as individual allotments, could be leased with the permission of the tribal council and Indian agent—subject to approval by the Secretary of Interior—for periods of five years for grazing and ten years for farming, 26 Stat. 795, § 3.

[91] Act of May 31, 1900, 31 Stat. 229; Cohen, *Handbook of Federal Indian Law*, 135-36.

[92] See Chapter 9.

[93] Chambers and Price, "Regulating Sovereignty," 1068-74.

[94] File—"Irrigation and Drainage," Irrigation records, 1913-34, YA, RG 75, BIA, NA-Seattle; Hurt, *Indian Agriculture in America*, at 156-58.

[95] See Table I: 6a, Appendix 1.

Indians—although some Japanese farmers seeking to escape alien land laws rented some reservation lands.[96] Lessees predominantly sought lands for farming and grazing, although some set up stock yards, orchards, and other businesses. Revenue from leasing averaged about $1.75 per acre per year, although "improved" lands and business leases generally yielded higher amounts.[97]

Leasing of Indian allotments and of unallotted tribal lands continued to expand through the twentieth century, but generally, the system did not work as promised, and the Bureau made little effort to ensure that Indians benefitted from the leasing programs.[98] Lessees usually had no long-term interests in the land, and sought to make as large a profit as possible before their lease expired. Lessees' short-term interests, moreover, precluded their making any long-term improvements in the land. In their haste to reap profits, farmers repeatedly overirrigated and created widespread problems with salinization.[99] Overgrazing of tribal land, both by lessees and by ranchers illegally grazing stock on the reservation, was also a problem throughout the period.[100]

Leasing provided small but steady revenues for Yakama lessors, most of whom did not control the disposal of their rental income because the agent retained the power to disburse it. Some Yakama sold their allotments for cash. The Dawes Act prohibited allotments from being alienated until the expiration of the trust period, usually 25 years. The provision was designed to give Indian landholders a measure of protection against tax collectors, land sharks and others. After the trust period expired, however, the land was alienable.[101] Under the Burke Act of 1906, Indians whom the Secretary of Interior deemed "competent" could obtain patents in fee for their allotments. Competency

---

[96] On Japanese lessees, see Miles C. Poindexter to Cato Sells, March 13, 1916, 79:1, MCPP. Poindexter quotes from a letter from F. Benz & Sons, Toppenish, Wash, "indicating the difficulties of the white citizens in that community who are leasing Indian lands, arising from competition of Japanese. The results of that competition would make a long story, but you are, I think familiar with the fundamental principles involved. It is really a great and serious problem." Poindexter recommended that OIA give preference to white citizens in leasing Indian lands.

[97] Petition, signed by 70 individuals, Feb. 1913, 76:13, MCPP, requesting that lease money be distributed in larger installments. Leasing revenues remained about $1.75/acre/year through at least 1911, and were little more than $5.00/acre/year for improved agricultural lands by the 1920s, see Tables I:6a-6b, Appendix 1.

[98] Hoxie, *Final Promise*, 85-87.

[99] *CIA-AR*, 1905, 370, Lynch reports that few lessees have "made anything from their leases and some have lost money." While the lessees say they need more land and longer leases, Lynch believed that they did not know how to farm or irrigate properly. See also Chapter 7.

[100] Gretta Gossett, "Stock Grazing in Washington's Nile Valley, Receding Ranges in the Cascades," *Pacific Northwest Quarterly*, 55 (July 1964): 119-27.

[101] 24 Stat. 389, § 5.

commissions roamed Indian Country between 1909 and 1920, declaring individuals competent and eliminating the trust protections on their allotments.[102] Between 1906 and 1911, for example, 78 trust patents were issued to Yakama.[103]

The effect, once allottees lost their trust protections, was almost always the same: Indians sold the land to pay previously accrued debts, taxes, or for their support, or the agent sold it for them. Sales of Yakama allotments were "constantly made to the highest bidder under sealed bids."[104] Once an allottee sold his or her land, the individual received a monthly allowance from the agent from the proceeds of the sale.[105] The Bureau also sold trust allotments on behalf of "non-competent" Indians, especially after 1917.[106]

Bureau rhetoric on Indian land sales resounded with Manifest Destiny tones. "Sturdy American citizens" are buying Indian lands and settling among Indians, declared the Commissioner's *Annual Report* of 1904, although only the previous year's report had noted the rampant speculation and land monopolies generated by allotment sales.[107] Other (perhaps less "sturdy") citizens "fleece the Indian of the last penny within a few hours after the agent has turned over to him the proceeds of a sale."[108] In any case, the Bureau continued to approve such sales on the grounds that penniless and landless Indians would be forced sooner or later by the "law of necessity" to survive in a capitalistic world.[109]

---

[102] Under Cato Sells, Commissioner of Indian Affairs from 1913-21, the process of terminating wardship status accelerated dramatically. Sells believed that ending Indian "wardship" was the solution to the "Indian problem." Under this policy, graduates of government schools and adults of less than half Indian blood were issued patents in fee automatically; to adults who had one half or more Indian blood, patents were issued after an investigation. The government issued 17,176 fee patents between 1917 and 1920—double the number it had issued in the previous decade. Cohen, *Handbook of American Indian Law*, 137; Hoxie, *Final Promise*, 180-83.

[103] Currently there are no accurate or complete compilations of trust patents issued to Yakama tribal members during the period.

[104] John T. Reeves, Acting Chief Land Division, to A. T. Thorson, Aug. 23, 1910, file 65118-10-308.1, DSJ, YA, BIA, RG 75, NA.

[105] C. R. Whitlock, Yakima Superintendent, to CIA, June 20, 1931, describing problems facing Indian land holders whose trust patent period had expired, folder—"Allotment of lands, 380, 1906-1955," DSF 360-391, YA, BIA, RG 75, NA-Seattle.

[106] Sales of "non-competent" Indian lands began in 1908. In 1909, one such 80 acre tract was sold for $6420; in 1911, 18 tracts, totalling 1367.37 acres, were sold for $37,866. There are no compilations of total sales of non-competent Indian land sales on the Yakama Reservation for the period.

[107] *CIA-AR*, 1903, 48; *CIA-AR*, 1904, 29.

[108] *CIA-AR*, 1904, 63-3.

[109] Hoxie, *Final Promise*, 183.

Additionally, inherited allotments were sold by relatives of the deceased because federal law prohibited inclusion of trust property in wills.[110] Agent Evan Estep noted in 1924 that "Every once in a while an Indian under one of those [irrigation] ditches dies. And we all know that as soon as he dies the heirs want to sell the land and get the money. When the land is sold it is always sold to a white man."[111] Although financially-strapped individuals often acquiesced in the sale of heirship lands for cash, some managed to reinvest the proceeds of the sale in the purchase of improved tracts.[112]

Louis Mann described the situation at Yakima in a 1909 letter to Commissioner of Indian Affairs Robert Valentine (1909-1912):

> [T]here are many poor Indians who have went to work and sold their Inherited land through Sup[erin]t[endant] or ag[en]t hand and this day many are suffering hard ship or starvation why because one ten dollars monthly payment is [illegible] a very small [...] I know no one on this earth would go to work sell his lands and get his payment that way and make his business go right and you law makers there you need not want Indians to starve.[113]

Just as the agent doled out annuity payments, agents distributed cash from Indian land sales. One $10 monthly payment in 1909—$15 in 1914—was simply not sufficient to support an individual.[114]

Louis Mann noted with dismay in 1916 that landsharks, with the approval of Department of Interior, were watching the reservation, ready to snatch up any available land.[115] Mann and other Yakama saw that federal law protected white interests; not those of Indians. Mann wrote angrily to Sen. Miles Poindexter that year, "how can we be brought into civilization by looking at our superiors let them rob us or do as they Damn please is this you white man call a Civilization or a law...[?]"[116] To Yakama such as Mann, federal Indian

---

[110] Hoxie, *Final Promise*, 159-60. Hoxie also notes that OIA did have a policy to assist families in retaining heirship lands. At Yakima, however, most such lands seem to have been sold.

[111] Statement in Report of Commission to investigate the claims of Indians along Simcoe Creek [hereafter cited as Report of Simcoe Creek Commission], June 9, 1924, file 77253-22-341, part 1-A, Central Classified Files, 1907-39, CCF, YA, BIA, RG 75, NA. (The pages of the report are not numbered consecutively, or in any identifiable order, so I have omitted them.)

[112] *CIA-AR*, 1920, 49. The Yakama Tribe began purchasing trust lands in heirship cases beginning in 1954. Schuster, "Yakima Indian Traditionalism," 264.

[113] Mann to Valentine, Nov. 8, 1909, file 7003-1909-307.4, DSJ, YA, BIA, RG 75, NA. See also Cohen, *Handbook of Federal Indian Law*, 136.

[114] *CIA-AR*, 1903, 47 (proceeds of sale paid in cash); cf. *CIA-AR*, 1904, 63-5 (proceeds of sale paid in monthly installments). Field matrons employed by OIA, as a comparison, were earning $60/month; agency farmers were earning $65/month.

[115] Mann to Poindexter, Feb. 2, 1916, 76:12, MCPPF; see also Mann to Poindexter, Feb. 7, 1916, ibid.

[116] Mann to Poindexter, Feb. 7, 1916, 76:12, MCPP.

land laws were "grafting" policies and violated the apparent sanctity of the Yakamas' 1855 treaty protections of their reservation land base.[117]

Conclusion: Yakama Wage Laborers

If their reservation had been an insular territory, protected from outside encroachment of all kinds, and sufficient to protect a subsistence resource base large enough to support their populations, tribes would have had little reason to participate in the market system. Yet this was emphatically not the case: The reservation was open to a variety of entries and other encroachments by non-Indians, Indians found it increasingly difficult to live on the proceeds of the subsistence round, and in order to support themselves they necessarily became tied to the larger capitalist economic structure. Taxes on land, cash for farming tools, materials, and food all required money. In order to obtain cash, then, Indians sold whatever they had, including land, their labor, and crafts.[118]

Yakama had been fishers for a long time, and some found that they could support themselves by marketing their catch to non-Indians. During the 1870s, Yakama sold salted fish and fresh berries to local residents.[119] Indians also sold—and still sell—fish to the many canneries lining the Columbia by the mid-1870s and early 1880s. These fishers took first for their own needs and sold the surplus to the canneries.[120]

Some, such as Sam Williams and Sam Tan-a-washa, worked for local canneries who provided them with fishing tools and equipment. Charley Dick provides a different example, in that he worked as a "boss" for the Winans Brothers Company cannery, overseeing a crew of ten to twelve Indian fishers.[121] Yet Yakama on the whole do not seem to have been as involved in commercial fishing as their counterparts in western Washington, such as the Lummi. There was significant tribal sentiment against fishing for the market.[122]

Yakama also worked as wage laborers in a variety of jobs. Federal policies encouraged Indians to work as laborers: Indian schools utilized an "outing" system by which children were sent into Euro-American homes to work, especi-

---

[117] See also Angie Deboe, *And Still the Waters Run: The Betrayal of the Five Civilized Tribes* (Princeton, Princeton University Press, 1972): 92-125, for a description of activities by such "grafters" among the Choctaws, Seminoles, Chicasaws, Creeks, and Cherokees.

[118] C. K. Jacobson, "Internal Colonization and Native Americans: Indian Labor in the United States from 1871 to World War II," *Social Science Quarterly* 65 (March 1984): 158-71.

[119] *CIA-AR*, 1870, 32.

[120] "Officials Make Survey of Diets, Families Average 1600 Pounds [of salmon] Yearly," n.p., Aug. 2, 1942, file—"Indians-Yakima-Government," Yakima Valley Museum [hereafter cited as YVM]. On Yakama commercial salmon fishing, see Chapter 8.

[121] Testimony of Sam Tan-a-washa, in *U.S. v. Winans*, transcript of record, 147-48; testimony of Charley Dick, ibid.; testimony of Sheppard Peters, Report of Simcoe Creek Commission.

[122] See Chapter 8.

Yakama mother with her children at hop farm, ca. 1900

Northwest Museum of Arts & Culture/Eastern Washington State Historical Society, Spokane Washington, American Indians of the Pacific Northwest Images Digital Collection, Negative # L93-72.56, used by permission

ally in domestic tasks.[123] Additionally, requirements for obtaining a pass from the Indian agent in order to leave the reservation did not apply if individuals were leaving to do wage labor. As early as 1878 the Bureau issued a circular instructing its agents not to allow Indians to leave the reservation without express permission. Those who left for off-reservation jobs required no

---

[123] For a discussion of the outing system, see Robert A. Trennert, "From Carlisle to Phoenix: The Rise and Fall of the Indian Outing System, 1878-1930," *Pacific Historical Review* 52 (Aug. 1983): 267-92.

permit.[124]

An extremely popular Yakama job was hops picking both east and west of the Cascades. Picking hops provided seasonal labor during September and October that fit easily into Yakama subsistence lifeways. Good pickers earned $1.50 to $2 per day in 1889.[125] By the early twentieth century pickers could ride the train into crop areas near Puget Sound. Yakama also worked as migrant laborers bringing in hay, potatoes, sugarbeets, and other crops.[126]

By 1934, then, the economic changes wrought on the reservation by the treaty and subsequent federal laws had not turned the Indians into yeoman farmers. Rather the efforts of federal officials had alienated through lease and sale a large portion of Yakama reservation lands, leaving the population to seek new methods to support themselves in a market economy for which they were ill prepared to participate.

Although by the end of the period, some Yakama had taken up ranching, others remained at tiny fishing villages year-round. Many individuals fell between these two extremes, pursuing subsistence fishing and berrying practices, and augmenting their harvest with produce grown on small farms or with foods and goods purchased with the proceeds of labor in hops fields or from selling fish and berries to local citizens. When crops failed, people dip netted salmon; when salmon runs were light, they resorted to wage labor or farming.[127]

Federal Indian farm policies encompassed more than simply rearranging patterns of land holding, however, just as the Euro-American property bundle had implications for social organization as well as human-nature relationships. Bureau policymakers tried to remake Indian life completely, including tribal governance and education in their efforts to bring agriculture into Native American lives. Yet here too, as in their efforts to turn Yakama into individualistic farmers, federal officials did not succeed.

---

[124] Those Indians who federal the agent wished to "reward" for "meritorious conduct and attention to labor" and whose visiting would not interfere with the "necessary work at agencies," also received permission to leave. OIA Circular no. 28, December 28 (?), 1878, cited in "Civilization," Indian Office Circular no. 43, B. J. Brooks, Acting CIA, 114:22, CRP. In 1880, the Indian Office required agents to issue written passes to those wishing to leave the reserve, Circular no. 43, 114:22, CRP. In practice the system worked imperfectly because the single agent on the reserve could not effectively police the activities of each tribal member. See, e.g., Knight, Acting CIA, to Thomas Priestly, Jan. 3, 1889, 115:22, CRP, ordering Priestly to stop Palouse Indians from visiting the Colville Reservation where they allegedly sold stolen horses, went hunting, got drunk, and gambled.

[125] *CIA-AR*, 1889, 291; *CIA-AR*, 1890, 234, reporting that agent is discouraging hop-picking because Indians get drunk and leave their farms.

[126] L. F. Michael, supervisor Yakima Indian reservation and schools, Feb. 20, 1915, file 26666-15-920, CCF, YA, BIA, RG 75, NA; "Wanapam way of life, September and October," Relander interview with unidentified Yakama [probably Frank Sohappy], n.d., 57:25, CRP; "At George Desmarais Hop Camp," Relander interview with Frank Sohappy, Sept. 4, 1956, 58:8, CRP.

[127] "Officials Make Survey of Diets," Relander, *Treaty Centennial*, 33-34.

5

"THE INDIAN BELONGS TO THE EARTH"

> The Indians of the Yakama Agency were as low at our beginning with them as humanity gets without getting into the pit that is bottomless. They were taken from the war-path, gathered upon the reserve, and fed at great expense by the government, clothed with annuity blankets and goods, living in idleness, using the goods furnished as a gambling-fund, drinking whisky, running horses on the Sabbath, stealing each other's wives, and, carrying out the practices of the low, degraded white men to great perfection. The Bible and the plow (which must never be divorced) have brought them up from the horrible pit, and put a new song into their mouths, and new hopes into their hearts. They are washed and clothed and in their right minds. Between five and six hundred are accepted members of the Methodist Episcopal Church.
> —J. H. Wilbur (1878)[1]

Missionaries knew early on that to restructure a people's religious beliefs involved far more than preaching the word of god. Those such as the Whitmans believed firmly that the Bible and plow went hand in hand in the effort to convert Native Americans to the ideal of "civilization" that they believed their own Euro-American culture to embody. Federal officials, too, recognized the connections between world view, economy and society. In their policies for reorganizing and administering tribal government, work, and education, Bureau officials hoped to further the assimilationist goals embodied in statutes regulating reservation land use. Through their work in each area, officials sought to instill and reinforce the image of an independent worker making a productive place for himself in society. Women, in that scenario, were to take up wifely and virtuous posts at the hearth, where, not unlike their Victorian counterparts, they would provide an example to their husbands and families. In the reformers new world every Indian would have a new place and each would learn his or her place in the larger society.

Thomas J. Morgan, Commissioner of Indian Affairs (1889–1893), summed up the goal of federal Indian policy in his 1889 report:

> It has become the settled policy of the Government to break up reservations, destroy tribal relations, settle Indians upon their own homesteads, incorporate them into the national life, and deal with them not as nations or tribes or bands, but as in-

---

[1] U.S. Commissioner of Indian Affairs, *Annual Report to the Secretary of the Interior, 1878* (Washington, D.C.: Government Printing Office, 1879) [hereafter cited as *CIA-AR*, year]: 141.

dividual citizens.[2]

The process of turning "tribal" Indians into "individual citizens" and farmers left no aspect of Yakama cultural or individual life untouched: work patterns, religion, family and home life—even clothing and home furnishings—became targets for reform. "The blanket must give way," declared E. A. Hayt, Commissioner, in 1877. "It is only tolerable in the rudest savage life. It is unfitted to be the garment of civilization and labor; and as the Indian is gradually brought to give up his nomadic life for one of labor and industry, the question of clothing becomes one of practical interest as bearing upon his advancement and civilization."[3]

Transforming human relationships to the land entailed a restructuring of the tools and techniques of Yakama subsistence practices as well as a restructuring of the social relationships within which people understood and organized their relationships with nature. Treaties contained all the provisions necessary to legalize this massive effort at social engineering. Treaties such as that of the Yakama did contain provisions acknowledging and protecting pre-contact subsistence practices such as fishing, gathering, hunting, and grazing; but, more importantly, they also set out a legal framework to manipulate Indian social and environmental relationships.

Yakama were not passive objects in this process of cultural transformation. Throughout the period they told federal officials their views about land, government, and appropriate education for children, even if federal officials often did not listen. Ultimately, however, federal policies did not destroy the Yakamas' belief that "the Indian belongs to the earth."[4]

Indian Views of Land and Law

Euro-Americans arriving on the Plateau brought with them a particular legal system and speedily imposed it on all of the region's inhabitants. According to Hahise Sawyahill, a Yakama woman testifying in an irrigation controversy in 1922, "When you white people come to our country [you] made laws and governed everything. You are not oldest in this country. And we have more right to talk about our country than the white man has."[5] Plateau inhabitants were no strangers to law: particular rules governed access to fishing and other

---

[2] *CIA-AR*, 1890, vi.

[3] *CIA-AR*, 1877, 5.

[4] Helen Hersh Schuster, "Yakima Indian Traditionalism: A Study in Continuity and Change" (Ph.D. diss., University of Washington, 1975): 418.

[5] Statement in Report of Commission to investigate the claims of Indians along Simcoe Creek [hereafter cited as Report of Simcoe Creek Commission], June 9, 1924, file 77253-22-341, part 1-A, Yakima Agency, Central Classified Files, 1907-39, Records of the Bureau of Indian Affairs, Record Group 75, National Archives, Washington, D.C. [hereafter cited as YA, CCF, BIA, RG 75, NA-branch]. (The pages of the report are not numbered consecutively, or in any identifiable order, so I have omitted them.)

subsistence grounds, the boundaries of each group's territory, and proper behavior in trading and other social and economic relationships.[6] Yet Euro-Americans—even had they recognized the existence of an indigenous legal system—were determined to impose their own laws on Native peoples. To survive within this world structured by white law, Indians needed to acquire familiarity with—and even fluency—in this new language.

Indians' adoption of a new and Europeanized view of land and the structure of human relationships toward land on the Columbia Plateau went hand in hand with a growing awareness of how the U.S. legal system could affect them. Indians who acquiesced to the terms proposed by U.S. treaty makers and other officials expected the federal government to honor the promises inherent in those agreements. Indians who became owners of private property needed both an appreciation for the protections offered to them by the legal system and a sense of caution as to its power over them—to compel them, for example, to pay taxes, to relocate, and even to forfeit their land.

It is very difficult to document the process by which Native Americans generally, and specifically the Yakama, came to understand the significance of law to their lives. Doubtless for some of them "law" and what officials said the law was were synonymous.

Others quickly found a distinction between the law as written and the law as implemented. To them, it was the treaty that was truly "the law": the treaty became the standard against which they evaluated the integrity and legitimacy of all future federal laws and policies. In this view, law was a static, nearly divinely sanctioned agreement among individuals. As Chief We-yallup Wayacika of the Ahtanum stated it in 1913,

> When the treaty was signed, the law was established that the land and water was given us. The law was satisfied. We were satisfied. This law is still there, but it is not regarded by the whites. I have not forgotten this law, but my people are passing away. I am grieved that the white man has not kept his word. When an Indian lies, Me-yay-way (God) is angry. When the white man lies, his God is not ashamed.[7]

Wayacika's statement makes clear that he expected some higher authority to hold humans accountable to the promises they made to one another through the law.

Similarly, Frank Selatsee told Assistant Commissioner E. B. Meritt in 1928, "Today we see white people trying to get them [our resources] away. We get just a few and the white people get more.... That is the reason I don't want to have my laws changed or the [Indian] Office to change my laws. As long as

---

[6] See Chapter 2.

[7] Wyallup Wayacika, Chief of the Ahtanum, to Miles C. Poindexter, April 13, 1913, Accession no. 3828, box 76, folder 8, Miles C. Poindexter Papers, University of Washington Library, Manuscripts Division, Seattle, Washington [hereafter cited as box:folder, MCPP].

the sun shines on the earth we want to keep our traditions and laws. We want our laws and traditions observed. It is the rule among the Indians that we have to come every year to protect our rights on different matters to this city."[8]

Here, law sanctified certain promises, a notion that Yakama expressed in the image of the law shining a light that revealed truth. As Louis Mann wrote to Senator Poindexter in 1916, "We want light of the law no blind work ... [we want the enactment of] good right laws for our light to live by no more Grafters Policy or political schemes...."[9] Mann's comment illustrates the perceived clear distinction between law and policy that characterized many Yakamas' evaluations of federal intentions toward them. The Yakamas' treaty of 1855 came to provide the measure of legitimacy against which they evaluated all subsequent federal law.

After 1855, federal statutes which provided for the division of the tribe's land base into individual allotments, and gave officials tools to promote the breakdown of tribal society, made the Yakamas' treaty seem like a document that offered protection to the Yakamas' culture and their resources. No wonder, then, that the Yakama repeatedly sought to hold federal officials to the 1855 agreement. Here, in the eyes of some Yakama, the treaty terms, and valid laws that would honor the treaty, contrasted sharply with the "grafting policy" promoted by members of Congress and reservation officials in order to fulfill the demands of white landowners and speculators. Louis Mann, secretary of Yakama Council, wrote in an angry letter to Senator Miles Poindexter in 1916:

> We Indians are Dispossessed and there always Exists big Evil by which we are tried to be blind folded and misrepresented into the hands of the Department of the Interior now let us all have same table to eat from white and red race ... and why men are put into our reservation to blind us when we can read an[d] write just the same as they do now....[10]

Some Yakama, such as Mann, could read and write and kept up with developments in Indian policy by reading the newspapers and obtaining federal reports from government offices, and frequently wrote letters to government officials expressing their views.

Similarly, when Yakama delegations travelled to Washington, D.C. throughout the 1910s and '20s, they requested that the federal government honor its pre-existing promises to the tribe.[11] The more Indians could read and learn for themselves, the more distrustful they became of what officials said.

---

[8] In "Hearing Held Before E. G. Meritt, Assistant Indian Commissioner," Feb. 2, 1928, file 6987-28-115, YA, CCF, General Records, 1907-39 [hereafter GR], BIA, RG 75, NA [hereafter cited as 1928 delegation hearing].

[9] Mann to Poindexter Jan. 25, 1916, 76:12, MCPP.

[10] Mann to Poindexter, Feb. 2, 1916, 76:12, MCPP.

[11] See for example 1928 delegation hearing, comment of Frank Selatsee noting that Yakama have come to Washington every year to protect their treaty rights. See also U.S. Congress,

In their petitions and letters to their congressional representatives or to officials in the Bureau of Indian Affairs, those Yakama repeatedly held officials accountable to what they saw as the higher law of the treaty. The treaty became the tribe's constitution, the document against which they would measure all change. When federal officials in 1916 denied individual allotments in timbered areas, including Cedar Valley, Mann reported for Yakima Council, "As to the timberlands in trying to obtain allotments these Government Officials blinded us by telling us these land [sic] were held [as] a reserve for the tribes, but we have found on the plot and maps, these lands was claimed by white homesteaders and such grave lies was put to us Indians and made us to sleep therefore whiteman's words on the Indian reservations are always trap for the Redman." Such skepticism colored all Yakama relations with federal officials throughout the period.[12]

Although Yakama often found the administration of the legal system questionable, they learned early that their only effective recourse was to use the system to promote their treaty-based interests; indeed this tactic provided a primary means by which they attempted to secure their claims to the land and other resources. The anthropologist Helen Schuster noted that at the same time as other Plateau groups turned to the Prophet religion and its derivatives as a way to counteract white aggression, Yakama turned to the courts and political realm. We can only speculate about the reasons for their choice.[13] Relative to many other tribes, they were a well organized group despite treaty depradations and disease suffered by the region generally. Perhaps they determined to make good on the rhetoric of Euro-American law that promised "justice and a square deal." Perhaps they saw in courts and political institutions their last chance to protect what lands and resources remained to them. Most importantly, Yakama realized early that rights once established in a court had significance for future rights.[14]

The U.S. legal system provided a vital tool by which some Yakama sought to protect their treaty-based claims, but it was also a tool by which virtually all federal officials expected to remake Native Americans into the image of white property owners. The image of land written into the Yakamas' treaty on its face is a Euro-American image of land as alienable, convertible into a monetary value, and useful only to the extent that it can be made productive. That image

---

Senate, *Payment of Expenses of Delegates of Yakima Confederated Tribes of Indians*, 73d Cong., 2d Sess., 1935, S. Rep. 1180, p. 2.

[12] Mann, addendum to YTC-WS report, Jan. 13-14, 1916, 76:12, MCPP. See also "Collier holds Six-Hour Talk With Redmen, Tribesmen Distrust 'New Plans' and feel though 'on edge great precipice,'" newspaper clipping, Dec. 17, 1934 [?], file—"Indians-Yakima-Government," Yakima Valley Museum, Yakima, WA [hereafter cited as YVM].

[13] Schuster, "Yakima Traditionalism," 263-64, 274.

[14] For a discussion of marginalized peoples' experiences in the U.S. legal system, see Peter Gabel and Paul Harris, "Building Power and Breaking Images: Critical Legal Theory and the Practice of Law," *New York University Review of Law & Social Change* 11 (1983): 369-411.

was one that federal officials hoped to instill in Native American hands and hearts.

Yet, throughout the period to 1934, and despite a massive federal effort to reeducate Indians, there was no more a unified Yakama view of land in the twentieth century than there had been in the mid-nineteenth.[15] Treaty participants had wavered between the notion of land inherent in the old sacred bundle of their tradition and the notion embodied in the Euro-American bundle of rights in property. Their twentieth century counterparts were equally equivocal. Many used the tenets of the Smohalla religion or the Yakamas' own Washat religion to fortify beliefs of an older time. These people tended to see the earth as a living entity which could not be partitioned and sold out of the hands of the people who lived upon it. In that view, the concept of selling land was distasteful, even if by now it was a coherent concept.[16]

A pair of meetings between the Yakima Tribal Council and two U.S. Indian Commissioners in 1897 and 1898 illustrates the range of views held by Indian participants. In both years the federal government sent commissioners to induce the tribe to sell "surplus," or unallotted, land remaining from the 1892 and subsequent allotments of Yakama reservation lands.

Columbia Wild Man, reflecting, the attitudes of Yakama who had pulled survey stakes out of the ground in 1897 to protest the very act of surveying the land, stated: "There is not one man that claims this reservation. Every living soul on this reservation, Indians, they claim this land. We claim this reservation as our father, we say this reservation is our mother as long as the [I]ndians live."[17]

Similarly, during the 1898 council, Caperty told the commissioners "we will not sell—never. All Indians say we never sell our land."[18] Pearn also argued. that "In old times they [the chiefs] would not go to Yakima to make

---

[15] See Chapter 3.

[16] See statement of Charles Colwash, in Council Proceedings of Yakima Indians, Fort Simcoe, Wash., June 2, 1913, folder "Councils and Meetings (Tribal) 1913-25," Tribal Records, 1897-1952, YA, BIA, RG 75, NA-Seattle [hereafter cited as June 2, 1913 Council]; Schuster, "Yakima Traditionalism," 318-19ff; Morris L. Uebelacker, *Time Ball: A Story of the Yakima People and the Land* (Yakima Indian Nation, Toppenish, WA, 1984); Uebelacker, *Land and Life in the Naches River Basin*, U.S. Forest Service, Region 6, Portland Oregon, 1980.

[17] Statement of Columbia Wild Man, in "Report of Council with Indians at Yakima Reservation by Commissioners Barge and Goodwin, Fort Simcoe, Feb. 20, 1897, folder "Yakima Council 1898," Tribal Records, 1897-1952, YA, BIA, RG 75, NA-Seattle [hereafter cited as Feb. 20, 1897 Council]. Columbia Wildman was married to Hadwesa, an "ancient faith priestess" and head root digger for the Wapato Longhouse, Charles Relander (Now Tow Look), *Drummers and Dreamers: The Story of Smohalla the Prophet and his nephew Puck Hyah Toot...*, with a foreword by Frederick Webb Hodge (Caldwell, ID: The Caxton Printers, 1956): 176-77.

[18] Statement of Caperty, in "Report of Council of Commissioners and Yakima Tribe of Indians," n.d., file "Yakima Council, 1898," Tribal Records, 1897-1952, YA, BIA, NA-Seattle [hereafter cited as Yakima Council, 1898].

talk. They stay at home. They not talk about land we hold it forever."[19] John Wesley held similar sentiments: "My Friend the land belong to the Indian. The law has taken it away from us.... Don't think to buy land. The government law put Indian on this Reservation same as God."[20] Here, humans and the earth continued in a sacred, living relationship that no law or notion of private property could break. The Rev. George Waters, a Yakama educated in Bureau schools, stated, "You have no right to put a price on the land. It is too small an amount." Waters' statement indicates his ambivalence toward the commissioners and their offer, but perhaps all prices would have been too small.

Others, however, accepted the premise of the market and the Euro-American property bundle. Yakama Chief White Swan (1868-1910), who requested $2,500,000 for the land for which the commissioners were offering $1,400,000, seemed to believe that the land could be priced and sold; a sentiment that earned him the wrath of many of his people.[21] White Swan's price was the product of his realization that federal officials always tried to buy Indian land at low prices, and his familiarity with current land prices as well.[22]

In subsequent years, such diverse views as council members expressed in the 1897-98 meetings continued to divide the tribe, and the division precluded any formation of a single "Yakama view" of the land. Such a range of viewpoints arose from several factors, some of which related to an individual's historical tie to the land.[23] Another factor was that Yakama, like other Plateau peoples, historically had cultivated each individual's own relationship to the spirit and natural world. Within that system, however, some may have held stronger claims to property associated with privilege than others. One example is the case of men who inherited the position of fishing headman from their fathers or grandfathers. Those men, such as Chiefs Skamiah, White Swan, and Thomas and Louis Simpson, asserted property rights to particular fishing locations which they had inherited with their titles.[24]

Tribal Government and Federal Power

Pre-contact Plateau societies used the flexible "task group" system to achieve cooperation among many small groups to complete large projects such

---

[19] Statement of Pearn, in Yakima Council, 1898.

[20] Statement of John Wesley, in Yakima Council, 1898.

[21] Schuster, "Yakima Traditionalism," 242.

[22] Statements of George Waters and Chief White Swan, in Yakima Council, 1898.

[23] See Chapter 2.

[24] Case of Chief Skamiah discussed in Carey & Kerr to Register and Receiver of the Land Office, Vancouver, Washington, April 21, 1910, file [?] 688-1910 [?]-115, YA, CCF, GR, BIA, RG 75, NA. White Swan and Thomas Simpson were the two Yakama plaintiffs in the case *United States v. Winans* (1905). Louis Simpson said that he had inherited rights to fish at the See-we-pam fishery from his father, who was chief. See Chapter 8.

as hunting and trading.[25] Cooperation was key to survival and socialization: politics stressed collaboration and consensus. Dispute settlement rested at the family level, with an emphasis on reparation for wrongdoing.[26] Blood revenge was an accepted response to murder, which explains why so many medicine people who failed to cure their diseased patients were killed at the turn of the century.[27]

Bureau officials were unimpressed with this system, and surely were disinclined to leave Yakama affairs in such unpredictable hands. For a variety of reasons, the Bureau wanted to ensure that it retained control over important tribal governing institutions such as council, courts, and police. A friendly tribal council could be relied upon to rubber stamp federal schemes to sell off reservation resources such as timber and "surplus" lands. Euro-American courts would not allow such practices as polygamy and blood revenge. Tribal police, also, would make sure that any reservation justice was ultimately in line with Euro-American ideals.

The Bureau's efforts to remake Yakama government unsurprisingly began at the top; the logical beginning point from the Euro-American perspective. Federal officials wanted a monarchical figure on which to pin responsibility for negotiating treaties and other agreements. To that end, Article 5 of the treaty postulated a "head chief" who would be responsible for all of the collected groups on the reserve, and who would be elected by tribal members. The chief was to be the contact point between federal agents and the rest of the tribe, and would "perform many services of a public character, occupying much of his time." For his efforts this man would receive a "comfortable house," "properly" furnished, and $500 per year from the federal government.[28] The treaty designated Kamiakin as Yakama chief although no one had elected him and Kamiakin himself refused to move to the reservation or to accept that position.[29] In 1868, Agent Wilbur called for an election in which Joe Stwire (Chief White Swan) was elected to the office.[30]

---

[25] See Chapter 2.

[26] Schuster, "Yakima Traditionalism," 53-59.

[27] *CIA-AR*, 1888, 232; J. D. C. Adkins to Priestly, April 13, 1888, box 115, file 21, Click Relander Papers, Yakima Valley Regional Library, Yakima, WA; *CIA-AR*, 1901, 395.

[28] Treaty with the Yakima, 12 Stat. 951, art. 5. The salary was to be paid for not more than 20 years.

[29] Agent Wilbur reported that Kamiakin remained "hundreds of miles from the reserve" and refused to come to the reservation and to accept his salary. *CIA-AR*, 1868, 100; Andrew Jackson Splawn, *Ka-Mi-Akin: Last Hero of the Yakimas* (Portland, OR: Kilham Stationery & Printing Co., 1917): 119-21. Splawn reported that one year after Kamiakin's death, vandals desecrated his grave and cut off his head and shoulders. His remains have been reburied at Toppenish Creek, near Fort Simcoe.

[30] *CIA-AR*, 1868, 101. Spencer, appointed by Superintendent Gery, served as head chief from 1859 to 1861, Schuster, "Yakima Traditionalism," 242.

Below the level of head chief were chiefs of the individual bands that made up the Yakama confederacy. The bands held their own elections to fill those positions. Representatives from all of the bands in the confederacy eventually made up the Yakima Tribal Council, which met collectively at the White Swan long house.

It seems clear that some pre-treaty practices continued to inform the selection of at least some local headchiefs. Men whose fathers and grandfathers had been headchiefs of fishing continued to exercise power over Indian fishers at inherited sites. Thomas Simpson and White Swan represented more than their own treaty fishing rights when they became plaintiffs against the Winans Brothers Company in the late 1880s: both men held inherited chieftainships in the fishery grounds at issue.[31] Such positions did not necessarily continue to carry authority with other tribal members: Where a Yakama fisher used his inherited fishing location to fish commercially, the Yakima Council sent the Indian police to threaten him with arrest if he continued.[32]

The reorganization of tribal government was designed to strengthen the OIA's voice in reservation affairs. In 1883, Agent Milroy divided the reservation into districts, each with its own representative, by way of replacing the old headman-based system.[33] The Dawes Act provided that individuals who accepted allotments would be preferred for public positions in reservation government and police.[34] Thus, Indians such as the Dreamers, followers of Smohalla, and the "Wild Yakima" who pursued subsistence lifeways along the river valleys had no representatives on the Council or tribal court.[35]

When Agent Walter Stabler organized a court of Indian offenses in 1890, he appointed men who had adopted Euro-American dress and habits. These men wore "while on the bench white shirts and standing collars, and otherwise conducting themselves with becoming gravity." Agent Stabler noted with satisfaction that "They favor the education of children and other progress in civilization."[36] Even with such hand-picked appointees, the agent retained authority to reverse all court decisions. The court imposed a Euro-American view of crime on reservation inhabitants: Agent Jay Lynch reported in 1893

---

[31] See Chapter 8.

[32] See Chapter 8.

[33] *CIA-AR*, 1883 153-55.

[34] 24 Stat. L. 388, 390 §5 (1887).

[35] Schuster, "Yakima Traditionalism," 259-60ff; Helen Spencer, personal communication, July 1989, Yakima, Washington.

[36] *CIA-AR*, 1890, 232. These men included Stick Joe, Louis Simpson, and Peal. See also Click Relander, "Indian Police Founded in '77," n.p., Feb. 22, 1951, file "Indians, Yakimas—Government," YVM; Linda Baker, "A Long Tradition of Justice," *Yakima Herald-Republic*, April 13, 1987, file—"Indians, Yakima—Government," YVM. For a discussion of the historical development of tribal councils and tribal court systems, see Vine Deloria, Jr. and Clifford M. Lytle, *American Indians, American Justice* (Austin: University of Texas Press, 1983).

that "All persons having two wives are promptly brought before the Indian court."[37] Additionally, the court policed liquor traffic, murder, and theft.[38]

Still, Yakama do not seem to have accepted the Bureau's involvement in their government without protest, or without frustrating Bureau plans in some cases. In 1895, following their receipt of allotments, some Yakama protested the agent's choice of judges, demanding that they be able to elect their own. Agent L. T. Erwin told them they could hold elections once allotment was completed.[39] And although the tribal council met when the agent convened it, and discussed issues that the agent designated, the council could thwart Bureau plans.

While the agent introduced topics for debate, he could not always dictate the outcome. For example, one well-organized conservative group was able to influence council decision making to some extent. When Indian Commissioners visited the reservation to purchase "surplus land" in 1897 and 1898, this conservative faction was instrumental in preventing the sale. At the same time, at least some council members also refused to discuss the land sale until the commissioners acknowledged their concerns about a resurvey of the reservation boundary, compensation for the federal purchase of the Wenatshapam fishery, and another fishing related problem.[40] In 1898, 1904, and 1917, some Yakama, including Yakima Council members, organized lobbying efforts (including petitioning) to press the Bureau to approve additional allotments for unallotted children on the reservation. Yakima Council lobbying was instrumental in securing congressional authorization to allot those children.[41]

Yet the power to bring issues to the attention of the Bureau was hardly the power to govern a tribe. The Yakima Council resembled a puppet government at best: it provided an official body with whom the federal government could negotiate, even if the members had no tribally recognized authority in the matter.

The sale of the Wenatshapam fishery to the federal government in 1894 provides a clear example of the Council's lack of power coupled with federally

---

[37] *CIA-AR*, 1893, 339.

[38] See, for example, case load of the court *CIA-AR*, 1890, 232-33. Although Lynch reported that the Court of Indian Offenses had been abolished in 1905, the Yakama continued to keep a tribal court system to the present. *CIA-AR*, 1905, 371; Linda Baker, "A Long Tradition of Justice," *Yakima Herald-Republic,* April 13, 1978, 3A.

[39] *CIA-AR*, 1895, 322.

[40] Yakima Council 1898; Feb. 20, 1897 Council; Schuster, "Yakima Traditionalism," 259-60.

[41] When L. V. McWhorter, a long time advocate of the Yakama, wrote to the Commissioner of Indian Affairs stating that the tribe was unsatisfied with the quality of lands allotted to the children, the Commissioner reminded him that subsequent allotments were a privilege, not a right. Allotment to children was "purely one of courteous and friendly interest by Congress; not being one that the Indians could insist on as a matter of right. You and the members of your tribe should be glad to avail yourselves of this additional privilege given you by Congress." File 57561-10-313, DSJ, YA, RG 75, BIA, NA.

acknowledged authority. The Wenatshapam fishery, on the Wenatchee River, near Cashmere, Washington, was a traditional fishing place of the Wenatchee Indians. The fishery encompassed an area "six miles square" and had been included in the land reserved to the Yakama tribe under their 1855 treaty.[42] The Wenatchi people, however, did not live on the reservation, nor were they represented in any of the discussions for the sale of that land.[43] Tom Pearn, a Yakima Council member, recalled the events of the sale:

> We had a council before once. I was standing before them myself, Pearn. Colonel Lane stood here before the Indians. He said before the Indians he wanted to buy a piece of land. I said no, I don't want to sell land. Colonel Lane said to me how much do you want for your land. I says $10.00 an acre. Well Colonel Lane he says no use, the government won't pay that. So I said all right, we will not sell to them. All these Indians represent me before Colonel Lane to set the price.... Now we have a fight about that money. Now we are robbed out of that money. Now the Indians feel bad about that money. Now we think to-day our Indian Agent is our enemy to-day.[44]

The federal government purchased the land and extinguished all Indian rights for $20,000, to be expended on the Yakama Reservation.[45] Congress eventually authorized the expenditure of the money on an on-reservation Bureau irrigation project. The Bureau informed the Wenatchi, in response to their petition for redress, that they could receive a share of the benefits of the land and fishery sale only if they accepted allotments on the reservation.[46] In response to their protest, Bureau finally secured homesteads in the area for most of them by 1903.[47]

---

[42] Treaty with the Yakima, art. 10.

[43] On the Wenatchi, see *CIA-AR*, 1898, 306, reporting that about 200 Wenatchi refuse to come to the reservation. In 1892 OIA completed a survey of the fishery, during which time white settlers in the area protested the creation of another reservation, leading Lynch to conclude that it would be easier to sell the land than to fight to maintain it in Indian ownership, *CIA-AR*, 1893, 100-01. See also *CIA-AR*, 1893, 340; *CIA-AR*, 1894, 326.

[44] Statement of Pearn, "Feb. 20, 1897 Council."

[45] Ch. 290, § 13, 28 Stat. 320-321 (1894).

[46] 28 Stat. 321; Oscar S. Lipps, Supervisor of Indian Schools, to CIA, July 7, 1911, file 59588-11-313, DSJ, YA, RG 75, BIA, NA, stating that the Wenatchee Indians have petitioned the Indian Office for compensation for the Wenatshapam fishery land; C. F. Hauke, Second Assistant CIA to John Hemilt and Louis Judge, July 29, 1911, ibid., advising that compensation to the Wenatchee Indians is in the form of their choice of allotments on the Yakama or Colville reservations.

[47] *CIA-AR*, 1903, 110-11. Seven landless Wenatchi were relocated to the Colville Reservation. The structure of YTC-WS today is as follows: A General Council is comprised of all eligible voters (enrolled Yakama tribal members over 18). The Yakima Tribal Council is the business committee of the tribe and is composed of 14 treaty band representatives, who are elected at by the General Council. See Click Relander, ed., *Treaty Centennial, 1855-1955: The Yakimas*,

104 • LAND DIVIDED BY LAW

Yakama Chief White Swan and Indian Agent Thomas Priestley on horses, Fort Simcoe, Washington, ca. 1888

University of Washington Libraries, Special Collections,
Negative # NA 4113, used by permission

1st ed., Washington State Historical Society and Oregon State Historical Society, published by authorization of the Yakima Tribal Council (Yakima, WA: Republic Press, 1955): 38; Baker, "Long Tradition of Justice," "Yakima Nation Organizational Chart," 3A.

The Indian agent was the field representative for the Bureau on each reservation, and had virtual sovereignty over the Indians on the reserve. The agent wrote out passes for leaving the reservation for visiting or making subsistence rounds; doled out rations and the seeds, tools, and other goods that made up federal annuity payments; and generally supervised or engineered the implementation of federal policies on the reservation.[48] The agent convened the council, represented Indian concerns to both state and federal officials, and assisted in helping Indians litigate claims in the state and federal courts. The position necessarily required a lot of personal discretion, which agents did not always exercise responsibly.

Agents possessed an enormous amount of power over Indians and employed that power to force Indians to adopt particular Euro-American practices. At Yakima, the agent commonly withheld rations from all except the aged and sick to force people to work for their support.[49] The agent also commonly disbursed annuity payments, in amounts too small to meet people's monthly expenses to create an incentive to work. Sometimes the agent promised money or goods to those who performed given tasks. While Indians built projects, often they never received the promised compensation. Captain Eneas noted in 1898:

> The Government promised to build houses and fence up the land. After the treaty was over the white man [turned] around and said we will not build your house unless you go to work and cut the logs down and our boys went to work. All those Indians that have got houses went to work, and rustled it themselves. All those head chiefs that wanted to see whether the Government would stick to their promise to build them a house have not got a house yet. These Indians around here are from those high chiefs' band. They are living in mat houses. They are waiting yet to see whether the Government will build them the houses or not.[50]

Others built irrigation works on the reservation in exchange for wages that the agent never paid out.[51]

The relationship between tribal, state, and federal law as it evolved over the period moved to marginalize Indian authority over all but purely internal tribal matters. Indians had authority to determine membership of the group,

---

[48] For a good discussion of the role of an Indian agent in practice, see Martha C. Knack and Omer C. Stewart, *As Long as the River Shall Run, An Ethnohistory of Pyramid Lake Indian Reservation* (Berkeley: University of California Press, 1984): 93-97.

[49] *CIA-AR*, 1875, 368; Report of Webster Stabler, Yakima Agent, in U.S. Department of the Interior, Census Office, *Report on Indians Taxed and not Taxed: 1890* (Washington, GPO, 1894): 607, 614, noting that of a total reservation population of 7,516 individuals, only 152 receive "any rations or aid from the government." Only the "old and infirm" received rations.

[50] Statement of Captain Encas, Yakima Council 1898.

[51] Chief Wyallup Wyacika to Poindexter, April 13, 76:8, MCPP; statement of Yallup, June 2, 1913 Council.

they also had jurisdiction over crimes committed by Indians within Indian territory. They had no jurisdiction over non-Indians who committed crimes on the reservation or against Indians off the reservation: states and the federal government divided this power.[52] Over time, states obtained an increasing amount of authority over off-reservation fishing and hunting, the rules governing inheritance of Indian trust property, and the administration of Indian water rights.

"The Blanket Must Give Way"

Federal efforts to impose Euro-American culture on Indian peoples went much deeper than merely fitting those peoples within Euro-American institutions; they included extensive programs of cultural literacy for both children and adults. Bureau education efforts undermined traditional Plateau methods of socialization and education, but ultimately left little in their place. Moreover, no amount of Indian education could combat the racism which colored the world in which the Bureau ostensibly sought to place its converts. Consequently, graduates of Bureau programs often returned to the reservation and to a culture within which they had grown no roots.

Additionally, Bureau policies were premised on the notion that Indians were racially inferior to Euro-Americans and genetically suited only for wage labor. Consequently, Bureau policies emphasized repetitive, uncreative work. Literacy was not necessarily a priority.[53]

In traditional Plateau society, children learned appropriate interpersonal relationships and relationships with nature through an oral tradition that conveyed knowledge about the world and human role within it through myth, ritual, and song.[54] Children learned by observing and imitating both nature and older group members.[55] The vision quest for a spirit partner was a significant part of Plateau socialization both into the human and natural-spirit worlds, and that process required an individual to draw upon knowledge acquired through the oral tradition and the example set by older community members. Yakama education necessarily was rooted in time and place. To acquire knowledge about the world and the human role within it, children required the collective knowledge of the group and opportunities to practice skills in the world.

---

[52] *United States v. McBratney*, 104 U.S. 621 (1882); *Donnelly v. United States*, 228 U.S. 243 (1913). See also Cohen, *Handbook of Federal Indian Law*, 264-66, 286-308, for a discussion of criminal jurisdiction in Indian Country.

[53] *CIA-AR*, 1904, 27-28, noting both blue collar and white collar jobs; Robert E. Bieder, *Science Encounters the Indian, 1820-1880: The Early Years of American Ethnology* (Norman: University of Oklahoma Press, 1986). Bieder discusses Euro-American views of Indians as culturally and mentally inferior to whites.

[54] Sue Whalen, "Nez Perces' Relationship to Their Land," *Indian Historian*, ser. 2, 4 (1971): 30-33; Helen H. Schuster, "Yakima Indian Traditionalism," 100-20.

[55] Yakima Indian Nation Cultural Center, 1989, Yakima, Wash.

Children were prime targets for federal efforts to impose Euro-American ways on Indians since they had not yet, or only partially, learned Indian ways.[56] Article 5 of the Yakamas' treaty provided:

> The United States further agree to establish at suitable points within said reservation, within one year after the ratification hereof, two schools, erecting the necessary buildings, keeping them in repair, and providing them with furniture, books, and stationery, one of which shall be an agricultural and industrial school, to be located at the agency, and to be free to the children of the said confederated tribes and bands of Indians, and to employ one superintendent of teaching and two teachers....[57]

In 1860, Rev. J. H. Wilbur, a methodist missionary, and newly appointed superintendent of the reservation school, set up the first school at Yakima. Wilbur was an efficient administrator, but he was a bigot, wholly intolerant of religious differences.[58]

He lost no time in setting up a school farm where he determined to teach the boys to grow crops:

> Provision was made to subsist the children of the school for eight months. I immediately gathered in the larger boys for school, and commenced my instruction in yoking the cattle, hitching them to the plow, and with my wild team and wild boys began making crooked furrows on the land chosen fora school farm. In starting out with unbroken team and uneducated drivers, I needed and had a boy or two for every ox in the team, and then it was difficult to keep them on an area of 80 acres. Patience and perseverance in the work soon tamed the cattle and instructed the boys in driving.[59]

The first year, according to his own account, Wilbur and the boys plowed 20 acres in fall and sowed wheat; they plowed 10 acres in the spring and planted corn, potatoes and "garden vegetables;" and they fenced 80 acres. At the end of that year they reaped 300 bushels of wheat, 500 of potatoes, 40 of corn, and enough vegetables to supply the school and provide seed for the school farm

---

[56] For discussions of federal Indian education programs, see Francis P. Prucha, *The Great Father: The U.S. Government and the American Indians*, 2 vols. (Lincoln: University of Nebraska Press, 1984): 2: 687-715, 814-40.

[57] Treaty with the Yakima, art. 5.

[58] Wilbur had come to the Methodist Oregon mission in 1846. For more information about Wilbur, see Grant L. Whitner, "Grant's Peace Policy on the Yakima Reservation, 1870-1882," *Pacific Northwest Quarterly* 50 (Oct. 1959): 137-42. See also Report of Samuel Ross, brevet colonel, U.S. Army, superintendent of Indian affairs for Washington Territory, *CIA-AR*, 1870, 21; Report of Lt. James M. Smith, U.S. Army, Yakima Agency, in *CIA-AR*, 1870, 31-33, noting Wilbur's intolerance of Catholicism and favoritism in his administration.

[59] *CIA-AR*, 1878, 139.

and those of the children's parents.[60]

Wilbur's school was more than a farm; it was a boarding school for twenty-nine boys and girls, and inside its rooms, children learned the ways of Euro-American children. It is significant that children boarded at the school: Away from their parents they could not learn ancestral ways.[61] In fact, Wilbur noted explicitly that in the first days of the school, "The children were taken from the camps of their parents in great destitution not having clothes enough to cover their nakedness." Wilbur's wife showed the girls how to "sew, spin, knit, to cut and make dresses, and clothing for the boys." One Mrs. Wright instructed the girls "in cooking, washing dishes, washing their clothes, and keeping their beds and rooms in order." Mr. Wright—"a Christian man, with great practical ability"—manned the schoolroom.[62]

All the children had assigned tasks that set them in place within Wilbur's school microcosm of the larger Euro-American society. And, according to Wilbur, the system worked like clockwork:

> The school-farm thus opened, and the children thus cared for at the boarding-house and school, operated like a mainspring to a watch to kindle a desire in the parents to have land and cultivate the soil. They asked for and received help in breaking new land, putting in seed, and instruction and assistance in fencing. The work thus begun in weakness has grown from year to year, until the Indians of the agency are well nigh self-supporting.[63]

After the first year, Wright and Wilbur instructed the boys in different mechanical arts, including wagon making, blacksmithing, harness-making, saddle making, carpentry, boot and shoe making, and painting.[64]

The Christian ideals that purportedly infused Wilbur's school administration soon found a wider forum as he accepted the position of Yakima Agent (1865–1869, 1871–1882). In 1870, under President Grant's "Peace Policy" toward Native Americans, the Bureau parceled out the administration of each reservation among the major U.S. religious denominations that were already carrying on missionary activities among Indians. The purpose of the peace policy was to provide a purportedly gentler approach to U.S.-Indian relations, as well as to stem the widespread corruption which characterized Bureau administration. Under the new policy, missionaries were appointed as Indian agents and supervised all aspects of agency life with attention to Christian

---

[60] *CIA-AR*, 1878, 139.

[61] The composition of the first school class was 30 students, aged 6 to 21; one fifteen-year old boy died the first year. The children came from at least 17 different families, with 20 boys and 10 girls, *CIA-AR*, 1865, 87.

[62] *CIA-AR*, 1878, 139.

[63] *CIA-AR*, 1878, 139-40

[64] *CIA-AR*, 1878, 140.

teachings.⁶⁵ The Yakima Agency, as well as fourteen others, were assigned to the Methodist Episcopalians.⁶⁶

If Wilbur's reports about the Yakama school-farm are accurate, Indians—and especially children—readily and rationally adapted Euro-American ways. A different picture emerges, however, from evidence outside Wilbur's reports.

An Indian child's first day of school was hardly a happy occasion; many children literally had been kidnapped from their families and sent to boarding schools far away from their homes. Although in 1894 the Bureau outlawed the withholding of rations to families to insure school attendance, agents found other ways of filling up schools. Yakama parents who refused to send their children to school were arrested by tribal police officers and punished by the agent by fine, imprisonment, or hard labor.⁶⁷ In 1885, Cotiakin, leader of one of the groups of "Wild Yakima," resorted to federal troops to protect him from Agent Milroy who himself had requested federal troops to force Cotiakin's son into the agency school. Cotiakin's victory, after a Bureau official declared that the Yakima Agent had no authority outside the reservation's boundaries, encouraged other Yakama parents to take their children outside the agent's jurisdiction as well.⁶⁸

Wilbur imposed a rigorous work routine on his charges, much different from Indian work patterns. Generally, the work at agency boarding schools was hard and many children died under the strenuous schedules combined with the psychological stress of being torn from their families.⁶⁹ Boys labored long hours in the fields or shops, while girls toiled inside, cooking washing, and sewing. Mrs. Merial Dorchester, a special agent for the Bureau, wrote "I have seen girls with wet feet, wet ankles, draggled skirts, working for hours in a room full of steam, and then we wonder why they sicken and die." Some agents also believed that to prepare children for the hard lives they would lead as adults they should not have fires in their dormitories, nor clothing enough to

---

⁶⁵ Whitner, "Grant's Indian Peace Policy," 135-36; Prucha, *Great Father*, 1: 501-33. Robert L. Utley, *The Indian Frontier of the American West 1846-1890*, Histories of the American Frontier Series (Albuquerque: University of New Mexico Press, 1984): 129-55. See also *CIA-AR*, 1870, 10-11; and Wilbur's report, in *CIA-AR*, 1873, 355.

⁶⁶ This sect was at that time the largest involved in the program. *CIA-AR*, 1873, 314; Whitner, "Grant's Indian Peace Policy," 135.

⁶⁷ *CIA-AR*, 1885, 200; *CIA-AR*, 1894, 6 (no withholding of rations); *CIA-AR*, 1901, 16 (agents have authority to compel school attendance).

⁶⁸ *CIA-AR*, 1885, 200-201.

⁶⁹ *CIA-AR*, 1891, 72, noting scarlet fever, measles, diphtheria, smallpox, sore eyes, and liver problems of children at OIA schools; *CIA-AR*, 1898, 307, report of Calvin Asbury, Yakima school superintendent, noting that several pupils died when they came to the boarding school; *CIA-AR*, 1804, 35-8, noting high incidence of tuberculosis at schools because of poor and unsanitary conditions. For a study of Navajo students, see W. T. Boyce and J. C. Boyce, "Acculturation and Changes in Health Among Navajo Boarding School Students," *Social Science and Medicine* 17 (1983): 219-26.

keep them warm.[70]

When not working, children were taught to shun Indian ways in favor of Euro-American ways. At times, that learning must have been purely imitative. Reverend R. H. Milroy (1882-1885), an admirer of Wilbur's and Wilbur's successor, reported in 1885 that although students in the school could read English, few understood what they were reading, and while they could write, their compositions were unintelligible.[71] Russell Jim, Yakama religious leader and tribal council member, recounted in 1978 that during the latter half of the nineteenth century, Yakamas who practiced their own religion were "incarcerated for days without food or water, or beaten and hanged. In mission schools ... talking in one's native tongue was actively discouraged through ridicule, punishment and even beatings. That philosophy carried over into the reservation's public schools during much of this century."[72] Behind the whitewashed facades of agency school buildings, teachers and other personnel carried on a systematic, brutal campaign to turn children against their culture.[73]

Wilbur had noted that children's education was effective where it trained youngsters and could "kindle a desire in the parents to have land and cultivate the soil." The Bureau had no intention of leaving adults' education to chance, however. Throughout the period, the Bureau employed farmers and field matrons to carry on that task. Farmers and matrons modeled appropriate behavior and taught skills necessary to instruct Indian men and women in their rightful place in Euro-American society. These Bureau employees also

---

[70] Report of Merial A. Dorchester, OIA "Special Agent, in *CIA-AR*, 1891, 544 [hereafter cited as Dorchester Report, 1891].

[71] *CIA-AR*, 1885; Dorchester Report 1891, 546, noting that children often were forced to master an education and a language, in that order. See also *CIA-AR*, 1887, xxii-xxiii, on English-only directives in boarding schools.

[72] Russell Jim, quoted in Mike Murphy, "Yakima Experience fits a Historical Pattern," newspaper interview, clipping, November 26, 1978, file—"Indians-Yakima-History," YVM. Jim recalled his own boarding school experience. He began at the school when he was five: "I spoke no English, just a few words.... I arrived at the school on a Saturday. On Sunday, they asked me 'what is your denomination?' Denomination? I thought. I didn't have any idea what that was and I couldn't answer. Finally one matron asked me, 'what church do we send you to?' Ah, I thought, church. I have heard that word and I know what it means. I said to them, church means Longhouse. 'Oh,' they said, 'one of those people from the Longhouse religion. Well we don't have longhouses here.' So they got a list of all the members of all the different denominations, looking for the churches that needed members. 'We are short of Lutherans,' they said. So they made me a Lutheran. For that whole year, I was a Lutheran."

[73] *CIA-AR*, 1902, 13-16 (discussion of "short hair" orders and recommending withholding rations and benefits to insure compliance). This order apparently was "bitterly denounced" by the press, ibid. See also Cohen, *Handbook of Federal Indian Law*, 142, n. 150. There have been several modern studies of federal Indian boarding schools and their impact on children. See Robert A. Trennert, "Educating Indian Girls at Non-Resident Boarding Schools, 1878-1920," in Roger L. Nichols, ed., *The American Indian: Past and Present*, 3d ed. (New York: Knopf, 1986): 218-31, and generally the literature cited in Boyce and Boyce, "Acculturation and Changes in Health."

modeled a gender-based division of labor that was different from that which had characterized pre-contact Yakama social organization.

Federal education policies focused on creating a new role for men as farmers. Article 5 of the Yakamas' treaty specified that the agency was to employ one superintendent of farming and two farmers.[74] The farmers' responsibilities included creating and maintaining model farms on the reservations which were intended to instruct Indians in farming methods; helping, people set up their own farms; and dispensing advice about farming. Farmers were supposed to travel around the reservation as a mobile source of advice.[75] With a monthly salary of $65 in the 1880s-90s, however, agents frequently reported that it was difficult to get good employees who would carry out their duties. Tecumseh Yakstowit told Indian Service Inspector E. B. Linnen in 1916 that neither the agency farmer nor field matron had ever come to his house. Others reported that Indian farmers sometimes were more knowledgeable and more willing to teach than those employed by the government.[76]

Reformers wanted more than to teach men farming skills, however. As part of their initiation into Christian and civilized life men could not remain polygamous, as the tribal court was already forcing reservation residents to acknowledge. Plateau peoples historically practiced polygamy. Cayuse men told Narcissa Whitman that they had many wives because then "they have plenty to eat, but where they have but one they have nothing."[77] Whitman took their statements as evidence that these men used their women as slaves, an interpretation that fit well within the nineteenth century stereotype of the "squaw drudge" who labored while her husband lay idle.[78] In the context of Pla-

---

[74] Treaty with the Yakima, art. 5. An additional support for such adult education came from the Act of March 3, 1819, 3 stat. LXXXV, by which Congress authorized an appropriation of $10,000 to assist Indians in becoming civilized.

[75] John D. C. Atkins, CIA, to Priestly, Sept. 24, 1887, file—"1881-99, Ahtanum Letters," Letters Received regarding irrigation matters, 1903-08, YA, RG 75, BIA, NA-Seattle, noting that the agency farmer should be traveling around the reservation assisting individual Indians, not spending all his time on the agency farm which the school superintendent was supervising. See also Hurt, *Indian Agriculture in America*, 155, 157.

[76] See, for example, statement of Tecumseh Yakstowit, in Indian Council Proceedings, Yakima Agency, Ft. Simcoe, WA, Nov. 11, 1916, file—"Councils and Meetings (tribal) 1913-25," Tribal Records, 1897-1952, YA, RG 75, BIA, NA-Seattle.

[77] Clifford M. Drury, *Elkanah and Mary Walker, Pioneers Among the Spokanes* (Caldwell, ID The Caxton Printers, Ltd. 1940): 128-29 (noting practice of polygamy); Narcissa Whitman to Parents, brothers, and sisters, March 30, 1837, May 3 entry, reprinted in Archer Butler Hulbert and Dorothy Printup Hulbert, *Marcus Whitman, Crusader: 1802-1839*, 3 vols. (Colorado Springs and Denver, CO: The Stewart Commission of Colorado College and the Denver Public Library, 1936): 1: 274-75.

[78] Joan Jacobs Brumberg, "Zenanas and Girlless Villages: The Ethnology of American Evangelical Women, 1870-1900," *Journal of American History* 69 (1982): 347-71; David D. Smits, "The 'Squaw Drudge': A Prime Index of Savagism," *Ethnohistory* 29 (Fall 1982): 281-306.

Yakama schoolgirls at Fort Simcoe, Washington, ca. 1910-1916

Northwest Museum of Arts & Culture/Eastern Washington State Historical Society, Spokane Washington, American Indians of the Pacific Northwest Images Digital Collection, Negative # L97-29.98, used by permission teau subsistence patterns, however, many wives meant many family connections which ensured access to alternative subsistence sites in times of local scarcity. Missionaries and federal officials did not understand that aspect of Plateau life, and in any case were not inclined to respect it.[79] Enough workers in the Washington Indian superintendency exploited the Plateau practice of polygamy to lead to a Bureau circular against concubinage and prostitution in 1861: "The practice of open prostitution and concubinage between the whites and Indians while degrading and demoralizing to both classes, is calculated to destroy that respect which is due from the Indians to their official protectors, to retard materially the gradual elevation of character among the natives, to diminish sensibly the efficiency of our means of ameliorating the condition of these pupils of our general, government...."[80]

In Yakama society, as in many other Native American groups, women traditionally kept gardens as part of their subsistence tasks. Such work might have included maintaining a small riparian garden, but it extended to women's work of burning forest lands to promote huckleberry and other crops. Women owned herds of horses, cattle, and sheep as well, Both men and women sought spirit partners through vision quests and there were no rigidly defined boundaries between men and women's work.[81] Yakama women held property in land in their own names following allotment.[82]

In the Euro-American world view, however, a society whose men hunted and fished while its women raised crops and babies appeared to be a society that enslaved women.[83] Further, given federal efforts to force men to take up farming, reformers soon took up the task of teaching women their own separate "sphere." Here, Indian women would learn to be tenders of the hearth and home while men worked in the larger outside world.

Congress first appropriated moneys to fund a field service aimed at Indian women in 1891. In her 1891 report, Mrs. Dorchester noted:

---

[79] *CIA-AR*, 1888, 233.

[80] Circular against concubinage, reprinted in *CIA-AR*, 1861, 177.

[81] See Chapter 2. On the role of Indian women in pre-contact agriculture, see Hurt, *Indian Agriculture in America*, 11-12ff; Gilbert L. Wilson, ed. *Buffalo Bird Woman's Garden* (St. Paul, Minnesota Historical Society Press, 1987). On the role of Indian women in pre-contact societies, see Joan M. Jensen, *With These Hands* (Old Westbury NY: The Feminist Press, 1981), 5, 31-32; Anna Moore Shaw, *A Pima Past* (Tucson: University of Arizona Press, 1974), 70-74, 109; George B. Grinnell, "The Wild Indian," *Atlantic Monthly* 83 (January 1899): 25-26; Barbara Welter, *Dimity Convictions* (Athens: Ohio University Press, 1976), 32; Irene Stewart, *A Voice in Her Tribe* (Socorro, NY: Ballena Press, 1980); Yvonne Ashley, "'That's the Way We Were Raised,' An Oral Interview with Ada Damon," *Frontiers* 2 (Summer 1977): 59.

[82] Report on the Conditions of Yakima Washington, 1912, file 120334-12-YA-341, Correspondence file 1970-39, CCF, BIA, RG 75, NA, 25.

[83] Smits, "The 'Squaw Drudge'"; Valerie Sherer Mathes, "A New Look at the Role of Women in Indian Society," *American Indian Quarterly* 2 (1975): 131-39.

> It is very clear to those most closely studying the 'Indian problem' that the elevation of the women is, to a greater degree than many realize, the key to the situation. That the men are from 15 to 25 years in advance of the women is a no more freely admitted fact than that the children start from the plane of the mother rather than from that of the father. Therefore the great work of the present is to reach and lift the women and the home.[84]

Pressure from non-Indian women whose missionary activities brought them in contact with Indian women, and from such groups active in missionary work as the Religious Society of Friends, led the Bureau to broaden its scope of attack on Indian culture to include women directly.[85] According to Thomas J. Morgan, Commissioner (1889-1893), "The position of field matron has been created in order that Indian women may be influenced in their home life and duties, and may have done for them in their sphere what farmers and mechanics are supposed to do for Indian men in their sphere."[86]

In 1891, with a $2,500 appropriation, the Bureau hired three field matrons who would work for $60 per month. In 1892, the appropriation increased to $5000, and paid for a staff of seven matrons.[87] The Bureau solicited recommendations for matrons from religious societies, and sent the first matrons to reservations where Indians were about to receive allotments, since officials believed that those peoples' needs for civilizing influences was most pressing. Since the Yakama were allotted in 1892, they were among the first to receive a matron.[88]

Commissioner Morgan outlined the ten tasks of a field matron in his 1892 report:

---

[84] Dorchester Report 1891, 542.

[85] For an account of the establishment of a field matron corps, see Lisa Elizabeth Emmerich, "'To respect and love and seek the ways of white women': Field Matrons, the Office of Indian Affairs, and Civilization Policy, 1890-1938" (Ph.D. diss., University of Maryland College Park, 1987): 15-41.

[86] *CIA-AR*, 1892, 101.

[87] *CIA-AR*, 1893, 54-57; Dorchester Report, 1891, 542. The small appropriation left no money for supplies such as fabric, soap, articles used for decorating houses, food and medicines; and tools such as sewing supplies, sewing machines, and washing machines. All those supplies were donated or purchased from moneys contributed by private charities, by friends, or from a matron's own funds. See Report of Dr. Emily C. Miller, in *CIA-AR*, 1892, 510; and Emmerich, "To Respect and Love," 161-63.

[88] *CIA-AR*, 1893, 56, noting that matrons had been sent to the Yakamas, Cheyennes, Arapahoes, Mission Indians, Poncas (Nebraska), Mexican Kickapoos, Sioux, Navajos, and Moquis. See also *CIA-AR*, 1896, 1084; *CIA-AR*, 1897, 24; Emmerich, "To Respect and Love," 59-71, 91-92. In 1891, the position of field matron—as well as all other major Indian agency personnel—came under Civil Service classification. Henceforth, those positions were filled via the Civil Service examination process. *Eighth Annual Report of the United States Civil Service Commission, July 1, 1890-June 30, 1891* (Washington, D.C.: Government Printing Office, 1891): 72; Emmerich, "To Respect and Love," 90-91.

1. Care of a house, keeping it clean and in order, ventilated, properly warmed (not overheated), and suitably furnished.

2. Cleanliness and hygienic conditions generally, including disposition of all refuse.

3. Preparation and serving of food and regularity of meals.

4. Sewing including cutting, making, and mending garments.

5. Laundry work.

6. Adorning the home, both inside and out, with pictures, curtains, home-made rugs, flowers, grass plots and trees, construction and repair of walks, fences, and drains....

7. Keeping and care of domestic animals, such as cows, poultry, and swine; care and use of milk, making of butter, cheese, and curds and keeping of bees.

8. Care of the sick.

9. Care of little children, and introducing among them the games and sports of white children.

10. Proper observance of the Sabbath; organization of societies for promoting literary, religious, moral, and social improvements, such as 'Lend a Hand' clubs, circles of 'King's Daughters,' or 'Sons,' Y.M.C.A, Christian Endeavor, and temperance societies, etc.[89]

Not only did Morgan's list outline the teaching responsibilities of field matrons, it was a blueprint for the proper role of all women within the larger society as tenders of the domestic sphere of daily life.[90] Morgan suggested that matrons use their influence "to give to the male members of the family kindly admonitions as to the 'chores' and heavier kinds of work about the house which in civilized communities is generally done by men."[91]

Just as children educated in boarding schools would spur their parents to take up Euro-American ways, women educated by the field matrons would prod and lure their husbands to become more like white men. If women learned to can fruit, and served this "healthful and tempting" dish to their

---

[89] CIA-AR, 1892, 101. Morgan made the list virtually inclusive of all domestic tasks in his comment "Of course, it is impracticable to enumerate all the directions in which a field matron can lend her aid in ameliorating the condition of Indian women. Her own tact, skill, and interest will suggest manifold ways of instructing them in civilized home life, stimulating their intelligence, rousing ambition, and cultivating refinement."

[90] Emmerich briefly discusses the influence, of the ideal of a "sphere of womanhood" on officials at the Bureau of Indian Affairs, "To Respect and Love," 45-54. On the sphere of womanhood, see Nancy F. Cott, *The Bonds of Womanhood: "Woman's Sphere" in New England, 1780-1835* (New Haven: Yale University Press, 1977); Mary P. Ryan, *Womanhood in America*, 3d ed. (New York: Franklin Watts, Inc., 1983); Barbara Welter, "The Cult of True Womanhood 1820-1860," *American Quarterly* 18 (1966): 151-74.

[91] CIA-AR, 1892, 101.

families, their husbands and sons would learn to grow fruit.[92] If women learned to use sewing and washing machines, their husbands might work harder so as to purchase those items.[93]

If Mrs. Dorchester believed Indian women were 15 to 25 years behind Indian men in their education into white ways, she—and other non-Indians—saw the potential of Indian women within Euro-American society as at least 25 years behind the potential of white women. By the 1890s white women had begun to take up work beyond the immediate domestic sphere of home and hearth, around which their lives had centered since at least the American Revolution. Women were active in missionary and charity work, increasingly obtained higher education, and worked for wages at a variety of different jobs.[94] Mrs. Dorchester observed, "Two years ago I was ready to say, 'Open every door of pleasure and profit to the girls in the schools as freely as you do the boys. Teach the girls telegraphy, shorthand, typewriting, bookkeeping, and fit them to go into offices, stores, shops, etc....' Now I can only say, teach them every industry which may be prosecuted at their homes, but do not shove them out of the home nest, poor and unsheltered as it may be. Only a few—mostly mixed bloods of the better type, or girls who have had especially good training ... are fitted to meet the outside life."[95] To Euro-Americans Indians were an inferior race, and women were the inferior sex; Indian women were doubly handicapped.

Romanticizing a narrowly defined sphere of womanhood was far from dead at the Bureau, which ironically employed a new generation of Progressive era women to promote the old Victorian image.[96] The Commissioner and Indian agents, and to a lesser extent the field matrons themselves, occasionally soliloquized about their work. One agent observed, "The benefits of her [matron's] work are evident in many ways. Some of the most desperate characters of the tribe who have come under her influence have developed into steady, hard-working men."

Daniel M. Browning, Commissioner (1893–1897), saw the matrons' work no less grandly: "[S]ewing schools, weekly clubs, and simple Sabbath services

---

[92] Dorchester Report 1891, 544.

[93] Dorchester Report 1891, 544; for references to sewing and washing machines, see Statement of Tecumseh Yakstowit, "Indian Council Proceedings, Yakima Agency, Ft. Simcoe, WA, Nov. 11, 1916, file—"Councils and Meetings (tribal) 1913-25," Tribal Records, 1897-1952, Yakima Agency, RG 75, BIA, NA-Seattle; Schuster, "Yakima Traditionalism," 243.

[94] Brumberg, "Zenanas and Girlless Villages"; Jill Conway, "Women Reformers and American Culture, 1870-1930," *Journal of Social History* 5 (1971-1972): 164-77; Keith Melder, "Ladies Bountiful: Organized Women's Benevolence in Early 19th Century America," *New York History* 48 (July 1967): 231-55; Julie A Matthaei, *An Economic History of Women in America* (New York: Schocken Books, 1982).

[95] Dorchester Report 1891, 542-43.

[96] Emmerich, "To Respect and Love," 39-41, 46-50; Jensen, "Zenanas and Girlless Villages," 358.

have brought to the young men and women self respect, something hopeful and widening in their narrow lives of poverty, dirt, and degradation, until they have dared to be 'progressive.'" The field matron would shape the very character of her clients, he believed: "Everywhere this field matron work modifies outward forms and touches the mainsprings of life and character, and slowly develops a finer womanhood, childhood, and manhood."[97] Such progress sprang from the matrons' own mature "finer womanhood" and her spirit of "self-denying, self-forgetting devotion to the interests of those among whom she labors."[98]

The reality of a field matron's work was, somewhat removed from the job's ideal. The Yakima Agency had employed a matron type position at least from the time that Wilbur first opened his boarding school in 1864. Those early matrons were financed by missionary groups, and they worked to teach cooking, cleaning, and clothes washing to girls at the school.[99] Dr. Emily C. Miller was the first federally appointed field matron at the Yakima Agency and worked at that position in 1891–1892. Miller received her degree from the New England Medical College for Women, and she practiced with her husband until his death. Unable to support herself by herself in private practice, she took a position as a dining hall matron at the Carlisle Indian School, in Pennsylvania. She did missionary work among the Yakama in 1890, and accepted the field matron position in 1891.[100]

When Miller first began her work, Indian women were so shy and afraid that to approach them she needed to chase after them into fields where they hid from her.[101] Gradually the women overcame their shyness, perhaps because of Miller's persistence and her willingness to learn the Sahaptin language. Women came to her for a variety of reasons, only one of which was learning white women's ways. Some came for food or other needed materials; some came simply because they were curious to see a white "Boston" woman and her house. While Miller made many visits to their houses, she found Indian women often were not interested in learning what she had to offer. "I went five times to teach one woman to make biscuit before she was ready to learn, though I had given her flour and baking powder."[102]

---

[97] *CIA-AR*, 1894, 18-19.

[98] *CIA-AR*, 1897, 24.

[99] Dorchester Report, 1891, 542, noting that two women working as matrons were doing so independent of any organization's support. See also W. B. Gosnell, Indian Agent, Washington Territory, in *CIA-AR*, 1861, 185, noting that Yakama girls assisted the matron "in the discharge of those labors so evidently the field for female industry."

[100] Emmerich includes brief background material on Miller in "To Respect and Love," 100-101, 100 n.16; Miller's Report, *CIA-AR*, 1891, 511.

[101] Miller's Report *CIA-AR*, 1891, 510; Relander, *Treaty Centennial*, 33.

[102] Miller's Report, *CIA-AR*, 1891, 510.

In her first year she visited 115 families, 97 of which lived in houses. The largest obstacles she saw to the Indians' adoption of white ways was general poverty and the unsuitability of reservation lands to sustain farms without artificial irrigation (which Indians could not afford). Women could not feed their families regular meals if they had no food; similarly they could not adorn their houses if they were so poor that they had not money for even a change of clothing.[103]

The same problems as plagued the position of agency farmer plagued that of the field matrons. Low wages, understaffing (Miller complained that the one field matron at Yakima had to cover 1,250 square miles of territory within which families had settled solely according to the availability of water), and incompetence were persistent problems. Tecumseh Yakstowit, one the first pupils of Wilbur's boarding school, complained in 1916 that

> Field Matron is riding around but never go into a house and show a woman how to cook and how to sew and how to use a sewing machine. Field Matron come to an Indian woman's home, sewing machine was out of fix; she asked the Field Matron whether she could fix it for her. Field Matron fooled around there a good while but could not do nothing. Field Matron did not know nothing. Same way with additional farmers.

A Bureau inspector agreed: "Many of the homes are dirty and unsanitary and need the services of a good matron very badly. And I have visited a good many Indian homes and there is nobody at home; nobody to take care of the chickens; the horses or nothing."[104] Neither the field matron service nor the agency farmer system provided a successful method for transforming Indian ways of life.[105]

It is doubtful whether the sphere for which federal officials sought to prepare women, and to a lesser extent men, was an attainable goal for Indians within the larger Euro-American culture. A 1910 U.S. census report of Indians over ten years of age employed in "gainful occupations" indicated that of 1,028 Yakama, 185 were so employed, or slightly under 18 percent.[106] "Gainful employment" included farming and wage labor, but did not include a variety of other jobs that traditionally were important in Plateau society, including

---

[103] Miller Report, *CIA-AR*, 1891, 510-511.

[104] Statement of Tecumseh Yakstowit, "Indian Council Proceedings, Yakima Agency, Ft. Simcoe, WA, Nov. 11, 1916," file—"Councils and Meetings Tribal 1913-25," Tribal Records, 1897-1952; YA, RG 75, BIA, NA-Seattle; statement of E. B. Linnen, Chief Inspector, in ibid.

[105] Emmerich, "To Respect and Love," 317-18, concludes that the field matron service did not change the lives of the women it targeted, and was a "near-total failure."

[106] The total Yakama population figure included 463 men and 565 women, with 162 men and 23 women employed. U.S. Bureau of the Census, *Indian Population in the United States and Alaska, 1910* (Washington, GPO, 1915): Table 103, "Number and Proportion of Indians of Each Sex 10 Years of Age and Over Engaged in Gainful Occupations, for Principal Stocks and Tribes," and 252.

hunter, fisher, and medicine man/healer.[107] Many contemporary observers noted that Indian children who finished their educations at Bureau schools returned to the reservations because there was no place for them in white society. The tasks included in the field matron position anticipated that result because matrons were to serve as reminders of white culture once children left school—a condition that acknowledged that those grown-up children would not be working and living away from the reservation.[108]

Conclusion

As Euro-Americans took control of more and more of the continent, most Native American groups within the boundaries of non-Indian control found themselves with a shrinking subsistence resource base, little cash income or wealth, and inadequate experience in a capitalist economy. Many people could not sustain themselves and were reduced to begging for money or food from whites. As Walker, a Yakama, noted in 1904: "[S]ometimes I go now [to the Winans Brothers commercial fishery] merely to beg for my people a few dried salmon."[109] Others viewed with bitterness the Bureau policies that systematically narrowed the scope of their 1855 treaty. One Yakama told Agent Thomas Priestly in 1897 that he was "getting to be the same as a white man and would soon be just like one;" that he had "learned to steal a little and lie a good deal.[110]

By 1910, or the end of the first half-century or more of federal control of Indian on-reservation life, the Yakima had not become an agricultural, or even predominantly market-oriented, people. Although all but the most isolated "Wild Yakima" participated to some extent in the cash economy, the majority of tribal members retained continuing ties to a traditional Plateau subsistence lifestyle in their preferences for food, clothing, religious participation, and language. Although almost all Yakama held allotments in trust, most were not themselves farmers: Many Yakama rented their allotments and used the cash to buy coffee, flour, and similar staples that supplemented subsistence foods.

---

[107] See U.S. Census Bureau, Indian Division, Tenth Census of the United States, Ennumerator's sheets, Yakima Agency, 1880, folder—"Relander as a collector, personal papers—U.S. Bureau of Indian Affairs, Yakima Indian Agency, Census (Yakima Indians)," 114:13-14, CRP, a number of respondents listed their occupations as hunter, fisher, farmer, medicine man, laborer. Unfortunately, the ennumerator's sheets do not include any detailed information about women.

[108] *CIA-AR*, 1893, 56; Emmerich, "To Respect and Love," 29-30. See also Wilbert Ahern, "'The Returned Indians'" Hampton Institute and its Indian Alumni," *Journal of Ethnic Studies* 10 (Winter 1983): 101-24.

[109] Testimony of Walker, *U.S. v. Winans*, transcript of record; E. L. Stevens, Acting CIA, to Secretary of Interior, May 16, 1885 [noting that if Indians cannot fish they will have to be supplied with government rations or starve], File 4799, *U.S. v. Winans*, Attorney General, Letters Received 1882-1886, Department of Justice, Record Group 60, NA.

[110] *CIA-AR*, 1897, 221.

In this mixed cash-subsistence reservation economy, both agriculture and traditional subsistence resources remained important. Thus, Yakama worked hard to secure a viable on-reservation irrigation system to supply their arid lands, while at the same time fighting to retain access to important resources such as fish, game, roots and berries, and grazing lands.

II

**EARTH'S HEART:
WATER**

6

SACRED WATER

> If I have known in a history that a white man brought that water to this great America when he landed I would not care to say a word I would keep quiet but it seems to me all is in a Prejudice against my Race and I beg your honor to assist me and to hold the bill back all of my tribes are considering this shameful Grafting Bill and as I say in behalf of my Tribes that my people will never consent to Jones Bill at no time on God's earth...."
> —Louis Mann (1912)[1]

The Yakima Basin was a complex system of interlinked yet discrete habitat regions that ranged from rich alluvial river bottoms to the varied ecology of canyons, ridges, volcanos, and glacial valleys.[2] The climate varied from arid lands in the extreme eastern portion of the reservation to a moist climate in the west where the Cascades began. Annual rainfall in the east, near the town of North Yakima was at a basin low of about 8 inches, while farther west, near Cle Elum it was more than tripled that figure. At the crest of the Cascades, rainfall averaged more than 100 inches annually.[3] Most agriculture, however, took place at or below the elevation of the foothills, where rainfall was insufficient to support crops, and which led non-Indian farmers to view every stream as a potential reclamation site.[4]

---

[1] Mann to Poindexter, Jan. 24, 1912, box 76, folder 13, Accession no. 3828, Miles C. Poindexter Papers, University of Washington Libraries Manuscript Collection, Seattle, Wash. [hereafter cited as box:file, MCPP].

[2] Morris Uebelacker defines habitat region as "a sub-unit of a larger human habitat which is distinguished from other sub-units by its biotic and physical characteristics. These are areas which Indian people recognize as broadly similar in physical form and/or biota and which are recognizable in the field, on topographic maps, and by people who live in the eastern Cascades." Uebelacker, "Geographic Explorations in the Southern Cascades of Eastern Washington: Changing Land, People, and Resources" (Ph.D. diss., University of Oregon, 1986): 9-10. For a discussion of Yakama Reservation ecology and geography, see ibid., 12-80. See also John Arthur Bower, "The Hydrogeography of Yakima Indian Nation Resource Use" (Ph.D. diss., University of Washington, Seattle, 1989): 6-9; George Otis Smith, *Geology and Water Resources of a Portion of Yakima County, Wash.*, Water Supply and Irrigation Papers of the U.S. Geological Survey, no. 55 (Washington, D.C.: U.S. Geological Survey, 1901): 12-26.

[3] Uebelacker, "Geographic Explorations," 5; Smith, *Geology and Water Resources*, 13.

[4] Most agriculture in Washington took place east of the Cascade mountains. John Fahey, *The Inland Empire: Unfolding Years, 1879-1929* (Seattle: University of Washington Press, 1986): 87-109; Donald W. Meinig, *The Great Columbia Plain: A Historical Geography, 1805-1910* (Seattle: University of Washington Press, 1968): 321-64.

The Yakama Reservation itself sloped toward the southeast—from 12,307 feet at the Cascade crest to 650 feet above mean sea level—and this created a drainage pattern in which water applied to the deep, brown soils of the area north of Toppenish Creek would run off toward the south.[5] Reservation soil conditions were "very generally underlaid by a deep stratum of free water bearing gravel which is covered generally by from one to ten or twelve feet ... [of] volcanic ash soil."[6] Increased runoff from irrigated land at Toppenish Creek and above became trapped in the deeper soils, where the hard clay pan underlying the area forced runoff to the south, and created chronic problems with swamping, flooding, and salinization on the reservation as early as 1901.[7]

Yakama believed that water imparted life to their lands; riparian gardens flourished in flood-irrigated patches where swollen streams spilled winter snowmelts every spring and soda springs held restorative powers for ailing health. Such irrigation required little manipulation of water. Yakama had sufficient water in the pre-contact world.

To traditional Yakama, water was to be conserved: Loss of water meant loss of life.[8] In tribal long house ceremonies to the present, water plays a very important role: each place setting at special meals has a cup of water. This water, designated by the Sahaptin word cús, is sipped before beginning the meal and again once the meal is finished, indicating its significance as a sacrament in Yakama life. "We drink water first, before we eat, because it was the first thing in our country, and rain brings everything out," one Yakama noted. Another observed, "water is the element which supplies all life, all plant

---

[5] Uebelacker, "Geographic Explorations," 5, noting that "[t]his steep elevation change and resulting climatic gradient explains, in part, why larger animals and people in the eastern Cascades follow a seasonal east-west migration route." See also J. W. Martin to W. H. Code, June [?], 1910, quoted in "Report on the Conditions of Yakima, Washington," p. 15, file 120334-12-341, Yakima Agency, Correspondence File 1907-39, Central Classified Files, Records of the Bureau of Indian Affairs, Record Group 75, National Archives and Record Service, Washington, D.C. [Hereafter cited as file, YA, CF, CCF, BIA, RG 75, NA-branch.]

[6] J. W. Martin to W. H. Code, June, 1910, quoted in "Report on the Conditions of Yakima, Washington," p. 15, file 120334-12-341, YA, CF CCF, BIA, RG 75, NA.

[7] Smith reported leaching in the reservation area in his 1901 report, Smith, *Geology and Water Resources*, 13-14; O. L. Waller, "A Report on Irrigation Conditions in the Yakima Valley, Washington," Washington State Agricultural College and School of Science, Experiment Station, Pullman, WA, *Bulletin 61* (Pullman: Allen Bros., 1904): 8-9, 17-19, reporting that "thousands of acres, in the Yakima valley are being seriously damaged by the use of great quantities of water on higher lands."

[8] Helen Hersh Schuster, "Yakima Indian Traditionalism: A Study in Continuity and Change" (Ph.D. diss., University of Washington, 1975): 414. On Native American attitudes toward water, see Charles Bowden, *Killing the Hidden Waters: The Slow Destruction of Water Resources in the American Southwest* (Austin: University of Texas Press, 1977); Ruth M. Underhill, et al., *Rainhouse and Ocean: Speeches for the Papago Year*, American Tribal Religions Series, ed. Karl W. Luckert, vol. 4 (Flagstaff, AZ: Museum of Northern Arizona Press, 1979): 17-70, 141-46; Donald J. Worster, *Rivers of Empire: Water Aridity and the Growth of the American West* (New York: Pantheon Books, 1985): 32-35.

and animal life."[9] Thus in a modern day, basin-wide adjudication of Yakima River water, Yakama have discussed including a claim to water based on its present, sacred significance to the tribe.[10]

While Yakama found in the landscape around them confirmation of their belief that water sustained life, Euro-Americans saw the same sagebrush speckled hills of the Yakima Valley as proof of nature's barrenness. Here, human intellect and technology would channel water from existing sources across the arid lands to make the desert "blossom like a rose."[11] Water was scarce in a world which valued only the potential of land to produce commodities. Irrigators constantly demanded more water to irrigate more lands, and this water came at the expense of other irrigators—especially of Indian irrigators.

To proponents of artificial irrigation in the basin, the land consisted of only two types: irrigable and non-irrigable. Irrigable lands were further broken down into valley lands and the "bench" lands that comprised the area lying along foothills and basin slopes.[12] Farmers spoke of the "duty" of water to irrigate land, and measured its presence in miner's inches, acre feet, and cubic feet per second. They measured one another by the relative amounts of water each diverted to his or her lands: the more water, the more land to irrigate and the more crops to produce for sale—so the logic went.[13]

The legal expression of that view of water was the doctrine of beneficial use, by which a landholder could divert as much water from a source onto his or her lands as could be used to raise crops, generate electricity, and the like.[14] Western states such as Washington recognized the state's role in regulating water use. Hence a clause in Washington's constitution of 1889 declared: "the use of the waters of this state for irrigation, mining and manufacturing purposes shall be deemed a public use."[15] The states—and not the federal government—were responsible for the creation and management of individual rights in water.

---

[9] Schuster, "Yakima Indian Traditionalism," 413-414.

[10] Dr. John Bower, personal communication, October 4, 1990; *Department of Ecology v. Acquavella*, 100 Wash. 2d 651 (1983), and subsequent litigation.

[11] *Benton v. Johncox*, 17 Wash. 277, 283 (1897).

[12] C. R. Olberg, "Investigation of Complaints of Board of Directors of Yakima Reservation Irrigation District in Regard to Wapato Project," 1929, file 42962-21-341 pt. 3A (marked 51656-20-341), YA, CF, CCF, BIA, RG 75, NA.

[13] See Waller, "Report on Irrigation Conditions in the Yakima Valley," 19-20. See also Worster, *Rivers of Empire*, 98-99.

[14] On the legal development of the appropriative water rights system, see Joseph L. Sax and Robert H. Abrams, *Legal Control of Water Resources: Cases and Materials*, American Casebook Series (St. Paul, MN: West Publishing Co., 1986): 278-413; Robert Dunbar, *Forging New Rights in Western Waters* (Lincoln: University of Nebraska Press, 1983) 60-62, 209-10; Worster, *Rivers of Empire*, 88-96, 104-11.

[15] Wash. Const. art. 21, § 1 (1889).

During the nineteenth century, the Euro-American bundle of property was transformed. Doctrines that previously had protected the quiet enjoyment of property came to promote productive—or "dynamic"—uses.[16] Federal and state policies began to vest individuals with rights in dynamic uses of property, including water, subject to an overarching concept of public good.[17] Indian irrigators who competed with non-Indians in the new game of "beneficial use" could only lose because they did not have the funds, expertise, or desire to develop water on the scale of Euro-Americans. At bottom, Indians were not included in the community in whose interest regulations to promote the "public good" ultimately operated.

Subsistence and Water

To the Yakama without water there could be no life. Water was a core element of their existence and carried primordial and sacred significance. "Water is life. Tahoma, the Big White Mountain! the source of water," Lucillus McWhorter quoted of Yakama Chief Sluskin in 1920.[18] Yakama creation stories illustrate the connection between water, people, and life. In an early story, Coyote fought a powerful beaver god, Washpoosh, who lived in Lake Cle Elum in a time before humans existed. Washpoosh terrorized the animal-people who lived nearby, killing and eating everyone who came his way. Coyote found the animal-people and decided to save them by killing Washpoosh. Their ensuing battle to the death of Washpoosh created the hydrological and geological features of the Yakima and Columbia river basins as we now know them. From the dead beaver god, Coyote cut pieces that he threw into the land and created the tribes that came to inhabit the area.[19] The birth of the Yakama, as well as

---

[16] James Willard Hurst, *Law and the Conditions of Freedom in the Nineteenth-Century United States* (Madison: University of Wisconsin Press, 1956): 3-32; Morton J. Horwitz, The *Transformation of American Law, 1780-1860*, Studies in Legal History (Cambridge, MA: Harvard University Press, 1977): 109-39.

[17] Harry N. Scheiber, "Property Law, Expropriation, and Resource Allocation by Government, 1789-1910," *Journal of Economic History* 33 (1973): 232-251; Harry N. Scheiber and Charles W. McCurdy, "Eminent Domain Law and Western Agriculture, 1849-1900," *Agricultural History* 49 (1975): 112-30; Charles W. McCurdy, "Stephen J. Field and Public Land Law Development in California, 1850-1866: Case Study of Judicial Resource Allocation in Nineteenth Century America," *Law and Society Review* 10 (1976): 235-66.

[18] Lucillus Virgil McWhorter (He-mene Ka-wan), *The Discards* (n.p. 1920): 21.

[19] Yohyowan, "Legend of the Origin of the Yakimas," typed manuscript, n.d., file "Indians-Yakima-History," Yakima Valley Museum, Yakima, WA, [hereafter YVM]. One "YowYowan" testified for the Yakama plaintiffs in *United States v. Winans*, which would place this particular narrative record at around 1900 if these names refer to the same person. See *United States v. Winans*, Transcript of Record [hereafter cited as *U.S. v. Winans*, transcript of record], enclosed in Attorney General to Clerk of the Supreme Court, Jan. 21, 1904, *Winans* Appellate Case File no. 19213, records of the Supreme Court, Record Group 267, NA, P. 117. Many Yakama witnesses testified in Sahaptin; I have indicated their use of an interpreter wherever possible.

the other Columbia River tribes, could not be separated from the creation of rivers through their lands and the power which released water into them.[20]

In a second creation myth—this one reportedly told by Chief Coteakun, son of Chief Kamiakin and a follower of the prophet Smohalla, to a U.S Army officer in 1884-85—strands of the biblical Genesis story have been interwoven into an older Plateau story. "In the beginning of the world, all was water. Whee-me-me-ow-ah, the Great Chief Above, lived in the sky, above the water, all alone. When he decided to make the world he went down to the shallow places and began to throw up great handfuls of mud. Thus he made the land."[21] The Great Chief created mountains, trees, roots, and berries. He also created a man, then a woman, instructing them how to hunt, fish, gather roots and berries, dress animal skins, weave baskets in beautiful designs, and cook food. Yet the people quarreled and were not happy. Consequently, following the Smohalla prophecy, the story predicts that the Great Chief will return one day to restore peace.[22] Here, again—although this story post-dates the arrival of non-Indians—water preceded all earthly life and sustained it in ensuing years.

The arrival of missionaries in the region did not lessen the spiritual significance of water to Yakama lives. Cayuse Chief Sam-ass-pello told members of Stevens' treaty commission that "They [missionaries] told me in taking water to drink I should think of God. This I have not learned of myself, it is what they have taught me and I keep it."[23] The practice of using water as a sacrament in ritual reinforced prevailing beliefs in the importance of water and remained a part of Yakama long house ritual to the present.[24] In the semi-arid Plateau landscape, people valued highly all existing water sources.

The origins of Yakama agriculture remain unclear. Agricultural practices may have predated the presence of missionaries who staffed the Catholic mission on the Ahtanum, or they may have been learned from such missionaries, from other missionaries, or from Hudson's Bay trappers.[25] Floodwaters of

---

[20] See "Coyote at the Mouth of the Columbia River," "Coyote Frees the Fish," and "Coyote and the Mouthless Man," three Wishram stories of the genesis of their people and their dependence upon fish for food, in Jarold Ramsey, ed., *Coyote Was Going There: Indian Literature of the Oregon Country* (Seattle: University of Washington Press, 1977), 47-51.

[21] Coteakun, "Creation of the Yakima World," in Ella E. Clark, *Indian Legends of the Pacific Northwest* (Berkeley: University of California Press, 1953), 142-43; William E. Coffer (Koi-Hosh), *Spirits of the Sacred Mountains: Creation Stories of the American Indian* (New York: Van Nostrand Reinhold Co., 1978), 74-75.

[22] On the Smohalla cult and its influence among the Yakamas, see Chapters 3 and 4.

[23] Isaac Ingalls Stevens, *A True Copy of the Record of the Official Proceedings at the Council in the Walla Walla Valley, 1855*, ed. by Darrell Scott (Fairfield, WA: Ye Galleon Press, 1985): 84.

[24] Schuster, "Yakima Indian Traditionalism," 413-14.

[25] George Gibbs, "Report on the Indian Tribes of the Territory of Washington," in *Reports of Explorations and Surveys to Ascertain the Most Practicable and Economical Route for a Railroad from the Mississippi River to the Pacific Ocean*, H.R. Ex. Doc. 91, 33d Cong., 1st

Ahtanum Creek, for example, supported gardens in pre-treaty times. Chief Kamiakin maintained a garden on the Ahtanum, irrigated from a spring. Chief Ow-hi maintained a similar garden on Wenas Creek. Others had small garden patches on riparian lands at Nanum, Wilson, and Tanum creeks as well. Here they grew rich pasturage for their horses and some crops, including Indian corn, barley, melons, squash, and potatoes.[26] Before white settlers ran ditches from Simcoe Creek, Hahise Sawyahill, a Yakama woman, recalled "We used to have grass and pasture for our horses. Now we can[']t use that land. Now when that drainage ditch went through our land water was down below and now nothing comes up on our allotment."[27]

The Yakima River and Ahtanum Creek were expressly designated as reservation boundaries in the Yakamas' 1855 treaty, although the treaty did not specify what rights Indians might have to the waters of those streams aside from fishing.[28] Narrowly defining Yakama entitlements to those streams became a major objective of white settlers who sought the water for their own uses beginning in the late 1880s. On-reservation farmers wanted access to those streams because they provided the only water for late summer and autumn agriculture when creeks in the reservation's interior dried up. Off-reservation water users, however, backed by the U.S. Bureau of Reclamation (Reclamation Service), appropriated waters from those sources for large, off-reservation irrigation projects whose beneficiaries did not include Indians.

Yakama, from early times, used "little springs" for drinking water. Some of those subsequently were included in reservation boundaries. Other springs, however, such as those used by fishers at The Dalles and along other Columbia fishing areas were not included in treaty provisions and they soon became subject to appropriation—often by the same individuals who asserted title to land encompassing fishery locations.

"The children used to crawl outside of the [Winans Brothers] fence for [spring] water and tear their clothes," recalled White Salmon Charley. "That is

---

Sess., 426 (1855). Gibbs speculated that the Yakama farms he observed were the legacy of Hudson's Bay personnel.

[26] A. J. Splawn, *Ka-Mi-Akin, Last Hero of the Yakimas* (Caldwell, ID: The Caxton Printers, Ltd., 1917, 1958): 16; Gibbs, "Report on the Indian Tribes of Washington," 421, 426 (1855). Gibbs reported that Yakama raised eight-rowed Indian corn, whose ears were about five inches long, and also raised at least three kinds of potatoes, among other crops.

[27] Testimony of Hahise Sawyahill, in "Report of Commission to Investigate the Claims of Indians Along Simcoe Creek," part 1-A [hereafter cited as "Report of Simcoe Creek Commission"], transmitted by letter, June 9, 1924, file no 77253-22-341, CCF, General Records 1907-39, BIA, RG 75, NA-Seattle.

[28] Treaty with the Yakima, art. 2, 12 Stat. 951. See also Council Proceedings, Fort Simcoe, WA, June 2, 1913, file "Councils and Meetings, Tribal, 1913-25," Tribal Records, 1897-1952, YA, BIA, RG 75, NA-Seattle.

the way Winans are stopping the Indians from getting in."²⁹ William Speedies described the spring further:

> Mr. Winans told me that I must not go down to this spring to get any water, where we had been in the habit of getting water, and we had to go up the fence about half a mile, but some times we stole through the fence, crawled under the wire to get our drinking water ... that spring has been there ever since I can remember, I have been carrying water there ever since I can remember, now I have to go there and steal water to get it to drink.... [It was a] small spring.... We used that only just for the purposes of drinking water. Whenever we want water any more than that it is right close to the river."³⁰

Those Columbia River bands who lived at the river year-round, such as the Wishram, felt this deprivation most deeply and believed that Yakama treaty rights included "springs, little springs in Yakima Indian reservation, not any rights to the whites [to those springs]."³¹ Yakama also utilized soda springs, which they believed carried medicinal properties.³² Springs also provided irrigation for some farmers.³³ Hahise Sawyahill who used a spring on her allotment for irrigation told a federal commission in 1924, "Those springs are ours. They will be there forever."³⁴

The importance of water in Yakama spirituality connected directly with its significance to sustaining daily life. Sawyahill recalled in 1924:

> When I was raised on this reservation there was not one white man on this reservation. I see my father and my mother when I was small girl. Whenever we needed water there was water in the well. My father and my mother used that water to raise me. My father and mymother [sic] raised me on that water. And when I got to be good age I never saw any [irrigation] ditches anywheres. God created water running through the natural streams. We all Indians was raised in this country by the water.³⁵

---

[29] Testimony in *U.S. v. Winans*, transcript of record, 135 (speaking through interpreter).

[30] Testimony in *U.S. v. Winans*, transcript of record, 176, 180 (speaking through interpreter).

[31] Statement of Louis Simpson, Council Proceedings of Yakima Indians, Fort Simcoe, WA, June 2, 1913, "Councils and Meetings (tribal), 1913-25," folder, Tribal Records, 1897-1952, YA, BIA, RG 75, NA-Seattle.

[32] Yakima Agent S. A. M. Young to Commissioner of Indian Affairs, Jan. 21, 1911, file 3699-10-341, part 1, CCF, General Records [hereafter cited as GR], YA, BIA, RG 75, NA; Lucillus Virgil McWhorter, *The Crime Against the Yakima* (North Yakima, WA: Republic Print, 1913): 26.

[33] Case of Yesmowit Yah-ho-tow-wit, who irrigated from springs on allotment no. 1587. Report of Simcoe Creek Commission, 5.

[34] Testimony in Report of Simcoe Creek Commission, 12.

[35] Testimony in Report of Simcoe Creek Commission.

Water, together with the mountains and fish, bear, deer and other game, were the stuff of the Yakamas' continuing life. "All these streams inside the reservation are from springs inside the reservation, and our friend Mr. Holt, we claim water to be ours," Frank Selatsee stated in 1924:

> That is the water that is supporting us. As long as I lived on this reservation, and as long as there is water in the vall[e]ys and in the fields I will be supported by it Thatis [sic] the reason I claim the water. That is where I get my food from.... You take good drink of water and your body is good. That is the way with Indians. Everything that grows up it is supplied by water.... When the reservation was estblsihed [sic] for Indians['] purposes the water was there already.[36]

For the Yakama, water, earth, and all life were bound together. It made no sense to talk of one without all of the others.

Some Native American peoples who lived in arid regions, such as the San Papago, held reverential attitudes toward water that seem to have precluded the notion that water could be manipulated to human ends.[37] The Yakama, however, had no such fear. Water—and its place in supporting life—deserved human respect to be sure, but people might also use water to their own purposes.

In the 1960s, some Yakama "traditionals" "expressed apprehension over the loss of part of their water resources" that would result as part of a tribal economic development program that included the construction of three dams.[38] How much manipulation was consistent with reverence toward water was open to debate. Many factors might influence individual attitudes toward water, including one's personal connection to the reservation land base, family history, participation in agency schools, religion, the economics of subsistence, opportunity, access to water, and access to ready cash.[39]

Pre-treaty Yakama water use required little complex technology and fit well within the small-group structure of Plateau societies. People carried drinking water from springs, streams, and rivers with buckets and baskets.[40] Flood plain and spring irrigation were simple and required few tools. Farmers waited for annual floods to deposit silt on their gardens and dug their seeds

---

[36] Testimony in Report of Simcoe Creek Commission.

[37] Bowden, *Killing the Hidden Waters*, 8; Underhill, *Rainhouse and Ocean*, 37-69; Bowden, *Singing For Power, The Song Magic of the Papago Indians of Southern Arizona* (Berkeley: University of California Press, 1938, California Library Reprint Series, cloth ed. 1976): 111-13. Both Bowden and Underhill describe the practice of Papago warriors to demonstrate their bravery by running into the ocean and submerging themselves up to their shoulders.

[38] Schuster, "Yakima Indian Traditionalism," 413-14.

[39] See Chapter 7.

[40] On use of buckets, see testimony of Bill Se-hi-am, *U.S. v. Winans*, transcript of record, 158.

into this rich soil.⁴¹ Sometimes Yakama dug channels from creeks to convey water to their gardens. Sampson Whitefoot, Noah Whitefoot and Edward Tenowit constructed such a ditch from Simcoe Creek before the reservation was allotted, to irrigate small garden patches.⁴²

While it is not clear whether this floodplain agriculture emerged from Plateau society itself or was introduced by missionaries, Yakama water use clearly included aspects of productive/economic, spiritual, and cultural significance.⁴³ Yakama had spatial and temporal rights to water similar to those they created in land and fisheries. Individuals depended upon annual flooding and stream water to support their gardens. Others utilized springs on their land to irrigate their hayfields. At the fisheries, people had access to water when they came to fish. Just as particular families exercised priority over the use of fishing locations, family members may have held entitlements to nearby water supplies. Yet Yakama water use for gardens and fishing does not appear to have been on a large enough scale to alter stream flow very much, nor does there appear to have been much competition among water users. Although Yakama had water entitlements, those were collectively and less exclusively defined than the Euro-American system of water rights that replaced them.

Water as Property

Euro-Americans had their own myths about the place of water in their societies and the structure of appropriate human relationships to water. Judeo-Christian tradition taught that water surrounded and preceded all life on earth: "In the beginning, when God created the heavens and the earth, the earth was a formless wasteland, and darkness covered the abyss, while a mighty wind swept over the waters."⁴⁴ God separated the waters, creating oceans on earth and a second body of water above the firmament of the sky. This celestial water provided rain and snow through the floodgates of the sky. Only after earth, sea,

---

⁴¹ On technologies employed by indigenous Native American societies, see R. Douglas Hurt, *Indian Agriculture in America: Prehistory to the Present* (Lawrence: University Press of Kansas, 1987), 1-26; Worster, *Rivers of Empire*, 32-35.

⁴² The "Moses Sampson Ditch" was one of the oldest on Simcoe Creek, according to the Commission's report. Report of Simcoe Creek Commission, 4.

⁴³ Narcissa Whitman to Mr. and Mrs. Stephen Prentiss, April 11, 1838, reprinted in "Letters written by Mrs. Whitman from Oregon to her Relatives in New York," Oregon Pioneer Association, *Transactions of the 19th Annual Reunion, 1891* (Portland, OR: A. Anderson & Co. Printers and Lithographers, 1893): 103, 105; Whitman to Mrs. Stephen Prentiss, May 2, 1840, ibid., 135; Marcus Whitman to Rev. Lyman T. Judson, Oct. 30, 1838, reprinted in Archer Butler Hulbert and Dorothy Printup Hulbert, eds. *Marcus Whitman, Crusader: 1802-1839*, 3 vols. (Colorado Springs and Denver, CO: The Stewart Commission of Colorado College and the Denver Public Library, 1936): vol. 1: 327; Whitman to Levi Chamberlain, Oct. 30, 1838, ibid., vol. 2: 133; Whitman to ABCFM, July 6, 1840, ibid., vol. 2: 177; Whitman to David Greene, April 7, 1843, ibid., vol. 2: 294-301. See also Bower, "Hydrogeography of Yakima Indian Nation Resource Use," 119-21.

⁴⁴ 1 Gen. 1: 1-2, New American Bible.

and sky had been organized did God create plants, animals, birds, and finally humans to populate this world.[45] Just as water preceded and gave meaning to Yakama life, so too did attitudes toward water and its mythical place in the world give meaning to human life within the Judeo-Christian tradition.[46]

Euro-Americans differed from Yakama, however, in that their myths tended to legitimize human dominion over the earth and its resources. Thus, like other resources such as land, humans might use water and mix their own labor with it to create individual property entitlements in water. Still, a certain understanding of water as linked to the well-being of human collective identity informs Euro-American water use, as we will see, and precludes—at least in theory—uses of water in ways that are detrimental to a community's common good.[47]

Euro-Americans expressed through law their view of water as both an individual property right and a community resource to be held in trust for the common good. In the U.S. federal system, the task of defining rights in water falls upon the states.[48] In the western territories, additionally certain federal laws provided for the allocation and use of water on public lands owned by the United States.[49] States drew upon two major water law systems in creating

---

[45] 1 Gen. 1: 6-32, New American Bible. In a second biblical creation story, Genesis, 2: 5-25, God creates Adam from clay formed near a stream welling up out of the earth.

[46] This section is necessarily brief; there is much more research to be done on attitudes toward nature and natural resources inherent in Judeo-Christian traditions. An alternative view to the traditional patriarchal and hierarchical views of God, humans, and nature is found in the Gnostic tradition. See Elaine Pagels, *The Gnostic Gospels* (New York: Random House, Inc., 1979; New York: Vintage Books, 1981); Carolyn Merchant, *The Death of Nature, Women, Ecology and the Scientific Revolution* (San Francisco: Harper & Row Publishers, 1980): 17-19.

[47] Sax and Abrams, *Legal Control of Water Resources*, xvii-xviii.

[48] *U.S. v. Rio Grande Dam Co.*, 174 U.S. 690 (1899) (states have power to define rules under which water will be appropriated, irrespective of common law); *California Oregon Power Co. v. Beaver Portland Cement Co.*, 295 U.S. 142 (1935) (state, and not federal law, governs use of water on public lands granted to the states or patented to individuals after the Desert Land Act of 1877). Certain federal powers preempt state regulation of water for commerce and navigation, however. U.S. Const., Art. I, § 8(3); *Gibbons v. Ogden*, 9 Wheaton 1 (1824).

[49] The Act establishing the Territory of Oregon recognized existing property rights of missionaries, Indians, and others, Act of August 14, 1848, 9 Stat. 323 § 14; 1 Lord's Oregon Laws, p. 46. Federal statutes that permitted the acquisition of appropriative rights on public lands provided the means by which many individuals continued to hold appropriative rights once the lands passed into private ownership. Such acts included "An Act Granting the Right of Way to Ditch and Canal Owners of the Public Lands...." of 1866, that provided for the opening of mineral lands to "exploration and occupation." The act noted that "whenever, by priority of possession, rights to the use of water for mining, agricultural, manufacturing, or other purposes, have vested and accrued, and the same are recognized and, acknowledged by the local customs, laws, and the decisions of courts, the possessors and owners of such vested rights shall be maintained and protected in the same...." 14 Stat. 251, § 1(9) (1866); 16 Stat. 217, § 17 (1870). The Desert Land Act of 1877 required individuals who filed under its

individual water entitlements: riparianism and the doctrine of prior appropriation. Both will be discussed below. In Washington, where the legislature recognized both systems until 1917, a complex, overlapping pattern of conflicting water rights emerged.

Riparian rights are property rights that entitle an individual to use water appurtenant to a piece of land by virtue of his or her ownership of that land. By the 1850s, common law doctrines governing water and other property use shifted from a system that promoted the "quiet enjoyment" of property to one that valued active use for commercial gain.[50] The legal historian Morton J. Horwitz termed this shift "the transformation of American law."[51]

While the common law traditionally had prohibited interference with a stream's natural flow, the new system did not. The courts evaluated individual use according to the concept of reasonable use, whereby the state could balance relative benefits of conflicting property uses in order to determine who should prevail, and, significantly, whether the loser had suffered any judicially recognized injury. Now injury to private landholders did not necessarily constitute grounds for legal redress. Those who did not employ their property industriously stood to lose it to others who would.[52] Although this transformation occurred in the eastern United States by about 1860, the change took place later and more rapidly in the West.

---

provisions to acquire water rights via prior appropriation by its very definition of desert lands as all those "which will not, without irrigation produce some agricultural crop." 19 Stat. 377 (1877), §§ 1, 2

[50] T. E. Lauer, "Reflections on Riparianism," *Missouri Law Review* 35 (1970): 4-11; Lauer, "The Common Law Background of the Riparian Doctrine," *Missouri Law Review* 28 (1963): 99-106. Morton Horwitz notes that "[t]he extensive construction of mills and dams at the end of the eighteenth and beginning of the nineteenth centuries gave rise to the first important legal questions bearing on the relationship of property law to private economic development, and it was here that the antidevelopmental doctrines of the common law first clashed with the spirit of economic improvement. As a result, the evolving law of water rights had a greater impact than any other branch of law on the effort to adapt private law doctrines to the movement for economic growth." *Transformation of American Law*, 34; Scheiber, "Property Law, Expropriation, and Resource Allocation by Government, 1789-1910," 239-40 (mill dam acts), 40-48 (common law changes).

[51] Horwitz, *Transformation of American Law*, 1-4.

[52] Horwitz, *Transformation of American Law*, 38. The common law traditionally had prohibited the interference with a stream's natural flow for two reasons. First, such "artificial" manipulation disrupted nature's plan. Second, riparian rights ran with an individual's property right. Consequently any one property owner's interference with streamflow in a significant way could injure other property owners' enjoyment of their riparian rights. At common law, the rule generally for property was "Sic utere tuo ut alienum non laedas," or use your own property so as not to injure that of another. For riparians, that rule was equally clear: "Aqua currit et debet currere, ut currere solebat," water runs, and ought to run, as it has used to run. Horwitz, ibid., 35, quoting from *Merritt v. Parker*, 1 Coxe L. Rep. 460, 463 (N.J. 1795). See also Lawrence M. Friedman, *History of American Law*, 2d (New York: Simon & Schuster, 1985): 178-82.

Many western states adopted common law doctrines, including those of riparian rights, when they entered the federal union or before. Washington explicitly adopted the common law in 1891 where it was not incompatible with existing state practices, and the state courts recognized the existence of both appropriative and riparian rights.[53] Between, roughly, Washington's statehood in 1889 and the mid-1920s, however, the state's water law moved from a somewhat protective, dual riparian and prior-appropriative system to an appropriation-based system that had as its centerpiece the beneficial use of state waters toward the highest public use.[54] In the new system, even riparians came to hold their water rights subject to their ability to diligently and beneficially apply, their water.[55]

Even as riparian rights were changing to meet the needs of an industrializing economy, a competing doctrine of appropriate water rights was emerging as a significant tool in the exploitation of western U.S. water resources. In the appropriative system, irrigators could acquire water rights from sources that were not necessarily adjacent to their lands. Anyone could appropriate the available waters in a lake or stream and transport them in any amount to any location. While Washington courts initially held would-be appropriators to a standard of property ownership, that requirement was relaxed over time as an appropriator's intent and "diligence in putting the water to a beneficial use" became the "controlling features."[56]

An appropriator derived the water right by making "beneficial use" of some quantity of water—that is, putting it to work in some way. As soon as the appropriator ceased to use the water beneficially, she or he lost the right. Thus, appropriative rights provided an important state subsidy only to those who had the capital and enterprise to develop them. Finally, appropriation doctrine provided that when there was not sufficient water in a stream to supply all users, the one who was 'first in time" was "first in right." That is, the person who first tapped into a water source had a priority of right over all subsequent

---

[53] Charles Horowitz, "Riparian and Appropriation Rights to the Use of Water in Washington," *Washington Law Review* 7 (Feb. 1932): 203-04.

[54] 1917 Wash. Laws 447, ch. 117, §§ 1, 4.

[55] *Benton v. Johncox*, 17 Wash. 277 (1897): 281, quoting with approval *Lux v. Haggin*, 69 Cal. 225, 390 (1886), noting that "Use does not create the [riparian] right, and disuse cannot destroy or suspend it." Cf. *State ex rel. Liberty Lake Irr. Co. v. Supr. Ct.*, 47 Wash. 310 (1907); and *Brown v. Chase*, 125 Wash. 454 (1923), moving toward a "need" based and finally beneficial use criterion for evaluating riparian rights.

[56] *In re Waters of Alpowa Creek*, 129 Wash. 9, 18. Cf. *Thorpe, et al. v. Tenem Ditch Co.*, 1 Wash. 566 (1889); and *Sander v. Bull*, 76, Wash. 1 (1913): 6, stating: "No rights flow from the diversion and use of water by a mere squatter." The Washington state Water Code of 1917, which left it an open question as to whether property ownership was a requirement for appropriation of water. See also Morris A. Arval, "Washington Water Rights—A Sketch," *Washington Law Review* 31 (1956): 243, 254-55.

appropriators—even if that meant that more "junior" water users got no water at all."[57]

As early as 1873, the Washington territorial legislature recognized that if non-riparian landowners were not permitted to appropriate water, the arid eastern lands of the state could not be developed. That year the legislature passed an act that allowed Yakima County farmers, miners, manufacturers— and anyone else who could use water for "beneficial purposes"—to construct diversion works necessary to convey water onto their non-riparian lands. Disputes were to be settled by the priority of the appropriation date.[58] In 1890, the new state legislature passed a statute that provided for the appropriation of any unclaimed waters "from any of the natural streams or lakes in this state" for irrigation and permitted the condemnation of rights of ways for ditches to carry the water.[59] Subsequent acts set out state-wide rules for constructing irrigation works and dams, organizing irrigation districts, protecting the quality and sources of municipal water supplies; and they provided for irrigation and other improvements on lands granted to the state.[60]

How would riparian rights mesh with appropriative rights? Some states, including Colorado, Idaho, Utah, and New Mexico, rejected the riparian doctrine outright wholly or partially on the grounds that riparian rights were useless in an arid region.[61] That ecological argument proved unpersuasive to Washington and California courts, however. As Justice Anders of the Washington Supreme Court noted in 1897, "It certainly, can not be true that a difference in climatic conditions or geographical position can operate to deprive one of a right of property vested in him by a well-settled rule of common law."[62] To Anders and others, riparian rights were too old and too integral a form of property rights to discard them before the advancing tide of prior appropriation. Yet the price of retaining both systems was high: California and Wash-

---

[57] Sax and Abrams, *Legal Control of Water Resources*, 278-79; Limerick, *Legacy of Conquest*, 75.

[58] "An Act Regulating Irrigation and Water Rights in the county of Yakima, Washington Territory," Nov. 13, 1873, 1873 Wash. Laws 520-22.

[59] 1890 Wash. Laws 706, § 1.

[60] Horowitz, "Riparian and Appropriation Rights," 202-08; Carl J. Bauer, "Labor Without Brains: Water Development, Law, and Policy in Washington State, 1890-1935" (M.S. thesis, University of Wisconsin-Madison, 1988): 56-60; Fahey, *Inland Empire*, 98-100.

[61] *Benton v. Johncox*, 17 Wash. 277, 282-83 (1897); see, e.g., *Coffin et al. v. Left Hand Ditch Co.*, 6 Colo. 443 (1882), where the Colorado Supreme Court rejected the riparian doctrine and adopted prior appropriation as the state's only system. For a discussion of prior appropriation in western states, see Sax and Abrams, *Legal Control of Water Resources*, 278-413; Dunbar, *Forging New Rights*, 60-62, 209-10.

[62] *Benton v. Johncox*, 17 Wash. 277, at 283.

ington quickly became battlegrounds where riparian landowners and prior-appropriators fought over access to and control of water.[63]

Until 1917, however, when Washington State finally adopted an administrative water code that recognized prior appropriation as the only means by which individuals could acquire water rights, there was no legislative direction for sorting out mounting disputes among riparian and appropriative water users.[64] One historian estimated that by about 1910 there were 7000 water claimants in Washington courts.[65] The pre-code system, according to contemporary observers, seemed designed only to ensure the over-appropriation of the state's water resources. "Under the present statute the only limit to the quantity of water an appropriator may claim and file upon is the measure of his greed," Professor O. L. Waller noted with disgust in his 1904 report for the governor's water code commission:

> [The appropriator] always wants to be sure to have plenty to satisfy all his present ambitions and any desires that may come afterwards. It is fortunate that the Deity has not furnished water in such liberal quantities as some of our appropriators have claimed. If He had, these same fellows would be trying to get a monopoly on the drainage. For, if all the water had materialized for which there were at one time valid filings, it would have been enough to supply about 2.2 feet of precipitation daily for the entire state, or if it could have been held on the ground for one year evenly distributed, the water would have stood about 800 feet deep over the state of Washington, or about 17 feet deep over the entire United States.[66]

To Waller, such calculations proved only "the total ineffectiveness of the present law."[67] Yet while Washington law failed to conserve the state's water resources, it proved very effective in channeling water toward those who would develop it.

Early Water Development at Yakima

The Yakima Basin, with its rich, fine volcanic ash-enriched soils, was an early target for both missionaries' and settlers' irrigation efforts. As both Indians and non-Indians began to use basin water for agriculture and other uses, conflicts rapidly emerged between the two groups. Indian Bureau En-

---

[63] For California, see *Lux v. Haggin*, 69 Cal. 255 (1886) (recognizing both riparian and appropriative rights within the state). This case is discussed in Dunbar, *Forging New Rights*, 65-68.

[64] Horowitz, "Riparian and Appropriation Rights," 208-11; 1917 Wash. Laws 447-68. On the history of the water code and its passage, see Fahey, *Inland Empire*, 99-100; Bauer, "Labor Without Brains," 58-62, 74-81.

[65] Fahey, *Inland Empire*, 99.

[66] Waller, "Report on Irrigation Conditions in the Yakima Valley, Washington," 19.

[67] Waller, "Report on Irrigation Conditions in the Yakima Valley, Washington," 19.

gineer Dwight Redman reported in August 1904, after viewing the nearly drained Yakima River, "Perhaps it might be well for [appropriators] to assemble together and pray for rain, but I apprehend their calls upon a Deity are being made in a far different spirit."[68]

Yakama farming, and specifically irrigation, intensified under the direction of Bureau agents. Sheppard Peters, an Indian living along Simcoe Creek in 1917, recalled that some Yakama had built a ditch and were irrigating from it before J. H. Wilbur arrived at the reservation in 1860 to take over the superintendency of the agency school. Under Wilbur's instruction, the boys at the agency school were "cultivating a large garden" in 1861.[69] Perhaps that is where Schuyler Colfax first learned the irrigation techniques that he recalled Wilbur had taught him.[70]

Yakama worked hard to maintain their own irrigation works. "When the first ditch [the Meninick/Shumit ditch on Simcoe Creek] was constructed," Homer James recalled in 1924, "we did not irrigate very much ground. Then later on we kept enlarging the ditch and plowing more ground. That was before any allotments."[71] James's recollections put the construction of the ditch at around 1867 at the latest:

> I worked three days with my team some time ago [to help build the ditch]. I helped my cousin, Caroline Schumit, work th[re]e days to help clean out the ditch to bring more water into that channel from Simcoe Creek. It seems that there was a new channel that formed a creek right where the Wahput ditch comes out, and formed a creek next to the hill and took water into that channel.... We had to dig deeper in order to bring the water out into the ditch.... There was two women worked there at that time, myself, Robert Scowitch was the husband of Caroline Schumit, and Charley Blain worked there. We carried lots of boulders from the hill into that channel which was going the other way, and forced the water over to come this way.[72]

Both James and others noted the participation of Yakama women in building and maintaining reservation irrigation works, and it seems likely that irrigation fit easily within women's gardening and gathering tasks.[73] By 1864, about 400 acres of riparian lands were irrigated on the reservation, and by

---

[68] Redman to Lynch, Aug 28, 1904, file "1902-03," Letters Received Re: Irrigation Matters, 1903-08, YA, BIA, RG 75, NA-Seattle.

[69] Testimony in Report of Simcoe Creek Commission.

[70] W.B. Gosnell, Yakima Agent, report, in *CIA-AR*, 1861, 185; Testimony in Report of Simcoe Creek Commission.

[71] Testimony in Report of Simcoe Creek Commission.

[72] Testimony in Report of Simcoe Creek Commission. See also testimony of Sheppard Peters, ibid.

[73] Testimony of William Colwash and Homer James, in Report of Simcoe Creek Commission.

1878, 15,000 acres of reservation land had been fenced and 5000 acres were cultivated.[74]

Most Indians who were to farm and ranch on the Yakama Reservation needed a supply of water. Within the Yakima River valley, the rich bottomlands along the Yakima and Ahtanum rivers and Toppenish and Satas creeks required no artificial irrigation. People who had received allotments along those streams, according to Agent Jay Lynch (1891-93, 1897-1908), were, "as a rule ... self-supporting, and some of their crops are equal to the whites." One Mrs. McCauliff, "Half-breed, raised 6 tons of alfalfa hay per acre last season in three cuttings," and others had produced equally magnificent crops of corn, wheat, oats, barley, potatoes, and onions.[75] Those productive claims, however, had been the first lands allotted, which left the arid, sagebrush-covered lands above the valley floor for subsequent allottees. Here, Lynch observed, it was difficult to crop or graze the land because of the lack of water. Federally funded irrigation works were the key to turning those lands and the entire valley into a "garden spot of creation," he believed.[76]

Irrigation became a significant part of federal Indian policy following the Dawes Act of 1887. The first federal appropriations for Indian irrigation works were made in 1876, but only during the early 1890s did Congress begin regular appropriations for on-reservation work. In general, the Bureau had neither the expertise nor the funds to undertake such projects on its own. Moreover, federal representatives of Indians had no special status in water claims actions; courts treated them merely as one of many, ordinary claimants. As a result, the Bureau often lost the race against non-Indian appropriators to secure water, and many of the projects failed to bring anything but hardship to the supposed beneficiaries.[77] The Bureau justified the work anyway because construction was an effective way of employing Indians who could not get off-reservation jobs. In addition, working for money was a way of teaching the importance of hard work and thrift.[78]

During a time when federal funds were in short supply and were more often spent to benefit non-Indians, the Bureau required Indians to pay for their own irrigation works. Proceeds from the 1893 sale of the Wenatchee Band's fishery on the Wenatchi River (reserved in the Yakamas' 1855 treaty), for ex-

---

[74] *CIA-AR*, 1864, 473; *CIA-AR*, 1878, 140.

[75] *CIA-AR*, 1895, 320-21. Other crops included turnips, beans and other vegetables, melons, pumpkins, hay, and butter, *CIA-AR*, 1896, 317.

[76] *CIA-AR*, 1898, 304.

[77] Daniel McCool, *Command of the Waters: Iron Triangles, Federal Water Development, and Indian Water* (Berkeley: University of California Press, 1987): 118-27; Donald J. Pisani, "Irrigation, Water Rights, and the Betrayal of Indian Allotment," *Environmental Review* 10 (1986): 158. Congress authorized the OIA's Irrigation Service to proceed with the Wapato project in 1913 (an on-reservation project supplied by the Yakima River and briefly incorporated in BuRec's Yakima Irrigation Project), and with the Ahtanum project in 1915.

[78] Pisani, "Betrayal of Indian Allotment," 159.

Sacred Water • 139

Agent L. T. Erwin with Yakama chief White Swan (right)
and Sinkiuse-Columbia chief Moses (left), ca. 1895

Northwest Museum of Arts & Culture/Eastern Washington State Historical Society,
Spokane Washington, American Indians of the Pacific Northwest Images Digital Collection,
Negative # L94-14.56, used by permission

ample, went to fund an on-reservation irrigation canal from which no Wenatchee benefitted.[79] Construction soon began on a canal that would take water from the Yakima River at a projected capacity of 150 cubic feet per second (c.f.s.). Agent Erwin looked forward to soon irrigating 30,000 acres of land in addition to improving Indian character: "first, they will get money for performing the work, and when the work is finished they will have an improvement that will not only be a blessing to them, but to their children and their children's children."[80]

As was typical of federal reclamation projects, however, things looked better on paper than they did in reality. By 1889, Agent Lynch, who had by then succeeded Erwin, reported that the "expensive canal" had come "far short of what was expected of it."[81] As a result of poor planning, the canal's headgates had been located and constructed during the spring when the Yakima River was at its highest stage. Consequently, during the summer, at low water, the canal was virtually dry, and no more than a foot of water flowed through it during July, August, and the rest of the autumn. Insufficient depth and "some other defects" had rendered the canal worthless in its present form, and Lynch predicted that it would "require considerable expense in money to remedy this evil."[82]

The failure of that first canal did not deter the Bureau from undertaking more ambitious irrigation works on the Yakama Reservation. Those projects, beginning in 1902 with a canal and lateral built at Union Gap on the Yakima River that would irrigate some 50,000 acres, were financed by congressional appropriations charged against a tribe's annuities. At Yakima, Wesley L. Jones, then an imaginative Washington congressman (he served in the Senate from 1909 to 1932), launched an ultimately unsuccessful scheme by which Yakama could finance irrigation by selling most of their allotted lands, thereby finally opening the reservation to homesteading.[83]

In 1906 Congress passed legislation introduced by Jones (and popularly known as the Jones Act) that provided for funding the on-reservation portion of the Reclamation Service's larger Yakima Irrigation project by allowing each allottee to sell 60 acres of his or her allotment to pay for bringing water to the remaining twenty acres under the project. As an additional injustice, as part of the Jones's package, land lost from the Yakama Reservation through erroneous boundary surveys was deemed compensated for by on-reservation federal

---

[79] *CIA-AR*, 1894, 326; *CIA-AR*, 1896, 317-18. For a discussion of the Wenatshapam fishery sale, see Chapter 5.

[80] *CIA-AR*, 1896, 318.

[81] *CIA-AR*, 1899, 364.

[82] *CIA-AR*, 1899, 364.

[83] On earlier attempts to open the reservation to non-Indians, see Chapter 4.

reclamation efforts up to 1906.[84] The Act required the consent of the allottee, but subsequent legislation authorized the Indian agent to sign for individuals deemed incompetent to decide for themselves. Even one insider must have felt a twinge of anxiety over whether this water grab might raise suspicion, urging the Commissioner of Indian Affairs to implement the terms quickly: "Please do not let this matter get into the legal grind and have it mutilated. It is all right and meets with the approval of the legal adviser of the Reclamation Service who is on the ground and knows the conditions, and technical objections should not be permitted to further delay the work."[85] Yakama were outraged at the Act, demanded that the Indian Bureau fund Wapato in other ways, and tirelessly petitioned and wrote letters protesting its terms.[86]

Between 1907 and 1909, the Indian Bureau and Reclamation Service attempted to frighten and deceive allottees into signing. Sometimes officials threatened to deprive an individual of all water and to declare them legally incompetent if they refused to sign. Sometimes officials told people they were signing papers to build on-reservation road systems. By 1912, 826 people had been signed up, but only 292 had signed on their own (and under what circumstances we do not know). The agent had signed for all the others.[87] Still,

---

[84] 34 Stat.L. 53, Act of March 6, 1906. On the Yakima Project and the Reclamation Service's (BuRec's) growing involvement in reclamation in Washington State during this time, see Bower, "Hydrogeography of Yakima Indian Resource Use," 348-62.

[85] Author unknown, to CIA, July 29, 1909, file 133266-09-341, YA, CCF, BIA, RG 75, NA, enclosing forms to petition for water rights under the Jones Act. The letter discusses how the Secretary of Interior could be empowered to act for minors and incompetents in his capacity as the Indians' trustee. According to the Act of March 27, 1908 (Pub. L. no. 70), interests of any minor Indian in any lands on reservation could be sold at the discretion of the Secretary, or upon approved petition of child's recognized guardian.

[86] Mann to Poindexter, Jan. 24, 1912, 76:13, MCPP; YTC-WS to CIA, petition, April 6, 1911, file no. 34334-11-341, YA, CCF, BIA, RG 75, NA; W. H. Code, Chief Engineer, OIA-Irrigation Service, to Sec. of Int., April 27, 1911, file no. 33123-11-341, YA, CCF, BIA, RG 75, NA.

[87] James Martin, Memo, to CIA, March 11, 1912, file no. 16201-12-341, YA, CCF, BIA, RG 75, NA (noting that of a total of 826 signatures, all but 292 were signed up by the Superintendent under rules for incompetents and minors):

- Schedule of petitions to acquire water right under Wapato project, March 17, 1911, file no. 23589-11-341, YA, CCF, BIA, RG 75, NA (5 Competent allottee, 1 competent heir; 2 competent heirs of minors; 1 white land owner; all 80-acre tracts);
- Schedule of petitions, June 29, 1911, file no. 57416-11-341, YA, CCF, BIA, RG 75, NA (9 competent allottees, 1 competent heir of minor);
- Schedule of petitions, Sept. 5, 1911, ibid. (1 white owner, with multiple tracts; 28 incompetent heirs signed by superintendent);
- Schedule of petitions signed to June 22, 1911, ibid. (competent Indians (132); minors w/incompetent parents (57); minor orphans (14); incompetent adults (327); minors w/competent parents (69); deceased Indians (67); white land owners (160)—everyone except in first and last category was signed by superintendent;
- Petition for water rights under Wapato project: total number of petitions submitted to April 26, 1910 was 648, 5 of which were allottees; everyone else was a white land

not enough people had signed to provide the Reclamation Service with sufficient funds to build the Wapato project, and by 1909 the agency unofficially terminated its involvement in the on-reservation project, leaving reservation water users without any immediate hope of getting water.[88]

All around the Yakama Reservation, non-Indian settlers and land companies were busy also, buying and staking land claims. Many hoped to resell at higher prices once irrigation works boosted property values. The Northern Pacific Railroad, for example, which had extensive holdings from railroad land grants, was in a prime position to develop irrigation projects along the Yakima River because its grants ran parallel to the river for about 135 miles on the east bank. Any reclamation projects diverting water west of the tracks necessarily ran across the Northern Pacific's property and the company charged fees for the right of way for all ditches, including those of the Indian Bureau and Reclamation Service.[89]

The Northern Pacific developed its own reclamation project through its subsidiary the Northern Pacific, Yakima and Kittitas Irrigation Company. The new company built irrigation works on railroad lands on the east shore of the Yakima River.[90] In 1890 the company filed on 2000 c.f.s. from the Yakima River, and amended it to 1000 c.f.s. the following year when it began construction of the Sunnyside irrigation project. Company officials declared that the Yakamas' treaty contained no reservation of water rights, thereby preventing reservation users from asserting any rival entitlements to water.[91] At an old Yakama dance house site, the Company built an adjustable dam in 1891 that Agent Jay Lynch believed was big enough to appropriate virtually the entire low flow of the Yakima River.[92] The Yakama protested that the dam would

---

owner on reservation, in S.A.M. Young to CIA, April 26, 1910, file no. 15608-10-341, YA, CCF, BIA, RG 75, NA.

See also *In Re Water Rights for Yakima Indian Reservation* memorandum brief to House-Senate Joint committee to investigate reservation water claims, Oct. 20, 1913, file no. 123855-13-341 YA, CCF, BIA, RG 75, NA, arguing that Indians were coerced into signing over property rights under Jones Act.

[88] S. A. M. Young to CIA, Feb. 17, 1910, file no 15608-10-341, YA, CCF, BIA, RG 75, NA. Young reported: "A large number of the Indians and some of the white owners seem to be immovable in their determination not to sign." He anticipated that it would take a long time to get the project moving, because Yakama "connect so many irrelevant things with the Wapato project and it is so difficult to get them to take a business-like view of the matter."

[89] Meinig, *Great Columbia Plain*, 340, 379-80; Bower, "Hydrogeography of Yakima Indian Nation Resource Use," 290-96.

[90] See Chapter 4. The Northern Pacific was the principal stock holder in the new company. See Fahey, *Inland Empire*, 87.

[91] P. H. Winston to Attorney General, March 30, 1892, file 4799, *Winans*, box 420, Attorney General, Letters Received, RG 60, Records of the Department of Justice [hereafter cited as AGLR, RG 60, DOJ], NA.

[92] Charles Relander (Now Tow Look), *Drummers and Dreamers: The Story of Smohalla the Prophet and his Nephew Puck Hyah Toot....*, with a foreword by Frederick Webb Hodge

deprive them of water and destroy their fisheries, and while Agent Lynch repeatedly requested that the Bureau suspend the project, no one at the Department of Justice defended the Yakamas' claims.[93]

In 1892, at the dedication of the first 25 miles of the Sunnyside canal, a local newspaper proclaimed that "The era of irrigation ... has opened in earnest for central Washington." The new "monster canal" was only a part of a much larger scheme that would eventually include a 60-mile main canal with 550 miles of laterals, and that would water 40,000 acres or more.[94] The company was well on its way to that goal: It had appropriated "the waters of the three lakes which sustain the Yakima river and Bumping lake, the source of the Natchez" from which it planned to run diversion works to water benchlands in the Sunnyside project.[95] By 1896—and despite the Northern Pacific's declaration of bankruptcy during the panic of 1893—an estimated 9,860 acres were irrigated under the auspices of a newly reconstituted company that now ran both the Sunnyside and Kennewick canals. "By 1905," historian John Fahey wrote, "the company operated more than seven hundred miles of canals and laterals watering 36,000 acres, and one of every five residents of the Yakima Valley lived on the Sunnyside project."[96]

Individuals, farmers' collectives, and ditch companies invested in their own small-scale irrigation systems up through the 1890s. Most private attempts to build large-scale irrigation systems during this time, however, were doomed. Low land prices and a lack of markets made it impossible for private investors to complete irrigation works on a scale that would make returns profitable.[97] Washington State had little better success at developing irrigation within the state. In 1894 Congress passed the Carey Act which allowed states to choose up to one million acres each of arid land for irrigation development. In 1895, Washington set up an Arid Lands Commission to investigate the possibility of developing lands between the Yakima and Columbia rivers, above the

---

(Caldwell, ID The Caxton Printers, 1956): 173; "The Era of Irrigation," *The Yakima Herald* [n.d., but probably March 26, 1892], clipping, file 4799, *United States v. Winans*, box 420, AGLR, RG 60, DOJ, NA; Bower, "Hydrogeography of Yakima Indian Nation Resource Use," 321-26.

[93] Jay Lynch to Harry S. Jones, April 29, 1913, box 1, file 3, Accession no. 3095, Henry J. Snively Papers, University of Washington Libraries Manuscript Collection, Seattle, Washington [hereafter cited as box:file, HJSP]. Bower notes that the Secretary of Interior appears to have been uninterested in the case, "Hydrogeography of Yakima Indian Nation Resource Use," 325.

[94] Fahey, *Inland Empire*, 88.

[95] The Era of Irrigation," *The Yakima Herald*, March 27, 1892.

[96] Fahey, *Inland Empire*, 90.

[97] Bauer, "Labor Without Brains," 25; Fahey, *Inland Empire*, 88; Meinig, *Great Columbia Plain*, 342-43, 473. In 1894, for example, the Prosser Falls Land and Power Co. had built a dam on the Yakima River, Bower, "Hydrogeography of Yakima Indian Nation Resource Use," 326-27. The company was sold by a receiver in 1899 after it went bankrupt.

Sunnyside project, but the long business depression of 1893-97 and competition with other water users for a share of Yakima River water derailed the state's plans. By the time the economic climate had improved, it was the federal government, through its new Reclamation Service, that had emerged as the dominant force in Washington's irrigation aspirations.[98]

The Newlands Act of 1902 created the Reclamation Service within the U.S. Geological Survey, in the Department of the Interior, where it functioned under the auspices of its own Director and the Secretary of Interior. The Service was empowered to provide planning, engineering, and financial assistance for irrigation projects.[99] The agency built new projects but also took over partially built irrigation projects, as it did with its 1906 purchase of the Sunnyside project built by the Northern Pacific, Yakima and Kittitas Irrigation Company.[100] The premise according to which the Reclamation Service operated was that if the federal government initially capitalized projects from a revolving fund, the beneficiaries would eventually repay the project costs over a fixed period of time. Non-Indian landowners, who held their land in fee simple, unlike Indians whose lands were mostly held in trust, could mortgage their lands to pay for irrigation development. Chronic underestimation of project costs and inflation kept the Reclamation Service's revenues far behind their costs."[101] Nevertheless after 1902 and until the Great Depression, the agency provided the primary water development force in the Yakima Basin.

The Reclamation Service's mission was to provide water to white farmers. Because both the Indian Bureau and Reclamation Service worked under the auspices of the Secretary of Interior within the Department of Interior, the Secretary was expected to balance somehow the conflicting tasks of acting as a trustee for Indian tribes and overseeing the development of western resources. The Department of Interior struck the balance consistently in favor of non-Indians. The conflict only heightened after 1908 when the Reclamation Service, now the Bureau of Reclamation (BuRec) organized as a separate

---

[98] Calvin B. Coulter, "The Victory of National Irrigation in the Yakima Valley, 1902-1906," *Pacific Northwest Quarterly* 42 (1951): 99-122; Bower, "Hydrogeography of Yakima Indian Nation Resource Use," 327-331; Bauer, "Labor Without Brains," 25; Fahey, *Inland Empire*, 91-94.

[99] Federal reclamation projects were predominantly irrigation-centered; multiple use projects that included hydroelectricity generation did not become the norm until after 1928, with Congressional authorization of the Boulder Canyon Project. Dunbar, *Forging New Rights*, 56-58.

[100] C. Brewster Coulter, "The Victory of National Irrigation in the Yakima Valley, 1902-1906," *Pacific Northwest Quarterly* 42 (1951): 113-15.

[101] On the organization of the Reclamation Service, see Dunbar, *Forging New Rights*, 46-56; McCool, *Command of the Waters*, 14-24, 28-35; Marc Reisner, *Cadillac Desert: The American West and Its Disappearing Water* (New York: Viking Penguin, Inc., 1986): 118-22ff. See also Sax and Abrams, *Legal Control of Water Resources*, 628-82, for a discussion of problems facing the Service.

organization within the Department of Interior, took over many Indian Bureau irrigation projects.[102] Indian water rights, in the Department of Interior's vision of the world, were non-existent and it was convenient to keep them that way.

Conclusion: "Farms for the Homeless"

Congressional passage of the Newlands Act rested on the prevailing belief that humans could employ technologies to make the desert "blossom as the rose," and in doing so would strengthen the agrarian foundations of American democracy.[103] While early writers on western lands such as John Wesley Powell, had suggested that western settlement conform to ecological constraints—most notably the lack of rainfall—such conservatives were overridden by more optimistic visionaries.[104]

With the technology to channel water to particular crops at particular times, the proponents of reclamation believed, human-engineered irrigation could streamline the inefficient natural hydrological cycle of western lands. Plants would receive water when people perceived that they needed it—not when nature saw fit to send rain.[105] The men who controlled this progressive West were a new breed, according to Smythe and others. "They are men of the Forward Look. They are clearing the intellectual forests, rooting up the social sage-brush, irrigating the arid wastes of politics and economics.[106] They

---

[102] On cooperation between OIA and BuRec, see 35 Stat.L. 70, Act of April 30, 1908. On conflict of interest and impact on Yakama in the case of Ahtanum Creek water allocation, see *United States v. Ahtanum Irrigation District*, 236 F.2d 321, 334-39 (9th Cir. 1956). See also Chapter 7.

[103] Worster, *Rivers of Empire*, 7ff, argues that western water development has centralized federal power in that region at the expense of democratic forms of social and political ordering. Compare the beliefs of many nineteenth century policymakers, such as William Ellesworth Smythe, who believed federal reclamation would lead to a more democratic society. See discussion below.

[104] John Wesley Powell, "The Reclamation Idea," (1878), reprinted in Roderick Nash, ed., *The American Environment* 2d ed. (Reading, MA: Addison-Wesley, 1976), 28-33. Powell suggested that agriculture would be suitable only on riparian lands, leaving the remaining arid lands as pasturage land, to be divided into minimum allotments of four-square miles or more. He noted that any large scale reclamation of arid lands would require "extensive and comprehensive plans, for the execution of which aggregated capital or cooperative labor will be necessary. Here," Powell wrote, "individual farmers, being poor men, cannot undertake the task," ibid., 33. Powell also advocated the division and regulation of available western waters into basins which would serve as the basis for irrigation districts. On the ideology of reclamation, see Donald J. Pisani, "Reclamation and Social Engineering in the Progressive Era," *Agricultural History* 57 (1983): 46-63; Pisani, *From the Family Farm to Agribusiness. the Irrigation Crusade in California and the West, 1850-1931* (Berkeley: University of California Press, 1984): 279.

[105] Smythe, *The Conquest of Arid America* (1899), Americana Library Paperbacks (Seattle: University of Washington Press, 1970): 47-48.

[106] Smythe, *The Conquest of Arid America*, xxvi-xxvii; Pisani, "Reclamation and Social Engineering," 46-63.

controlled the nation's destiny as surely as they controlled nature, firmly linking ecological to social change.

At a practical level, however, federal expertise and capital conflicted with state authority over water rights and also with the individualism of most western residents. Proponents of irrigation such as Francis Newlands, William Ellsworth Smythe and Frederick Newell ignored the omnipotence of federal power in the projects in their fervent belief that arid lands could foster small-scale agrarian communities.[107] "The essence of the industrial life which springs from irrigation is its democracy," Smythe wrote in his popular 1899 book, *The Conquest of Arid America*. "Where water is the foundation of prosperity it becomes a precious thing, "to be neither cheaply acquired not wantonly wasted ... it is a thing to be carefully husbanded, to be fairly distributed according to men's needs, to be wisely expended by those who receive it...."[108]

Arid lands, Smythe thought, because of the expensive irrigation necessary to make them productive, would be unattractive to large farmers and speculators but were ideally suited to small-scale family farming. The vision of those farms clustered together across the west provided the best of both eastern small-town society and rural independence.[109] Legislators banked on such reasoning in the Newlands Act. The act contained a 160-acre limitation on landholdings eligible for federal water, although that limitation proved ineffectual, and individuals regularly were able to receive federal water for landholdings above the limit.[110]

Those who peopled the new "farm villages" would be migrating landless urban workers, tenant farmers, and other easterners looking for a better life. As Senator Jones put it, reclamation offered "farms for the homeless [and] homes for the farmless."[111] Somehow, that disgruntled crew would learn to combine the sturdy ideals of yeoman farmers with the progressive tools of "truly scientific agriculture" to make up the ranks of new western settlers.[112]

---

[107] On conflicts between federal reclamation and state water rights systems, see McCool, *Command of the Waters*, 18-19; Limerick, *Legacy of Conquest*, 138-39ff; Worster, *Rivers of Empire*, 117-25.

[108] Smythe, *The Conquest of Arid America*, 43. See also introduction by Lawrence B. Lee, ibid., xxix-xliii.

[109] According to Smythe, irrigation increased the potential productivity of the land to such an extent that a family would require only a small (20-acre) plot to support themselves. *The Conquest of Arid America*, 45-46.

[110] Historians have pointed out that the 160-acre limit encouraged speculation rather than curbed it. For a discussion of the acreage limitation and the Newlands Act, see Pisani, *From Family Farm to Agribusiness*, 316-17; Clayton Koppes, "Public Water, Private Land: Origins of the Acreage Limitation Controversy, 1933-1953," *Pacific Historical Review* 47 (1978): 607-36. See also Dunbar, *Forging New Rights*, 46-51.

[111] Jones, quoted in Fahey, *Inland Empire*, pp. 90-91.

[112] Smythe, *The Conquest of Arid America*, 47; Pisani, *From Family Farm to Agribusiness*, 316-17.

Yet the westward journey transformed few easterners into expert farmers, and one local asserted that such greenhorns, faced with a quantity of Yakima benchlands, would swiftly conclude that "starvation stares him in the face, and if he has money enough to go back, he does."[113] Even westerners—many of whom prided themselves on their supposed inherent ability to conjure fruit from the desert—often understood the mechanics of irrigation in hazy terms at best.[114]

Despite the rhetoric about scientific agriculture, reclamation systems did not deliver water with respect to soil conditions and many individuals who irrigated did not know how to apply water to their lands, nor how much water to use According to H. M. Gilbert, a white man who had farmed reservation land since 1900, "The partial and inadequate system of irrigation existing on the reservation at present I fear is doing almost as much harm as benefit. The water is being distributed without any system in a very reckless manner, and large areas are being 'swamped' every year."[115] Indians fell prey to the same misconceptions held by their white counterparts. Thomas Sam, a Yakama living along Simcoe Creek, noted in 1924, "I have some kind of soil on my allotment, I don[']t care how much water I put on it, [nothing] will [g]row on it."[116]

Indians were a cursed people in this brave new world. Euro-Americans saw them as inferior peoples, lagging behind in the intellect, skills, and ambition to embrace civilized ways. That perception fueled sentiments expressed by non-Indian settlers and many federal officials in both the Reclamation Service and Indian Bureau that Indians could not develop their resources as quickly, efficiently, or profitably as whites. In the case of land holding, that thinking provided a convenient excuse for the transfer of large amounts of Indian land and other resources to whites under federal treaties, statutes such as the Dawes General Allotment Act, and laws providing for the lease and sale of individual allotments.

Indian water rights were no different. Non-Indians believed that they could put water to better use than could Indians, and that assumption became a self-executing prophecy. Indians could not secure sufficient water to develop agriculture or other industries on their lands, and non-Indians who observed their depressed economic state believed that to recognize any larger legal entitlements to resources would be to waste them on a backward people and stunt the growth of the nation's economy. As long as Indian irrigators had to compete with state water users to make their appropriations, Yakama were

---

[113] Testimony in 51st Cong., 1st Sess., S. Rept. 928, Pt. 1 (1889-90), p. 283, quoted in Meinig, *Great Columbia Plain*, 342.

[114] Waller, "Report on Irrigation Conditions in the Yakima Valley," 18-21.

[115] C. F. Larrabee to W. H. Code, quoting from letter of H. M.Gilbert, to W. L. Jones, file no. 1902-03, Letters received re: Irrigation Matters, 1903-08, YA, BIA, RG 75, NA-Seattle.

[116] Report of Simcoe Creek Commission.

disadvantaged because they had neither the capital nor the expertise to make beneficial use of water on the terms dictated by non-Indians.[117]

---

[117] Pisani, "Betrayal of Indian Allotment," 160; McCool, *Command of the Waters*, 127.

7

COMMAND OF THE WATERS

> You may say you are not trying to put Indians out of their right. I went down to Toppenish. An Indian told me down at Toppenish that when you Indians hold your hands up to tell whole truth, down there at White Swan, you give your water away to Reclamation. We not hold up our hands and sell our water right.
> —Sheppard Peters (1924)[1]

William Colwash, a Yakama who lived with his wife along Simcoe Creek, recounted in 1922 how, several years before, a white man dammed his irrigation ditch to divert the water. When Colwash tore the dam out, a deputy sheriff arrived at his house and fired three shots at him before Colwash's wife chased the deputy away with an axe.[2] Hahise Sawyahill, another Yakama living along Simcoe Creek recalled in the same year, that BuRec was draining a spring on her allotment as part of its off-reservation Yakima Project and she would soon have no water.[3] Both Colwash and Sawyahill's water uses were threatened by state and federally sanctioned water projects that promoted the beneficial use of water for a higher public good that excluded Indians from its calculus.

In theory Indians had reserved their lands under federal protection. But what about the water necessary to sustain the communities on those lands? In the 1908 case of *Winters v. United States*, the U.S. Supreme Court held that Indians had reserved water rights even where their treaties made no express mention of water.[4] Although the case upheld Indian rights in theory, in practice it was a difficult rule to enforce. *Winters* was an ambiguous victory for Indian water rights because the decision did not suggest how much water Indians had reserved—nor did the Court suggest how future water users ought to apportion water so that Indian reservations received a fair share.[5]

---

[1] Peter's testimony in Report of Commission to investigate the claims of Indians along Simcoe Creek [hereafter cited as Report of Simcoe Creek Commission], June 9, 1924, file 77253-22-341, part 1-A, Yakima Agency, Central Classified Files, 1907-39, records of the Bureau of Indian Affairs, Record Group 75, National Archives and Record Service, Washington, DC [hereafter cited as YA, CCF, BIA, RG 75, NA]. Note: the pages of the report are not numbered consecutively, or in any identifiable order, so I have omitted them.

[2] Report of Simcoe Creek Commission.

[3] Report of Simcoe Creek Commission.

[4] 207 U.S. 564 (1908). The case involved the Assiniboine and Gros Ventre tribes of the Fort Belknap Reservation in Montana.

[5] Norris Hundley, Jr., "The Dark and Bloody Ground of Indian Water Rights: Confusion Elevated to Principle," *Western Historical Quarterly* 9 (1978): 454-82; Hundley, "The

A deeper underlying problem of the case was that while it recognized the unquantified and unexercised water rights of Indians, it did so within a system that valued exclusively the active use of water in ways that promoted the highest public benefit. No justice expected non-Indians to put their agricultural or industrial development schemes on hold until Indians might quantify their water rights. And once Indian water rights became an issue for litigation, the vested rights of other water users could not be overlooked. Consequently, *Winters* promised but did not deliver water to reservations such as that of the Yakamas.

In the first thirty years of the twentieth century, Yakama water rights did not fare well against the claims of other water users. On-reservation reclamation in conjunction with reservation farming developed slowly and on a smaller scale than did the projects of neighboring non-Indian settlers. After *Winters*, the Bureau and Reclamation Service attempted to diffuse the Yakamas' still-undefined treaty rights to water in order to protect the future of non-Indian reclamation efforts in the Yakima Basin. The result was the marginalization of Yakama rights to waters of the Yakima River and Ahtanum Creek, and the irreversible transformation of the world of plentiful water that the Yakama had known before the arrival of non-Indians.

Indian Water Rights in the Courts

By Professor Waller's calculations in 1904, appropriative filings in Yakima and Kittitas counties far exceeded the available water in streams and storage facilities, leaving "not even enough to water a thirsty dog."[6] Both before and after Washington passed its water code in 1917, water users were locked into a fierce competition for every available drop and were demanding ever-increasing storage facilities to exploit still-untapped sources. User conflicts often ended up in the courts, although it was not unusual for individuals to settle matters on their own with guns, axes, or dynamite. In 1905, Washington Irrigation Company engineers, on their attorneys' advice, blew up a storage dam run by the Union Gap Irrigation Company at Lake Cle Elum when insufficient water threatened to destroy crops in the Sunnyside Project.[7] Yet such spectacular tactics were not the rule, and the bulk of everyday water user disputes took place between farmers and the ditchrider—an individual who both administered and policed water running into irrigation ditches. While the Reclamation Service supplied water "within a reasonable distance" of the

---

'Winters' Decision and Indian Water Rights: A Mystery Reexamined," *Western Historical Quarterly* 13 (1982): 17-42.

[6] O. L. Waller, *A Report on Irrigation Conditions in the Yakima Valley, Washington*, Bulletin 61 (Pullman, WA: Washington State Agricultural College and School of Science Experiment Station, 1904): 22 [hereafter cited as Waller Report].

[7] *State v. Tiffany*, 44 Wash. 602, 87 P. 932 (1906). See John Fahey, *The Inland Empire: Unfolding Years* (Seattle: University of Washington Press, 1986): 99-100, for a description of the "irrigation war."

highest point of each piece of land, farmers had to build their own sublaterals to move the water around their property. Ditchriders were responsible for dividing water among many users and "turning out a head" of water for each farmer, an inexact process which prompted many disputes and occasionally required a state hydrographer to intervene.[8] Amid that turmoil, Indian water rights were an unwelcome competitor for an already over-taxed resource.[9]

In the Yakima Basin, Ahtanum Creek, Yakima River, and many smaller streams were quickly appropriated. Because people were taking more water out of the rivers than ever before—for irrigation, hydropower, and municipal use—competition among water users grew steadily. Despite Washington's Water Code, appropriative filings continued to pile on top of one another with little coordination of their implementation.[10]

Conflicts over water rights involving Indians no doubt often were motivated by the same tensions that fueled water disputes among non-Indians. Yet controversies involving Indians differed in one important respect: Indians did not acquire their water rights from the state, and prior to the *Winters* decision in 1908 there was little agreement on what other basis, if any, Indians could assert such rights. The Yakama experience provides a vivid example. Although their Treaty of 1855 contained provisions that could not be carried out without water, nowhere in the document was there an explicit water right.[11] Because Indians were wards of the government and held their land in trust, they could not make appropriations of water on their own and had to rely on the agent to make appropriations on their behalf.

Until 1903, the Bureau's policy was not to file notices of appropriations under state law on the reasoning that states had no authority over water on federal public lands. While legally promising, on the ground this theory was quickly made moot by the ample claimants who were filing under state law. Because off-reservation appropriations were draining streams bordering the reservation without any regard for Indians' prior (unrecorded) diversions, in

---

[8] C. A. Olberg, "Investigation of Complaints of Board of Directors of Yakima Reservation Irrigation District in Regard to Wapato Project" [hereafter cited as Olberg "Investigation"], 1929, file 42962-21-[341], pt. 3A (marked 51656-20-341), YA, CCF, BIA, RG 75, NA, 12. On modern ditchriders, whose tasks include making sure that sufficient instream flows remain to protect fish, see Kate Campbell, "Ditch Tender Keeps the Water Flowing," *PG&E Progress* (Jan. 1990): 4-5.

[9] For a detailed chronology and examination of water rights disputes involving the Yakama Nation, see John Arthur Bower, "The Hydrogeography of Yakima Indian Nation Resource Use" (Ph.D. diss., University of Washington, Seattle, 1990).

[10] Fahey, *Inland Empire*, 100.

[11] Treaty with the Yakama, 12 Stat 951 (1855). Art. 2 provides that the reservation, which is bounded by the Yakima River and Ahtanum Creek, is "reserved ... for the use and occupation" of the tribe. By Art. 3, the tribe reserved "The exclusive right of taking fish in all the streams, where running through or bordering said reservation." Arts. 4, 5, and 6 provide for Yakama to take up farming. Art. 10 reserves to the tribe the Wenatshapam fishery.

1903 the Bureau requested that the Yakima Agent file on new appropriations with the state as a precaution against conflicting claims. Consequently, Agent Lynch filed a notice of appropriation from the Yakima River to supply a Bureau canal.[12] After 1905, when Washington reserved all remaining unappropriated waters of the Yakima River for the Reclamation Service's exclusive use, the question of what rights the tribe had to the river became much more complicated.[13]

Non-Indian water users had many reasons to believe that Indians had restricted water rights or none at all, and they acted accordingly. For example, irrigators on the north side of Ahtanum Creek virtually drained the stream where it bordered the reservation in 1889 and 1891, leaving Yakama there with no water for their stock, farms, and fishery.[14] When Bureau officials attempted to re-divert water to the reservation in the dry summer of 1892, the northside users brought suit.

Northside users argued that Yakama had no rights to Ahtanum Creek water because they were mere occupants of the reservation. Further, because the treaty made no specific mention of a reservation of water, Indians should be made to appropriate water under state law as everyone else did, they thought.[15] Additionally, as Washington's common law of water rights moved toward a beneficial use standard for both riparian and prior appropriators, most non-Indians believed that the Indians had forfeited any rights they may have had because of non-use.

The Supreme Court's 1908 *Winters* decision, although it left many questions unanswered, recognized for the first time the existence of treaty-based Indian water rights. "The Indians had command of the lands and the waters—command of all their beneficial use.... Did they give up all this?" the Court asked.[16] In determining that tribes would not have agreed to confinement on reservations without the necessities to support their lives there, the Court found that the tribes had reserved water by treaty even where the treaty made no explicit mention of water. Since treaties were agreements among sover-

---

[12] "McGC," Memo, Jan. 10, 1912, YA, CCF, BIA, RG 75, NA. In February 1908, OIA instructed Lynch to file on unappropriated waters of Toppenish, Simcoe, and Satus creeks. Code to Sec. of Int., Feb. 19, 1908, file 12670-08-341, YA, CCF, BIA, RG 75, NA; C.F. Larrabee, acting CIA, to Lynch, March 12, 1908, ibid.; Larrabee to Code, March 12, 1908, ibid. See also BuRec Director to CIA May 19, 1910, file 41663-10-341, YA, BIA, RG 75, NA.

[13] On BuRec's jurisdiction over certain Washington waters, see Fahey, *Inland Empire*, 92-94; Carl J. Bauer, "Labor Without Brains: Water Development, Law, and Policy in Washington State, 1890-1935" (M.S. thesis, University of Wisconsin-Madison, 1988): 58.

[14] P. C. Sullivan, Asst. U.S. Attorney, Tacoma, to W. L. Stabler, Yakima Agent, Dec. 27, 1890, box 116, folder 3, Click Relander Papers, Yakima Valley Regional Library, Yakima, Wash. [hereafter cited as box:file, CRP]; *CIA-AR*, 1889, 293; *CIA-AR*, 1891, 462.

[15] W. H. Code to Secretary of the Interior, Oct. 17, 1907, file 85193-07-341, YA, CCF, BIA, RG 75, NA.

[16] 207 U.S. 576 (1908).

eigns, Indian rights were federally protected and superior to state law. Thus, Indian water rights did not depend on state definition under the doctrines of appropriative or riparian rights.[17]

While *Winters* recognized an Indian water right, it did not specify what quantity of water the Indians held.[18] Much as the Supreme Court's 1905 Yakama fishing rights case had recognized a tribal right to fish superior to state law yet subject to state regulation, *Winters* affirmed a lower court decree that stated whites "can acquire no right to the exclusion of the reasonable needs of the Indians."[19] The Court did not define what "reasonable needs" were, nor to what extent non-Indian water use could curtail that of Indians. A subsequent federal decision in 1908 held that the tribes were entitled to sufficient waters to meet present and future uses.[20] Although in later years federal courts held that Indians could use their water rights for more than simply agricultural uses and were entitled to amounts necessary to develop reservation resources, during the period between *Winters* and 1934 there was no rule for determining the quantity of water to which tribes might be entitled.[21]

Winters confused the question of whether the tribes or the federal government had the power to reserve water.[22] While some federal-tribal mixture of authority had set Indian water rights above state law to the extent that tribes would not lose their water rights through non-use or inability to use "diligence" in putting the water to "beneficial use," Indian rights still functioned in a system of state-created rights where those standards applied to everyone else. Those waters that Indians failed to appropriate had already filled the

---

[17] 207 U.S. at 577-78. See also Felix S. Cohen, *Handbook of Federal Indian Law* (1982 ed.) (Charlottesville: The Michie Company, 1982): 581-85. In *Winters*, even though settlers along the Milk River near the Fort Belknap Indian reservation had appropriated water and beneficially applied it before members of the Assiniboine and Gros Ventre tribes had done so, the Indians could still assert a paramount claim on the basis of an implied right to water in their treaty of 1888.

[18] On the history of *Winters*, see Hundley, "The 'Winters' Decision and Indian Water Rights."

[19] Quoted in Hundley, "The 'Winters' Decision and Indian Water Rights," 36.

[20] *Conrad Investment Co. v. United States*, 161 F. 829, 831 (9th Cir. 1908). In *Arizona v. California*, 373 U.S. 546, 600 (1963), the Court employed the *Conrad* rule. See also *Cappaert v. United States*, 426 U.S. 128, 141 (1976), noting that "The implied-reservation-of-water doctrine, however, reserves only that amount of water necessary to fulfill the purpose of the reservation, no more."

[21] Cohen, *Handbook*, 588-589, discusses some of the purposes for which tribes have been able to apply their water rights. This was determined in *Winters* itself, 207 U.S. 577. For the subsequent scope of tribes' reserved water rights, see Cohen, ibid., 588-89, and notes 73-79.

[22] 207 U.S. at 577-78. "The power of the Government to reserve the waters and exempt them from appropriation under the state laws is not denied, and could not be," McKenna wrote for the Court. The issue of whether federal or tribal authority provided the basis of the Indians' rights was also an ambiguous question in *United States v. Winans*, 198 U.S. 371 (1905) (another McKenna opinion). See Hundley, "Dark and Bloody Ground," 469-70; Hundley, "The 'Winters' Decision and Indian Water Rights," 33-35; and Cohen, *Handbook*, 590-91.

ditches and canals of others. When tribes were ready to exercise their dormant water rights it was unlikely that they could bring successful claims to condemn vested property rights of non-Indian water users who had worked to develop the resource:[23]

The reserved rights articulated by the Court in *Winters* were more like the anachronistic riparian rights to "quiet enjoyment" of property without a requirement of beneficial use, than like the new water rights advanced by western states. While *Winters* recognized that Indians often would not be able to make beneficial use of water before their non-Indian counterparts, even asserting explicitly that this did not matter to the integrity of the right, it certainly interfered with the vested water rights of hundreds—even thousands—of other water users who stood to lose their water when Indians finally made their appropriations. *Winters* thus established the existence of Indian reserved rights to water, but did not address how much water had been reserved, who had reserved it, or the relationship between the reserved water rights and vested rights under state law.

The Chilling Effect of *Winters*

In the years following *Winters*, Indian water rights at Yakima were determined more by what the case did not say than what it promised. Non-Indian water users perceived the Yakamas' potential water rights as a threat and they worked with their congressional representatives, especially Senator Jones, to head off any attempt to settle Yakama water rights in the courts. Moreover, the decision played to the institutional conflicts within the Department of Interior, as the Secretary—acting both for tribes and for the Bureau of Reclamation constituents—was left to work out the practical effect of the Court's rule. Although Yakama worked tirelessly to begin *Winters*-based litigation on their own, without the permission of their trustees they could achieve little through the courts.[24] Thus, despite the paramount place guaranteed to Indian water rights by the *Winters* decision, on the Yakama Reservation, *Winters* had a chilling effect on the tribe's ability to litigate their water rights.

The Secretary of Interior had ultimate authority over Indian affairs, including water rights, because of the oversight of Indian affairs vested in that office by Congress.[25] The Dawes Act of 1887, for example, authorized the

---

[23] *United States v. Ahtanum Irr. Dist.*, 236 F.2d 321, 327-28 (1956).

[24] In 1913, a group of Wenatchee Indians living on Mission Creek near Cashmere, Washington, hired a law firm to protect their rights to water in the Yaksum irrigation ditch. OIA approved of their suit, but did not appear on their behalf because the Indians held their lands in fee, thereby terminating federal trust responsibility for the property. Oscar H. Lipps, Supervisor, to CIA, May 17, 1913, file 24718-13-341, CCF, YA, BIA, RG 75, NA. Lipps noted that the Indians were able to pay the $150-200 fee for handling the case. It would be worthwhile to do a search of lower state court records to determine whether Indian plaintiffs took more such cases into court on their own.

[25] 236 F.2d at 334-35.

secretary "to prescribe such rules and regulations as he may deem necessary to secure a just and equal distribution" of water necessary to irrigate allotments.[26] Yet the Department of Interior's primary mission throughout the period was to foster speedy white western settlement and the development of the West's resources.

Reclamation Service officials decided as early as 1905 that Indian irrigation was at most a worthless endeavor in the Yakima Valley and at the least a stumbling block to its Yakima River Project and the Valley's water development generally.[27] While Reclamation Service officials recognized that Yakama had treaty claims to water following *Winters*, they wanted to suppress them to ensure the success of off-reservation projects. Ralph Williamson, a Reclamation Service attorney, noted that Yakama litigation of Ahtanum Creek waters would unravel the entire system of water rights in the Basin because a Yakama victory would throw the rights of all other users into question.[28] Similarly, W. H. Code, chief engineer of the Indian Bureau's own Irrigation Service, reported in 1907: "The reclamation engineers in charge of the Yakima project are very anxious that litigation may be avoided on the Ahtanum, fearing that a start made in this direction might ultimately spread to the Yakima Valley, and involve the country in a sea of litigation which might stop all reclamation work."[29]

Non-Indian water users off the reservation generally saw their interests as being pitted against those of Yakama farmers and on-reservation white irrigators. Because those off-reservation users relied upon the Reclamation Service's golden eggs, they rallied against any threat to their goose. In 1913, as litigation of Yakima River water rights seemed imminent, One North Yakima newspaper declared that any litigation of Indian water rights was "an attack—and an unnecessary attack—upon every interest of the Yakima country." Such litigation would spell the end of all Basin water rights as "50 attorneys"

---

[26] 24 Stat. 390, § 7 (1887).

[27] Bower notes that by August 1905 BuRec officials believed that Yakama water rights, if adjudicated, (1) would diminish any water rights BuRec could acquire when it took over the Sunnyside project, (2) would hamper its ability to deliver water on existing contracts for Sunnyside, (3) would make it impossible to get white water users to sign limiting agreements, (4) would destroy the future of the Yakima reclamation project. Bower, "Hydrogeography of Yakima Nation Resource Use," 361-62.

[28] Williams to Lynch, Jan. 20, 1908, folder "1902-03," Letters Received re: Irrigation Matters, 1903-08, YA, BIA, RG 75, NA-Seattle; Williams to Joseph Jacobs, BuRec district engineer, Sept. 25, 1907, file 85193-07-341, YA, CCF, BIA, RG 75, NA; "Historic Agreement of 1908 Is Basis for Half-Century of Court Debate on Splitting Ahtanum Water Rights," *Yakima Herald*, Nov. 15, 1957, 76:5. See also Bower, "Hydrogeography of Yakima Resource Use," 408-09, citing correspondence in the Records of the Bureau of Reclamation, Record Group 115, National Archives.

[29] Code to Secretary of Interior, Oct. 17, 1907.

litigated for decades to settle the issues.[30] A Toppenish paper, whose circulation reached primarily on-reservation water users, accused North Yakima citizens—led by Senator Jones—of conspiring to steal water rights.[31]

The Indian Bureau was well aware that Yakama had rights to water in light of *Winters'* conclusion that treaty provisions which referred to agriculture meant water to support it.[32] Yet the Bureau was all-too willing to allow the tribe to suffer rather than threaten the existing scheme of off-reservation water rights. Although Acting Commissioner C. F. Larrabee believed that the Yakamas could win the entire low flow of the Yakima River if they went to court, he noted:

> The office would also greatly regret an outcome which would deprive the settlers who have been there for many years of all low water and render their lands useless. These settlers certainly have equities if not legal rights against the Indians and I am heartily in favor of any settlement, which, while fair to the Indians, will not wholly deprive the settlers of water for irrigation.[33]

The Indian Bureau actually used its willingness to compromise treaty rights as a bargaining point with non-Indian water users, whom they reminded were likely to get a much better deal for themselves under compromise agreements than if Indians were allowed to litigate.[34]

Yakama consistently protested the marginalization of their water rights claims, especially following the notorious Jones Act.[35] In 1911 the Yakama

---

[30] *Yakima Republic*, Oct. 29, 1913.

[31] "Overdue Anxiety," *Toppenish Review*, Oct. 31, 1913; "Yakima Foam," *Toppenish Review*, Nov. 7, 1913.

[32] E.B. Meritt, OIA law clerk, Memo, Jan. 20, 1913, file 131730-13-341, YA, CCF, BIA, RG 75, NA. Meritt's memo relied upon both the Yakamas' treaty of 1855 and the Secretary of Interior's authority to reserve water for Indian agriculture under 24 Stat. 390, § 7. Although Meritt's memo recommended that OIA and DOI take "every proper action necessary to recover and secure to the Yakima Indians all water rights to which they are entitled," he also wrote that "The decisions of the Federal courts would, no doubt, be calamitous to the present status and arrangement [of water rights]." Meritt believed that even if OIA chose to ignore the Yakamas' *Winters* claim, the tribe could still win 50 percent of the Yakima River based on such Washington case law as *Benton v. Johncox*. Meritt's memo also raised the issue of whether Yakama should receive their water from the Yakima River's natural flow or from storage waters on the river. The issue of storage versus natural flow is a complex question, discussed in Bower, "Hydrogeography of Yakima Resource Use," 370-72ff.

[33] Larrabee to Secretary of Interior, n.d., but 1908, quoted in "Historic Agreement of 1908," 76:5, CRP.

[34] Code to Secretary of Interior, Oct 17, 1907, file 85193-07-341, YA, CCF, BIA, RG 75, NA.

[35] W. H. Code to Secretary of Interior, April 27, 1911, file 33123-11-341, YA, CCF, BIA, RG 75, NA. Code reported a growing "feeling of antagonism on the part of many Indians" as well as white reservation land owners who did not want to sell their lands to secure water. "The situation is growing critical on the reservation and many meetings of whites are being held, also councils among the Indians."

Council appointed a committee of 14 members to confer with the Secretary of Interior about lands, tribal moneys, and what DOI planned to do about building an on-reservation irrigation project.[36] In 1913 the Council elected a 20-man committee "to represent our business on this water question[;] we estimate our Irrigation waters are stolen by the reclamation service is worth to eight millions of dollars we are not going to sleep and be blindfolded no we are going to make fight with Senator Jones no flies about it[.]"[37] Yakama continued to lobby, organize, and petition for the recognition of their water rights throughout the period.[38] The Yakama Tribal Council especially targeted U.S. Senator Miles C. Poindexter as their ally in this fight.[39]

Officials worried that Yakama eventually would force them to recognize their rights under *Winters*. A 1912 Indian Bureau memo noted, for example, that "[t]here are some intelligent Indians among the Yakimas and at any time this [Yakima River water rights] matter may be brought into court...."[40] Bureau and Department of Interior officials also worried that they might be seen as giving Indian rights away. "This grant of a right of way to the Klickitat Company [for irrigation development] never appealed to me," wrote one official in 1912. "It looks as though we are giving away valuable water rights, or water power, from the Indians to the non-Indian settlers within the Horse Heaven country. It appears that we can't use the water now, but in 15 or 20 years conditions may change and it would be a Pima situation over again, with charges of our having given away the water of the Indians."[41]

---

[36] R. S. Holt, to W. L. Fisher, Secretary of Interior, June 17, 1911, file 57024-11-341, YA, CCF, BIA, RG 75, NA.

[37] Mann, corresponding secretary, Yakima Tribal Council, White Swan [hereafter YTC-WS], to Poindexter, May 2, 1913, 76:13, MCPP. See also Mann to Poindexter, Jan. 24, 1912, 76:13, MCPP.

[38] See, for example, Chief Saluskin petition to CIA, Feb. 19, 1913: "We ... claim and know all our property rights are absolutely ours regarding the irrigation upon Yakima Indian Reservation.... We claim positive rights to all creeks upon this Reservation...." 76:13, MCPP.

[39] Mann to Poindexter, Nov. 18, 1914, 76:13, MCPP; Mann to Poindexter, Jan. 25, 1916, 76:12, MCPP (discussing Chief Alex Sluskin's trips to Washington, D.C.); Mann to Poindexter, Feb. 2, 1916, 76:12, MCPP; Mann to Poindexter, Feb. 29, 1916, 76:12, MCPP; E. B. Meritt to Chief Saluskin, Kiutus James, et al., Feb. 5, 1916, 76:12, MCPP. On Poindexter's efforts on behalf of Yakama interests, see, for example, Poindexter to Mann, March 6, 1914, 76:13, MCPP; Poindexter to Yakima Indians, May 28, 1919, 76:12, MCPP.

[40] "McGC," Memo, Jan. 10, 1912, file 131730-13-341, YA, CCF, BIA, RG 75, NA, noting that it is not seen how further delay on the part of this Office to, protect the Reclamation Service and the white settlers would be justified."

[41] Chief Land Division, DOI, Memo, March 1, 1912, file 3699-10-341, pt. 1, YA, CCF, BIA, RG 75, NA. In his 1913 memo on *Winters* as a basis for Yakama water rights, Meritt, enclosed a copy of a letter regarding OIA's actions on the Pima reservation, where officials had been accused of giving away Indian water rights. Meritt, memo, Jan. 20, 1913, file 131730-13-341, YA, CCF, BIA, RG 75, NA.

Commissioner Valentine, too, looking at letters from a reservation filled with angry water users, had glimpsed the bleak results of the Yakama water rights compromises. "The Indians' rights to water have not been acknowledged by the Reclamation Service," he wrote in a 1912 letter to the Secretary of Interior "and this Office has pursued a quiescent and conciliatory policy of not encouraging any belief that their rights would be asserted and protected, as a result of which the [Yakama] reservation has borne the hardships incident to the shortage of water in the valley."[42]

While officials debated the appropriate course, irrigators on the reservation battled one another with both firearms and law. William Colwash's story of being assaulted by a deputy sheriff was not unique. "There are men who carry revolver guns in their [fields]," Louis Mann complained in 1913. "[A]nd ... if our white rentors [sic] brother want to scare us out of our Irrigation waters [we] wish you could put him out of our reservation to avoid all the troubles." Charles Myers "always has a gun in his person" and patrols the Indians' Yemowat ditch on the Ahtanum Creek preventing Indians from getting water onto their lands.[43] Non-Indians who purchased allotments increased water use on the properties, leaving lower riparians without adequate (or without any) water.[44]

Off-reservation irrigators resorted to local courts to obtain injunctions against Yakima Agency officials to prevent them from diverting water onto the reservation.[45] OIA officials and Yakama implemented their own ad hoc justice by ripping out dams that interfered with reservation facilities. Two Yakama were arrested and jailed in 1912 because they "broke open the headgates" of a canal diverting water away from their land.[46] Such violence continued through the period.[47]

---

[42] CIA to Secretary of Interior, March 15, 1912, file 16201-12-341, YA, CCF, BIA, RG 75, NA.

[43] Mann to CIA, May 14, 1913, file 55328-13-341, YA, CCF, BIA, RG 75, NA. See also complaint against Frank Fox, who allegedly stole water rights belonging to Yakama, Jacob Hunt, leading to a DOJ investigation, Acting CIA to Carr, Dec. 20, 1912, file 133661-12-115, YA, CCF, GR, BIA, RG 75, NA.

[44] Don Carr to CIA, Jan. 23, 1913, referring to Alex Tio's and Chief Stwire's water complaints, file 2129-13-341, YA, CCF, BIA, RG 75, NA; Carr to Francis A. Garrecht, U.S. Attorney, Spokane, April 6, 1915, ibid.

[45] Bower, "Hydrogeography of Yakima Resource Use," 359-62ff.

[46] The individuals were Sam Ashue and Paul Hoptowit. Council Proceedings of Yakima Indians, Fort Simcoe, WA, June 2, 1913, folder "Councils and Meetings (tribal) 1913-25," Tribal Records, 1897-1952, YA, BIA, RG 75, NA-Seattle.

[47] Estep to CIA, May 11, 1929, file 9225-1936-341, part 0-1, YA, CCF, BIA, RG 75, NA, noting that things are getting violent on reservation; incidents include a ditchrider being verbally and physically attacked by a lessee. Estep was concerned because it was not yet even July, when real water shortages usually began. In 1927, after off-reservation users flagrantly violated the 1908 Ahtanum Creek agreement, CIA Burke ordered Agent Estep to divert as much water as the Yakama required (intervention by Sen. Jones stopped Estep from taking

In a 1913 Yakima Tribal Council meeting, Harvey Shuster expressed the frustration felt by many Indian water users: "It seems that the white people has the full control of that water down there and the Indians have very little voice in the water...."[48] Louis Mann put it this way: "Now just as if I had a piece of bread in my mouth and the whiteman he comes up and pulls that out of my mouth, now how am I [going] to get a living that way[?]"[49]

Yakama lobbying efforts and the potential for public accusations of mismanagement succeeded only in driving Bureau officials into the waiting arms of the Reclamation Service and Washington congressmen who were ready to bargain away Yakama water rights outside the courts. As a result, the tribe's water rights to the Yakima River and Ahtanum Creek were determined in a series of ad hoc arrangements among the Reclamation Service, Department of Interior, and off-reservation water users and their congressional representatives, and with the Indian Bureau's acquiescence. These compromises will be treated in turn. The specter of unexercised Indian water rights was not powerful enough to challenge the existing distribution of water rights in the Valley until well after 1934.

In 1905, Yakama were limited to 147 cubic feet per second (c.f.s.) flow of the Yakima River according to an order of the Secretary of Interior, while white non-Indian users received 2065 c.f.s. Reservation users received this small amount because the Reclamation Service and Indian Bureau agreed to limit on- and off-reservation users to the amounts they used in 1905, a year during which reservation users were restricted by at least two injunctions stopping them from diverting more.[50]

On-reservation irrigators—both Indian and non-Indian—immediately protested. On-reservation non-Indian irrigators saw their own interests aligned with Indian irrigators because they correctly believed that any successful treaty claims to water would reduce the cost of getting water on their lands. Large landholders also saw treaty water rights as a way to circumvent the 160-

---

action), *United States v. Ahtanum Irr. Dist.*, 236 F.2d 321, n. 12. In fact, non-Indian diversions were increasing, as their land holdings increased.

[48] Council Proceedings of Yakima Indians, Ft. Simcoe, Wash., June 2, 1913, folder "Councils and Meetings (Tribal) 1913-25," Tribal Records, 1897-1952, YA, BIA, RG 75, NA-Seattle.

[49] Council Proceedings of Yakima Indians, Fort Simcoe, Wash., June 2, 1913, folder "Councils and Meetings (Tribal) 1913-15," Tribal Records, 1897-1952, YA, BIA, RG 75, NA-Seattle. An interesting question raised here is whether lack of water among on-reservation users led to, inter-tribal disputes. I came across only one case: Bill Charley and Martin Speedis both led small factions that clashed over the use of water (as well as fishing rights, see Chapter 8), file 133661-12-115, YA, CCF, GR, BIA, RG 75, NA.

[50] See R. G. Valentine to Secretary of Interior, Mar 15, 1912, file no 16201-12k341, YA, CCF, BIA, RG 75, NA; Jay Lynch to Harry S. Jones, April 29, 1913, box 1, folder 3, Henry J. Snively Papers, Accession no 3095, University of Washington Libraries Manuscript Collection, Seattle, Wash [hereafter HJSP, box:file]. Lynch's letter gives background to the events leading up to the 147 c.f.s. allocation, which he believed may have originated in the amount of unallocated water left in the river after all other appropriations had been tallied.

acre irrigated acreage limitation of the Reclamation Act.[51] "We are to all intents and purposes as much wards of the Government under present conditions as are the Indians," one white farmer wrote in 1914.[52]

Yakama were not unified in their views of how best to promote their irrigation claims. Yakama Tribal Council members, for example, argued that the tribe should be supplied from natural flow, not storage, which would have eliminated significant storage costs borne by other water users. Yakama were well aware that non-Indian users intended to reap the benefits of their legal entitlements, and so they petitioned the Bureau to exclude non-Indians from benefitting from any on-reservation irrigation projects.[53] Yet non-Indian, on-reservation farmers had political power which the tribe had not, and some Yakama saw that they could further their own interests through cooperation.[54] To Secretary of Interior Walter L. Fisher (1911-1913), cooperation was infinitely preferable, from the standpoint of the Reclamation Service's future in the basin, to having the tribe force litigation to resolve an indefinite treaty right to the Yakima River.[55]

In 1912, the Reservation Water Users Association, a joint white-Indian group, hired an attorney to bring suit on the Yakama's claim to half the Yakima River flow. The threat of this litigation and the Reservation Water Users Association's pressure on Congress to take some action finally resulted in a 1914 legislative provision that increased the reservation's water entitlement to 720 c.f.s. during minimum flow; or sufficient water to irrigate 70,000 acres at 40 acres for each allottee.[56]

---

[51] W. H. Code, Chief Engineer, OIA-IIS, to Secretary of Interior, April 27, 1911, file 33123-11-341, YA, CCF, BIA, RG 75, NA.

[52] Secretary, Yakima Reservation Water Users Association, to Franklin K. Lane, July 17, 1914, file 73870-14-341, YA, CCF, BIA, RG 75, NA.

[53] YTC-WS to CIA, petition, enclosed in L. V. McWhorter to CIA, April 13, 1911, file 34334-11-341, YA, CCF, BIA, RG 75, NA.

[54] There were at least three on-reservation irrigators' associations, the Yakima Indian Water Users Association, Ahtanum Creek Indian Water Users Association, and the Reservation Water Users Association. It would be useful to compare the memberships and agendas of these groups.

[55] Bower, quoting Fisher letter, Jan. 23, 1913, in "Hydrogeography of Yakima Resource Use," 442.

[56] Act of Aug. 1, 1914, 38 stat. 604-05. The 1914 Act authorized OIA to purchase water from BuRec's storage projects to create an on-reservation, low-water supply of at least 720 c.f.s., which was sufficient to provide each allotment with irrigation water for 40 acres. The arrangement, worked until 1921 when BIA and BuRec negotiated a new purchase agreement. In 1930 BIA considered litigation again after BuRec threatened to limit the reservation's water supply unless BIA paid for the construction of further storage projects. Thereafter, the two agencies continued to muddle through ad hoc arrangements while skirting litigation. Bower, "Hydrogeography of Yakima Resource Use," 442-48.

Meanwhile, on Ahtanum Creek, Yakama water users faced the same problems as had their counterparts on the Yakima River.[57] Fear of litigation at Ahtanum eventually resulted in a 1908 Interior Department order that divided the Creek's waters by the amount of acreage irrigated by north and south side users, respectively; a 75 percent–25 percent allocation.[58] Yakama repeatedly asserted that they had never agreed to the allocation established in the 1908 decree and they did not understand why they should settle for less than half of the creek waters, which they believed they could get in a *Winters*-based claim.[59] Yet the Bureau would not start an adjudication of their rights.[60]

---

[57] The Indian Irrigation Service completed a dam and ditch for reservation use on the Ahtanum in 1894, and Yakama had built several small ditches on the Ahtanum as well. Bower notes that by 1894, white settlers on the north side of the creek had run "nearly 80 ditches," all of which ran water continuously. See "Hydrogeography of Yakima Indian Nation Resource Use," 396. For a detailed history of the Ahtanum Creek water rights disputes, see ibid. at 391-428, 448-62.

[58] The estimated actual irrigated acreage was 4,500 acres (northside/whites) and 1,500 (southside/reservation). On the agreement and Secretarial Order, see Wathen to Collier, [n.d.], file 9225-36-341, YA, CCF, BIA, RG 75, NA; Frank Pierce, Acting Secretary of Interior, to CIA, July 3, 1908, enclosing contract between the United States and white water users (May 11, 1908), file 85193-07-341, YA, CCF, BIA, RG 75, NA; "Historic Agreement of 1908," 76:5, CRP. See also Holt to CIA, Sept. 4, 1923, file 9225-26-341, part 0-1, YA, BIA, RG 75, NA, noting that "I further know that the white owners have never lived up to the agreement entered into in 1908, which I understood was largely for the benefit of the whites and to keep the matter out of the courts at that time." See also Holt to CIA, April 27, 1931, file 9225-36-341, Part 0-3, YA, CCF, BIA, RG 75, NA, arguing that DOI's Solicitor had no idea of what the real situation was on the reservation and that Yakama water rights should run to the thread of the stream, giving them a 50 percent share of the flow.

[59] The following petitions were sent by Yakama:

—Petition of allottee and land owners on Ahtanum Project, Sept. 11, 1923, file 9225-26-341, part 0-1, YA, CCF, BIA, RG 75, NA.
—Petition of Ahtanum water users to BIA, May 15, 1929, file 9225-1936-341, part 0-1, YA, CCF, BIA, RG 75, NA. The petition was signed by 56 Indians and 28 whites, who stated that the 1908 agreement was unfair and that a *Winters*-based claim likely would result in a 50-50 division. They demand action. Estep to CIA, May 11, 1929, ibid., suggested that people signing this petition did not know what they were signing.
—Petition of Noah Saluskin, Frank Selatsee, and at least 37 other Yakama owning land under the Ahtanum Irrigation Project, June 22, 1931, file 9225-36-341, Part 0-3, YA, CCF, BIA, RG 75, NA (this petition is signed by both men and women).
—William Adams, Chairman Ahtanum Indian Water Users Association, to Henry J. Scattergood, Asst. CIA, Jan. 21, 1932, file 9225-36-341, YA, CCF, BIA, RG 75, NA, demanding litigation in federal court to, secure 50 percent of Ahtanum flow.
—Ahtanum Indian Water Users Association to CIA, March 4, 1932, file 9225-36-341, YA, CCF, BIA, RG 75, NA, stating that the temporary agreement was "forced upon our local officials" and that no Indian water users could attend the meeting. They requested litigation on the basis of *Winters*, noting that "we know this matter, will never be settled only in court from all indications."
—Petition of Indians at White Swan to CIA, 1936, file 9225-26-341, part 0-1, YA, CCF, BIA, RG 75, NA, asking for an investigation of using the Klickitat River as a source for

Each time Yakama pointed out that the existing allocation was unfair, water users on the north side of the creek and their allies in Congress stalled the proceedings and secured temporary agreements, a pattern which continued through the 1930s.[61] Non-Indian water users even tried to get Congress to ratify the 1908 agreement to remove it from potential litigation.[62] "Several hundred farmers face total destruction of crops and inevitable bankruptcy," Senator Jones wrote in 1931, voicing his constituents' fears of the potential impact of Yakama water rights adjudication. To Jones, the only issue of importance in the division of Ahtanum Creek Waters in favor of non-Indian irrigators.[63] One Bureau official suspected that state authorities were secretly encouraging white off-reservation water users to take a hard line approach to Yakama water rights in order to discourage Indian claims.[64]

---

supplying Indian farms in Medicine Valley, where the Toppenish-Simcoe project will not reach.

Even Senator Jones admitted that the 1908 agreement was never put before the Yakama. See also 236 P.2d 332, nn. 17-18, quoting testimony of Sen. Jones before the Senate Committee on Indian Affairs.

[60] *United States v. Ahtanum Irr. Dist.*, 236 F.2d 321, n. 12 (1956).

[61] In 1931, a temporary agreement postponed litigation, John H. Lynch to M. T. Albertson, et al., May 21, 1931, file 9225-36-341, part 0-3, YA, CCF, BIA, RG 75, NA. This temporary agreement was in place for the 1932 irrigation season, Wathen to Collier, [n.d.], ibid. Under the agreement, 50 percent of all flow above 60 c.f.s. would go to reservation users; when the flow was between 40 and 60 c.f.s., BIA could divert all but 30 c.f.s.; for flow below 40 c.f.s., OIA received 25 percent plus an additional c.f.s. for the South Fork diversion; for flow less than 25 c.f.s., BIA assumed 25 percent of the losses due to seepage and evaporation, Reed to Maj. W. S. Post, Nov. 30, 1931, ibid; Redman to W. S. Post, BIA director of irrigation, Jan. 22, 1932, ibid. BIA hoped that the temporary agreement could become part of a consent decree eventually to be entered by a federal court, Rhoads, CIA, to C. C. Dill, March 3, 1932, file 9225-36-341, YA, CCF, BIA, RG 75, NA. By 1933 both DOJ and BIA saw litigation as the only solution to continuing difficulties, Watham, Memo on Ahtanum Irrigation Project, [no file] box 24, class 341, YA, CCF, BIA, RG 75, NA.

[62] The legislation failed. See Hearing before the Committee on Indian Affairs, U.S. Senate, 72d Cong., 1st Sess. on S. 3998/ H.R. 10351, April 20, 1932; Wathen to Collier, [n.d.], file 9225-36-341, YA, CCF, BIA, RG 75, NA. During the hearings it became clear that DOI and BIA disagreed over the allocation of water. By this time, CIA Rhoads believed that the Secretary of Interior did not have authority to enter into the agreement, and he knew Yakama petitioners were protesting ratification of the agreement, John H. Lynch to Sen. C. C. Dill, Feb. 8, 1932, file 9225-36-341, YA, CCF, BIA, RG 75, NA. See also Ahtanum Indian Water Users Association to CIA, March 4, 1932, ibid.; William Yemowat, president Yakima Indian Water Users Association, to Sec. of Int., April 19, 1932, telegram, ibid.; *Yakima Morning Herald*, clipping, Feb. 29, 1932.

[63] Jones to President, June 2, 1931, file 9225-36-341, pt. 0-3, YA, CCF, BIA, RG 75, NA.

[64] W. M. Reed, BIA special irrigation engineer, to Major W. S. Post, Nov. 25, 1931, file 9225-36-341, pt. 0-3, YA, CCF, BIA, RG 75, NA (reporting on a meeting between north and south Ahtanum Creek water users, Nov. 25, 1931). A second meeting was held on November 28, at which participants (including the attorney for north side users, Redman, George Clark, OIA-IIS attorney, and Reed) reached a one year agreement that could be extended if practicable. It

Bureau officials agreed that north side users at times took more than their 75 percent allocation of creek waters, even though they did not need that much water and ended up running it back into the creek or swamping their lands with it.[65] Often non-Indians took the water to prevent Indians from getting it. "Every ditch and channel on the white side is running full of water, while the farmer on this side can only get a small amount," wrote Agent Evan Estep (1923-1930) wrote in 1929.[66] Although during the years after 1908 reservation users were able to increase their share of Creek waters, they still received a relatively smaller share than did off-reservation users.

Yet water users, the Reclamation Service, and the Department of Interior steadfastly maintained that no Yakama litigation should be allowed to disturb these "vested" water rights, even though Indian ditches were often dry and white water users themselves were litigating among one another over the distribution of their share of Ahtanum waters through at least 1926.[67] As John H. Lynch, speaking for the north side water users, put it, a successful Indian suit "would open the door to litigation of the whole Yakima River allocation. It would, at least, cast a cloud on all White water rights in the Yakima Valley."[68] The power of the rights set out in the *Winters* decision thus proved no match for the vested property rights of non-Indian water users.

Throughout the period, Yakama farmers on both Ahtanum Creek and the Yakima River received less water than did their non-Indian counterparts. Yakama tirelessly protested the relative distribution of water, which continued to favor non-Indians. "They have complained and quarrelled for so long that the I[n]dian Office is tired of listening to them...," an exasperated Estep wrote in 1924.[69]

---

was not formally signed and the group decided to keep it secret until tempers on both sides cooled.

[65] On off-reservation users over-appropriating water, see Holt to CIA, Sept. 4, 1923, file 9225-26-341, Part 0-1, YA, CCF, BIA, RG 75, NA, noting that Indian lands are in good shape, but much land on north side of creek is alkalied and whites are using water for stock purposes and subirrigation. See also Nealy N. Olney to Sen. Lynn Frazier, chair Indian Affairs Committee, April 30, 1932, telegram, file 9225-36-341, Part 0-3, YA, CCF, BIA, RG 75, NA, stating that whites are letting water go to waste on north side of stream and asking for an increased allocation for the reservation. See also Holt to CIA, April 27, 1931, file 9225-36-341, Part 0-3, YA, CCF, BIA, RG 75, NA, noting that northside irrigators are using two to three natural channels as canals (instead of one, as per agreement) and have only provided weirs and headgates to a limited extent (which they are supposed to do under the agreement).

[66] Estep to CIA, May 11, 1929, file 9225-36-341, Part 0-1, YA, CCF, BIA, RG 75, NA.

[67] Northside water users adjudicated their 75 percent share of the creek in the Washington Supreme Court in *In re Water Rights in Ahtanum Creek*, 245 Pac. 758 (1926). The case assumed the validity of the 1908 agreement.

[68] John H. Lynch to Sen. C. C. Dill, Feb. 8, 1932, file 9225-36-341, YA, CCF, BIA, RG 75, NA. See also American Fruit Growers, Inc. to CIA, telegram, file 9225-36-341, Part 0-3 YA, CCF, BIA, RG 75, NA.

[69] Report of Simcoe Creek Commission.

The more time that passed, however, the harder it was to challenge rights that had vested under the ad hoc agreements of the 1910s. Non-Indian water users near the reservation "will accept a compromise in an emergency and after a little while will claim it as a right and feel badly used when we insist on them living up to their part of the agreement," Estep wrote.[70] In the nearly three decades following *Winters*, the patchworked compromises of Indian water rights retarded reservation agricultural development, especially for Indian farmers, and led to widespread ecological changes in the Yakima River Basin.

Vested Rights and the Yakima Landscape

In the world created by the ad hoc agreements on the Yakima River and Ahtanum Creek, Yakama had no vested rights to water. E. C. Finney, Solicitor for the Department of Interior, wrote three separate opinions between 1929 and 1931 upholding the validity of the 1908 Ahtanum agreement, each turning on the necessity of protecting the vested rights of north side users. In Finny's view, even if the Secretary of Interior had not had authority to make the 1908 agreement, the interests of non-Indian water users were now well-established and could not be disturbed.[71] To Finney and others, Indians potentially had treaty rights under *Winters*, but they remained potential and therefore insignificant in comparison to the established rights of non-Indian users.

Many Yakama certainly wanted to farm their lands, as is evidenced by their numerous petitions and letters over the period. Yet federal officials and non-Indian water users persisted in believing that Indians were poor farmers, and that their resources would be better allocated to non-Indians. This racial bias went hand-in-hand with the rest of the colonial view of Indians as inferior because they lacked an apparent history of settled agriculture.

The financial dependence of Indians on the federal government prohibited them from capitalizing their farms to the same extent as their non-Indian counterparts, or even retaining their lands once the trust period on allotments had expired. Even where Indians were supposed to benefit from Bureau or Reclamation Service projects, many could not afford to pay water delivery and maintenance charges. Chief We-yal-lup Wa-ya-ci-ka complained in 1911 that when the government incorporated his old ditch in a new canal, he was charged $40.00 and $64.00 in 1910 and 1911, respectively, to get his water: "my water rights has been unlawfully Deprived my water has been taken away from me with out grace," he wrote to the CIA Valentine. "I wish you would at the earliest date to Release my water for my use free because why my water

---

[70] Estep to CIA, May 11, 1929, file 9225-36-341, Part 0-1, YA, CCF, BIA, RG 75, NA.

[71] E. C. Finney, DOI Solicitor, opinion on Ahtanum water use, June 7, 1929, file 9225-36-341, Parts 0-1 and 0-3, YA, CCF, BIA, RG 75, NA; Finney, opinion, May 24, 1930, in Wathen to Collier, [n.d.], file 9225-36-341, YA, CCF, BIA, RG 75, NA; Finney, opinion, March 18, 1931, file 9225-36-341, Part 0-3, CCF, BIA, RG 75, NA.

had been already in use thirteen years to my ranch." Wy-ya-ci-ka noted that he would seek an injunction against the government in order to protect his water rights.[72]

Indian agriculture also lagged behind that of non-Indians because Indians were consistently deprived of sufficient water to raise crops as valuable or as extensively as non-Indian water users. Lucillus V. McWhorter, an advocate for Yakama water rights noted in 1920, "It takes no careful observer to ride through the Ahtanum Reservation lands and pick out the Indian tilled lands from those of white owners and lessors. The former invariably present a withered appearance, while those of the whites show fine crops, resultant from sufficient water."[73] To reservation farmers, such contrasts were old news: in 1907, Yakama watched their "crops burn in the sun as water gushed past Sunnyside dam and presumabl[y] on to the sea," William Redman reported.[74]

Many Yakama farmers never received water at all. One Bureau official estimated that only 600 (out of more than 3200 allottees) received any benefit from irrigation projects.[75] John Grinder reported in 1919 that although he had held an allotment near a government ditch for twenty years, he never received water. The Indian agent informed him that if he wanted water, he should pump it onto his land from a drainage ditch.[76] Thomas Sam noted in 1924 that "There is lots of this land [allotted] where there is not water," and an official estimate that year found that allottees on 18,000 acres of land to that date had never received water.[77] The fact that non-Indians believed Yakama farmers were unimportant in the overall development of the basin, therefore, was a self-fulfilling prophecy from which Yakama could not easily break free.

Under the terms of the Yakima River and Ahtanum Creek agreements, less water was delivered to reservation farmers than to off-reservation farmers, as we have seen. But the pattern of water distribution differed as well. Reservation irrigators received most of their water early in the growing season, from natural flowage, before the low flow period set in. Not only did off-reservation users receive more water generally, their supplies were augmented from storage reservoirs. This enabled water delivery to crops throughout the low-flow period. One Bureau official reported in 1949 on the longterm effects of that allocation: "Under present conditions of water use, the development of

---

[72] Wy-ya-ci-ka to Valentine July 24, 1911, file 66121-11-341, YA, CCF, BIA, RG 75, NA.

[73] L. V. McWhorter, *The Discards* (n.p., 1920): 5. See also McWhorter, *The Crime Against the Yakima* (North Yakima, WA: Republic Print, 1913).

[74] Redman to A. L. Smith, water commissioner, Prosser, Wash., Aug. 22, 1907, file 34334-11-341, YA, CCF BIA, RG 75, NA.

[75] McChesney to CIA, report, May 6-20, 1910, file 43398-10-341, YA, CCF, BIA, RG 75, NA. McChesney estimated that upon completion, the Wapato would benefit 1800 allottees, or 56 percent of all reservation allotments.

[76] Agent to John Grinder, Oct. 1919, file 97678-19-341, YA, CCF, BIA, RG 75, NA.

[77] Report of Simcoe Creek Commission. That comes out to 225 allottees of 80 acres apiece.

Indian lands is restricted primarily to alfalfa, grains and hay meadows. Little or no sugar beets, hops or fruit can be raised successfully. The few cases where fruit is grown have required supplemental water from wells or is restricted to early fruit such as cherries."[78] Most Indian farmers grew wheat, and at most could take two cuttings of hay or alfalfa per season. "In other words," L. M. Holt observed in 1927, "the land produces about one half what it would with an adequate water supply."[79]

Additionally, Indian farmers usually did not have the time, capital, or financial security necessary to develop stands of lucrative orchard trees that only began to bear three to five years after planting. Non-Indian lessees, too, kept to short-term crops such as grains and hay, because of their short-term investment interest in the land. "The high prices on hay existing in this valley for the past few years [have] caused a very strong desire on the part of the white people to lease and farm these Indian allotments," J. W. Martin, Superintendent of Irrigation at Yakima, noted in 1910: "And I understand that about 8000 acres were added the past year to the already existing cultivated area which previously to this additional acreage, was very close to the limit that could be taken care of by the amount of water available from the summer low water flow of the Yakima River.[80] Lessees continued to favor grains and other short-term crops throughout the period.[81]

Because the ad hoc water agreements of the 1910s had largely ratified the existing distribution of water to Indian and non-Indian water users, there was little opportunity or incentive for water users to cut waste or improve the efficiency of their water use.[82] Repeated over-irrigation of land north of the reservation created widespread swamping and alkalinization of vast tracts on the reservation.[83] On-reservation lessees, too, had little incentive to conserve their water supplies, nor did many adequately prepare their land for irrigation.[84]

---

[78] "A comparison of the crop reports from 1931 to 1948 shows that the per acre value of the Ahtanum project averaged 52% of the per acre value of the Wapato project," A. L. Wathen to CIA, Memo, Jan. 1949, [no file], box 24, class 341, YA, CCF, BIA, RG 75, NA.

[79] L. M. Holt, testimony for Inspector Trowbridge, June 1927, quoted in American Indian Defense Assoc., Inc., April 1932, "The Yakima Bill, Interior Department's Mock Moral Fervor Suddenly Evaporates," file 9225-36-341, Part 0-3, YA, CCF, BIA, RG 75, NA.

[80] J. W. Martin, OIA superintendent of irrigation, to CIA, Aug 24, 1910, file 72186-10-341, YA, BIA, RG 75, NA.

[81] See Appendix I, Crop Yields, Yakima Reservation, 1918-1935.

[82] See for example, *United States v. Ahtanum Irr. Dist.* 236 F.2d 321, 341 (9th Cir. 1956), noting that at the time of the 1908 agreement dividing Ahtanum Creek water, "irrigation water diverted by the defendants [was] permitted to run to waste upon highways, diverted through open channels with no headgates or measuring devices, old river beds and sloughs used in place of ditches, and the like."

[83] Smith, "Geology and Water Resources of a Portion of Yakima County," 13-14.

[84] OIA-IIS, Indian Irrigation Service, District no. 1, *Annual Report*, file 78600-15-341, YA, CCF, BIA, RG 75, NA, noting, "The entire system, as well as the farmers themselves, are very

In 1909, the Reclamation Service began incorporating drainage structures in the Yakima Irrigation project, but by that time, according to Special Indian Agent Thomas Downs, seepage from irrigation works was "causing a good deal of damage to the low lands." He reported that "under the present plan, nearly as much land is being rendered unfit for farming from seepage as is being benefited by irrigation." He estimated that 12,000 acres, mostly allotments, could no longer be farmed and "the damage is still in progress."[85] By 1915, a report on the Wapato project stated that "Approximately 40,000 acres below the irrigated area has become alkalied and partly submerged."[86]

As salt grass crept over formerly fine pasturelands, benchlands developed severe erosion problems and southern farmers saw their lands transformed into alkali wastelands, contemporary observers pointed at the wasteful irrigation practices going on throughout the basin. According to Waller,

> The drainage problems would be simple if men had to buy water as they buy other commodities. If vested rights did not interfere, the simplest way to cure over irrigation evils would be to fix a limit to the amount of water lands could receive and then sell it to the owner by the acre foot. When a man pays for what he gets he is not so likely to waste it. On the other hand, when there no limit placed on the supply, or his greed, and neither restriction nor penalty for drowning out his neighbor, he spends little time studying how to apply water economically.[87]

Not only did the gravel-based reservation canal and lateral system act as a sieve, but on-reservation farmers themselves were "very wasteful."[88] On the

---

wasteful, inasmuch as the greater part of the canals and main laterals are in gravel, and in the case of the farmers, where the majority lease their land under high rentals, we can hardly expect them to place the land in proper shape for economical irrigation." See also *CIA-AR*, 1905, 370, in which Lynch reported that many lessees were not making profit on their lands and some were losing money. Lessees argued that the leases were not long enough, but Lynch wrote, "...I am inclined to think that but few know how to handle water for irrigating, and that the lands are not put in proper condition and properly leveled to begin with; also that most of the lessees rent and try to cultivate more land than they can properly care for and cultivate."

[85] Thomas Downs, OIA special agent, "Report of Inspection of Yakima Indian School," July 23, 1909, file 85193-07-341, YA, CCF, BIA, RG 75, NA.

[86] OIA-IIS, Indian Irrigation District no 1, *Annual Report*, 1915, file 78600-15-341, YA, CCF, BIA, RG 75, NA. Professor Waller, in a 1904 report, estimated that the damage to lands along the lower Ahtanum totalled "several thousands of acres" alone, Waller, *Report*, 18. See also Snively to John McPhaul, OIA, Dec. 22, 1914, case file "reopening of Yakima Indian Reservation, 1914-15," 1:8, HJSP, noting that "a number of allotments that three years ago were very valuable for agricultural purposes, at least worth $100.00 per acre, are now worth no more than probably $5.00 to $10.00 per acre for pasture, the salt grass having taken them." He advocated state-administered drainage districts.

[87] Waller, *Report*, 19,

[88] OIA-IIS, Indian Irrigation Service, District no. 1, *Annual Report*, file 78600-15-341, YA, CCF, BIA, RG 75, NA; Downs, "Report on Inspection of Yakima School," noting that the main canal on the side of Ahtanum ridge is "quite a distance above the land to be irrigated. As a

reservation, non-Indian lessees made up the majority of farmers, and everyone agreed that they had neither the time nor the economic incentive properly to prepare or irrigate their lands.[89] The problem was endemic to the Basin. "Water users in the valley have been using as much as 10 and 12 acre feet of water per year per acre and in some cases more. This has been largely due to inadequate levelling, improper distribution systems and ignorance or indifference of crop needs."[90] As Waller put it, "Water has been used in lieu of cultivation."[91]

Drainage efforts never caught up with water damage.[92] The problem was one of both constructing a coherent delivery and drainage system in the midst of a "sort of patchwork of development" of inefficient canals and laterals, and training farmers to practice better irrigation methods.[93] Until 1913, ranchers still regularly ran their waste water into reservation roads, where the resulting mudholes trapped unsuspecting travelers and new motorists.[94] Although Yakima Agents tried to enforce rules regulating waste water disposal on the reservation, they could do little about off-reservation water use that damaged or destroyed reservation land. In 1914, for example, Carr called in the Commissioner of Indian Affairs to press Toppenish municipal officials to install a septic system to stop the town from dumping sewage into a reservation

---

result, when the water is applied, the current is so strong that the soil is washed away." He recommended building flumes to slow the water down.

[89] Holt, Report of the Simcoe Creek Commission.

[90] "Proposal for Initiation of a Soil Conservation Program, Yakima Agency," July 17, 1945, file 9228-36-341, YA, CCF, BIA, RG 75, NA.

[91] Waller, *Report*, 16.

[92] *CIA-AR*, 1911, 16; OIA-IIS, Indian Irrigation District no. 1, *Annual Report*, 1915, file 78600-15-341, YA, CCF, BIA, RG 75, NA. Drainage work in 1915 lowered the water table in some places by four feet in one year.

[93] Secretary, Yakima Reservation Water Users Association, to Franklin K. Lane, July 17, 1914, file 73870-14-341, YA, CCF, BIA, RG 75, NA. An Indian Service project, costing $250,000 in reimbursable funds, was constructed to run reservation water back into river, and provided an important water source for Prosser and users below the reservation, Jay Lynch to Harry Jones, April 29, 1913, 1:3, HJSP.

[94] Carr to C. Haskell, June 27, 1913, "Haskell, C." file, Irrigation Records, 1913-35, YA, BIA, RG 75, NA-Seattle. See also S. A. M. Young to All Lessees of Indian Allotments, Aug. 30, 1909, file 72408-09-112, YA, CCF, BIA, RG 75, NA, noting: "A few lessees are still negligent as to the disposal of waste water. They will be held accountable for this, and will be dealt with as rapidly as definite evidence can be obtained against individual offenders." See also C. F. Larrabee to Code, quoting from H. M. Gilbert to W. L. Jones, 1908, file "1902-03," Letters received re: Irrigation matters, 1903-08, YA, BIA, RG 75, NA-Seattle: "The present situation here [on the reservation] is deplorable. The partial and inadequate system of irrigation existing on the reservation at present I fear is doing almost as much harm as benefit. The water is being distributed without any system in a very reckless manner, and large areas are being 'swamped' every year." Gilbert noted that large areas west of Toppenish are "nearly ruined owing to the large amount of water turned loose in a reckless manner on lands higher up."

drainage canal where the effluent ended up in a slough used by allottee for household and irrigation purposes.⁹⁵

Drainage systems had a dual impact on reservation farmers. Efforts to install disposal canals and excavate formerly alkaline lands brought large areas back into crop production, but the same systems often injured Indian irrigators who had long depended upon some seepage and spring water to support their rich hay and pasture lands. Cordelia Olney complained to Secretary of Interior Franklin Lane in May 1913:

> Before the big drainage ditch was made my land didn't need any water. It grew fine alfalfa but now it has to have water. The water men threaten to shut it off immediately if I don't pay for the water. I have not got the money to pay for it and I am not able to work. If it is shut off my crops will burn up. I am trying to farm it myself. I believe that I should have water free under these circumstances or have more time to pay for the water.⁹⁶

Similarly, Hahise Sawyahill protested in 1924 that "nobody asked my permission to run ditch through that allotment" when a drainage ditch cut off seepage water. "Now, everything is gone from that allotment. What became of the grass that was on that allotment? We used to have grass and pasture for our horses. Now we can[']t use that land."⁹⁷ Irrigators sometimes received compensation for the loss of their water or ditches, but could not necessarily pay for water under the new systems.⁹⁸ Indian users also were charged higher rates for water delivery in expanding systems, even if they had used the water for many years.⁹⁹

---

⁹⁵ Carr to Holt, March 4, 1914, in "Sewer–Toppenish" file, Irrigation Records, 1913-35, YA, BIA, RG 75, NA-Seattle; clippings from Toppenish Rev. Jan. 9, 1914, ibid.; Clipping "To Construct Septic Tank," ibid; Carr to Cain, Sept 6, 1912, ibid.; Oscar Cain, U.S. Attorney, to Carr, Sept. 11, 1912, ibid., noting that it is not illegal to empty raw sewage into a stream, but it might be to do it in an artificial waterway.

⁹⁶ Olney to Lane, May 18, 1913, file 72902-13-341, YA, CCF, BIA, RG 75, NA.

⁹⁷ "I like to have Mr. Holt leave us Indians alone not to make so many drainage. We like to have our grass[ ] in our fields for our support," she said. Report of Simcoe Creek Commission. See also testimony of Schuyler Colfax, ibid., noting that he has had no water on his lands for two years.

⁹⁸ Estep to CIA, Nov. 1, 1928, file 50991-28[?]-115, YA, CCF, RG 75, NA. See also testimony of Thomas Sam, Report of Simcoe Creek Commission, noting that he wants his legal entitlements to seepage water which he has confirmed on a trip to Washington, D.C. Sam also noted that "Mr. Reed told us Indians, we Indians, Yakimas and Klickitats, has legal right to that water. That is what I am talking about. As long as Reclamation is bucking against our rights we are going to talk about it. We got a claim on it and we are not going to let it go to any company." Ibid.

⁹⁹ Yalup, a Yakama tribal member, noted in 1913: "Now the white people are outside that country there and take the water from us; they build a dam right above our canal. This Ahtanum ditch was made by the Indians with our own labor and they put their own dam and was take water from them and after that time—well since that time or after that time there

Reclamation projects, with their power to change water flow and drainage patterns, had a major impact on the ecology of the Basin. Storage reservoirs constructed on numerous streams beginning in the late 1890s altered or entirely eliminated the former rhythm of spring floods that nourished riparian lands.[100] "More water flowed in Ahtanum creek in early days than now," attorney J. H. Lynch noted in 1901. "The watershed had not been burned off nor grazed excessively by sheep, hence there was more water. The runoff was also later, coming mostly after July 1."[101] Indian fisheries in the Yakima River, Ahtanum, Simcoe, and Satus creeks bore the costs of water development just as did Yakama farmers. In 1908, the state fish commissioner asked the Reclamation Service to include fish ladders at Yakima project dams, but was told that fish ladders were not feasible, nor was the Reclamation Service responsible for meeting state fishery laws.[102] Not until the late 1940s would reclamation and later hydropower development projects include fishery mitigation programs.[103]

Conclusion: Post-1933 Yakama Water Rights

By 1933, the Yakama had come little closer to establishing treaty-based water rights than they had been before *Winters*. Certainly many water users and federal officials had felt the dormant power of Yakama water rights, yet Indian farmers were still among the poorest and their lands were among the driest in the basin. Yakama had energetically petitioned and lobbied for treaty-based water rights, but their voices were only indirectly, considered in the decisions allocating Yakima River and Ahtanum Creek. Even on the wholly on-reservation streams federal reclamation plans preempted pre-existing Indian

---

was another canal put right on top of ours, leaving our dam right under theirs," in Council Proceedings of Yakima Indians, Fort Simcoe, Wash., June 2, 1913, folder, "Councils and Meetings (Tribal), 1913-25," Tribal Records, 1897-1952, YA, BIA, RG 75, NA-Seattle; Chief Wa-ya-ci-ka to Valentine, July 24, 1911, file 66121-11-341, YA, CCF, BIA, RG 75, NA; Report of Simcoe Creek Commission, Yakama irrigators complained of loss of control over old ditches and being made to pay a fee for use of water.

[100] Bower lists major BuRec dams in the Yakima Basin with their dates of completion: Kachess dam, 1910; Bumping Lake dam, 1910; Clear Creek dam, 1914; Keechelus dam, 1917; Tieton dam, 1925; Cle Elum High dam, 1933; Easton diversion dam, 1929 (to Kittitas Main Canal in 1929); North Branch Canal, 1931; Prosser dam modified (dam constructed 1904, canal in 1912); Kennewick main canal completed 1956, "Hydrogeography of Yakima Indian Nation Resource Use," 431.

[101] "Yakima Attorney Outlines Ahtanum District History, clipping, [n.d.], 76:5, CRP.

[102] Bauer, "Labor Without Brains," 61-62. In 1915, the Wapato project was generating a surplus of 7,000 h.p., OIA-IIS, Indian Irrigation District no. 1, *Annual Report*, 1915, file 78600-15-341, YA, CCF, BIA, RG 75, NA.

[103] Commissioner of Fisheries, Report, in *Bonneville Dam and Protection of the Columbia River Fisheries*, Sen. Doc. no. 87, 75th Cong., 1st Sess., July 22, 1937; Michael Blumm, et al., "The Fish and Wildlife Coordination Act and Columbia Basin Water Project Operations," *Anadromous Fish Law Memo* 6 (1980): 7.

irrigation facilities and generally ignored Yakama interests and economic realities.[104] Frank Selatsee observed in 1924, "Reclamation people they want to make money from the Government. They are the ones asking for construction on Simcoe and Toppenish, not the Indians."[105]

Non-Indian water users throughout the first three decades of the twentieth century managed to postpone litigation over Indian treaty rights, but the situation had changed after the Great Depression. The Reclamation Service ceased to be an expansive force in the Basin, and rising numbers of diverse water users competed for shares in the water system for everything from hydropower and irrigation to commercial and sport fisheries, recreation, and wildlife protection.[106] The post-1933 period marks the beginning of a series of water rights adjudications in the Basin in which Indian rights were finally and squarely at issue.[107] In 1956, a U.S. district court held that the Yakamas' share of Ahtanum Creek waters should be determined according to the amount the tribe needed in 1915, at the completion of the Ahtanum Project, while the off-reservation users would be limited to the amount used by individuals named in the 1908 agreement in that year.[108]

---

[104] One Yakama, Bill Charley, was a member of the three-person committee to investigate Yakama claims along Simcoe Creek. It is not clear how representative Charley was; the Charley family fished commercially using fish wheels at a tribal fishing place to the detriment of other Yakama fishers, and arousing the anger of more "traditional" tribal members, see Chapter 8.

[105] Chief Saluskin to CIA, Feb. 19, 1913, indicated that he did not want Toppenish Creek developed, 76:13, MCPP. Compare Holt statement that some Yakama wanted those streams developed, in Report of Simcoe Creek Commission.

[106] High Country News, *Western Water Made Simple* (Washington, D.C.: Island Press, 1987): 47-105; Gus Norwood, *Columbia River Power for the People: A History of the Policies of the Bonneville Power Administration* (Portland, OR: U.S. Department of Energy, Bonneville Power Administration, 1981); Lewis E. Queirolo and William A. McNamee, "The Columbia-Snake: Challenges for Multiple-Use River Management," *Pacific Northwest Bulletin* 212 (WA: Pacific Northwest Cooperative Extension, 1981); Philip R. Wandschneider, "Control and Management of the Columbia-Snake River System," *Bulletin* no. 0937 (Pullman, WA: Agricultural Research Center, Washington State University, 1984).

[107] Irrigation districts also fought among one another for shares of water. See *Ickes v. Fox*, 85 F.2d 294 (D.C. Cir. 1936), which held that BuRec was obliged to deliver water to users in the Sunnyside Irrigation District according to priorities established under Washington state law. A 1945 consent decree further defined U.S. obligations to deliver water to irrigation districts, *Kittitas Irr. Dist. et al. v. Sunnyside Irr. Dist. et al.* (E.D. Wa., So. Div., Civ. Action no. 21, 1945), allotted 611,342 acre-feet of water per year to the on-reservation Wapato-Satus Irrigation project. The 1945 consent decree allocated 90 percent of available irrigation water within the Yakima Project, but tribe was not a party, Mike Murphy, "Indian Water Accord," *Yakima Herald-Republic*, Feb. 21, 1979, p. 3.

[108] *United States v. Ahtanum Irr. Dist.*, 236 P.2d 321, 339-42 (9th Cir. 1956). The court directed the water master to adjust the non-reservation water users' allocations to take into account the excessive waste of irrigation water. In *United States v. Ahtanum Irr. Dist.*, 330 F.2d 897 (9th Cir. 1964), the court determined that the off-reservation users need for water

As the tribe asserted more control over their own and on-reservation water use, their claims increasingly were inseparable from the larger issue of managing Basin water. Now Yakama treaty rights were only one of many unresolved issues facing disparate water users.[109] However, because Yakama still held so much of their lands in trust (for example, 80 percent of the reservation was held in trust in 1989), during the time period of this study, the tribe still had to rely on federal officials to bring suit on their behalf.[110]

In 1977, the Yakama filed an action in federal court seeking to assure that all reservation water needs be met before water was allocated to other water users in the Yakima Irrigation Project. The tribe asked for a minimum streamflow for fish of 500 c.f.s. and 655,000 acre-feet annually for on-reservation farmlands.[111] Washington requested that the case be moved into state court for adjudication of water rights, under the McCarran Amendment, and the court agreed. Washington State then began a suit in Superior Court of Yakima

---

was less than the 75 percent allocation they received under the 1908 agreement, and moreover, that because the need for water to those lands had decreased between 1908 and 1957, the share of water allocated to those users should also be decreased. The court also found that the off-reservation users' rights to water were limited to the time between the beginning of the irrigation season and July 10; after which, reservation users would have all the stream waters. The Northside settlers got 46.96 c.f.s., with any water above that to go to the reservation (the court found that the normal low flow of Ahtanum creek before July 10 was 62.59 c.f.s.).

[109] In 1978 the Yakama implemented their own water code, regulating on-reservation water use, and met with much hostility from non-Indian on-reservation water users. In *Holly v. Totus* 655 F. Supp. 548 (E.D. Wash., 1983), the tribe was enjoined from enforcing the tribal water code against on-reservation non-Indian water users who were using water in excess of the code's provisions. See also Murphy, "Yakima Nation Water," *Yakima Herald Republic*. In *United States v. McIntire*, 101 F.2d 650, 654 (9th Cir. 1939), the court held that states cannot regulate individual or tribal water use on Indian lands with respect to any reservation purpose. As early as 1912, Yakama had formed a committee to study the reservation irrigation system, see R. G. Valentine to Secretary of Interior, Mar. 15, 1912, file 16201-12-341, YA, CCF, BIA, RG 75, NA.

[110] For Yakama attempts to litigate their Ahtanum water rights in the 1940s, see: Kenneth R. L. Simmons, BIA District Council, to A. L. Wathen, Director of Irrigation, May 13, 1940, file 9225-36-341, Part 0-4, YA, CCF, BIA, RG 75, NA; M. A. Johnson to CIA, April 1, 1940, file 9225-36-341, YA, BIA, RG 75, NA (denial of tribal funds to pay for attorney); YTC-WS, Tribal Resolution, May 29, 1942, enclosed in Johnson to CIA, June 2, 1942, file 9225-36-341, Part 0-5, YA, CCF, BIA, RG 75, NA (decision to hire attorney anyway). The resulting action was *Frank Totus, Thomas Sam, et al. v. United States*, bill of complaint, District Court, eastern District of Washington, Southern Division, 28 June 1940, file 9225-36-341, Part 0-5, YA, CCF, BIA, RG 75, NA. For Order granting motion to dismiss entered Oct. 9, 1941, see Norman N. Littell, Assistant A. G., to Southworth, Acting BIA Director of Irrigation, Oct. 10, 1941, file 9225-36-341, Part 0-5, YA, CCF, BIA, RG 75, NA; M. A. Johnson to CIA, April 1, 1940, file 9225-36-341, Part 0-4, YA, CCF, BIA, RG 75, NA. BIA officials tried to prevent YTC-WS from hiring the attorney, arguing that he was incompetent, even though no one at BIA was familiar with the attorney.

[111] The action would have reviewed the consent decree established in *Kittitas Irr. Dist. v. Sunnyside Irr. Dist.* (E.D. Wa., So. Div., Civ. Action no. 21, 1945); Murphy, "Indian Water Accord," Feb. 21, 1979, *Yakima Herald-Republic*.

County which is presently at the discovery stage.[112] In 1982, a federal court set aside minimum flows for fish in the Yakima River.[113]

Yakama met with greater success in asserting treaty-based water rights in the post-1933 period than earlier, but they could not undo the past. *Winters* did not create vested rights in water for the Yakama, and both the tribe and the basin suffered for it. Because federal land and water policies did little to promote Indian agriculture but did much to injure it, the proceeds of subsistence remained an important source of food and cash to Yakama throughout the period.

---

[112] The McCarran Amendment allows the federal government to be joined as a party in suits involving the adjudication of water systems by waiving the sovereign immunity of the United States for this specific purpose. Act of July 10, 1952, ch. 651, § 208, 66 Stat. 549, 560 (codified at 43 U.S.C. § 666). See *Department of Ecology v. Acquavella,* 100 Wash. 2d 651 (1983).

As a modern postscript, the Washington State Court website has this note about the continuing *Acquavella* litigation: "The *Acquavella* litigation, underway since 1977 and due to be wrapped up in the next few years, is addressing 4,000 water right claimants. State-wide, however, approximately 170,000 other water right claims still need adjudication. It has been estimated that at the current pace it will take over 200 years to fully adjudicate all the water right claims in the state." See "Water Issues: General Water Right Adjudications and Water Courts: Background Information," at http://www.courts.wa.gov/committee/?fa=committee.display&item_id=425&committee_id=109 (last accessed Nov. 16, 2014).

[113] *Kittitas Irr. Dist. v. Sunnyside Irr. Dist.* (1945). The 1945 agreement did not discuss the fishery, but the court maintained continuing jurisdiction, and in 1982 it amended the consent decree to provide minimum flows for fish. See Bower, "Hydrogeography of Yakima Resource Use," 447-48.

III

**LIFE AND BREATH OF THE EARTH:
FISH AND WILDLIFE**

8

SEATED TOGETHER AT THE GREAT TABLE OF THE COLUMBIA RIVER

> I am telling you that all the Indians has been raised by the spirit of god and same spirit of god has made salmon for all the Indians to get to make the[ir] living by fishing and that[']s why I do not want to have any white race around here to have me buy license before I go fishing. I don[']t like to buy no license for my own fishing rights. Salmon has been made for us Indians by god early times ago the time the[re] was no white People.
> —Chief Skookum Wallahee, 1914[1]

To Euro-Americans, the solution to the "Indian Problem" of the nineteenth and early twentieth centuries was assimilation of tribes into the dominant society. Indian Bureau land and water policies for Indians publicly promoted agriculture as an acceptable "civilized" lifestyle for Indians, yet they assisted few people in becoming successful farmers. On the Yakama reservation, many people left the farming to non-Indian lessees who had the capital and political power necessary to build irrigation works and to make the land productive. Yakama earned their wages as field hands; it was hard work, but it fit roughly into the seasonal pattern of subsistence life.[2] Seasonal work left time to fish, hunt, and gather the foods that were the traditional support of Yakama peoples.

Yakama subsistence strategy was mobility. Hunters and foragers sought out game and important root and berry grounds when their yields were highest. Fishers timed their trips to the rivers when fish appeared. Salmon, probably the most important food fish in the Columbia River system, are anadromous fish, that is, fish that are born in freshwater, migrate to saltwater where they spend part of their lives, and then return to freshwater to spawn and to die. Five species of Pacific salmon inhabit Columbia Basin waters during their lives: Chinook, silver, sockeye, pink, and chum. All the species possess a "homing instinct" to some extent that enables them to return to spawn in their particular stream of birth. The trait ensures diversity among the

---

[1] Wallahee to E. B. Meritt, assist. CIA, Dec. 30, 1914, file 120088-14-115, Yakima Agency, Central Classified Files, General Records, 1907-39, Records of the Bureau of Indian Affairs, Record Group 75, National Archives, Washington, D.C. [hereafter cited as YA, CCF, GR, BIA, RG 75, NA-branch].

[2] See "At George Desmarais Hop Camp," field notes, Sept. 4, 1956, box 58, file 8, and "Wanapum Way of Life," narrative of Yakama work in hops fields, transcribed by Click Relander, n.d., but ca. 1950s, box 57, file 25, both in Click Relander Papers, Yakima Valley Regional Library, Yakima, Washington [hereafter cited as box:file, CRP].

wild stocks, even among members of the same species who are distinctly adapted to their homestream, and who have different migration routes and times. Fishers counted on that trait to bring the fish to predictable places year after year.[3]

Fishing, especially for salmon, was a key component of Yakama subsistence—as well as Plateau peoples' subsistence generally—both before and after Euro-American contact. Yakama and other native fishers regulated fishing to some extent through familial and village-based affiliations. At many fishing locations inherited rights determined where fishers could work, and in what order families fished. In other places fishing took place without such determinative structure: when one family had caught enough for its winter supply, another group took its place.[4] As Yakama Doctor Shea-wa recalled in 1918, there was no trouble over such sharing of the fishery: "[T]he Columbia River, was a table between [the tribes].... Everything was free.... The river, I might say, was a table for both sides of the river. It laid right in between them and they came and ate and were gone."[5]

Euro-Americans who fished in Columbia Basin waters in the latter half of the nineteenth century had different relationships to the fisheries from those of the Indians. Euro-Americans also created rights to the fisheries, but in this instance access depended upon an individual's ownership of land along the banks of the fishery itself, and, later, upon the purchase of a state license to fish. Such rights entitled fishers to work during certain time periods at specified locations and, early on at least, to catch an unlimited amount of fish. As the state became the primary regulator of the relationship between individuals

---

[3] The preceding discussion is based on the following sources: Anthony Netboy, *The Columbia River Salmon and Steelhead Trout: Their Fight for Survival* (Seattle: University of Washington Press, 1980); Netboy, *Salmon: The World's Most Harassed Fish* (Tulsa, OK: Winchester Press, 1980): 209-56; R. J. Childerhose and Marj Trim, *Pacific Salmon and Steelhead Trout* (Vancouver, B.C.: Douglas & McIntyre, 1979); Pacific Salmon Commission, *Pacific Salmon Commission, Handbook* (Vancouver: Pacific Salmon Commission, 1988), Natalie Fobes, "The Saga of Salmon, an Epic Struggle to Survive Man," *Seattle Times*, special report, Nov. 22, 1987. See also Bruce Brown, *Mountain in the Clouds: A Search for the Wild Salmon* (New York: Simon and Schuster, 1982). For a profound pictorial study of salmon lifecycles, see Atsushi Sakurai, *Salmon* (New York: Alfred A. Knopf, 1984).

[4] Plateau peoples shared with Northwest Coast peoples a dependence on salmon for food, although the structure of rights to fisheries—both fin and shell—appears to have been more highly structured among coastal peoples. See Hiliary Stewart, *Indian Fishing: Early Methods on the Northwest Coast* (Seattle: University of Washington Press, 1977); Daniel L. Boxberger, "The Lummi Island Reef Nets," *Indian Historian*, 24 (1980): 48-54; Boxberger, *To Fish in Common: The Ethnohistory of Lummi Indian Salmon Fishing* (Lincoln, NE: University of Nebraska Press, 1989): 13-24; Eugene Hunn, "Mobility as a Factor Limiting Resource Use in the Columbia Plateau of North America," in Nancy M. Williams and Eugene Hunn, eds., *Resource Managers: North American and Australian Hunter Gatherers*, AAAS Selected Symposium 67 (Boulder, CO: Westview Press, 1982): 31-4.

[5] Quoted in *United States v. Seufert Bros. Co.*, U.S. brief, March 16, 1916, file 93689-13-115, YA, CCF, GR, BIA, RG 75, NA, p. 64 [hereafter cited as *U.S. v. Seufert*, U.S. brief].

and the fishery, laws governing access to state fisheries came to protect the interests of white fishers who systematically excluded those groups with whom they competed, often by alleging their depredations on the resource.[6] Moreover, as states came to regulate all aspects of the commercial fishery, officials argued that state-licensed fishers had more legitimate entitlements to the resource than did unregulated Indian fishers.[7]

The Yakima Nation's treaty of 1855 reserved to the tribes

> the exclusive right of taking fish in all the streams, where running through or bordering said reservation ... as also the right of taking fish at all usual and accustomed places, in common with the citizens of the Territory, and of erecting temporary buildings for curing them....[8]

As Euro-American fishers stationed themselves along the Columbia and elsewhere at many traditional Native fishing sites, interracial conflict over access to the fishery became an issue of widespread public concern, and one that soon found its way into state and federal courts, as well as other branches of Washington's state government. As some Yakama fishers took jobs as fishers for local canneries, intertribal conflicts erupted that Yakama also attempted to channel into the courts.

Yakama efforts to protect their treaty fishing rights received support from Bureau officials who recognized them as important property rights capable of providing a source of income to tribal members. Unlike hunting and gathering, which were also important Yakama subsistence activities, fishing held the potential to become a commercial enterprise that might bring fishers within the embrace of a market economy and civilization.[9] Some officials, such as Col.

---

[6] On non-Indian fishers excluding other ethnic groups from fisheries under the guise of conserving the resource, see Courtland L. Smith, *Salmon Fishers of the Columbia* (Corvallis, OR: Oregon State University Press, 1979): 39-40. In the California fisheries, see Arthur F. McEvoy, "In Places Men Reject: Chinese Fishermen at San Diego, 1870-1893," *Journal of San Diego History*, 23 (1977): 12-24; and McEvoy, *The Fisherman's Problem: Ecology and Law in the California Fisheries, 1850-1980* (Cambridge: Cambridge University Press, 1986): 75-90.

[7] *State v. Towessnute*, 89 Wash. 478, 479, 482 (1916). This theme was prevalent in later twentieth-century fishing disputes involving Yakama and other tribes. See *Sohappy v. Smith*, 302 F. Supp. 899, 907 (1969); *Tulee v. Washington*, 315 U.S. 682, 864ff (1942); *Department of Game v. Puyallup Tribe*, 414 U.S. 43 (1973).

[8] Treaty with the Yakima, 12 Stat. 951, Art. 3. Other treaties that Stevens arranged with Pacific Northwest Tribes contained similar provisions that reserved tribal access to both fin and shell fishes. See Daniel L. Boxberger, *Handbook of Western Washington Indian Treaties: With Special Attention to Treaty Fishing Rights*, Contributions to Aquaculture and Fisheries, Occasional Paper 1 (Lummi Island, WA: Lummi College of Fisheries, 1979); American Friends Service Committee, *Uncommon Controversy: Fishing Rights of the Muckleshoot, Puyallup, and Nisqually Indians* (Seattle: University of Washington Press, 1970): 18-40.

[9] George W. Gordon, *Report upon the Subject of the Fishing Privileges etc. guaranteed by Treaties to Indians in the Northwest, with Recommendations in Regard Thereto*, Jan. 19,

Thomas Lang, of the Bureau, and Francis Garrecht, U.S. Attorney in Spokane, viewed Yakama fishing rights as a question of justice on the non-economic principle of fairness under the 1855 treaty, but this perspective was not the dominant one.

Although Yakama came to articulate their position in fishing conflicts through the language of rights, they meant something different from the Euro-American understanding of rights as severable entitlements to discrete resources located firmly in space and time. Whether Yakama fished for subsistence or sold or traded some of their catch, most of them believed that their treaty protected fishing as part of its larger protection of their subsistence way of life; hence fishing rights became a shorthand way of designating the rights to eat, to work, and to participate in Yakama culture. Consequently, while Yakama subsistence fishers and non-Indian commercial fishers alike talked of fishing "rights," they were not talking about the same thing. Nor is it surprising that Yakama would see the protection of their rights to hunt and to harvest subsistence plants as an extension of the rights they had begun to secure to fish.

During the period from 1855 to 1933, Yakama and Euro-American conflicts over access to the Columbia River salmon fisheries went through several phases. Until roughly the 1880s, conflict among Native and Euro-American fishers was sporadic and localized; Washington commercial fishing was still establishing itself as a major state industry. But beginning in the 1880s, user conflicts moved from local courts into state and federal courts.

While in its 1905 decision in *United States v. Winans*, the U.S. Supreme Court asserted the supremacy of Yakama treaty rights to fish at an important off-reservation site, Yakama fishers continued to have trouble asserting their rights against state-licensed fishers in virtually every place they fished.[10] The root of the difficulty inhered in the very structure of the decisions, which subordinated tribal sovereignty to state and federal power and thus legitimated the further marginalization of Indian peoples within the U.S. legal and political system. Courts systematically refashioned fishing rights to be compatible with state regulation of commercial fishing. The appropriate roles of both state and tribal regulations in shaping treaty fishing rights after 1906, is the central issue in Yakama fishing conflicts through 1933 and into the present.

Subsistence Fisheries

Yakama, like other Plateau peoples, knew well the different fish species that inhabited their world.[11] Yakama fished for salmon, suckers, Dolly varden,

---

1889, U.S. Department of Interior, Branch of Fisheries, typed transcript, 1986, [hereafter cited as Gordon Report]: 146-147; Gordon to CIA, Jan. 12, 1889, ibid., 33-34; Estep to CIA, March 12, 1926, file 8324-26-115, YA, CCF, GR, BIA, RG 75, NA.

[10] 198 U.S. 371 (1905).

[11] Eugene Hunn, "Sahaptin Fish Classification," *Northwest Anthropological Research Notes* 14 (1980): 1.

trout, lamprey, sturgeon, and sculpin, depending upon the season.[12]

Suckers, which appeared at about the same time fresh plants became available in the early spring, provided welcome relief when winter stores ran low. Salmon, making their way upstream from the ocean, appeared about six to eight weeks later, and the successive runs were a fluctuating presence in Columbia Basin waters until the fall because new runs entered the river system and because some fish had to travel longer distances depending upon how far upstream they had to travel to spawn.

Chinook arrived earliest, in March and could be caught into until November. Steelhead also may have presented a continuous presence in Basin streams. Coho and Sockeye runs entered the river in the fall. Columbia River salmon migrations historically coincided with the river's own flow patterns, producing two separate, major "runs" of salmon in the mainstem Columbia; the first in June and July and the second in October and November.[13] Yakama families returning from hunting and berrying expeditions in the Cascades could return to the rivers in the fall to harvest from the autumn runs.

All Plateau groups made some accounting for the presence of salmon in their rivers. A Wishram story recounted the time Coyote, the trickster, disguised himself as a baby and set himself adrift on a pond where two women kept fish. When the two women took him home and believed he was sleeping, he went back to the pond and released the fish through a passageway that became the Columbia River. When the women discovered what he had done, they accused Coyote of making them poor. He replied: "Soon now ... people will come into this land; those fish will be the people's food."[14] In another account, Coyote gave humans mouths and taught them to prepare and to eat salmon, as well as other fish.[15] In each version, the origin of human life coin-

---

[12] Hunn, "Sahaptin Fish Classification," 6; Morris L. Uebelacker, "Geographic Explorations in the Southern Cascades of Eastern Washington: Changing Land, People, and Resources" (Ph.D. diss., University of Oregon, 1986): 112-19.

[13] Uebelacker, "Geographic Explorations," 112-16; L. A. Fulton, *Spawning Areas and Abundance of Chinook Salmon (Oncorhynchus tshawytsha) in the Columbia River Basin—Past and Present* (Washington, D.C.: U.S. Department of the Interior, 1968); Fulton, *Spawning Areas and Abundance of Steelhead Trout and Coho, Sockeye and Chum Salmon in the Columbia River Basin—Past and Present* (Washington, D.C.: U.S. Department of the Interior, 1970); R. F. Schalk, "The Structure of an Anadromous Fish Resource," in Lewis R. Binford, ed., *For Theory Building in Archaeology: Essays on Faunal Remains, Aquatic Resources, Spatial Analysis and Systemic Modeling* (New York: Academic Press, 1977): 207-49. Uebelacker points out that the present composition of fish populations in Basin streams is much different from that of the pre-contact period. Much of the change stems from the Euro-American agricultural system imposed on the region, which has lowered instream water quality. Trout, salmon, and other species are artificially propagated and planted in Basin waters at present. Uebelacker, "Geographic Explorations," 118-19.

[14] "Coyote Frees the Fish," in *Coyote Was Going There: Indian Literature of the Oregon Country*, ed. Jarold Ramsey (Seattle: University of Washington Press, 1977): 47-48.

[15] Ramsey, *Coyote Was Going There*, 49-51.

cided with the arrival of fish in the rivers, and from those fish humans derived their sustenance.

Salmon provided roughly one third of Yakama diets, although that varied with annual fluctuations in stocks. "Some years we could have fed Lincoln's Army with fish; some years nobody," Yakama fisher J. H. Covington remembered in 1904.[16] There are no exact figures on Plateau peoples' annual salmon harvests, but average figures for the nineteenth century put the catch in the millions of pounds. One researcher estimated that per-capita fish consumption on the Columbia-Fraser River Plateau totalled from 50 to 900 pounds per year, depending upon Native group, with the average per-capita consumption at 438 pounds. With a population of 62,000, for example, fishers would have harvested more than 27 million pounds of fish annually.[17] Salmon remained an important part of Yakama diets throughout the period and after. A 1941 Bureau of Indian Affairs survey found that the average Yakama family consumed 1,800 pounds of salmon per year, making an annual total consumption of 900,000 pounds for the tribe.[18]

Salmon provided both physical and spiritual nourishment. "Salmon makes a man look fresh and stout," stated Yakama fisher Chief Louis Simpson, who was one of the Yakama plaintiffs in the 1905 *Winans* suit. "The Indians that were raised [at the See-we-pam and Wisham fisheries] were fat. I am a fat looking man myself. I eat salmon and berries. That is what the treaty gave me."[19] Similarly, Chief White Swan, or Joe Stwire, also a plaintiff in *Winans*, explained that the Yakama "want salmon all the time." "I can[']t myself get along without the salmon, I don[']t know how to eat hog meat, I don[']t like it very well myself and that is the way with the other [I]ndians I suppose."[20]

---

[16] *U.S. v. Winans*, Transcript of Record, Testimony and Final Report of Examiner, enclosed in Attorney General (AG) to Clerk of the Supreme Court, Jan. 21, 1904, Appellate Case File no. 19213, Records of the Supreme Court, RG 267, NA, p. 232. [Hereafter cited as *U.S. v. Winans*, transcript of record.] The transcript has several sets of page numbers. I have used the handwritten page numbers that have not been crossed out. I have also indicated the use of interpreters where Yakama were not speaking in English.

[17] Hunn, "Sahaptin Fish Classification," 2; Gordon W. Hewes, "Indian Fisheries Productivity in Pre-Contact Times in the Pacific Salmon Area," *Northwest Anthropological Research Notes* 7 (1973): 133-55; U.S. Department of the Interior, Bureau of Reclamation, *The Columbia River, Comprehensive Report on Development...* (Washington, D.C., 1947), 353, cited in American Friends Service Committee, *Uncommon Controversy*, 4 n. 3. Yakama fisher Lancaster Spencer recalled that families would store 600-700 pounds or more of dried salmon for winter use, testimony in *United States v. Winans*, transcript of record, 141; testimony of Covington, ibid., 231.

[18] "Officials Make Survey of Diets," clipping, Aug. 2, 1942, folder "Indians-Yakima-Government," Yakima Valley Museum, Yakima, WA [hereafter folder, YVM]. These figures do not include the Yakama commercial catch.

[19] Testimony of Louis Simpson, *U.S. v. Winans*, transcript of record, 132.

[20] Testimony in *U.S. v. Winans*, transcript of record, 103.

Yakama marked their connection to the fisheries in two "first foods" ceremonies, the first honoring suckers and the first fresh roots in the spring, and the second honoring salmon when the fish arrived at traditional fishing locations during the summer. While anthropologists have made much of "first salmon ceremonies" held by some Plateau groups, Yakama apparently did not treat their first salmon of the year in any special way, although in pre-contact times no one could fish until the fishing chief of a village group gave permission.[21] The number of fish passing by a particular fishing location, the water level of the river, and seasonal changes from year to year all continued to condition the commencement of fishing at any given place into the twentieth century.[22] It is possible that regulation of fishing by headmen had a conservative effect on Yakama fishing, but it is more likely that the finite storage capabilities of fishing groups, together with a subsistence pattern that required people to move constantly to harvest different resources, worked to prevent Indian fishers from depleting stocks.[23]

Over time, Yakama fishers identified the best fishing places. Those were cliffs alongside waterfalls where the fish could be speared and caught with dip nets, such as the Cascades and The Dalles about 150 miles upriver and Celilo Falls about 200 miles upriver, three large fisheries used by Yakama. Here as many as 3000 people would come together at the peak of a salmon run. Yakama fishers used other fisheries at Priest Rapids, Umatilla Rapids, and Kettle Falls, as well as sites along Wenatshapam River, and the Yakima River and its tributaries.[24] In shallow places, fishers could work using seines, weirs,

---

[21] On Yakama first foods ceremonies, see Helen Hersh Schuster, "Yakima Indian Traditionalism: A Study in Continuity and Change" (Ph.D. diss., University of Washington, 1975): 70, 432-36; Hunn, "Sahaptin Fish Classification," 13; Click Relander, "Celilo Fishery Notes, Manuscript I," 18:2, CRP. On first salmon rituals, see Erna Gunther, "An Analysis of the First Salmon Ceremony," *American Anthropologist* 28 (1926) 605-17; Gunther, "A Further Analysis of the First Salmon Ceremony," *University of Washington Publications in Anthropology* 2 (1928): 129-73. Gunther does not discuss the religious significance of the ceremony.

[22] On Yakama fishers discussing river conditions affecting the timing and location of fishing efforts, see *United States v. Winans*, transcript of record, 108, 121, 157-58.

[23] Hunn, "Mobility as a Factor," 33-35; Schalk, "Structure of an Anadromous Fish Resource," 241-42; J. H. Fairchild, clerk, to James H. Wilbur, May 21, 1881, 115:2, CRP [hereafter cited as Fairchild Report]. Fairchild wrote that he observed that Yakama fishers stopped fishing each day when they had taken as many fish as they could process in one day, giving their places to others.

[24] Click Relander, "Place Names: Fisheries," typed transcript of interviews, [n.d. but ca. 1952-53], 58:8, CRP; Edward G. Swindell, *Report on Source, Nature and Extent of Fishing, Hunting, and Miscellaneous Rights of Certain Indian Tribes in Washington and Oregon* (Los Angeles: U.S. Department of the Interior, Office of Indian Affairs, Division of Forestry and Grazing, 1942) [hereafter cited as Swindell Report]; Schuster, "Yakima Indian Traditionalism," 70-72; Hunn, "Mobility as a Factor," 34. Uebelacker, "Geographic Explorations," 115, notes that we have no information about fish distribution or use on smaller and intermittent streams in the Basin.

and traps.[25] Women then processed and preserved the fish by cooking, sundrying, and smoking them, although some was eaten fresh.[26]

Many different bands came together to feast, celebrate, and lay in winter stores at the fishing grounds. Some fishing took place communally, with no apparent structure to allocate time and space among fishers. In certain places, most notably at Celilo Falls and The Dalles, fishers held entitlements, based on family ties, to fish at particular rocks or other sites. Priority at those locations depended upon family ownership of the site, or connections that fishers had to other groups based on marriage or other relationships. Such rights passed generationally within families, from father to sons. Thus it is not surprising that Yakama plaintiffs in fishing rights cases were individuals whose family fishing sites were at issue. Yakima Agent Evan Estep (1923-1830) observed in 1924 that a "number [of Indians] claim a sort of common law right to fish at particular places, and exclude other members of the tribe from these points."[27] Before the beginning of the twentieth century, intra- and intertribal disputes over, fishing sites appear to have been extremely rare.[28]

Summer fishing coincided with large intertribal trade and social gatherings, especially at The Dalles. Families arrived at the fishing places with tents, equipment for processing fish, and herds of horses, which were both a mode of transportation and a mark of social status. With winter stores packed away, people had time to trade, gamble, hold horse races and other contests, socialize, and exchange news. Among the goods traded by Yakama were fish, which indicates that some surplus catch was part of subsistence fishing from pre-contact times. Yakama widely traded bags of dried pounded salmon with Chinook, Nez Perce, and other groups, for example.[29] Thus Yakama fishing

---

[25] For a nicely illustrated description of Northwest fishing gear, see Stewart, *Indian Fishing*.

[26] Testimony of Charley Dick, *U.S. v. Winans*, transcript of record, 104; Testimony of Lancaster Spencer, ibid., 141; Schuster, "Yakima Indian Traditionalism," 72.

[27] Estep to CIA, June 9, 1924, file 39001-24-115, YA, CCF, GR, BIA, RG 75, NA. See also testimony of Moses Strong, in *U.S. v. Winans*, transcript of record, 112; testimony of Louis Simpson, ibid., 131, noting that "See-we-pam and Wisham are together and it belonged to me personally my father was chief"; testimony of Charley Colwash, ibid., 138; testimony of Bill Charley, ibid., 162; Deward E. Walker, Jr. "Mutual Cross-Utilization of Economic Resources in the Plateau: An Example from Aboriginal Nez Perce Fishing practices," Washington State University, Laboratory of Anthropology, *Report of Investicetations*, no. 41 (1967): 15-39; Schuster, "Yakima Indian Traditionalism," 85, noting Yakama held reciprocal rights to fish at the Wenatshapam fishery, owned by the Wenatchee band of Yakama. The Wenatshapam fishery was ceded to the United States as a result of an Act of Congress of 1894. See Agreement with the Yakima Nation of Indians in Washington, 28 Stat. 320 (1894) and discussion in Chapter 5.

[28] Hunn, "Mobility as a Factor," 34. Click Relander describes one ancient dispute over gear and location in *Drummers and Dreamers* (Caldwell, ID: The Caxton Printers, 1956): 25, 308.

[29] Walker, "Mutual Cross-Utilization," 16-17, 18; Schuster, "Yakima Indian Traditionalism," 94-98; Smith, "Salmon Fishers of the Columbia," 13; Alvin M. Josephy, Jr. *The Nez Perce Indians and the Opening of the Northwest*, abridged edition (Lincoln: University of Nebraska

historically had both nutritive and trade value, and both were part of a much larger social, spiritual, and economic system, outside of which fishing had no meaning.

Conflict at the Table

Before the 1860s, when canning technology made it possible to store large quantities of salmon for long-distance transport, Euro-Americans fished Columbia River waters sporadically. Fur traders and settlers disliked fish as long as meat was available, and early marketing attempts aimed at international trade rather than local markets, which only emphasized the inadequacy of storing and shipping techniques. The Hudson's Bay Company, for example, tried to sell salted salmon internationally during the 1830s, but beyond Hawaii few buyers found the product desirable.[30]

The development of canning techniques, and the discovery that consumers found chinook and sockeye salmon more palatable and attractive than other species, launched the commercial salmon industry in the Pacific Northwest. Canning operations soon lined both banks of the Columbia River: in 1873 there were seven; by 1875 there were 14, and by 1880, there were 35, in addition to at least 12 fishing stations between Cape Disappointment and the Cascades. By 1882, *The Morning Oregonian* reported that "salmon packing is the largest industry, save wheat growing, in the northwest, when more salmon is put up on the Columbia river than in all other localities in the world."[31]

Although fish had economic importance to both Euro-Americans and Native Americans, Euro-Americans perceived and used the fisheries in different ways than did their predecessors. Commercial fishers were in business to take fish from the river and sell them to consumers for profit. The sole value of the fish was equal to the value fish could bring in a market. Fishers caught salmon quickly and in large numbers. The catch went to canneries near the river to be processed and preserved for shipping. The market for canned salmon was Europe until the early 1880s, when a domestic market began to develop. Marketing remained difficult until it was possible to make direct shipments of fish from the river via the railroads.[32] That transport system made regular commercial shipments possible and profitable.

Press, 1971): 21, 28; Robert H. Ruby and John A. Brown, *The Chinook Indians: Traders of the Lower Columbia River*, The Civilization of the American Indian Series (Norman: University of Oklahoma Press, 1976): 21ff. See also *Washington v. Washington State Commercial Passenger Fishing Vessel Association*, 443 U.S. 658, 658 nn. 6-7 (1979), noting commercial and trade uses of salmon historically.

[30] Meinig, *The Great Columbia Plain: A Historical Geography, 1805-1910* (Seattle: University of Washington Press, 1968) 59; Boxberger, *To Fish in Common*, 35.

[31] "The Salmon Interest," *Morning Oreaonian*, Jan. 1, 1882, 1-2; see also Smith, *Salmon Fishers of the Columbia*, 15-23.

[32] "The Salmon Interest," *Morning Oregonian*, 1.

Yakima fishers at Celilo Falls, Oregon

Northwest Museum of Arts & Culture/Eastern Washington State Historical Society, Spokane Washington, American Indians of the Pacific Northwest Images Digital Collection, Negative # L94-14.50, used by permission

Commercial fishers employed tools and techniques of an extractive industry. Gill netting, mostly done at night, was the principal method of Euro-American salmon fishing.[33] But seines, fish traps, and fish wheels were also used.[34] Commercial fishers used fish wheels on the Columbia between 1879 and 1934, when net fishers finally pushed through a Washington voter initiative that curtailed fixed gear fishing, including wheels—Oregon voters had banned wheel fishing in 1926.[35] The fish wheel, a giant water wheel with three or more cavernous wire baskets scooped fish out of the river continuously and could "take in a good day's run 10 or 20 tons," according to Thomas Lang, a resident of The Dalles and later a special agent for the Indian Service.[36] Water-powered wheels could be moved around on the river once attached to scows. Owners often blasted rocks from which Yakama historically had fished to position their wheels on flat ground. "There was a standing rock there fishing ground," Thomas Simpson testified in the *Winans* litigation, "and that was all blasted out [by Winans Bros.] and is now a fish wheel instead of a standing place."[37] The wheels could take an enormous quantity of salmon: One large wheel caught 200 tons of salmon during the 1906 season alone.[38]

The social organization of Euro-American fishing flowed from the extractive nature of the industry. Fishers were largely men who traveled to the Columbia for the business of fishing. Non-indians worked as boat masters, and at other oversight jobs, while thousands of Chinese immigrants and other minorities toiled in the canneries until increased mechanization did away with many of those jobs in the early 1900s.[39] The industry largely took resources and

---

[33] "The Salmon Interest," *Morning Oregonian*, 1.

[34] Smith, *Salmon Fishers of the Columbia;* Robert J. Browning, *Fisheries of the North Pacific: History, Species, Gear and Processes* (Anchorage: Northwest Publishing Co., 1974). Fishing boats with nets were an investment of at least $50,000 in 1882, according to "The Salmon Interest," *The Morning Oregonian*, 2.

[35] 1927 Ore. Laws 17. See also *P. J. McGowan & Sons, Inc. v. Van Winkle*, 21 F.2d 76, 77 (D. Ore. 1927); Brown, *Mountain in the Clouds*, 152-53; Ivan J. Donaldson and Frederick K. Cramer, *Fish Wheels of the Columbia* (Portland, OR: Binfords & Mort, 1971): i, 111-13.

[36] Lang to CIA, June 14, 1887, cited in *U.S. v. Seufert*, U.S. Brief, 40.

[37] Testimony of Thomas Simpson, *U.S. v. Winans*, transcript of record, 90.

[38] Donaldson and Cramer, *Fish Wheels of the Columbia*; Smith, *Salmon Fishers of the Columbia*, 36; *U.S. v. Winans*, transcript of record, 120, 136. For a detailed discussion of canning technology, see Patrick W. O'Bannon, "Technological Innovation in the Pacific Coast Canned Salmon Industry, 1864-1924" (Ph D. diss., University of California-San Diego, 1983).

[39] Chinese workers were employed beginning in 1872, Smith, *Salmon Fishers of the Columbia*, 23; Netboy, *Columbia River Salmon and Steelhead*, 28-29; Cekay, A Chinese Memory, Northwest Magazine, *Sunday Oregonian*, Aug. 28, 1983, p. NW 10. Citizenship was a requirement for fishing in Washington under 1891 Wash. Laws § 171, 1902 Wash. Laws §§ 5313-5314. A machine called the "Iron Chink" began displacing workers in the canneries in 1905, with one machine able to do the work of 30-40 laborers. By 1918, a "Model G" machine could bone and slice a salmon for canning at the rate of 60 fish per minute. Smith, ibid., 23-25.

revenues out of state. "It makes some men rich, it gives many men daily bread, it builds but few homes," an 1882 newspaper wrote.[40]

While some Yakama continued to fish solely for their own subsistence, some began to find employment at the canneries.[41] Catching fish for sale was not a new concept to Yakama. Yakama had historically traded surplus catch with other Plateau peoples, and arrangements to sell excess fish to canneries or local residents was not outside the realm of their subsistence way of life. Canneries paid for fish, an important consideration for the chronically cash-poor Yakama. There are no figures on Yakama subsistence and market fishing before 1937.[42] An Indian Office estimate in 1940 set the Yakama take at Celilo Falls as 60 percent subsistence and 40 percent market.[43]

---

[40] "The Salmon Interest," *The Morning Oregonian*, 2. Courtland Smith studied the 1880 census for Clatsop County—taken in May, at the height of the fishing season—and found that of 1,293 fishers who lived in the county, 91% were single; 86% boarded at local rooming houses; 13% were born in the United States; and 1% were born in Oregon. Of the foreign-born fishers, 44% were from Scandinavia. There were an estimated 2,500 fishers in Washington State in 1880. Smith, *Salmon Fishers of the Columbia*, 26-27.

[41] In 1917, Agent Carr described a group of Rock Creek Indians who followed pre-contact subsistence patterns as they traveled to Fall Bridge, Wash. to fish for salmon in the spring, living along the river until they went to the mountains in the summer for berry gathering, returning to the river in the fall to secure a winter's supply of fish, and finally returning to Rock Creek for the winter. Carr to CIA, Feb. 26, 1917, file 14373-17-115, YA, CCF, GR, BIA, RG 75, NA.

[42] Construction on Bonneville Dam began in 1933 and was completed in 1937, at which time fish ladders were first installed. Between 1933 and 1937, there were no attempts to mitigate damage to fisheries. Because most Indian fisheries lie above Bonneville Dam, any Indian fishing after 1933 would have been affected by some destruction of the stocks. The total poundage of all salmon species caught with dip nets and set lines on the Columbia (the U.S. Bureau of Fisheries estimated that 99.9 percent of the fishers using those methods were Indians) was as follows for 1928 to 1936: 1928, 168,278 pounds; 1929, 413,242; 1930, 660,004; 1931, 860,848; 1932, 245,415; 1933, 864,695; 1934 (dip nets only) 531,700; 1935 (dip nets only) 1,650,900; 1936 (dip nets only) 454,430. These figures do not include fish taken for food and trade, and the figures include fish taken by all Indian fishers, including Yakama and Umatilla fishers, and others as well. Kenneth R.L. Simmons, District Counsel, to William Zimmerman, Jr., Assist. CIA, Nov. 5, 1938, folder 115B "General Wildlife Correspondence and Circulars, box 351, YA, Decimal Subject File 921, BIA, RG 75, NA [hereafter cited as Simmons to Zimmerman]. See also "Schedule of Totals from 1937 Fishing Permits Issued on the Yakima Reservation," noting that 345 received permits to fish at Mt. Adams Lake, Fish Lake, Klickitat River, Logy-Satus Creek, and Medicine Valley, catching 5,258 fish. Another 8,000 fish were caught by Indians employed in the Civilian Conservation Corps, Indian Division, and another 10,000 fish were caught by Indians without permits, making a total of 23,268 fish caught total, folder 115B "General Wildlife Correspondence and Circulars," box 351, YA, Decimal Subject File 921, BIA, RG 75, NA.

[43] "Minutes of Meeting of Indian Service Personnel in the Pacific Northwest to Discuss Indian Hunting, Fishing, and Trapping Problems," meeting held May 6-7, 1940, reported in office of Indian Affairs, Circular of Information to Superintendents, Wildlife Conservation Officers, etc., May 28, 1940, folder 115B "General Wildlife Correspondence and Circulars," box 351,

For Yakama, commercial fishing never eclipsed subsistence fishing in importance.[44] "Most of our Indians are opposed to fishing by wheel, traps, and the like and for commercial purposes, although nearly all of them do sell a few fish at times, or trade fish for salt and provisions," Agent Estep wrote in 1927.[45] For most Yakama, Indians who fished solely for the canneries or for their own businesses were no better than "white game hogs" who recklessly destroyed wildlife populations for sport.[46] Worse, Indian market fishers set up their wheels or other equipment at historic fishing locations, justifying their actions on the basis of inherited rights. Conflict between subsistence and market fishers within the Yakama Nation increased during the early twentieth century just as did conflict between Yakama and non-Native fishers.

Commercial fishing rapidly depleted the Yakamas' table of plenty. Between 1866 and 1883, the annual landings of Columbia River salmon increased from 272,000 pounds to a record high of 42,799,000 pounds.[47] Thereafter the commercial catch exceeded the 1883 record only 5 times between 1895 and 1919, and after 1919 the annual catch usually remained well below the old record.[48] The high catch levels occurred despite the decline of salmon stocks because canneries and fishers constantly increased the scale of mechanization of their operations. If fishers caught more fish than canneries could handle they simply dumped the dead fish back into the river to rot—and thousands of fish were wasted in this manner every year.[49] Overfishing, in addition to degradation of the salmon habitat by logging, farming, and mining, made competition for a share of the declining stock more intense.[50]

Decimal Subject File 921, YA, BIA, RG 75, NA-Seattle [hereafter cited as Circular on Indian Hunting and Fishing, 1940].

[44] Circular on Indian and Hunting and Fishing, 1940.

[45] Estep to CIA, Nov. 14, 1927, RG 75, CCF, file 39001-24-115, YA, CCF, GR, BIA, RG 75, NA; Testimony of Bill Charley, *U.S. v. Winans*, transcript of record, 173 [speaking through interpreter], noting that he sometimes sold a "sack full" of fish to "hotels around town."

[46] Estep to CIA, June 9, 1924, file no. 39001-24-115, YA, CCF, GR, BIA, RG 75, NA.

[47] The annual pack on the river had increased every year, with the exception of 1877, to a record 550,000 cases. "The Salmon Interest," *Morning Oregonian*, 1.

[48] Netboy, *Columbia Salmon and Steelhead Trout: Their Fight for Survival*, Table I, "Landings of Columbia River Salmon and Steelhead trout, excluding troll catches, by species, 1866-1977." See also below, Appendix II, "Columbia River Salmon Fishery Commercial Catch, 1866-1934."

[49] Smith, *Salmon Fishers of the Columbia*, 30; Brown, *Mountain in the Clouds*, 152. Canneries set landing limits beginning in the mid-1880s.

[50] Hewes, "Indian Fisheries Productivity," 144-149; Smith, *Salmon Fishers of the Columbia*, at 20-22. On the dynamics of commercial fisheries in relation to fish stocks, see James A. Crutchfield, "Management of the North Pacific Fisheries: Economic Objectives and Issues," *Washington Law Review* 43 (1967): 283-307; Russel L. Barsh, *The Washington Fishing Rights Controversy: An Economic Critique*, rev. ed. (Seattle: Graduate School of Business Administration, University of Washington, 1977).

Fishers, and a variety of state regulatory agencies created in Washington and Oregon during the 1890s, consistently viewed the solution to the problem of declining stocks as one of augmenting wild salmon stocks with hatchery-bred salmon rather than curtailing fishing. Although beginning in 1918, Washington and Oregon began to coordinate their regulation of Columbia salmon fishing through licensing, fixed seasons, and gear restrictions, enforcement remained sporadic and ineffectual.[51] The Oregon Master Warden complained in 1903, "I found that fishing was being carried on in all directions and no pretense whatever being made to respect the law."[52] Fishing restrictions appeared more unnecessary where hatcheries held the potential to supply unlimited quantities of fish, although hatcheries had negligible and even detrimental affects on wild salmon stocks because techniques for raising the fish were severely limited by lack of knowledge.[53]

In the midst of this fishing frenzy, rival groups of fishers—distinguished by their gear type and ethnicity—attempted to bar one another from fishing, often by citing the alleged waste and unconscionable depredations committed on the fishery by the target group. Oregon gill netters vied against Washington pound net operators; net fishers attacked fixed gear fishers; and white fishers sought to bar non-whites from the fishery. The effort against Chinese in Washington was successful: An 1891 Act made citizenship a requirement for fishing, and Chinese were systematically excluded from participating in the industry in any capacity save cannery workers.[54] "Fishwheel men" were banned from operating on the river by both Washington and Oregon in the 1920s and 1930s by rival groups, as we have seen. The effort against Indians, including Yakama, was long and bitter, and unsuccessful, although it is not yet finished.[55]

---

[51] In 1915, because of increasing conflict between Oregon and Washington regulations, the states adopted a uniform fish code that stipulated neither state would alter its regulations without the consent of the other. Elmer Wollenberg, "The Columbia River Fish Compact," *Oregon Law Review* 18 (1938): 94. Congress approved this joint regulation in 1918, 40 Stat. 515 (1918).

[52] *Annual Report of the Department of Fisheries of Oregon to the Legislative Assembly* (1903): 7, quoted in Charles F. Wilkinson and Daniel Keith Conner, "The Law of the Pacific Salmon Fishery: Conservation and Allocation of a Transboundary Common Property Resource," *Kansas Law Review* 32 (1983): 34 n. 92. On Washington and Oregon fishing regulations, see Wilkinson and Conner, ibid., 33-34; Netboy, *Columbia Salmon and Steelhead Trout*, 34-36.

[53] On fish hatcheries in Washington, see Brown, *Mountain in the Clouds*, 146-47; Netboy, *Columbia Salmon and Steelhead Trout*, 105-07.

[54] On rival fishing groups, see Brown, *Mountain in the Clouds*, 152-53; Donaldson and Cramer, *Fish Wheels of the Columbia*, 111-13; Smith, *Salmon Fishers of the Columbia*, 27, 39-40; Netboy, *Columbia River Salmon and Steelhead Trout*, 19-36.

[55] See American Friends Service Committee, *Uncommon Controversy*; Fay G. Cohen, *Treaties on Trial, The Continuing Controversy over Northwest Indian Fishing Rights*, a report prepared for the American Friends Service Committee (Seattle: University of Washington Press, 1986).

To non-Indian fishers, Yakama were visible and unwelcome predators on the commercial fishery. Yakama and other Native fishers flocked to their historic fishing places every year where their dramatic dip net fisheries provided an exotic attraction for tourists and locals alike. Their campgrounds, drying houses, and herds of horses spread Indian activities from the river banks onto adjoining lands, where they drew the ire of landowners whose neat orchards and newly fenced pastures marched riverward to meet the edges of the canneries' riverbank claims. The combined Yakama and Umatilla fisheries represented less than one percent of the total commercial harvest on the Columbia River between 1928 and 1937.[56] Yet as early as 1916, the Washington Supreme Court voiced a common public sentiment when it wrote that "the salmon industry of this state must be grievously wounded in its very nurseries, because the Yakimas and other tribes ... claim many such [fishing] spots on various waters to be exempt" from state regulation.[57]

Not all state residents hated Yakama fishers. Some, such as Thomas Lang, a long-time Dalles resident and later a special agent for the Indian Office, saw tragedy in the Indians' struggle against giant canneries. In 1887, Lang wrote "at the request of many citizens" to Thomas J. Morgan, Indian Commissioner (1889-1893):

> I wish, dear sir, you could see the Indians as they sit about the rocks adjoining the fisheries, and see tons of [salmon] going into refrigerating cars, caught by wheels lowered into the eddies in which this beautiful fish rest in their way up through the rapids.... These Indians come constantly to me and beg me to write to you for them.[58]

The sight of Indians watching the huge harvest and waste of commercial fishing operations from the vantage points of their old fishing places became common in the following years. Similarly, on an evening in late July 1889, Special Agent Henry Marchant, observed a group of hungry Yakama Indians watching commercial fishers extract 38,000 pounds of salmon from the river and load it into railroad cars.[59]

---

[56] Estimated from statistics in Netboy, *Columbia River Salmon and Steelhead Trout*, Table I, "Landings of Columbia River Salmon and Steelhead Trout, Excluding Troll Catches, by Species, 1866-1977;" Simmons to Zimmerman, Nov. 5, 1938.

[57] *State v. Towessnute*, 89 Wash. 478, 479 (1916).

[58] Lang to Morgan, June 14, 1887, cited in *U.S. v. Seufert*, U.S. brief, 40. Two years later, Lang was moved to write, "It is hard for 15 to 30 Indians to go and stand on the rocks at their old fishing berths and see 20 tons of salmon turned out by machinery at a single berth, and they not allowed to take one." Lang to Edward Atkinson, Aug. 15, 1889, file 4799, *Winans*, box 419, Attorney General Letters Received, Records of the Department of Justice [hereafter AGLR, DOJ], RG 60, NA.

[59] Marchant to Attorney General, July 31, 1889, file 4799, *Winans*, box 419, AGLR, DOJ, RG 60, NA.

C. C. Hutchins, a "scenic photographer" and member of the White Salmon Commercial Club in White Salmon, Washington, took up the case of several Klickitat who sought to obtain dead salmon from the Underwood Hatchery for food in 1919, arguing that the Bureau should protect the Indians' access to fish.[60] To Lang, Hutchins, and others, Yakama were tragic and "noble savages" of a sort; whose elderly chief and their peoples deserved consideration at the least because they had believed U.S. treaty promises.[61]

Indian Fishers in the Courts

The Yakamas' principal fisheries on the Columbia were off their reservation and were clustered along both sides of the Columbia River between the Dalles and Celilo Falls. Indian fisheries, however, extended all along the river and its tributaries. The same qualities that made certain locations attractive to Indians, also made those sites ideal for fish wheels. "Fishwheel men" stationed their contraptions specifically by observing dip net fishers on the Columbia, primarily between the Cascades and Celilo Falls. Here, at Tum Water and The Dalles in Yakima territory, ancient lava channels and natural eddies harbored fish resting before their journeys forced them upstream over spectacular falls.[62] Fish wheels appeared in this area first in 1883-84.[63]

The off-reservation Columbia fisheries continued to attract Yakama fishers not only because these were traditionally fished places, but on-reservation fisheries became less productive during the period. Charley Ike, a Yakama fisher, stated that fish wheels on the Columbia had destroyed many of the smaller salmon runs that normally travelled into reservation creeks by way of the Yakima River. Chief Louis Simpson stated that there were no fish in streams near Toppenish by 1904.[64] While commercial fishing depopulated fish stocks, so too did the numerous irrigation projects on the Yakima River and

---

[60] Hutchins did not argue, however, that Indians should be allowed to fish for themselves. C. C. Hutchins to CIA, Sept. 6, 1919, file 781531-19-115, YA, CCF, GR, BIA, RG 75, NA. See also Carr to CIA, Dec. 10, 1919, ibid.; and Hutchins to CIA, July 21, 1920, ibid.

[61] See "Let Us Be Just to the Red Man," and other clippings enclosed in Francis Garrecht to AG, Feb. 26, file 58718-14-115, YA, GR, CCF, BIA, RG 75, NA; "Pow Wow in Senate," *Ledger*, Tacoma, WA, Jan. 23, 1921; "Yakima's Pleading for Treaty Rights," *Seattle Times*, Jan. 29, 1921; "Ancient Fishing Rights Upheld," *Spokane Chronicle*, Mar. 23, 1921.

[62] "Approximate Location of Indian Fisheries as Described in the Gordon Report," map, in Gordon *Report*; Donaldson and Cramer, *Fish Wheels of the Columbia*, 72; *U.S. v. Seufert*, U.S. brief, 51-53ff; Swindell Report.

[63] Donaldson and Cramer, *Fish Wheels of the Columbia*, 83. Gill nets were primarily used on the lower Columbia, below present-day Bonneville Dam; gill-netters still dominate there, see Smith, *Salmon Fishers of the Columbia*, 27. Trollers began to dominate the ocean salmon harvest in the twentieth century, once gasoline powered engines became available, see Wilkinson and Conner, "Law of the Pacific Salmon, Fishery," 32, n. 78.

[64] Testimony in *U.S. v. Winans*, transcript of record, 140-41; testimony of Louis Simpson, ibid., 133; testimony of Lancaster Spencer, ibid., 141-42.

smaller streams. Here—where an estimated 90-97 percent of Yakima river water passed through irrigation works—unscreened ditches led thousands of migrating fish to their death in fields.[65] Increased sedimentation and pollution of streams from farming also destroyed prime salmon spawning areas.

Control of land was an important aspect of commercial fishers ability to exclude Indians from off-reservation fisheries. By 1888, "All the lands along the river bank [at The Dalles] have passed out of the control of the United States to individual settlers," observed John D. C. Atkins, Commissioner (1885-1888), "and the Indians are not allowed to pass from the state highway to the river to fish. Barbed wire fences securely locked or guarded effectually bar their access to the river."[66]

Indians had for five years repeatedly attempted to scale the fences, and in 1886 they finally tore them down and "forced a passage to the river." A public meeting held at Dalles City resulted in a temporary passageway to the fishery, that the landowners quickly refenced.[67] Federal public lands legislation granting tide and shorelands to the states and state laws that allowed individuals to file on those lands invited the privatization of riverbanks suitable for fishing or other development.[68]

Federal officials were well aware that non-Indian settlers were claiming shorelands along Indian fisheries but lacked any coherent authorities to prevent this. In 1884, for example, the War Department ordered the Land Office at Vancouver, Washington, not to recognize homestead or other entries on lands along the Columbia River, including specifically lands bordering the Tum Water fishery.[69] John O'Kane, the receiver of the Vancouver office from 1885 to 1889, recalled that he had never seen the directive.[70] No one took

---

[65] Dennis Winn, Field Superintendent to Commissioner of Fisheries, Dec. 8, 1919 [enclosing photographs], file 110573-19-341, YA, CCF, GR, BIA, RG 75, NA. Winn wrote that current estimates held that "there are less than 5 per cent of fish ascending the Yakima River each year in comparison with ten years ago." See also L. M. Holt to CIA, Jan. 30, 1920, ibid.; W. M. Reed to L. M. Holt, May 5, 1920, enclosing advertisement for "Aitken Revolving Self-Cleaning Fish Screen," ibid. Although by the early twentieth century Washington law required screens on irrigation ditches, the law was not enforced.

[66] *U.S. v. Seufert*, U.S. Brief, 40, quoting Atkins to Secretary of Interior, Feb. 20, 1888.

[67] *U.S. v. Seufert*, U.S. Brief, 40.

[68] On state sales of shorelands, see 1895 Wash. Laws 527, repealing Act of March 26, 1890.

[69] Testimony of James O Kane, *U.S. v. Winans*, transcript of record, 241-49; Circular to Registers and Receivers, May 31, 1884, reprinted in ibid., 247. See also discussion of 1884 letters from General Land Office to Vancouver Land Office, in ibid., 247-49; and U.S. Department of Interior, General Land Office, Circular Relative to Lands in the Possession of Indian Occupants, Oct. 26, 1887, 115:20, CRP. Hubert Howe Bancroft records that non-Indian settlement occurred at Tum Water as early as 1847, Bancroft, *The Works of Hubert Howe Bancroft*, vol. XXXI: *History of Washington, Idaho, and Montana, 1845-1889* (San Francisco: The History Co., 1890): 6-10.

[70] Indian Office Circular, May 31, 1884, stating that on non-reservation lands along the Columbia River the Registers/Receivers in the land office are not supposed to allow entries

notice until non-Indians had bought up or staked claims on virtually all the land along the fishery.[71]

The Tum Water Fishery, about 60 miles from the Yakama Reservation, became the first focus of conflict between Yakama and non-Indian fishers, and the resulting litigation culminated in the Supreme Court's *Winans* decision in 1905, recognizing Yakama treaty rights to this important off-reservation site. Tum Water was situated on the Washington side of the Columbia, about five miles from The Dalles, Oregon.[72] The site was a "[f]irst class natural fishery," large enough to accommodate 67 to 100 individuals at a time. Lancaster Spencer, a Yakama fisher, noted in 1904 that "a thousand Indians" came to the site every year.[73] Frank Taylor, a farmer and commercial fisher, purchased 2000 acres of land adjacent to the fishery and had partially fenced the land by 1884.[74] When Yakima Agent R. H. Milroy (1882-1885) asked Taylor to allow Indians to "take and cure fish" on his lands and "to approach such fishery in whatsoever way they saw fit, and to pasture their ponies," on the land, Taylor closed the fences, fearing that his land would be worthless if Indians had unlimited access.[75]

In July 1884, several Yakama assisted by Milroy, brought suit against Taylor in the Washington territorial district court at Yakima, where they lost.[76] On appeal in 1887, the Washington Territory Supreme Court reversed, holding that land patented under federal laws dated after a treaty had been ratified were subject to the treaty's terms.[77] Thus, Taylor had to allow Indians to camp and fish from his shorelands because the Yakamas' treaty of 1855 reserved to

---

and filings, quoted in *U.S. v. Winans*, transcript of record, 246-249; testimony of O'Kane, ibid. See also Plaintiffs' Exhibit B, T. I. Anderson, acting CIA, to Register and Receiver of the Vancouver Land Office, in ibid., 376; and Plaintiffs' Exhibit C, A. B. Upshaw, Acting CIA, to Secretary of Interior, May 24, 1888, in ibid., 377.

[71] Testimony of James O'Kane, *U:S. v. Winans*, transcript of record, 244.

[72] The fishery encompassed lands along the Columbia in Tp. 2 N. R. 13 E. Willamette Meridian (sections 25, 35, and 36); and Tp. 2 N. R. 14 E. Willamette Meridian (Sections 19 and 30). The land in question in *Winans* is Tp. 2 N. R. 13 E. Willamette Meridian (esp. sections 25 and 36); and Tp. 2 N. R. 14 E., Willamette Meridian (esp. sections 19 and 30); this is a subset of the original area at issue in *Taylor*.

[73] Gordon Report, 65; testimony of Lancaster Spencer, *U.S. v. Winans*, transcript of record, 145.

[74] William Taylor purchased 99 acres along the fishery for $123.75 in 1869, receiving a patent in 1870. William Murphy purchased adjacent lands, and Frank Taylor purchased these lands, and more, under federal preemption and homestead laws. Testimony of James O'Kane, *U.S. v. Winans*, transcript of record, 241-42; *U.S. v. Taylor*, 3 Wash. Terr. 88, 95 (1887); Franklin P. Mays, Oregon U.S. Attorney, to AG, Sept. 25, 1890, file 4799, *Winans*, box 419, AGLR, DOJ, RG 60, NA.

[75] Mays to AG, Sept. 25, 1890, file 4799, *Winans*, box 419, AGLR, DOJ, RG 60, NA.

[76] Gordon *Report*, 42; 3 Wash. Terr. 88.

[77] 3 Wash. Terr. 88.

them this "usual and accustomed" site.[78] The court relied on the district court to work out a decree to implement its decision.[79]

Consistent with the Supreme Court's decision, the resulting 1889 decree recognized an easement across Taylor's property for Yakama fishers, whom Taylor and his workers were not to disturb or harass. More significantly, however, through the decree, the lower court imposed several restrictions on Yakama to make their fishery more compatible with commercial fishing and private property ownership. First, the court imposed a set "season" on Yakama fishers, who could now fish only from June 1 to September 1. Second, the court established Tum Water's geographic boundaries by designating trails Yakama were to use to get there and by marking out a ten acre area for campsites, grazing, and drying houses.[80] By imposing "seasons" and confining fishers to a designated area, the court wrote into law a Euro-American version of Yakama fishing as firmly located in time and place as needed to fit them into an overall scheme of privately held, state-regulated rights.

The *Taylor* litigation foreshadowed a judicial pattern of subordinating Indian interests to those of Euro-Americans, even as the Washington courts upheld the superiority of federally secured treaty rights as against the rights of settlers. Although Bureau officials believed treaty fishing rights had valuable commercial potential, Yakama fishers were not capitalizing on that opportunity, and no one expected subsistence to impede state commercial fishing operations.[81] Consequently, the lower court reserved the right to intercede in Yakama fishing and required Taylor to set aside his most marginal lands for a campsite. The site, "is inundated during high water, and when dry is devoid of vegetation. It would not pasture a goat, and is worthless to the Indians for grazing uses for their horses," observed DOJ agent Crawford.[82] To Yakama families, who required land enough for pasturage, camps, and thirty-five drying houses, the decree was a cruel joke.[83]

---

[78] If, as Taylor contended, the fishing rights clause of the Indians' treaty reserved rights to fish "in common" with non-Indians at any of the territory's fisheries, the court believed that the servitude imposed on non-Indian lands by the Yakama treaty would have been much more extensive than if Indian rights were recognized to exist only at "usual and accustomed" fishing places, as the *Taylor* court held, 3 Wash. Terr. 98.

[79] 3 Wash. Terr. 98.

[80] Decree, *U.S. v. Taylor* (Feb. 8, 1889), enclosed in John B. Allen, U.S. Attorney, Washington Territory, to Garland, AG, Feb. 21, 1889, file 4799, *Winans*, box 419, AGLR, DOJ, RG 60, NA.

[81] The Washington Supreme Court's opinion observed that "the court knows as a matter of common knowledge, that these Indians were always tenacious in adhering to past customs and traditions," even where newer methods would prove to be "of more avail than the old." 3 Wash. Terr. 97-98.

[82] Crawford to AG, Jan. 6, 1891, file 4799, *Winans*, box 419, AGLR, DOJ, RG 60, NA; Gordon also complained of the site, "there is not pasturage enough to keep one animal, it being composed almost entirely of gravel and rock." Gordon Report, 38-40.

[83] Crawford to AG, Jan. 1891, file 4799, *Winans*, box 419, AGLR, DOJ, RG 60, NA.

The *Taylor* case and resulting decree failed to alleviate conflict between Yakama and the succession of landowners who purchased the Tum Water site. Orson D. Taylor, a Baptist minister and no relation to Frank Taylor, purchased Frank Taylor's land in 1886, allegedly without knowing about the *Taylor* decision and decree. Orson Taylor, by his own account, had moved his family west to take advantage of a "Providential opportunity to teach [the Indians] how to better their condition physically, morally and spiritually."[84]

Taylor had more than a spiritual stake in Tum Water: he leased the site to two men with fish wheels, and the pair reportedly attempted several times to defraud the Yakama of their claims to the fishery.[85] Taylor and his men also used more violent tactics to keep Indians away, including stringing barbed wire across trails, tearing down or burning houses and camps, stealing horses, threatening to have fishers arrested, and beating them. One of the most notorious incidents involved one of Taylor's employees who was convicted in a local court for "unmercifully beating an Indian boy for catching salmon on [the Indians'] own ground where he had a written permit from the Yakama [sic] Agent to go and to fish."[86] Attempts by Thomas Lang, made a deputy special Indian agent in 1889, and a series of special agents of the Department of Justice only succeeded in escalating the violence.[87] Linneaus and Audubon

---

[84] O. D. Taylor to J. H. Mitchell, Aug. 27, 1889, file 4799, *Winans*, box 419, AGLR, DOJ, RG 60, NA. On O. D. Taylor's land purchases, see testimony of John O'Kane, *U.S. v. Winans*, transcript of record, 243. Taylor wrote that his own ministry to the Indians led him to set aside a ten-acre tract of land along the fishery that he allowed the Indians to use on the condition that "they should abstain from the use of liquor and from harboring criminal Indians and from interfering with the rights of white men on the fishery...," ibid.

[85] Those two men probably were Linneaus and Audubon Winans. O. D. Taylor to J. H. Mitchell, Aug. 27, 1889, file 4799, *Winans*, box 419, AGLR, DOJ, RG 60, NA. Taylor to Mitchell, box 419, AGLR, DOJ, RG 60, NA. On Taylor's attempts to defraud Indians of the fishery, see Henry Marchant to AG, July 31, 1889, file 4799, *Winans*, box 419, AGLR, DOJ, RG 60, NA [hereafter cited as Marchant Report, 1889]; O. D. Taylor to Thomas Priestly, Aug. 31, 1887, 115:20, CRP.

According to Special Agent Crawford, Marchant's successor at The Dalles, Taylor's motivations were more "shylockian" than Christian. Crawford reported that Taylor arrived at The Dalles in financial straits, and was taken in by Baptists who gave him a house and made him their pastor. He concocted various schemes to get rich, including insurance and land frauds, and money lending ventures. Probably his most imaginative success was getting the church trustees to mortgage the church and parsonage to him for back pay. When the trustees became disenchanted with him and asked him to leave, he threatened to foreclose on the property. Despite, or perhaps as a result of, his "sagacious rascality," Taylor become influential in the region, and among the wealthiest along the coast.

[86] Marchant Report, 1889.

[87] Federal officials won temporary injunction against Taylor in May 1890, but Judge C. H. Hanford acquitted Taylor of contempt charges in November, finding that Taylor's fish wheels did not obstruct Indian fishers. *In re O. D. Taylor* (U.S. Cir. Ct., So. Dist. Wash.), file 4799, *Winans*, box 419, AGLR, DOJ, RG 60, NA. Agent Crawford reported of the trial that testimony for the defense "was from beginning to end a tissue of the most rank falsehood." Taylor's

Winans, two brothers who leased Tum Water from Taylor in 1888 and who owned the property by December 1890, continued to use such tactics.[88]

To federal officials, the Yakama appeared to retreat in the face of conflict. "The Indians are timid and ignorant, and are not inclined to assert and maintain their rights as a white person would," wrote W. H. White, U.S. Attorney for Washington Territory.[89] Winnear, a Yakama, reported that "The Indians just stand now and do nothing.... The old women now they set down and cry."[90] A man came to T-Wash-pam's house near the fishery,

> and he says to me, if you don't get out of here, I will tear your house down. I did not believe him, that he would do it; pretty soon he put a lasso on our house, I got scared and cried, and put a little barrel on my back and took that and went away crying; he said, if you go to make any more trouble around here I will put you in jail; I said all right you can take me, that is all I said to him; what little things I had I was picking up and taking away, I was crying.[91]

Other fishers reported that threats of jail or violence kept them away from the fisheries, and from staking their own homestead entries at Tum Water.[92]

"gold forms the barrier which wards off the shafts of justice hurled at him." Crawford to AG, Jan. 6, 1891, ibid. The day after the trial ended, Crawford took his story to the local newspapers and was sharply censured by the Department of Justice and transferred to Fort Craig, N.M. See also White to Attorney General, June 30, 1889, ibid.

Taylor's attorneys were Mays and Huntington, of which Franklin Mays, former attorney for Frank Taylor, was still a consulting member while serving as Oregon U.S. Attorney; and Huntington was then Commissioner of the U.S. Circuit Court. See also Frank B. Crosthwaite, examiner, DOJ, to E. C. Foster, General Agent, Sept. 22, 1890, ibid.; and Winston to AG, Nov. 25, 1890, ibid.

[88] On the Winans brothers' purchase of the Taylor property, see Crawford to AG, Jan. 6, 1891, file 4799, *Winans*, box 419, AGLR, DOJ, RG 60, NA. The brothers purchased the land from Taylor as early as December 1890.

There is a mountain of documentation on abuses against Yakama fishers at Tum Water between 1889 and the early 1900s. See *CIA-AR*, 1889, 296; White to AG, June 30, 1889, file 4799, *Winans*, box 419, AGLR, DOJ, RG 60, NA; Henry Marchant, Special Agent, DOJ, to AG, July 31, 1889, ibid.; Thomas Priestly, Yakima Agent, to T. J. Morgan, March 19, 1890, ibid.; Caleb Smith, Secretary of Interior, to AG, March 28, 1895, ibid.; Yakama plaintiffs in *U.S. v. Winans*, transcript of record, 86-249.

[89] White to AG, June 30, 1889, file 4799, *Winans*, box 419, AGLR, DOJ, RG 60, NA.

[90] Testimony of Winnear, *U.S. v. Winans*, transcript of record, 126-27.

[91] *U.S. v. Winans*, transcript of record, 183-84 (speaking through interpreter).

[92] On threats against Yakama fishers, see testimony of Jo Ko-lock-en, *U.S. v. Winans*, transcript of record, 150 (speaking through interpreter); testimony of Charley Cath-lum-it, ibid., 154-55 (speaking through interpreter); testimony of William Speedies, ibid., 176-78 (speaking through interpreter). On problem of Yakama homesteads near Tum Water, see conflict between N. Whealdon and John Selatsee: Lang to Thomas Priestly, May 17, 1889, 115-23, CRP; Lang to Priestly, June 26, 1889, ibid.; *In the Matter of the Contest of the Homestead*

Although Yakama fishers clearly were frightened, Winnear and others also reported that they would "go and steal fish" at Tum Water when white men were not looking. Winnear recalled:

> I went there [Tum Water] and they told me dont you go down the river, you cant go there any more. They told me if I went there if Winan[s] seen me going in there he would put me in jail. And of course myself I stand up and went down. Two men told me not to go. If you raise the wire you will be arrested. I told them I am hungry for salmon and I went down and raised the wire myself.[93]

Jo-Ko-lock-en attempted to fish at Tum Water despite Winans' threats to jail him.[94] Some Yakama were jailed after crossing the Taylor-Winans property.[95]

Yakama required the assistance of a "competent white man" to protect them at Tum Water and elsewhere because their rights were open to debate, federal officials believed.[96] As Yakama saw it, the 1855 treaty clearly delineated their entitlements and they wanted enforcement. Chief White Swan stated in 1904, "If at that time during the treaty the government didn't agree to give us these fisheries we never ... would have agreed with the government."[97] Bill Charley stated:

> [W]hen the treaty had been made the old people had said, we want this, this is our privilege this fishing right, this place, we want this always to be laid out for us, and my people to fish, that is where that wheel is today. We are going around there with tears in our eyes, just looking at him [Winans]; the law said when they made the treaty ... you shall be never disturbed in your rights; this is just the same as you or me, and that is the reason we always come there and stay there.[98]

Yakama were not a violent people, and they continued to look to federal officials to enforce their rights. Yakama held "many councils" on the fisheries and "urged the inspector, the special agent, and myself to use every effort to

---

Entry no. 6273 of John Selatsi, U.S. Land Office, Vancouver, WA, May 1889, ibid.; Story & Bradshaw to Priestly, May 8, 1889, ibid. Selatsi, a Yakama, won his claim.

[93] Testimony of Winnear, *U.S. v. Winans*, transcript of record, 125. See also testimony of Bill Se-hi-am, ibid., 159-60 (speaking through interpreter).

[94] Testimony of Jo Ko Lock-en, in *U.S. v. Winans*, transcript of record, 151; testimony of Bill Se-hi-am, ibid., 160; testimony of William Speedies, ibid., 177 (speaking through interpreter). See also William Speedies, noting that he now steals water from a spring that the Winans brothers fenced, in ibid., 180 (speaking through interpreter).

[95] See for example testimony of Jo Ko lock-en, *U.S. v. Winans*, transcript of record, 152.

[96] White to AG, June 30, 1889, file 4799, *Winans*, box 419, AGLR, DOJ, RG 60, NA.

[97] Testimony of White Swan, *U.S. v. Winans*, transcript of record, 100; see also testimony of Bill Charley, ibid., 163 (speaking through interpreter).

[98] Testimony in *U.S. v. Winans*, transcript of record, 163.

restore to them their accustomed fishery," Agent L. T. Erwin (1893-1897) reported in 1894.[99]

Yakama litigants and Yakima Council members clearly saw the solution to the fishing conflicts in a court settlement. Yet one effect of litigation was to channel the broad political issue of how Yakama subsistence life could fit into a market society into discrete problems of whether Indians could prove to a court that they had fished in a particular place in the past: "What constitutes a usual and accustomed place will depend entirely upon the facts which may be presented as the case arises."[100] Because the cases left ambiguous what powers the tribe had to reserve off-reservation resources, state officials repeatedly asserted that state power was superior to tribal authority. The federal policy that treated Indians as "dependent wards," and married federal and tribal sovereignty in treaties, only blurred the line separating federal sovereignty from that of the tribes.

Consequently, *Taylor* and its progeny failed to quiet contention over Yakama rights to fish anywhere, and Agent Estep complained that the fishing litigation seemed endless: "it seems impossible for the courts to render any decision which does not again come up in some different form."[101] The Tum Water dispute continued into 1918, as Yakama secured the assistance of the Bureau and Department of Justice in bringing suit first against the Winans brothers, who purchased Taylor's lands, and second against the Seufert Brothers Company, a cannery and fruit packing firm that succeeded Winans and owned property on both the Washington and Oregon sides of the Columbia near Tum Water.

In *United States v. Winans*, a case that worked its way to the U.S. Supreme Court during 1894-1905, Washington state officials argued that the Yakamas' treaty fishing rights could not survive Washington statehood in 1889.[102] The state argued that because it was entitled to enter the federal union upon "an equal footing" with other states, neither the tribes nor the federal government could enter into an agreement that precluded the state from exercising complete sovereignty over the natural resources within its borders.[103] The Supreme Court rejected that argument and held that Yakama or

---

[99] *CIA-AR*, 1894, 326.

[100] F. H. Abbott, Acting CIA, to Carr, March 19, 1913, file 133661-12-115, YA, CCF, GR, BIA, RG 75, NA.

[101] Estep to CIA, June 9, 1924, file 39001-24-115, YA, CCF, GR, BIA, RG 75, NA.

[102] A brief litigation history of the case can be found in the following: *U.S. v. Winans*, 193 U.S. 371, 379-80 (1905); *U.S. v. Winans*, 73 F. 72, 74-75 (1896); *CIA-AR*, 1895-96, 319; U.S. Attorney for District Washington to AG, June 16, 1903, file 4799, *Winans*, AGLR, box 420, DOJ, RG 60, NA; Acting Secretary of the Interior to AG, Aug. 3, 1903, ibid. [decision to appeal]; CIA to Secretary of the Interior, July 30, 1903, ibid.

[103] Charles H. Carey and Franklin P. Mays, brief for respondents, *U.S. v. Winans*, 198 U.S 371, 375-76(1905); see also *Geer v. Connecticut*, 161 U.S. 519 (1896); and Thomas Lund, *American Wildlife Law* (Berkeley: University of California Press, 1980): 35-46.

the federal government had reserved by the 1855 treaty a perpetual easement to Tum Water that statehood could not affect.[104] The treaty, Justice McKenna wrote, "fixes in the land such easements as enables the right to be exercised" both on and off the reservation.[105]

Despite the seeming victory of Yakama treaty rights over state power in *Winans*, the Court clearly resolved the balance of tribal and state power in favor of the states:

> And surely it was within the competency of the Nation to secure to the Indians such a remnant of the great rights they possessed as 'taking fish at all usual and accustomed places.' Nor does it restrain the State unreasonably, if at all, in the regulation of the right.[106]

The Court's decision had made clear that while Yakama had treaty rights, these rights would be regulated and manipulated to suit the needs of the state and its own licensed fishers. Moreover, the decision wavered on the issue of who had reserved the fishing rights for the tribe. Justice McKenna's ambiguity on that point, coupled with his conviction that the states could regulate Yakama fishing, suggested that he believed tribal sovereignty to be subordinate to that of the states as well as the federal government.[107]

As in *Taylor*, the decree that implemented *Winans* protected the Yakamas' access to Tum Water while further reshaping their fishery to conform to commercial fishers at the site. The Winans Brothers Company could retain its three fish wheels at Tum Water (although it could build no additional ones), and Yakama fishers were not to interfere with the wheels by fishing within 200 feet of them. The decree allowed Yakama to camp and fish from the site, exactly as had *Taylor*.[108]

Yakama fishers customarily fished from both banks of the Columbia, and necessarily came in conflict with Oregon fishers as well. The Seufert Brothers Company purchased both Wah Sucks and Tum Water, where their plant turned out 32 tons of canned salmon per day during the season and boxed

---

[104] *U.S. v. Winans*, 198 U.S. 371, 381-83 (1905).

[105] 198 U.S. at 384.

[106] 198 U.S. at 384. See also Ralph Johnson, "The States versus Indian Off-Reservation Fishing: A United States Supreme Court Error," *Washington Law Review* 47 (1972): 207-36.

[107] Recall how Justice McKenna also blurred federal and tribal sovereignty in *Winters v. United States*, 207 U.S. 570 (1908), in which it is unclear whether the tribes, the federal government, or both, reserved water necessary to supply the reservation. See Norris Hundley, Jr., "The Dark and Bloody Ground of Indian Water Rights: Confusion Elevated to Principle," *Western Historical Quarterly* 9 (Oct. 1978): 465-72; Hundley, "The 'Winters' Decision and Indian Water Rights: A Mystery Reexamined," *Western Historical Quarterly* 13 (Jan. 1982): 33-39. See also Chapter 7.

[108] Estep to CIA, June 9, 1924, file 39001-24-115, YA, CCF, GR, BIA, RG 75, NA.

cherries, peaches, apricots, prunes, and peas during other times.[109] The company owned 19 stationary wheels, 17 scows, and 4 seines at one time, and owned "practically all of the shore lands along the Columbia River on both sides of the river for a distance of several miles from The Dalles, Oregon."[110] Sam Williams, a Yakama fisher and minister of an Indian Shaker church he had established at The Dalles, was one of many Yakama who fished at Wah Sucks until the company began a campaign to drive away those who did not contract to sell their fish to the cannery. Williams was a unique case in that he had operated a fish wheel for the Seufert cannery, but he engendered the company's hostility when began selling his fish elsewhere.[111]

The Bureau responded to Williams' request for assistance, but only after he had endured abuse ranging from verbal insults to attempts on his life—and had hired his own attorneys.[112] Letters written by other Yakama complained of Seufert's actions but not Williams' wheel operations, indicating that some members of the tribe saw Williams' conflict as more than his personal problem.[113]

Williams and the Yakama won their claim that the 1855 treaty protected their right to fish on the Oregon side of the river. Moreover, the district court's decree protected Yakama fishing for "food, domestic, and other purposes." The court also expressly "encouraged [Yakama] to adopt the more modern and advanced methods and means of prosecuting their fishing enterprises."[114] The

---

[109] Donaldson and Cramer, *Fish Wheels of the Columbia*, 84, 96.

[110] Carr to CIA, March 4, 1915, file 93689-13-115, YA, CCF, GR, BIA, RG 75, NA. Carr reported that the Seufert Co.'s operations "seriously affects the food supply of the Indians." See also Donaldson and Cramer, *Fish Wheels of the Columbia*, 83.

[111] Williams to CIA, Feb. 12, 1915, file 93689-13-115, YA, CCF, GR, BIA, RG 75, NA; See also "Report of [Robert A.] Rankin's [Assistant U.S. Attorney, Portland] Investigation," Aug. 25, 1914, enclosed in Assist. AG to Secretary of Interior, Sept. 1, 1914, ibid. [background and status of case]; Carr to CIA, May 18, 1914, ibid. For background on Sam Williams, see Ray Harmon, "The Indian Shaker Church The Dalles," *Oregon Historical Quarterly* 72 (1971): 151-57.

[112] See for example, Williams to CIA, telegram, May 6, 1914, file 93689-13-115, YA, CCF, GR, BIA, RG 75, NA; Williams to CIA, telegram, Aug. 1, 1913, ibid.; Williams to CIA, Feb. 12, 1915, ibid. See Frank A. Seufert to Clarence L. Reames, U.S. District Attorney, Portland, June 13, 1914, file 93689-13-115, YA, CCF, GR, RG 75, NA.

[113] Louis Simpson to Franklin K. Lane, Secretary of Interior, Feb. 4, 1915, file 93689-13-115, YA, CCF, GR, BIA, RG 75, NA; Chief Martin Speedies to E. B. Meritt, Jan. 26, 1915, ibid.; Garrecht to Carr, July 22, 1914, ibid.; Carr to Garrecht, Sept. 29, 1914, ibid. See also "Indians Are Here to Defend their Rights to Fishing Interests," clipping, ca. Jan. 1916, ibid.; "Gave Indian Choice of Underselling or Ceasing to Fish," Portland (OR) *Journal*, Jan. 26, 1916.

[114] *United States v. Seufert Bros. Co.*, decree (D. Ore. July 31, 1916), file 93689-13-115, YA, CCF, GR, BIA, RG 75, NA; cf. *United States ex rel. Sam Williams v. Seufert Bros. Co.* Order (D. Ore., Feb. 3, 1916), ibid., stipulating that Seufert Company was not prevented from operating its fish wheel at the location in conflict; that Sam Williams was limited to net fishing (no wheel fishing for Indians), and that only six Yakama—to be chosen by the agent—

Seufert Company quickly appealed the decree and Yakama rights to fish at Wah Sucks, were just as problematic as ever during the 1920s. In fact, the company ran its most lucrative wheels at the site until they were banned under a 1927 Oregon voter initiative which outlawed wheel fishing.[115]

By 1919, the Yakama had established two fishing sites as "usual and accustomed" under their 1855 treaty. Robert Rankin, the assistant U.S. Attorney in Portland, noted that Wah Sucks "is about the last place on the Columbia River between The Dalles and Celilo Falls to which the Indians are able to attach any right" to fish.[116] Following *Seufert*, Yakama claims to a traditional fishing area appeared in the federal courts once more, in a 1938 case establishing Celilo Falls on the Oregon side of the river.[117] The peak of federal intervention in assisting Yakama to assert fishing rights to new places was over, however. By 1919, Yakama had taken most of their important Columbia River sites to court. In the years following *Seufert*, the most contentious issues facing the tribe occurred over regulation of their fishing rights.

From Treaty Right to Regulation

Two different regulatory problems faced the tribe during the first three decades of the twentieth century. The first was how to protect its fishers from state officials who wanted to control Indian fishing by imposing licensing requirements, gear restrictions, and poundage taxes. This problem was the direct result of federal fishing cases that had left unresolved the political status of the tribes in relation to state authority. The second problem was one of internal tribal politics involving how best to regulate members' fishing when it

---

could use the fishery per season. Seufert Bros. Co. appealed the decree and the case continued, see George B. Guthrie to Carr, Jan. 26, 1917, ibid. On Jan. 29, 1917, a new decree, adverse to Williams was entered in the case, see Assistant AG to Secretary of Interior, April 7, 1917, ibid.

[115] Williams to CIA, March 17, 1920, file 93689-13-115, YA, CCF, GR, BIA, RG 75, NA; Carr to CIA, May 15, 1920, ibid. See also *P. J. McGowan & Sons, Inc. v. Van Winkle*, 21 F.2d 76 (D. Ore., 1927), upholding Oregon law banning fish wheels on the Oregon side of the river. Following the decision, the Seufert Co. painted a huge sign on its roof declaring: "It took forty seven years to build this business which was destroyed in one day by a law of Oregon sponsored by the Oregon Grange and American Federation of Labor." See Donaldson and Cramer, *Fish Wheels of the Columbia*, 112, for a photograph of the Dalles packing plant.

[116] Rankin to Meritt, Aug. 3, 1915, file 93689-13-115, YA, CCF, GR, BIA, RG 75, NA; Rankin to Sells, Feb. 7, 1916, ibid.

[117] *United States v. Brookfield Fisheries*, Inc., 24 F.Supp. (D.Ore. 1938). The Celilo site was submerged as part of a federal hydroelectric power project. For a discussion of tribal litigation and federal compensation for the flooded Celilo fishery, see Wilkinson and Conner, "Law of the Pacific Salmon Fishery," 41 and 46, and accompanying notes; *Whitefoot v. United States*, 293 F.2d 658 (Ct.Cl. 1961), *cert. denied*, 369 U.S. 818 (1962) (the federal Court of Claims holding that individuals were compensated for loss of Celilo fishery by the condemnation award paid to the tribe).

ranged from very traditional subsistence methods to commercial fishing. Those two problems will be treated in turn.

Justice McKenna's *Winans* decision in 1905 left open the possibility that the state could regulate Yakama treaty fishing rights as long as it was consistent with exercise of the right. State-licensed fishers and many Washington officials saw this as an opportunity to legislate treaty fishing rights out of existence. Yakama responded by turning to Bureau officials, much as they had done in the disputes over fishing locations, but for various reasons that will be discussed below, those officials would no longer take up Yakama claims. Yakama accordingly developed new tactics that included taking their own cases to court and working out ad hoc agreements with local officials.

By the turn of the century, Washington and Oregon fishers were already facing depleted salmon runs which only worsened over time. As rival groups fought over the remaining fish, Indians became natural targets for state regulation. Indians had no recognized voice in state politics and provided a prime scapegoat for hamstrung state-licensed fishers who did. The state effort to suppress Indian fishing coincided a related campaign to eliminate all Indian off-reservation hunting.[118]

Washington Fish Commissioner Leslie Darwin expressed widespread public sentiment when he wrote in his 1913 annual report for the Washington Department of Fisheries (WDF):

> After an examination of the various Indian treaties..., this Department became convinced that the Indians off the reservation have no rights superior to those of the Whites.
>
> Practically every Indian has an allotment of land, and a home of his own. This is very much more than is possessed by the average fisherman of this state. It would seem unfair, therefore, to tax the White person for a license and not require one of the Indians, particularly where the Indian engages in competition with the White man.
>
> But much more objectionable yet is the insistence of the Indians upon their right to disregard the closed season which our laws establish....[119]

Darwin and his successors campaigned tirelessly to force Indian fishers to purchase fishing licenses. This effort accelerated after the federal government conferred citizenship on all Indians in 1924.[120]

---

[118] See Chapter 9.

[119] Darwin, Washington Department of Fisheries, *Annual Report*, 1913, quoted in Brown, *Mountain in the Clouds*, 140-41. The anti-Indian position of state officials extended back at least to 1892, when Washington made it illegal for non-citizens to fish for salmon, sturgeon, or any "other food fish." 1902 Wash. Laws, § 5313, licenses to fish sold only to citizens, § 5274.

[120] Estep to CIA, Dec. 2, 1924, file "Hunting and Fishing, 1923-25," General Correspondence 1923-25, YA, BIA, RG 75, NA-Seattle.

Indian agents gave certificates to fishers that stated that the bearer was an Indian fishing at "usual and accustomed" place, but those garnered little to no respect among white fishers and WDF authorities at the river. Yakama objected to both the cards and to state policies to require purchasing licenses, which Chief Skookum Wallahee described in 1915 as buying "my own rights."[121] Salmon were part of Indians just as cows, hogs, sheep, and chickens were part of white people, thought Louis Mann. No human law could change that ancient relationship.[122]

Some Yakama, such as the Rock Creek band whose members lived off the reservation, mostly did secure state licenses. Other groups, especially subsistence fishers living on the reservation were more likely to challenge regulations or sit out jail terms for breaking the law.[123] Many Yakama were English-illiterate at least through the 1910s, and could not read (or understand) state fishing codes or posted signs.[124] Yakama fishers, thus, both knowingly and unwittingly violated state regulations.

The question of whether Yakama required state licenses to fish off the reservation repeatedly came before the Washington state courts during the 1910s and 1920s, and the court consistently ruled against Yakama fishers.[125] In those cases, the Court drew on the earlier Supreme Court decisions in *Winans* and *Seufert,* to hold that the state could regulate all fishers who used state waters, just as the state could regulate all game takings within its borders.

---

[121] Wallahee to E. B. Meritt, Assist. CIA, Feb. 25, 1915, file 120088-14-115, YA, CCF, GR, BIA, RG 75, NA; Even Estep to CIA, June 9, 1924, file 39001-24-115, YA, CCF, GR, BIA, RG 75, NA. See for example Yakama identification card for fishers and a copy of a permit issued by Indian agent which allowed an Indian fisher to go off the Umatilla reservation both in file 10150-39-931, CCF, GR, BIA, RG 75, NA. Interestingly, O. D. Taylor suggested to Yakima Agency officials as early as 1888 that Yakama fishers should receive passes from the agent to fish. Gordon to Priestly, May 12, 1888, personal papers, 115:21, CRP.

[122] Louis Mann to Miles Poindexter, April 19, 1916, box 76, folder 12, Accession no 3828, Miles C. Poindexter Papers, University of Washington Libraries Manuscript Collection, Seattle, WA [hereafter cited as box:folder, MCPP].

[123] Carr reported that Chief Black Wolf's band of Rock Creek Indians, who lived on public domain land, complied with state fishing laws and took out licenses. Carr to CIA, March 20, 1914, file 14373-17-115, YA, CCF, GR, BIA, RG 75, NA.

[124] Louis Mann to Miles Poindexter April 19, 1916, 76:12, MCPP.

[125] *State v. Towessnute,* 89 Wash. 478 (1916); *State v. Meninock,* 197 P. 641 (S.Ct. Wash., 1921). The Washington courts were busy with Indian fishing cases throughout the state during this time: *State v. Allen* [Indian fishing in Skokomish River held contrary to state law], 80 Wash. 83, 141 P. 292, rehearing en banc, 82 Wash. 698 (1914); *State v. Alexis* [Lummi Tribe held to require state licenses for off-reservation fishing], rehearing en banc, 89 Wash. 492 (1916). See also *State v. Wallahee* [Yakama off-reservation hunting held contrary to state law, resting on *Towessnute* and *Meninock*], 143 Wash. 117, 255 P. 94 (S.Ct. Wash., 1927). In the 1930s, the Washington Supreme Court upheld Indian on-reservation fishing without licenses, see *Pioneer Packing Co. v. Winslow* [Quinault Reservation], 294 P. 557 (S.Ct. Wash., 1930); *State v. Edwards* [Swinomish Reservation], 62 P.2d 1094 (S.Ct. Wash., 1936).

Significantly, the state court also found fuel in the Supreme Court's obvious ambiguity on the question of tribal sovereignty in the previous cases. The state court boldly declared in its 1916 ruling against Alex Towessnute, a Yakama fisher:

> The premise of Indian sovereignty we reject. The treaty is not to be interpreted in that light. At no time did our ancestors in getting title to this continent ever regard the aborigines as other than mere occupants, and incompetent occupants, of the soil.... True, arrangements took the form of treaty and of terms like 'cede,' 'relinquish,' 'reserve.' But never were these agreements between equals.[126]

The decision is threaded with a deeply racist view against the "savage tribes, whom it was generally tempting and always easy to destroy," and who now were in danger of "grievously wound[ing]" the salmon industry of the state.[127] And despite all this, the court's position did not conflict with federal court rulings that had left ambiguous the nature of Indian sovereignty.

The state's anti-Indian position received no outright challenges from the Bureau or Department of Justice until the 1940s, despite constant pressure on these agencies by Yakama to test state actions in federal court. Federal officials retreated from interfering in state regulations following a 1916 Supreme Court decision ruling that a group of Seneca Indians had to follow New York fishing regulations while off their reservation.[128] While some individuals, most notably Francis Garrecht, the U.S. Attorney in Spokane, were willing to challenge the state court decisions, Bureau officials could not agree that this was an acceptable course.[129] Without federal help, however, Yakama did not have the money or power to get into federal court, and were left to try their cases—when they could—in the hostile state courts.

Washington's Department of Fisheries also attempted to impose other restrictions on Indian fishers besides licensing requirements. Between 1915 and 1917, Commissioner Darwin closed the Klickitat River and several other major tributaries of the Columbia to food fishing—but not sport fishing—ostensibly to

---

[126] 89 Wash. 479, 481-82.

[127] 89 Wash. 479, 482.

[128] *New York ex rel. Kennedy v. Becker*, 241 U.S. 556 (1916), citing *United States v. Winans*, 198 U.S. at 564. The Court rejected the notion that the sovereignty of the state over the wildlife within its borders could be compatible with the tribes' exercise of sovereignty over the hunting and fishing conducted by its own members, ibid., 241 U.S. at 563. For a discussion of the effect of *Becker* on federal officials, see Garrecht to E. B. Meritt, Sept. 8, 1916, file 58718-15-115, YA, CCF, GR, BIA, RG 75, NA.

[129] Sells to Secretary of Interior, March 4, 1916, file 587118-15-115, YA, CCF, GR, BIA, RG 75, NA; Garrecht to Meritt, Sept. 8, 1916, ibid., noting that he, Garrecht, would be open to appealing the *Towessnute* decision. See also Bo Sweeney, assistant secretary of the Interior, to AG, May 2, 1916, ibid. Cf. Meritt to J. W. Brooke, May 11, 1918, stating that the Office will follow *Towessnute*.

protect salmon runs in those streams.[130] State officials also tried to prevent Yakama fishers from fishing near state dam projects at Prosser Falls and Sunnyside.[131] Another means of curtailing Indian fishers was through laws that made it illegal to use certain equipment, such as gaff hooks and nets, that non-Indian fishers did not use.[132]

Yakama fishers sometimes successfully negotiated agreements with local authorities to protect themselves from hostile non-Indian fishers. For example, at the homestead owned by Little Dave, a Yakama Indian who lived along the Klickitat River, there was a small waterfall traditionally used as a fishing place, and which non-Indian sport fishers began to use in June 1918. When non-Indians began harassing Indian fishers, Sam and Caples Dave, two of the complainants, posted trespass notices instructing non-Indians that they could fish until eleven o'clock in the mornings, after which time the Indians would have exclusive use of the fishing site. In this case, the Agent Carr and a justice of the peace backed up the Indians' actions, and the case apparently was settled.[133]

Thus, despite the Yakamas' seeming victory in *Winans*, Bureau officials during the 1910s and 1920s followed a policy of pressuring Indians to buy licenses and follow state regulations on fishing.[134] Charles Burke, Commissioner (1921-1929), stated the policy clearly: "Indians hunting and fishing outside the limits of their reservation, either on ceded lands the title to which has passed to the state, or on other state lands, are required to observe the state game and fish laws the same as all other persons."[135]

A second regulatory question that faced the tribe during the early twentieth century was how to regulate fishing by their own members. Many Washington tribes enacted fish codes at the turn of the century. Some of them—like

---

[130] Darwin to Carr, July 27, 1915, folder "Fishing Matters State, 1915-23," box 78, General Correspondence, 1908-27, YA, BIA, RG 75, NA-Seattle; Carr to Darwin, July 22, 1915, ibid.; Carr to W.L. Maple, Aug. 2, 1915, ibid.

[131] Carr to CIA, May 9, 1923, folder "Fishing Matters State 1915-23," box 78, General Correspondence, 1908-27, YA, BIA, RG 75, NA-Seattle. At Prosser Dam, Yakama actively petitioned Governor Lister for relief following the Court's *Towessnute* decision of 1916 that upheld state regulations banning Indian fishers from working near Prosser Dam. In 1919, the Washington legislature passed a "personal use" fishing act that allowed Yakama to fish for personal consumption at Prosser Falls, 1921 Wash. Laws, ch. 58, § 5774. That act was repealed by Wash. Laws, ch. 12, § 87.

[132] See, for example, 89 Wash. 478. See also Department Game of Washington v. Puyallup Tribe, 414 U.S. 165 (1977).

[133] Sam Dave and Caples Dave, to Secretary of Interior, June 17, 1918; and Carr to CIA, Aug. 20, 1918, both in file 52474-18-115, YA, CCF, GR, BIA, RG 75, NA.

[134] See, for example, Warcomac to CIA, Jan. 23, 1917, file 10238-17-115 part 2, YA, CCF, GR, BIA, RG 75, NA; Mary Warcomac to CIA, April 25, 1917, ibid.; Carr to CIA, June 19, 1917, ibid.; Meritt to Mr. and Mrs. Warcomac, July 13, 1917, ibid.

[135] Burke to N. Sinnot, May 29, 1924, file 39-001-24-15, YA, CCF, GR, BIA, RG 75, NA.

that of the Quinault enacted in 1907—were more comprehensive than state regulations of the time.[136] At best, such codes organized both on- and off-reservation fishing and provided for conservation of salmon stocks by ensuring that fishers did not take all available fish in a run.

The Yakama enacted no such codes during the period to 1933.[137] In pre-contact times, fishing disputes among Plateau groups were rare, and there appears to have been no formal structure for resolving conflict because none was needed. But as Yakama fishers pursued different fishing styles that ranged from the pre-contact styles of the "River People," or "Wild Yakima," to the savvy market fishing of Sam Williams and others, the tribe's reasons for fishing were too complex to boil down into a unified relationship to the fisheries.

Yakama retained family ownership of specific fishing locations through the early twentieth century at least. Here, fishers required an inherited right or a family connection to fish.[138] Where ancestral lines became blurred and Yakama faced their own shortages of fish, people were less willing to tolerate the relatively free sharing of fishing sites that had characterized pre-contact times. Agent Estep reported in 1926 that Yakama "have a lot, of quarreling" over access to the sites.[139] In 1926, Olie Charley and Mussey Charlie went to a Klickitat County Court to settle their dispute over priority at an inherited fishing rock.[140]

One of the hardest problems facing the tribe was how to regulate members who fished primarily for commercial use. Men such as Sam Williams, Bill Charley (Olie Charley's father), and Joe Estabrook fished in part for canneries.[141] The Charley family, at least, fished at an inherited fishing location at Se-

---

[136] Brown, *Mountain in the Clouds*, 138 (discussing Quinault regulations). The Tulalip, Taholah, Warm Springs, and Colville were among tribes that had fish and game regulations as of 1940, discussed in Circular on Indian Hunting and Fishing, 1940.

[137] In 1949 the Yakima General Council passed a resolution providing for some regulation of treaty fishing. During the 1950s, a Yakama committee addressed Celilo Falls fishing, before this location was flooded by federal hydroelectric development work. In 1963 the tribe established the Columbia River Fish Commission. Yakima General Council, "Columbia River General Council Fish Commission of the Yakama Indian Nation 1855," October 1967, 112:1, CRP.

[138] Testimony of Sam Tanawasha, *U.S. v. Winans*, transcript of record, 149; testimony of Bill Charley, ibid., 162 (speaking through interpreter).

[139] Estep to CIA, Mar. 12, 1926, file 8324-26-115, YA, CCF, GR, BIA, RG 75, NA; Estep to CIA, Aug. 19, 1927, file 39001-24-115, YA, CCF, GR, BIA, RG 75, NA.

[140] Estep to Paul W. Childress, Mar. 26, 1927, folder "Hunting and Fishing, 1926-52," Decimal Subject File 921, BIA, RG 75, NA-Seattle; Estep to CIA, March 12, 1926, file 8324-26-115, YA, CCF, GR, BIA, RG 75, NA [these letters probably refer to the same case]. It is possible that there are more such cases in the trial court records in Klickitat County, and this line of research would be well worth pursuing.

[141] It is important not to jump to conclusions about these Indian commercial fishers because market considerations do not appear to have been the sole motivation for their actions. Sam Williams was the pastor at a Shaker Indian church he established at Tum Water and was an

we-pam.[142] Following Oregon's banning of fish wheels, the Seufert Bros. Co. tried to employ Indians to run fish wheels at "usual and accustomed" fishing locations on the possibility that Indians were exempt from the law. They were not.[143]

Nor did the Yakima Council support those commercial operations. In 1913, two members of the tribal police force threatened to arrest Bill Charley and his son if they did not stop wheel fishing to the detriment of other Yakama.[144] Many Yakama objected to fishing on the scale of the Charleys' operations. True, most Yakama sold part of their catch, but they disdained large scale fishing, which they associated with greedy whites.[145]

Non-Indian commercial fishers like N. Whealdon, a former employee of both O. D. Taylor and the Winans Brothers (and who had beaten the Indian boy at Tum Water), argued that Bill Charley and his son exemplified the "civilized" Indians that the Bureau had been trying to encourage. Unlike other Indians who were content to "wear a blanket and sleep around the rocks," Bill and Olie Charley could dynamite fish and run wheels alongside the most ambitious commercial fishers.[146]

---

active participant in this faith. See Harmon, "Indian Shaker Church The Dalles," 153-54. Bill Charley, too, apparently viewed his operations through lenses of an older way of life. See notes 140 above and 142 below.

[142] Bill Charley, testimony in *U.S. v. Winans*, transcript of record, 162 (speaking through interpreter). Charley noted: "When I was grown up to be a man my grand-father told me, and my father told me that is our fishery; this fishery is named Se-we-pam...." Se-we-pam was a fishery located in Wisham territory and was as important to this band as Tum Water.

[143] Estep to CIA, Nov. 14, 1927, file 39001-24-115, YA, CCF, GR, BIA, RG 75, NA. Estabrook was wheel fishing. See Burke to Estabrook, Sept. 21, 1927, ibid.; Estep to CIA, Nov. 14, 1927, ibid.; Estep to CIA, Dec. 22, 1927, ibid.; Estep to Estabrook, Jan. 14, 1928, ibid.

Yakama fishers operated three fish Wheels on the Columbia in 1924. Estep to Cary W. Ramsey, April 15, 1924, folder "Fishing Matters Along the Columbia River, 1924," box 78, General Correspondence, 1908-27, YA, BIA, RG 75, NA-Seattle.

[144] N. Whealdon to Carr, April 8, 1913, folder "Wishram Fishery 1913-24," box 79, General Correspondence, 1908-27, YA, BIA, RG 75, NA-Seattle. See also Bill Charley to "friend," Dec. 28, 1912, stating that he falsely accused Dick Tom Hart Skonawa of murder after he objected to Charley's wheel fishing, in ibid.; Carr to CIA, Feb. 13, 1913, file no 133661-12-115,-YA, CCF, GR, BIA, RG 75, NA. According to his testimony in 1904, Bill Charley was not wheel fishing nor selling his catch to canneries. See *U.S. v. Winans*, transcript of record, 173. Some background on the Charleys' fishing operations can be found in Carr to CIA, Feb. 13, 1913, ibid.

[145] Carr to CIA, Feb. 13, 1913, file 133661-12-115, YA, CCF, GR, BIA, RG 75, NA. For a discussion of another tribe which came to fish largely for market, see Daniel L. Boxberger, "In and Out of the labor Force: The Lummi Indians and the Development of the Commercial Salmon Fishery of North Puget Sound, 1880-1900," *Ethnohistory* 35 (1988): 161-90; Boxberger, *To Fish in Common*.

[146] N. Whealdon to Carr, April 8, 1913, folder "Wishram Fishery 1913-24," box 79, General Correspondence, 1908-27, YA, BIA, RG 75, NA-Seattle. See also Carr to CIA, Feb. 13, 1913, file no 133661-12-115, YA, CCF, GR, BIA, RG 75, NA.

Whealdon further argued that Yakama commercial fishing should be subject to state regulations, and now he used the need to protect less "progressive" subsistence fishers as the justification for more regulation. Commercial Yakama fishers ought not to be allowed to "trample on the rights of the tribal or less capable Indians, who do not fish in a commercial way, and to whose benefit the treaty reservation of the right to fish at all 'usual and accustomed places' should, in my opinion, apply," he wrote. Whealdon was more interested in protecting his own fishing interests from Yakama competition than in promoting any Yakama rights to fish.

Just as some Yakama were willing to develop the subsistence fishery into a commercial enterprise, others refused to modernize at all. These "Wild Yakima" lived close to river bottoms, growing hay to sell and pursuing a predominantly pre-contact subsistence way of life.[147] To them, the Tribal Council was too willing to adapt white ways. The tension among different groups of Yakama fishers continued to characterize the tribal fishery into the present.[148]

Conclusion: Salmon and Yakama Life

Yakama fisher Bill Se-hi-am, who lived at the Tum Water fishery, had been reared by salmon: "the fish kept me alive; that is what raised me." As salmon became increasingly scarce under the unrelenting pressure of the wheels, traps, nets, and lines of Columbia River fishers, Se-hi-am's life changed markedly: "I am hungry. Salmon hungry."[149] T-wash-pam, who could not get to the fishery because of the Winans' fences, declared, "There are lots of

---

[147] See for example *CIA-AR*, 1881, 174, noting that there were 276 "Disaffected Indians" living off the reservation and subsisting on fish and game, and 598 Indians living off the reservation most of the time and subsisting in the same way (out of a population of 3,400); *CIA-AR*, 1897, 222, describing a group of Yakama who refused to take allotments on the reservation and prefer to live by hunting and fishing.

[148] The Tribal Council registered fishers after 1967, but not everyone agreed to register. The Columbia River Fish Commission attempted to represent their interests as well by making available to them a portion of a "bail and defense fund" to assist fishers who had been arrested for violating state laws. Leo R. Alexander, Secretary Columbia River Fish Commission, "Columbia River & Yakama Indian News, October 1968," enclosed in Alexander to Click Relander, 18 Oct. 1968, 112:1, CRP. For later consideration of state regulation in relation to treaty fishers (and rejecting the state's broad authority to regulate the treaty right under an 'equal footing' claim), see the *Sohappy* litigation, establishing that state regulation of treaty fishing must be necessary for the conservation of the fishery, cannot discriminate against Indian fishers, and must meet appropriate standards. *Sohappy v. Smith*, 302 F. Supp. 899 (D. Ore., July 8, 1969), *Sohappy v. Smith*, 529 F.2d 570 (9th Cir. 1976).

[149] *U.S. v. Winans*, transcript of record, 158, 161 (speaking through interpreter) See also testimony of Louis Simpson, ibid., 132, noting that Indians have "dry mouths" without salmon.

time I wished to get something to eat, such [ ] as salmon. Now I have given up all hopes, and have made up my mind I am going to starve myself to death."[150]

For Se-hi-am and others, not having access to fish meant starvation on many levels: cultural, spiritual, and physical. People who had sagebrush allotments and little chance of securing a dependable water supply were unable to support themselves through farming even had they wished to learn it. Fish—along with berries, roots, and game—were familiar foods and the birthright of every Yakama. Even as Yakama entered the market as wage laborers, many viewed such participation as part of a larger and older subsistence pattern that continued to define their identities as Yakama people.

Salmon were important to Yakama during the period to 1933. Those who could not fish because of fences, angry landowners, commercial fishing operations, hydroelectric projects, and other obstructions that barred their access to the rivers bought fish from non-Indians who could supply them, or begged for fish. People went to hatcheries through the 1910s and '20s to obtain dead salmon used for spawn; some women continued to go despite being abused by hatchery workers.[151] Many fishers endured—and continue to endure—threats and violence for fishing.[152] Why? Because salmon was and remains as much part of the Yakama as "the atmosphere they breathed."[153]

Salmon was part of a larger subsistence pattern that encompassed other foods such as berries and game, and that had social and spiritual aspects as well as economic ones. Salmon were so integral to this pattern that fishing—and the right to fish—stood for this larger subsistence system. During the period through 1933, Yakama attempted to apply rights won in the fishing cases to protect their access to historic hunting and gathering sites. Here, as in the case of fishing, Yakama and their Euro-American neighbors differed in both their understandings of law and of the appropriate relationships humans should cultivate toward nature.

---

[150] *U.S. v. Winans*, transcript of record, 184 (speaking through interpreter). He stated also, "They [Yakama] all feel very bad about not getting any salmon, and they think themselves to death."

[151] Celia Frank to Carr, Oct. 25, 1923, folder "Fishing Matters, *State of Washington v. Allen* (1914), General Correspondence, 1908-1927, box 78, YA, BIA, RG 75, NA-Seattle. On Yakama obtaining hatchery fish for food, see Charley Quaerupts to Carr, Sept. 25, 1919, ibid.; correspondence in file 78153-19-115, YA, CCF, GR, BIA, RG 75, NA. See also testimony of Moses Strong, *U.S. v. Winans*, transcript of record, 113 (he bought one fish for 25 cents at Se-we-pam fishery from white commercial fishers).

[152] See discussion above. See also testimony of Walker, a Yakama fisher, describing how N. Whealdon hit him in the head with a rock when he found him fishing on the Winans' property. *U.S. v. Winans*, transcript of record, 123.

[153] Brown, *Mountain in the Clouds*, 154, quoting U.S. Supreme Court.

9

FORAGERS IN A FARMERS' WORLD

> The fish are gone.
> The game are gone.
> Who got them all? The White man. He destroyed all and now he tries to bring them back by keeping the poor Reds from his few fish and fewer deer.
> —Louis Mann (1912)[1]

Yakama fishing was an important subsistence practice that the Bureau believed would have continued significance to the tribe as it increasingly took up "civilized ways." Unlike fishing, wide-ranging hunting and gathering practices were not easily converted into spatially and temporally defined—or economically defensible—rights. Federal and state officials tended to perceive Yakama hunting and gathering rights as intimately connected to Indian tribalism and old subsistence practices. By linking the hunting and foraging provisions of the Yakamas' treaty to the maintenance of an "uncivilized" society, the Bureau justified its decision not to help Yakama protect their access to game, berries, and roots. Just as the inferior, "uncivilized" nature of Native peoples had provided the initial justification for Euro-American subjugation of those peoples, the conquest mentality continued to shape the legal doctrines governing specific areas of Native American law, including subsistence rights, throughout the period 1840-1933 and beyond.[2]

Sahaptin peoples had long asserted the importance of hunting and gathering to their way of life and self-definition. Cayuse leader Young Chief told Stevens during the 1855 Council that "I think the land where my forefathers are buried should be mine.... That is what I love, the place we get our roots to live upon (meaning the Grande Ronde)."[3] Frank Selatsee and Chief Noah James Saluskin, two Yakama delegates to visit Washington, D.C. in 1928, testified to the continuing importance of hunting and berrying to their people:

---

[1] Mann, quoted in L. V. McWhorter, newspaper clipping, Aug. 1, 1912[?], file 20332-16-115, Yakima Agency, Central Classified Files, General Records, 1907-39, Records of the Buteau of Indian Affairs, Record Group 75, National Archives. [Hereafter cited as YA, CCF, GR, BIA, RG 75, NA-[branch].]

[2] See generally Robert A. Williams, "Documents of Barbarism: The Contemporary Legacy of European Racism and Colonialism in the Narrative Traditions of Federal Indian Law," *Arizona Law Review* 31 (1989): 237.

[3] Darrell Scott, ed., Isaac Ingalls Stevens, *A True Copy of the Record of the Official Proceedings at the Council in the Walla Walla Valley, 1855* [hereafter cited as Official Proceedings of the Walla Walla Council] (Fairfield, WA: Ye Galleon Press, 1985): 89. The Cayuse, Walla Walla, and Umatilla bands were resettled on the Umatilla reservation.

"When there were no white people in the United States we had deer, game of different kind, and berries on which we were raised. We consider them as a remedy for our life and body and we want to reserve all those for ourselves." Saluskin believed that "my forefathers reserved the right to fish and hunt, gather roots outside the reservation on ceded lands and I think I have a right to gather roots and berries ... [today]."[4] The U.S. Supreme Court's 1905 *Winans* decision remained visible proof to Yakama that hunting and gathering, because they were part of the same subsistence complex as fishing, would be protected under federal law.

According to Article 3—the so-called "fishing clause"—of the 1855 Treaty, the Yakamas reserved to themselves "the privilege of hunting, gathering roots and berries, and pasturing their horses and cattle upon open and unclaimed land."[5] At the treaty proceedings at Walla Walla, Stevens told the headmen present,

> *You will be allowed* to pasture you[r] animals on land not claimed or occupied by settlers, white men. *You will be allowed* to go on the roads to take your things to market, your horses and cattle. *You will be allowed* to go to the usual fishing places and fish in common with the whites, and to get roots and berries and to kill game on land not occupied by the whites. All that outside the reservation.[6]

According to Stevens, then, the federal government was permitting the Yakama to continue their off-reservation hunting and gathering only as long as whites had not appropriated the areas utilized by Indians.

The question of whether Yakama had off-reservation hunting and gathering rights had different answers to Indians and non-Indians. Just as they had off-reservation fishing rights, so too did Yakama believe that they had they retained other off-reservation rights.[7] Washington officials in the Departments of Fish and Game, followed by the Bureau and Department of Justice, interpreted the treaty language to mean that Yakama had off-reservation hunting rights equal to those of state residents. The treaty, they argued, gave Yakama no special privileges to state wildlife. That policy was consistent with the state's position on off-reservation fishing, and it turned on a narrow definition of tribal sovereignty in relation to the state's power.[8]

During the period through 1933, the Yakama fought to retain access to their off-reservation subsistence grounds and to protect important plant

---

[4] Statements by Selatsee and Saluskin in "Hearing Held Before E. G. Meritt, Assistant Indian Commissioner," Feb. 2, 1928, file 6987-28-115, YA, CCF, GR, BIA, RG 75, NA [hereafter cited as 1928 Delegation Hearing].

[5] Treaty with the Yakima, 12 Stat. 951.

[6] *Official Proceedings of the Walla Walla Council*, 67 (emphasis added); see also ibid., 98.

[7] *United States et al. v. Winans*, 198 U.S. 371, 384 (1905).

[8] See Chapter 8.

collection sites from hoards of cattle and sheep belonging to non-Indian ranchers. The proceeds of hunting and gathering—just as fishing—provided needed fresh foods to Yakama diets and spiritual well being. Unlike in the case of the Yakamas' fisheries, however, the Bureau and Department of Justice attached little importance to hunting and gathering. Consequently, the state's role in regulating off-reservation subsistence activities went largely unchallenged by federal law or through the courts. Yakama responded by writing letters, travelling to Washington to lobby officials directly, going to state court, and willfully violating state laws and going to jail. No state law could erase the conviction that "Nature's Gift" to them was the perpetual right to hunt and gather.[9]

Native Hunting and Gathering Patterns

Plants provided the bulk of foodstuffs in Sahaptin diets at contact; roots alone provided more than sixty percent of average caloric intake. Mobility was the key to Native peoples' ability to make use of the wide range of plant resources in the Columbia Basin. Foragers sought out edible plants as they ripened. Families spent winters, springs, and early summers in lowland areas, then traveled to higher elevations in late summer and early fall when berry crops ripened in the Cascade mountains, and returned to river valleys again in late fall. Not only did the logic of this subsistence system make use of the maximum range of subsistence resources available, constant movement of populations during the year reduced pressure on any particular species.[10]

While mobility rather than a "conservation ethic" likely precluded Sahaptin overharvesting, there is some evidence that Yakama and other Plateau peoples did manage certain resources. Communities structured the timing and location of salmon fishing, for example, by creating inheritable rights to certain fishing rocks and designating a salmon chief to oversee the harvest.[11] Yakama organized their hunting and gathering activities in similar ways. Yakama women, for example, could hold the position of "head root digger" of a household, a position necessarily based on an individual's extensive knowledge of

---

[9] Louis Mann to Miles C. Poindexter, Dec. 17, 1915, box 76, file 13, Accession no. 3828, Miles C. Poindexter Papers, University of Washington Libraries Manuscript Collection, Seattle, Wash. [hereafter cited as box:file MCPP].

[10] Eugene Hunn, "Mobility as a Factor Limiting Resource Use in the Columbia Plateau of North America," in Nancy Williams and Eugene Hunn, eds., *Resource Managers: North American and Australian Hunter Gatherers*, AAAS Selected Symposium 67 (Boulder, CO: Westview Press, 1982): 35-36; Hunn, "On the Relative Contribution of Men and Women to Subsistence among Hunter-Gatherers of the Columbia Plateau: A Comparison with Ethnographic Atlas Summaries," *Journal of Ethnobiology* 1 (1981): 129-31.

[11] See Chapter 8.

the area and success in locating foods from year to year, as well as family position.¹²

Women cultivated huckleberries by burning areas in which huckleberries grew in the fall. Burning not only promoted huckleberry production, but provided ecotones favored by both mountain goats and deer which people hunted. The high pre-contact populations of both of those game species may have resulted from such efforts to increase berry yields, whether or not Indian consciously employed burning to achieve that effect.¹³ After the turn of the century, when many of the huckleberry areas fell under U.S. Forest Service management, Yakama were forced to abandon that practice.¹⁴

Sahaptin peoples divided the useful plants in their world into several categories they still use today. In roughly their order in the seasonal round, they are "Indian celeries," "foods which are dug," and "foods which are picked."¹⁵ Indian celeries are those plants that provide fresh sprouts, stems, and shoots, including Gray's lomatium and bare-stemmed lomatium. Foods that are dug include all those plants, particularly roots, bulbs and corms, that Indian women dug using special digging sticks, often made of scrub oak. Bitterroot, Canby's lomatium, and camas, were root staples, in addition to a variety of other secondary types. Foods that are picked include berries, fruits, and

---

¹² See, for example, Charles Relander (Now Tow Look), *Drummers and Dreamers; The Story of Smohalla the Prophet and his Nephew Puck Hyah Toot...*, with a foreword by Frederick Webb Hodge (Caldwell, ID: The Caxton Printers, 1956): 176-77, for a discussion of Hadwesa, a Yakama woman, who was both a Washat priestess and head root digger for the Wapato Long House.

¹³ On Yakama use of fire to increase huckleberry yields, see Morris L. Uebelacker, "Geographic Explorations in the Southern Cascades of Eastern Washington: Changing Land, People, and Resources" (Ph.D. diss., University of Oregon, 1986): 51-52, 100; D. H. French, "Aboriginal Control of Huckleberry Yield in the Northwest," Paper read at the American Anthropological Association Annual Meeting, Chicago, 1957, cited in Hunn, "Mobility as a Factor"; Click Relander, ed., *Treaty Centennial, 1855-1955: The Yakimas*, 1st ed., Washington State Historical Society and Oregon State Historical Society, published by authorization of the Yakima Tribal Council (Yakima, WA: Republic Press, 1955): 52; cf. Hunn, "Mobility as a Factor," 34. Western Washington tribes may have been more active in their use of fire and other cultivation techniques, see Hunn, "Mobility as a Factor," 34. On the effects of burning on game populations, see Gary Dills, "Effects of Prescribed Burning on Deer Browse," *Journal of Wildlife Management* 34 (July 1970): 540-44.

¹⁴ Harold K. Steen, *The U.S. Forest Service: A History* (Seattle: University of Washington Press, 1976): 127-35, 188-89; U.S. Office of Indian Affairs, *Handbook of Fire Control*, circular no. 3212 (Washington, D.C.: Government Printing Office, 1937). On the perception of fire as detrimental, rather than beneficial, to forests, see Stephen J. Pyne, *Fire in America: A Cultural History of Wildland and Rural Fire* (Princeton, N.J.: Princeton University Press, 1982).

¹⁵ "Indian Celeries" is an Anglo term for some species of Lomatium, and is used by present-day Sahaptin peoples. Hunn, "Mobility as a Factor," 25; Hunn and David H. French, "Lomatium: A Key Resource for Columbia Plateau Native Subsistence," *Northwest Science* 55 (no. 2) (1981): 87.

lichens and mosses. Golden currents, dogwood, chokecherries and serviceberies augmented crops of more important huckleberries and blueberries that Indians picked in the Cascade range from mid-August through September.[16]

Huckleberries remained an important staple of Native diets throughout the period and beyond 1933. Agent Don Carr (1912-1923) noted in 1917:

> Many more Indians from Yakima, Warm Springs, Umatilla and the public domain were in these berry patches than I had any notion would go so far to gather huckleberries and the few days that I was able to be in the hills convinced me that the Indians attach more importance to the berry patches in the vicinity of Mount Adams than is the general understanding.[17]

Yakama to the present still hold berries and roots as important cultural as well as nutritional foods. Helen Schuster and William Hunn, whose combined field research on the Yakama spans 1950 to the present, noted the importance of berries both to daily diets and as an honored food in first food feasts.[18]

Gathering greens, roots, and berries were women's work and the tools and proceeds of this work were women's property to be used and given away at the discretion of the particular gatherer. An average Plateau family of four would consume 1600 kilograms of roots per year[19] Women gathered roots and tubers in special bags, and collected berries in fern-lined baskets. Once dried, and depending upon the type, roots might be stored whole or ground, dried and shaped into "finger cakes." Women also baked roots in underground fires

---

[16] The preceding discussion is based on Hunn, "Mobility as a Factor," 25-33; Hunn and French, "Lomatium: A Key Resource," 87-94; Click Relander, typed transcripts of interviews with Yakima [n.d., but ca. 1950], files in boxes 57 and 58, Click Relander Papers, Yakima Valley Regional Library, Yakima Washington [hereafter cited as file:box, CRP]; and L. V. McWhorter to Professor Sperlin, June 20, 1930, verifax, Washington State University Library, in "Indians-Yakima-History," folder, Yakima Valley Museum, Yakima, Washington [hereafter cited as folder, YVM]; Uebelacker, "Geographic Explorations," 119-30; N. Turner, "Economic Importance of Black Tree Lichen (Bryoria fremontii) to the Indians of Western North America," *Economic Botany* 31 (1977): 461-70; Helen H. Schuster, "Yakima Indian Traditionalism: A Study in Continuity and Change" (Ph.D. diss., University of Washington, 1975): 75-80.

[17] Carr to CIA, Feb. 26, 1917, file 14373-17-115, YA, CCF, GR, BIA, RG 75, NA.

[18] *The Yakimas, 1855-1955*, 52; elsewhere, Relander notes that Yakama held a huckleberry feast at the first quarter of the moon in August. Relander papers, 58-8; Schuster, *Yakima Indian Traditionalism*, 432.

[19] Hunn and French, "Lomatium: A Key Resource," 92. They estimated that root digging (of L. canbyi and L. cous) would yield 4700 Kilocalories (KCal) per hour of work; huckleberry picking yielded 1000 KCal per hour of work. See also Hunn, "On the Relative Contribution of Men and Women," 130-31. The caloric yields of salmon varied widely depending upon how late in a salmon's up-river spawning journey it was caught. Fraser River sockeye, for example, lose up to 75 percent of their caloric value during the spawning migration. Hunn, "On the Relative Contribution of Men and Women," 127-28.

or boiled them. Berries, too, were eaten fresh and the surplus dried over slow burning fires and later stored for winter use.[20]

Roots and other plants yielded food, but also medicine, insect repellents, perfume, and the raw materials for basket making.[21] Because Yakama women held as individual property all of the foods and materials they gathered—as well as those that they processed, such as skins, blankets, and clothing—many women were wealthier in material goods than were men. By generously giving of this wealth, women enriched others and built their own alliances. By trading surplus goods, they created their own trade networks with Plateau women outside their own kin groups.[22] The gender division of labor and of forms of property still were a coherent, operative system during the 1960s and 1970s. Thus, Yakama women adopted European foods and crafts into their own work and trade patterns.[23]

Hunting was a year-round activity for men. The proceeds supplemented the more seasonal fish catch and provided protein when caches of dried fish ran low in winter. Elk; deer, including Columbia blacktail, mule, and whitetail deer; mountain goat; and bear were important game species. Hunters followed mule deer and mountain goats in the fall when the animals moved upslope into the higher elevations as did Indian families in search of ripening berries. Hunters took a variety of other smaller game as well, including beaver, squirrels, rabbits, and wildfowl.[24] "We used to roast beaver in pits," Mary Chapman, a Palouse-Wanapam Indian, recalled in 1952. "We would dig a pit and heat rocks. We wrapped Swicht [Bunch Grass] around beaver and put it in pit and cover up. It would take two or three hours to cook."[25] Small game provided a

---

[20] Hunn, "Mobility as a Factor," 29; Hunn and French, "Lomatium: A Key Resource," "Table 1," 90; Relander, "Huckleberries, Naches place names, words, Field trip with Puck-Hyah-Toot," typed transcript [July 29, 1951], 25:57, CRP [hereafter cited as Relander, "Field trip with Puck-Hyah-Toot,"]; Relander, "Satus, Definition of Camps, Huckleberry Fields," typed transcript, July 20, 1950, 14 58, CRP; Relander, typed transcript, interview with Mary Chapman, March 28, 1952, 8:58, CRP [hereafter cited as Relander, Mary Chapman Interview]; Schuster, "Yakima Indian Traditionalism," 80-81. Schuster notes that now that fires are illegal because of Forest Service policy against forest fires, Yakama preserve berries by freezing and canning, ibid. at 80. See Schuster, ibid., at 432-36, for description of first roots feast, ca. 1960. See also H. Newell Wardle, "Certain Rare West-Coast Baskets," *American Anthropologist*, n.s., 14 (1912): 287-313.

[21] Hunn and French, "Lomatium: A Key Resource," 90.

[22] Schuster, "Yakima Indian Traditionalism," 129, 130-33.

[23] See Chapter 5. On women's roles in Yakama society generally, see Schuster, "Yakima Indian Traditionalism," 120-34ff.

[24] Uebelacker, "Geographic Explorations," 93-112; Hunn, "Mobility as a Factor," 33; Relander, Mary Chapman Interview; Relander, "Field trip with Puck-Hyah-Toot."

[25] Relander, Mary Chapman Interview.

supplemental winter food source. All animals, as other natural objects, were spiritual companions and teachers to Plateau peoples as well.[26]

Just as Plateau fishers held traditional fishing locations and established an order of access to the salmon fisheries, family and bands had some traditional rights of use to certain hunting and gathering grounds. While rights to hunt and gather do not appear to have been as completely defined as in fishing entitlements, newcomers required a headman's permission to use his bands' berrying and camas grounds, or hunting areas. Camping families used traditional sites and probably collected within established boundaries.[27]

Yakama and other Plateau groups' hunting and gathering practices took them over long distances every year. People might travel one hundred kilometers or more from their winter villages to reach favorite sites. Yakama hunters often went to hunt bison on the Plains, a journey that could last years and take them into the territories of the Blackfoot and other Plains tribes. The horse made such travel an ordinary part of the subsistence round.[28] The subsistence system also bound together the disparate Plateau bands and reinforced the spiritual and secular aspects of individual life.[29]

The Subsistence System in Conflict

While the Plateau subsistence system was orderly and remained fairly consistent from year to year, Euro-Americans who settled in the region found the Indians' way of life to be an increasing annoyance to farming, grazing, mining, and settlement. Even after non-Indians instituted the reservation system, Yakama continued to make their annual subsistence treks, often accompanied by a traditional entourage of stock, horses, and equipment. As long as Indians remained in constant pursuit of "the spontaneous productions of nature," no settler could count on the inviolability of his or her claim.[30]

The number of Yakama hunters undoubtedly declined following contact, as a combined result of disease epidemics and Euro-American pressure on

---

[26] Uebelacker, "Geographic Explorations," 106-09; Hunn, "Mobility as a Factor," 33; Wasco-Warm Springs Tribes, "Little Raccoon and His Grandmother," and Lower Chinook, "Wren Kills Elk," both reprinted in Jarold Ramsey, ed., *Coyote Was Going There: Indian Literature of the Oregon Country* (Seattle: University of Washington Press, 1977): 58-63. See also Chapter 2.

[27] Schuster, "Yakima Indian Traditionalism," 69; Hunn, "Mobility as a Factor," 34; H. Aoki, "Nez Perce Texts," *University of California Publication in Linguistics*, 90 (1979): 81-85; A. G. Marshall, "Nez Perce Social Groups: An Ecological Interpretation" (Ph.D. diss, Washington State University, Pullman, 1977): 117.

[28] Hunn, "Mobility as a Factor," 32. See Chapter 2.

[29] Angelo Anastasio, "The Southern Plateau: An Ecological Analysis of Intergroup Relations," *Northwest Anthropological Research Notes* 6 (1972): 102-229; Schuster, "Yakima Indian Traditionalism," 100-80ff.

[30] U.S. Commissioner of Indian Affairs, *Annual Report to the Secretary of Interior* [hereafter cited as *CIA-AR*], 1859, 384.

Plateau animal populations. Many Yakama had stopped hunting because the only remaining game now stayed deep in the Cascades out of easy reach of hunters, Yakima Agent Thomas Priestly (1886-1890) reported in 1888.[31] Priestly was over-optimistic about the number of Indians who had given up hunting.

Many Yakama indeed accepted cattle and allotments, but continued to hunt, fish, and gather as a regular part of their way of life. Not only the "Wild Yakimas"—a group of more than 200 individuals who carried out a traditional way of life throughout the late eighteenth and early nineteenth centuries— valued the proceeds of subsistence. Almost 2,000 of the 3,400 Yakama depended upon subsistence foods for at least a part of their diets, Agent Wilbur estimated in 1881.[32] Indian feelings at the time of the treaty were not different more than fifty years later: "I do love my own food.... Chief White Swan (Joe Stwire) (1868-1910) noted in 1904: "I love to go and get my deer and berries up in the mountain, therefore I do not like to go to the little reservation and leave my fish."[33] Yakima Agent Evan Estep (1923-1930) reported in 1928 that "even the old almost helpless Indians would rather go to the berry patches than stay at home on three full meals a day. It is not poverty that causes them to make these trips ... but they go just the same, hundreds of them each year."[34]

Euro-Americans wanted land, and while they got it under a variety of federal and state statutes as we have seen, they fixed covetous eyes on the rich rangelands lying within the confines of Indian reservations. Throughout the last quarter of the nineteenth century, pressure from non-Indian ranchers and farmers, in conjunction with the land-grab policy of the Dawes General Allotment Act, significantly reduced the land area held by Indians throughout the Pacific Northwest.[35] In 1880, there were three reservations in eastern Washington: the Colville and Columbia, to the north of the Columbia's Big Bend, and the Yakama. Together the three comprised 6,592,240 acres; 800,000 acres in the Yakama Reservation alone. While the Yakama still held about 800,000 acres in 1890, the total reserved area for Indians in eastern Washington had fallen by almost half, to 3,777,820 acres.[36]

---

[31] *CIA-AR*, 1888, 230.

[32] *CIA-AR*, 1881, 174.

[33] White Swan made these comments while recounting how Indians had felt at the Treaty Council. *U.S. v. Winans*, Transcript of Record, Testimony and Final Report of Examiner, enclosed in Attorney General to Clerk of the Supreme Court, Jan. 21, 1904, Appellate Case File no. 19213, Records of the Supreme Court, RG 267, NA, pp. 97, 103. On the recalcitrance of the "Wild Yakima," see *CIA-AR*, 1884, 173-74; *CIA-AR*, 1885, 200; *CIA-AR*, 1894, 325-27; *CIA-AR*, 1897, 222.

[34] Estep to Commissioner of Indian Affairs [hereafter cited in notes as CIA], Nov. 1, 1928, file 50991-28[?]-115, CCF, GR, BIA, RG 75, NA.

[35] See Chapter 4.

[36] J. Olin Oliphant, "Encroachments of Cattlemen on Indian Reservations in the Pacific Northwest, 1870-1890," *Agricultural History* 1 (1950): 24, reprinted in Paul Gates, ed., *The*

The Yakama, thus, were comparatively fortunate. While throughout Oregon, Washington, and Idaho federal officials approved sales of "surplus" lands left over following allotment and "restored" reservations such as the Columbia and Malheur (in Oregon) to the public domain, the Yakama peoples managed to retain almost their entire land base. Yakama organization and their determination to extend the allotment period to children effectively eliminated a fund of "surplus" lands.[37] Non-Indian ranchers and farmers also were able to achieve access to Yakama lands without necessitating the abolition of the reservation, and could actually benefit from the reservation status of lands they used.[38]

As early as 1878, Yakima Agent Wilbur had begun to permit "stockgrowers" to graze their animals near the agency and on the reservation for a fee, the proceeds of which he used to buy machinery for a reservation lumber mill.[39] Non-Indian grazers paid a small fee, for example, one dollar per head, in 1889, for cattle fattened up on reservation grass before they were shipped to market out of Toppenish Station.[40] Some grazers, such as the large Snipes and Allen operation, took advantage of their contracts by grazing more stock than they paid for. Others made private arrangements with Indians to pasture stock for them, thereby avoiding county taxes as well as reservation grazing fees.[41] All around the reservation, sheep and cattle growers allowed their animals to range freely, with the expectation that the animals would "go graze on the Indian lands."[42] Indeed, Indian groups throughout the Pacific Northwest at this time found that non-Indian ranchers simply ignored their reservation boundaries.[43]

Yakama complained that trespassing cattle and sheep prevented their own stock from grazing, and threatened important root gathering grounds on

---

Rape of Indian Lands, The Management of Public Lands in the United States Collection (New York: Arno Press, 1979): 43.

[37] See Chapter 5.

[38] This is not to say that Washington residents supported Indian reservations. In 1871, 1877, 1883, 1886, and 1888 the Washington territorial and then state legislature adopted resolutions advocating the reduction of the Yakama and Colville reservations. See Oliphant, "Cattlemen on Indian Reservations," 53, n. 66, citing Washington, Oregon, and Idaho legislative resolutions to reduce reservations during the period 1870-1890.

[39] *CIA-AR*, 1878, 141; Two grazing contracts, both dated Jan. 1882, 115-6, CRP; Oliphant, "Cattlemen on Indian Reservations," 50.

[40] Allen and Chapman Drug. Co. to Priestly, April 26, 1889, 115-22, CRP.

[41] *CIA-AR*, 1890, 233; Oliphant, "Cattlemen on Indian Reservations," 51-52.

[42] Oliphant, "Cattlemen on Indian Reservations," quoting CIA to C. S. Voorhees, June 25, 1888, Land Division, Letter Book 175, pp. 142-43. See also Gretta Gossett, "Stock Grazing in Washington's Nile Valley, Receding Ranges in the Cascades," *Pacific Northwest Quarterly* 55 (1964): 119-27. Gossett includes descriptions of many local grazing operations based on her interviews with residents of the area.

[43] Oliphant, "Cattlemen on Indian Reservations," 55.

the reservation. Until 1910, the reservation range, as well as those lands bordering the Yakama Reservation were heavily overgrazed through the combined efforts of sheep, cattle, and horses. Severe winters and depressed markets kept livestock numbers of both Indians and non-Indians down between 1910 and 1930 but did not prevent overgrazing. No reservation leasing program for grazing existed before the 1930s.[44] Yakama policed their range as best they could. Yakama who collected trespassing cattle charged one dollar per head—according to federal law—to return them to their owners, a practice that non-Indians protested but to no avail.[45]

Just as state-licensed fishers attempted to better their own access to shrinking Columbia River salmon stocks by trying to exclude Indians from the fishery, so cattle and sheep ranchers tried to eliminate Indian competition on the range. Cattle ranchers skirmished with sheep ranchers for a dwindling share of range, and conflict intensified after the Forest Service began issuing grazing permits on National Forest lands in 1906.[46] Both kinds of ranchers wanted access to reservation lands and wanted to keep Indians from using off-

---

[44] "Grazing Land Report Given By Saluskin," *Yakima Herald*, Nov. 21, 1963, p. 33. In 1954, the BIA set up a Branch of Land Operations which took on range management, previously handled by the Branch of Forestry. Since then, Tribal Council and Branch of Land Operations have jointly attempted to restore range lands. Federal policies on grazing on the public lands were just getting underway at the turn of the century, but failed to stem widespread over use and destruction of rangelands. Paul W. Gates, *History of Public Land Law Development* 1968 (New York: Arno Press, reprint edition, 1979): 495-529, 607-34.

[45] According to 4 Stat. 730, § 9 (June 30, 1834): "[I]f any person shall drive, or otherwise convey any stock of horses, mules, or cattle, to range and feed on any land belonging to any Indian or Indian tribe, without the consent of such tribe, such person shall forfeit the sum of one dollar for each animal of such stock." See also CIA to Miles C. Poindexter, copy [n.d.] box 78, folder 5, Accession no. 3828, Miles C. Poindexter papers, University of Washington Libraries Manuscript Collection, Seattle, Wash. [hereafter cited as box:file, MCPP]; Petition signed by 74 settlers along boundary of Yakima reservation, enclosed in C. S. Voorhees to Indian Department, April 28, 1888, enclosed in Atkins, CIA, to Thomas Priestly, May 7, 1888, 115:21, CRP; reply, quoted in Oliphant, "Cattlemen on Indian Reservations," 51.

[46] The General Land Office, which managed the Forest Reserves before the Forest Service was created in 1897, required sheep grazers in Oregon and Washington to apply for permits to use the reserves before 1906. Much public land suitable for grazing—and that was not homesteaded and grazed—was incorporated into National Forests for management purposes prior to the Taylor Grazing Act of 1934. Gates, *History of Public Land Law*, 511-27; Charles F. Wilkinson and H. Michael Anderson, *Land and Resource Planning in the National Forests* (Washington, D.C.: Island Press, 1987): 98-99. On competition for access to rangelands, see Gates, *History of Public Land Law*, 517-29, 617-18; Wilkinson and Anderson, *Resource Planning in the National Forests*, 95-100; Gossett, "Stock Grazing in Washington's Nile Valley," 122-25; Donald W. Meinig, *The Great Columbia Plain: A Historical Geography, 1805-1910*, The Emil and Kathleen Sick Lecture-Book Series in Western History and Biography (Seattle: University of Washington Press, 1968): 284-93; William D. Rowley, *U.S. Forest Service: Grazing and Rangelands: A History*, 1st ed. (College Station, TX: Texas A & M University Press, 1985).

reservation lands, a situation that left the Yakama perpetually on the defensive.

From 1917 through 1929, Yakama repeatedly petitioned the Bureau to increase the on-reservation range allocated to Indian grazers at the expense of non-Indian grazers, and to stop issuing permits for grazing in important subsistence grounds. A 1919 petition to Secretary of Interior Franklin K. Lane (1913-1920), requested that the Olney, Ahtanum, and Satus root digging grounds all be removed from rental as grazing land:

> The Indians prize these roots very greatly and each year dig them in very great quantities. Cattle and sheep destroy them. We feel under the treaty we should have a right to use these ranges as best suits out [sic] habits, and want to utilize them, and they will give the greatest benefit and happiness to our tribe.[47]

The Bureau's policy was to give Indian grazers precedence over non-Indians where there was a conflict over reservation grazing, but Yakama interests in sufficient grazing land and maintaining root grounds went largely unrecognized by reservation agents, especially Carr, and by higher Bureau officials.[48] The Bureau "has been acting very cavalierly with the Indians, and certainly not within the spirit of the May treaty," one local attorney wrote in 1919.[49]

Although on-reservation root gathering grounds were difficult to protect, excluding grazing animals from berrying grounds proved much more difficult because most berrying areas were in the Cascade range, where part of the disputed reservation boundary line met the borders of the Rainier and Gifford Pinchot National Forests.[50] The Forest Service issued grazing permits on

---

[47] Indian allottees to Franklin K. Lane, Secretary of Interior, et al., May, 1919, box 1, folder 2, Henry J. Snivley Papers, Accession No. 3095, University of Washington Manuscript Collection, University of Washington, Seattle, Wash. [hereinafter referred to as box:folder HJSP]. See also Petition to Carr, n.d., 1: "General Correspondence re: Indian Matters," HJSP, requesting that the root digging grounds in the Ahtanum and Olney ranges be reserved for tribal use.

[48] CIA to Poindexter, copy [n.d.] file 78:5, MCPP; Hauke to Carr, April 27, 1917, file 14373-17-115, YA, CCF, GR, RG 75, NA; Chief Jim Saluskin to C. C. Dill (Wash.), Nov. 3, 1929, discussing Butte Meadows and Pearne's cattle ranch, 1:2 "General Correspondence re: Indian Matters, 1919-30," HJSP. Saluskin's grazing lands in Mosquito Valley was taken by Charlie Wilson, a Scotsman who grazed his sheep there. Gossett, "Stock Grazing in Washington's Nile Valley," 123-24. See also Chief Joe Moses to Poindexter, March 13, 1916: "And it is spring time and I don't want the sheep to be grazing round in the reservation," 78:15, MCPP.

On Yakama complaints against Don Carr and the Indian Office, see, for example, George Meninock, Watson Homer, and Showona Cotiakin letter to Poindexter, May 10, 1919, 1:2, MCPP; Snively to Poindexter, June 23, 1919, 1:2, MCPP.

[49] Snivley to Poindexter, June 23, 1919, 1:2, MCPP.

[50] Rainier National Park, for example, was established in 1899, two years after the area had been designated the Mount Rainier Forest Reserve. Although it became a park, management for the area remained with the same group that had administered it as a Forest Reserve.

upland rangelands especially favored by sheep ranchers, and Yakama argued that sheep trampled and ate the bushes so they would not bear fruit.[51] In 1911 several tracts near Mount Adams, including Peterson Prairie, South Prairie, and Little Huckleberry Mountain, were closed to grazing specifically to allow Yakama to use the areas for huckleberry gathering, but conflict between Indians and non-Indian sheep ranchers continued.[52]

Yakama were often unsuccessful in protecting both root and berry grounds because their claims were difficult to map out in space and time. Yakama had root and berry grounds everywhere, both on and off the reservation, and state and federal officials were unwilling to set aside each of those subsistence areas.[53] At its fundamental level, Yakama requests to set aside hunting and gathering grounds rested on the Tribe's unique culture and the treaty protections they believed were in place to protect it, while state and Bureau officials did not perceive that as a valid basis for limiting property rights of Euro-Americans.

The Forest Service and Bureau denigrated Yakama petitions to restrict grazing in the berry patches by accusing the tribe of using berrying as an excuse to graze their animals for free in the National Forest.[54] Yakama historically traveled with a large number of horses when making their subsistence rounds. The fact that Yakama traveled with a reputed average of ten to twelve horses per person annoyed federal officials who believed that one horse per person should be sufficient for anyone.[55] Assistant Commissioner C. F. Hauke

---

Sheep grazing on the eastern slopes of the Cascades range was permitted in the park; an area that was also used by Yakama foragers. Gossett, "Sheep Grazing in Washington's Nile Valley," 125.

[51] Carr to CIA, Feb. 26, 1917, file 14373-17-115, YA, CCF, GR, BIA, RG 75, NA. Carr noted that "the bushes and berries are very materially damaged through grazing." He thought it would take only a few years before the Indians are barred from berrying in any areas except those "too remote for sheep men to get to."

[52] Carr noted in 1917, "The Indians agitate the question of protecting these berry patches on every occasion and it would be but fair and right if certain areas could be set aside and the sheep prohibited from ranging therein...." Carr to CIA, Feb. 26, 1917, file 14373-17-115, YA, CCF, GR, BIA, RG 75 NA.

[53] Sec. of Agriculture to Sec. of Interior, April 5, 1917, file 14373-17-115, YA, CCF, GR, BIA, RG 75, NA.

[54] Sec. of Agriculture to Sec. of Interior, April 5, 1917, file 14373-17-115, YA, CCF, GR, BIA, RG 75, NA. See Wallahee to Meritt, Dec. 30, 1914, file 120088-14-115, YA, CCF, GR, BIA, RG 75, NA, noting, "I am not telling these [things] to you about my old way for purpose, I am telling you true about my old way."

[55] Sec. of Agriculture to Sec. of Interior, April 5, 1917, file 14373-17-115, YA, CCF, GR, BIA, RG 75, NA. The Rock Creek band of Yakama apparently took only one horse per person with them. Perhaps on-reservation Yakama had more horses and better access to grazing land than did the Rock Creek band. Carr to CIA, Feb. 26, 1917, file 14373-17-115, YA, CCF, GR, BIA, RG 75, NA; Carr to CIA, Nov. 13, 1913, file 94359-13-308.1, YA, Decimal Subject Files [hereafter cited as DSF], BIA, RG 75, NA.

advised Chief Skookum Wallahee (1913-?), of the Skin Band of Rock Creek Indians in 1913, that his people should "not expect to be permitted to take along a large number of horses and graze them free of charge:

> The forest lands are leased to white persons for pasturage and if the Indians take a large number of surplus horses with them when they go berrying this interferes with the rights of the lessees. There would be no trouble at all if the Indians would comply with the regulations of the Forest Service and take just a reasonable number of horses on their trips.[56]

Hauke wanted Wallahee to act "reasonable," i.e., like a white person, thereby rejecting the Indian nature of the Yakamas' claims.

Forest Service officials also marginalized Yakama demands by pointing to the many berries that went unpicked.[57] Yakama, however, did not claim any entitlement to pick all available berries. They were concerned that continued overgrazing by white people's sheep would destroy areas that they had used for years and make access to bearing bushes increasingly difficult.

"[T]he white people always take there [sic] sheep up into my huckleberry patches and destroys my food," Wallahee reported to the Commissioner in 1914:

> Every year during the summer times the sheep they take up into mountains and gets right into huckle berry patches and now to-day huckleberry patches is most best of the huckle berry patches is about all dried out on account that sheep has been on it are destroyed every thing in mountains such as grass and water goes dry from sheep going on it. The ground is getting bad in all those places where sheep herder hold his sheep when he takes his sheep away from place to place on the first place his sheep has been herd and then it's smells full of manure as Indians don't like smell of it, and that's why I don't like to have sheep to be on those places, from now on next summer I do not want no sheep to be taking into mountains again where sheepherder have been making troubles against us Indians[.][58]

---

[56] C. F. Hauke to Wallahee, Feb. 4, 1913, file 133661-12-115, YA, CCF, GR, BIA, RG 75, NA.

[57] Sec. of Agriculture to Lane, April 5, 1917, file 14373-17-115, YA, CCF, GR, BIA, RG 75, NA. C. F. Hauke to Wallahee, Feb. 4, 1913, file no 133661-12-115, YA, CCF, GR, BIA, RG 75, NA. Hauke noted: "The question of the Indians using these lands has been up the last year or more and the Forest Service has no objection whatever to the Indians gathering the huckleberries as it is said that the bushes yield so many berries that thousands of gallons go to waste every year."

[58] Wallahee to E. B. Meritt, Dec. 30, 1914, file 120088-14-115, CCF, GR, BIA, RG 75, NA. See also Wallahee to OIA, March 16, 1915, noting that "I have no objections to the sheep going as far as Mt. Adams, but in other places they ruin the berries." "The Indians wish the berries to be taken care of and we have only tried to keep them from being destroyed." Wallahee to OIA, March 6, 1915, file 120088-14-115, YA, CCF, GR, BIA, RG 75, NA.

Wallahee argued that the Forest Service and Bureau were obligated to protect the areas for Yakama use because subsistence activities were sanctioned by a higher authority than U.S. law: "nobody here in these world has made all this game in the mountains. God has to say all about these for all what he has made in this world," he wrote.[59] From that perspective, Yakama had a reciprocal relationship with the berries and other resources and a responsibility to protect them. "The Indians wish these berries to be taken care of," Wallahee wrote in 1915, and Forest Service and Bureau grazing policies clearly were destroying them for all to see.[60]

Wallahee and others also complained that Indians who arrived to pick berries in late fall, after herders had already moved sheep into berry areas, became targets for sheepherders who would countenance no more competition once they had secured hard-won grazing permits.[61] Incidents of Yakama pickers who were verbally or physically abused by herders continued throughout the 1920s.[62]

Overgrazing and the discontinuance of burning reduced huckleberry yields, and made Yakama access to the bearing bushes more important.[63] Additionally, animals such as deer, elk, and mountain goats, which depended

---

[59] Wallahee to Meritt, Dec. 30, 1914, file 120088-14-115, YA, CCF, GR, BIA, RG 75, NA. Wallahee wrote that the world was created for Indians, and everything would be newly created after the old earth was destroyed. Until then, the treaty promised protection for Indian use of the forests and other subsistence locations.

[60] Wallahee to OIA, March 6, 1915, file 120088-14-115, YA, CCF, GR, BIA, RG 75, NA; Wallahee to Meritt, Dec. 30, 1914, ibid. Carr reported that extensive damage to huckleberry bushes in Pinchot National Forest, in Carr to CIA, Feb. 26, 1917, file 14373-17-115, YA, CCF, GR, BIA, RG 75, NA.

[61] Wallahee complained in 1913 that a group of Indians, including William Stayhie and his wife, and Wahpasset Whiz, were attacked by a sheep herder when they set up camp to pick berries. The herder hit the horses, trying to get them to move away, but the Indians remained there, and the herder moved the next day. Carr to CIA, Nov. 13, 1913, file 94359-13-308.1, YA, DSF, BIA, RG 75, NA. See also CIA to Black Wolf, Feb. 13, 1917, relative to Black Wolf's complaint about limited access to huckleberry and root fields, and Don Carr to CIA, reporting on Black Wolf's complaint, Feb. 26, 1917, file 14373-17-115, CCF, GR, BIA, RG 75, NA; Rev. S. Ewing to Hon. John Summers, Oct. 11, 1928, relative to Indian huckleberry fields on U.S. forest land, file 50991-28-115, YA, CCF, GR, BIA, RG 75, NA; Carr to CIA, Feb. 26, 1917, file 14373-17-115, YA, CCF, GR, BIA, RG 75, NA.

[62] Estep, Memo, Aug. 8, 1923, sheep interfering with berry patches in Rainier and Columbia national forests, folder "Councils and Meetings, Tribal, 1913-25," Tribal Records, 1897-1952, YA, BIA, NA-Seattle; Rev. S. Ewing to Hon. John Summers, Oct. 11, 1928, relative to Indian huckleberry fields on U.S. forest land, file 50991-28-115, YA, CCF, GR, BIA, RG 75, NA.

[63] See Petition of George E. Smith, et al. to Poindexter, March 25, 1912, enclosed in Poindexter to Henry S. Grayes, chief forester, Department of Agriculture, May 4, 1912, 59:1, MCPP, alleging that sheep grazed in Colville National Forest by one McAllister "a resident sheep owner[,] used this area holding his sheep upon it for such long intervals that the grass was eaten almost into the ground." Gossett, "Stock Grazing in Washington's Nile Valley," describes the McAllister brothers' sheep operation, p. 24.

on ecotones maintained by regular burning, suffered habitat loss through range expansion and as a result of the federal and state anti-fire stance.[64] Elk probably were exterminated by 1870; mountain sheep by 1900. Other species including grizzly bears, black bears, wild horses, antelope, bison, and mountain goats either disappeared altogether or are present now only in small numbers.[65]

Not only did on and off-reservation ranching destroy native plants and grasses important to Yakama peoples, ranchers' notorious efforts to kill predators reduced the diversity of wildlife populations on the Plateau.[66] Under the auspices of the U.S. Bureau of Biological Control and Washington's Department of Game, hunters systematically exterminated wolf, coyote, bobcat, and various smaller mammal populations in the area in order to protect livestock.[67] Loss of those predator species resulted in increases of deer and then elk (after a group of elk was transplanted to the Cascades from Yellowstone National Park in 1913) and further reduced the available range.[68]

Both Yakama and Euro-Americans hunted and trapped, and so it is not clear to what degree each group contributed to the decline of certain species, including elk, antelope, and deer during the period of initial contact in the 1840s and 1850s.[69] Plateau peoples had been involved in the European fur trade to various degrees since contact, and Yakama took part in this trade to some extent.[70]

---

[64] Uebelacker, "Geographic Explorations," 97-101, noting that the declining populations of mountain goat and bear may be linked to fire prevention; Helmut K. Buechner, "Some Biotic Changes in the State of Washington, Particularly During the Century 1855-1953: *Washington State College Research Studies* v. 21 (1953): 160-61, 163 (noting that prong-horned antelope were declining even as whites arrived), 172-85.

[65] Uebelacker, "Geographic Explorations," 93-105; Washington state authorized the killing of 5000 wild horses, promoted by cattle interests, Schuster, "Yakima Indian Traditionalism," 299; Buechner, "Some Biotic Changes in the State of Washington," 172-85.

[66] On changes in native grasses, see Buechner, "Some Biotic Changes in the State of Washington," 166-72.

[67] Smaller target animals included badgers, foxes, skunks, moles, rats, crows, sparrows, and blackbirds. See generally monthly reports on predator extermination program for Washington and trappers' reports, in box 351, DSF 921, BIA, RG 75, NA-Seattle. See also Gossett, "Stock Grazing in Washington's Nile Valley," 121.

[68] Buechner, "Some Biotic Changes in the State of Washington," 181-82.

[69] Uebelacker, "Geographic Explorations," 103; Buechner, "Some Biotic Changes in the State of Washington," 172-85.

[70] Because Yakama were not on a major trade or communication route in the early contact period (before 1850), they had only limited interactions with Anglo-Europeans. On the fur trade in the Northwest, see Ross Alexander, *Fur Hunters of the Far West*, 2 vols. (1855) (republished, Norman: University of Oklahoma Press, 1956); Theodore J. Karamanski, *Fur Trade and Exploration: Opening the Far Northwest, 1821-1852* (Norman: University of Oklahoma Press, 1983). There is an enormous literature on North American Indian hunting and how it was affected by contact with Euro-Americans. See the classic and controversial

By the twentieth century, Yakama women sold buckskin gloves as "one of their most important sources of revenue," according one Bureau official in 1914.[71] Toward the end of the 1920s, Yakama had "done a considerable business in trapping ... [and] the price of a beaver pelt has materially assisted the Indians in their provisions who otherwise would have been much shorter in the food line than they had been."[72] Since Yakama hunting pressure on wildlife had been limited by their mobility before contact, it is not evident whether and how they regulated their takings once they were more confined to the reservation; nor is it clear to what extent Yakama contributed to the overall depopulation of wildlife species in Washington following contact.

The Yakama Reservation, because of its federal status, became a peculiar battleground during the early decades of the twentieth century for state fish and game officials, state licensed hunters, and the Yakama. Federal law prohibited non-Indians from hunting on the reservation, which led state officials to use the reservation regularly as a haven for pheasant, bass, and other wildlife populations that were to be seeded in the wild to augment declining native species.[73] It was impossible to police the entire boundary of the reservation, and because a significant portion of the border was in dispute for decades, non-Indian hunters habitually used the reservation with impunity.

The result was that the reservation truly became an unregulated commons for non-Indian hunters who believed that any laws were suspended once they got onto the reservation. The Yakima County Auditor issued 3500 hunting licenses for the 1911 season alone, and an unknown number had been issued by the state.[74] F. H. Abbott, Acting Commissioner, observed in 1912 that "it appears that previous to this season ... [non-Indian] hunting on the reservation

---

study by Calvin Martin, *Keepers of the Game: Indian-Animal Relationships and the Fur Trade* (Berkeley: University of California Press, 1978); Sheppard Krech, III, ed., *Indians, Animals and the Fur Trade: A Critique of Keepers of the Game* (Athens, GA: University of Georgia Press, 1981).

[71] Charles Redfield to CIA, Feb. 14, 1914, file 19049-14-115, YA, CCF, GR, RG 75, BIA, NA. Chief Black Wolf asked Redfield to write to the Indian Office stating that Indians have right to kill deer and to have deer hides in their possession whenever they wanted. Redfield wrote that "[i]n some instances the Indian women have bought deer hides of white men, other white men have found the women with these hides in their possession, and have confiscated the hides and put the women in jail, presumably through due process of law. This was manifestly unjust, as these Indian women had neither intended nor done anything wrong." Redfield also noted that game was the only source of fresh meat for Indians.

[72] Estep to CIA, Feb. 15, 1929, file 8940-29-115, YA, CCF, GR, RG 75, BIA, NA.

[73] Non-Indian on-reservation hunting was prohibited by 4 Stat. 730, § 8 (June 30, 1834), which formed the basis for parallel regulations by the Indian Office. On state use of the Yakama Reservation as a game haven, see F. H. Abbott, Asst. CIA, to J. W. Rider, Nov. 22, 1912, file 87608-12-115, YA, CCF, GR, RG 75, NA.

[74] Carr to CIA, Aug. 28, 1912, file 87608-12-115, YA, CCF, GR, BIA, RG 75, NA.

has been indulged in to such an extent that certain game has become practically extinct."[75]

The situation remained unchanged, despite Carr's determination to post more guards and charge non-Indians for hunting on the reservation.[76] "[W]henever the game season is open a white man comes in on the reservation and does the hunting; kills all kind of game," 'Tecumseh Yakatowit complained at a council meeting in 1916.[77]

Agent Estep described opening day of the Washington pheasant hunting season of 1923 as a shooting frenzy:

> [H]unters from all of the surrounding towns and from Seattle, Tacoma, Pendleton, and possibly from farther places, flocked to the reservation with automobiles and automatic guns and, flagrantly violated the game laws of the State in many respects, particularly the law which prohibits shooting on public highways. A very large number of these hunters were wholly irresponsible and criminally negligent of the rights of the Indians and whites. I was out on the reservation that day and how any pheasant or any other game bird escaped the onslaught of this army I do not know.[78]

"Not all of the accidents have been reported," Estep wrote, "but the net result was the death of two men, the shooting of a horse, and several Indians being threatened by white men."[79]

As animals important to their subsistence became increasingly scarce,

---

[75] F. H. Abbott, Acting CIA to Rider, Nov. 22, 1912, file 87608-12-115, YA, CCF, GR, RG 75, NA; "Cattle are Killed by Bird Hunters," *Yakima Morning Herald*, Oct. 10, 1913. See also C. F. Hauke, 2d Asst. CIA to S. A. M. Young, April 22, 1911, authorizing a $1.00 fee for non-Indian campers; the money to go to the Yakama tribe's Miscellaneous receipts class III, file 26883-1911-113.1, YA, DSF, BIA, RG 75, NA.

[76] Hauke to Carr, Sept. 12, 1912, file 87608-12-115, YA, CCF, GR, BIA, RG 75, NA; J. W. Rider, Sec. Yakima Valley Business Men's Association, to CIA, October 28, 1912, file 87608-12-115, YA, CCF, GR, BIA, NA, and reply, F. H. Abbott, Acting CIA, to Rider, Nov. 22, 1912, file 87608-12-115, YA, CCF, GR, RG 75, NA, stating that there can be no exceptions to the ban on non-Indian hunting on the reservation.

[77] Statement in Indian Council Proceedings, Yakima Agency, Fort Simcoe, WA, Nov. 11, 1916, in folder "Councils and Meetings (tribal) 1913-25," Tribal Records, 1891-1952, YA, BIA, RG 75, NA-Seattle.

[78] Estep to CIA, Nov. 13, 1923, file 89707-23-115, YA, CCF, GR, BIA, RG 75, NA.

[79] Indians, according to Estep, were employed as range riders where found "competent," Estep to CIA, Nov. 7, 1923, excerpt copy from file 87454-1923, filed in file 89707-23-115, YA, CCF, GR, RG 75, BIA, NA. In the same letter, Estep noted that "[t]here seems to be the impression that the reservation is a sort of game preserve for this class of hunters and that the State laws are inapplicable to their offenses on the reservation." Estep wrote in 1923 that "personally, I know of no place where it [Section 2137] really needs to be invoked more than on this reservation." Estep to CIA, Nov. 13, 1923, same file as above.

Yakama necessarily hunted off the reservation to secure food.[80] During the 1920s, Yakima Agents attempted to set up reciprocal "gentleman's agreements" with state authorities, whereby whites could hunt on the reservation as long as Indians could hunt off the reservation. Those arrangements were consistently unsuccessful because Washington's Department of Game was unwilling to tolerate off-reservation Indian hunting on any grounds.[81] The state's hostile attitude toward Indian hunters was not in opposition to federal policy, rather it was the result.

State Law and Off-Reservation Foragers

Most Yakama believed that roots, berries, fish, and game were protected equally under their 1855 treaty. Because all those resources were part of the subsistence complex, it made no sense to think of one without the others. It made still less sense to Yakama to seek permission of non-Indians to pursue their subsistence ways that they had been divinely given long before Europeans had arrived. Chief Wallahee wrote in 1914:

> I want you Assistant Commissioner to help me to tell all the white people all those living around here in Indian Country I do not want to have white people to raise any trouble with us Indians about our own names that's in this Columbia National Forest."[82]

Frank Selatsee angrily told Assistant Commissioner Meritt in 1928, "It is the rule among the Indians that we have to come every year to protect our rights on different matters to this city. Now the Great Spirit has put all this game, fish and deer there for the Indians and we were raised by those resources and we don't want an act or law to destroy our property."[83] Just as Euro-Americans might claim that they held natural rights to liberty and property, Yakama claimed fundamental rights to their subsistence base that no white person could revoke. As Yakama Louis Mann put it, "game ... is my Nature[']s gift."[84]

---

[80] Carr to CIA, Nov. 10, 1917, file 97414-17-115, YA, CCF, GR, RG 75, BIA, NA, noting that large animals on the reservation are very scarce.

[81] Estep to H. Sylvester Garvin, Assistant U.S. Attorney, Spokane, Jan. 12, 1925, "Hunting and Fishing, 1923-25" folder, box 81, General Correspondence, 1908-27, YA, BIA, RG 75, NA-Seattle; Estep to Lee C. Delle, Asst. U.S. Attorney, Yakima, Dec. 10, 1924, box 81, "Hunting and Fishing, 1923-25," General Correspondence, 1923-25, YA, BIA, RG 75, NA-Seattle. Virtually all of the complaints I found against Indian hunters were based on their violation of state set seasons, not their violation of private property entitlements; in fact, Yakama had a reputation for being very respectful of private property off the reservation.

[82] Wallahee to E. B. Meritt, Dec. 30, 1914, file 120088-14-115, YA, CCF, GR, RG 75, NA.

[83] Statement of Selatsee, 1928 Delegation Hearing.

[84] Mann to Poindexter, Dec. 17, 1915, 76:13, MCPP.

Selatsee, Wallahee, Mann, and others believed that the Supreme Court's 1906 and 1916 rulings in the *Winans* and *Seufert Bros.* fishing rights cases stood for the legal recognition of all their off-reservation fishing, hunting, and gathering rights. "[M]any a time I get white brother game warden angry but I am friendly every where[. Since] fishing time last [M]ay we have had a considerable trouble," Mann wrote in a 1915 letter describing his annual "outing trips." "State Officers fight us in the Courts but we beat them our tribes went on fishing unmolested [...] many are poor Indians who do not understand how to farm like I do my self...."[85] Similarly, when Chief Saluskin and a party of his people entered the Rainier National Park in order to hunt in 1916, they told the rangers who ejected them under protest that the park was part of their ceded territory on which they had reserved the right to hunt and fish without restraint.[86]

The Yakamas' position that they could hunt and gather throughout their ceded territory threatened private property rights and the state's police power over wildlife within its borders; a formidable combination that few federal officials were willing to challenge. Moreover, the Yakamas' treaty appeared to guarantee their hunting, berrying, and grazing uses of "open and unclaimed" land, rather than "usual and accustomed places," which weakened the Yakamas' claims according to some Bureau and Department of Justice authorities. Others argued that a right to fish off-reservation but not to do other activities there made no sense.[87]

The Supreme Court's decisions in the *Winans* fishing rights case, and *Ward v. Race Horse* (1896) and *New York ex rel. Kennedy v. Becker* (1916), two off-reservation hunting rights cases, made it clear that the Court would allow state regulation of Indian treaty hunting rights.[88] The Bureau, following the Department of Justice's recommendation, would not take Yakama claims into the federal courts because no one thought the cases were winnable.[89]

---

[85] Mann to Poindexter, Dec. 17, 1915, 76:13, MCPP; Mann wrote in 1916 that "once in every year I go out on my outing trips and everytime I was in trouble [with state officials]." Mann to Poindexter, Jan. 5, 1916, 76:13, MCPP.

[86] Carr to CIA, Nov. 10, 1917, file 97414-17-115, YA, CCF, GR, BIA, RG 75, NA. See also Acting Director National Park Service to CIA, Oct. 18, 1917, file 97414-17-115, YA, CCF, GR, BIA, RG75, NA, reporting that in early October, four men and two women, all Yakama, with twenty horses went into Rainier National Park and killed a deer before they were arrested and park rangers confiscated their rifles; Carr to CIA, Oct. 1, 1917, same file, reporting that Simeon Harry, a Yakama, accidentally crossed the boundary to the park and had three rifles confiscated even though he had not killed any game.

[87] Burke, CIA, to Estep, Dec. 10, 1923, file 89707-23-115, YA, CCF, GR, BIA, RG 75, NA; Frank R. Jeffrey, U.S. Attorney, Spokane, to Lee C. Delle, Assist. U.S, Attorney, Yakima, Dec, 22, 1924, folder "Hunting and Fishing, 1923-25," box 81, General Correspondence, 1923-25, YA, BIA, RG 75, NA-Seattle.

[88] 198 U.S. 371 (1906); 163 U.S. 504 (1896) 241 U.S. 556 (1916).

[89] Burke to Estep, Dec. 10, 1923, file 89707-23-115, YA, CCF, GR, BIA, RG 75, NA.

Further, the Bureau viewed hunting and gathering rights as more diffuse and wide-ranging than fishing rights, and therefore more difficult to assert and protect. Thus officials encouraged Indians to follow state hunting and fishing laws, thereby creating the public impression that Indians had no valid treaty rights to do so.

Subsistence hunting and gathering were uncivilized activities unworthy of the protection they would require and the antagonism they would engender among state-franchised property owners, federal officials believed. Assistant Commissioner E. B. Meritt told Chief Wallahee in 1915:

> The office well knows that once upon a time Indians took game, picked berries, and in fact did as they liked in every respect throughout the entire country, but those days are past, reservations of land have been made for the benefit of the Indians and the balance of the areas once occupied by the Indians has been thrown open to the general public and is now under state control. The Indians have a right to go upon and use the lands off the reservation on the same terms that white people have the right to go upon and use such lands and on no other terms. It appears that this is not satisfactory to you, but nevertheless it is a fact which cannot be changed and the Office suggests that the sooner you make up your mind to accept the situation as it is the less trouble you will have.[90]

As long as Indians continued to hunt and gather, the thinking went, they would never learn white work habits and would remain a burden to society in general. Bureau Inspector E. B. Linnen preached a gospel of work to sixty Yakama in 1916, telling them that they could all be rich farmers if only they would stop "going out into the mountains and hunting and fishing and getting berries. He [the smart Indian] must stay at home and attend to his crops and attend to his garden and chickens and everything he has got and in that way he will succeed...."[91]

The attitude of subsistence work as inferior to agriculture informed Bureau policies throughout the period. Charles Burke, Commissioner (1921-1929), echoed Meritt and Linnen more than a decade later when he advised the 1928 Yakima Council delegation that times had changed since their 1855 treaty and it was time they changed too. They should teach their children "to take up active work, to make use of the lands which they have in much the same way as the whites do ... and, in a comparatively few years, they will find themselves gradually growing independent and well-to-do."[92]

---

[90] Meritt to Wallahee, Feb. 12, 1915, file 120088-14-115, YA, CCF, GR, RG 75, BIA, NA.

[91] Indian Council Proceedings, Yakima Agency, Fort Simcoe, WA, Nov. 11, 1916, folder "Councils and Meetings (tribal) 1913-25, Tribal Records, 1897-1952, YA, BIA, RG 75, NA-Seattle.

[92] Burke to Noah James Saluskin, Frank Selatsee, Alva Cleparty, Feb. 4, 1928, file 6987-28-115, YA, CCF, GR, BIA, RG 75, NA. See also Carr to CIA, Nov. 10, 1917, file 97414-17-115, YA,

Maintaining respect for state conservation laws provided the perfect excuse for relegating Indian hunting, fishing, and gathering to the hands of state authorities. "[I]t has been the policy of the Office to follow the State law in the matter of killing game, as far as practicable, inasmuch as it is realized that unless some regard is had for the game laws, particularly with reference to the larger game such as deer and bear the supply will soon be exhausted," Assistant Commissioner Meritt wrote in 1914.[93] Washington's Departments of Game and Fish were already hard at work trying to restock game species at a rate that could keep up with state-licensed users.[94] To state officials, Indians were a group that could be excluded easily from access to the state's game population when pressure on the resource from other users became too great. Indians had no recognized voice in the political process: "I am not a Tax payer or voter," wrote Warcomac, a Yakama living at Hamilton Creek. "[S]o I can't appeal to the county to get any help...."[95] Thus, state officials lost no time in vigorously applying state laws to Indian hunters and fishers.

Federal policy to acquiesce to state regulation of Indian subsistence activities encouraged state officials to take a hard line approach to off-reservation Yakama subsistence generally, even though some local officials occasionally seemed more willing to accommodate Yakama interests.[96] Most state officials wanted Indians to take out licenses and observe seasons, just like residents. Chief Wallahee complained in 1914 that "[o]ur game warden of this district is too strict on us Indians all time make us trouble no want us to kill any deer. He wants us to pay licenses."[97] In the Washington Supreme Court's 1916 *Towessnute* decision, the Court resurrected the old equal footing doctrine to establish that Yakama treaty rights to fish did not survive Washington's statehood.[98] The

---

CCF, GR, BIA, RG 75, NA, noting that he will ask the "more prominent, educated Indians" to inform the others to abide by state and federal law.

[93] Meritt to Carr, Mar. 11, 1914, file 19049-14-115, YA, CCF, GR, BIA, RG 75, NA; see also Meritt to Wallahee, Dec. 14, 1914, file 120088-14-115, YA, CCF, GR, BIA, RG 75, NA.

[94] See, for example, George E. Mitchell, Washington Department of Game, to Lew Evans, June 17, 1938, folder 115B, "General Wildlife Correspondence and Circulars," box 351, DSF 921, BIA, RG 75, NA-Seattle.

[95] Warcomac to CIA, March 16, 1917, file 10238-17-115, YA, CCF, GR, BIA, RG 75. NA: Stahy to [Evans], Nov. 17, 1924, "Hunting and Fishing, 1923-25" folder, General correspondence, 1908-27, box 81, YA, RG 75, BIA, NA-Seattle.

[96] Evan Estep wrote to the CIA in 1929 that "the County Game Commission and the County Game Warden are not in accord with the State's attitude in this matter [of Indian off-reservation hunting] and they have cooperated with us in every way possible in reducing the causes for friction between Indian and white hunters by strong advice and caution to the members of the different sportsmen's organizations, but the State seems to be pressing down on the local organizations, evidently with a view to assuming entire charge of the hunting and fishing proposition throughout the State." Estep to CIA, Feb. 15, 1929, file 8940-29-115, YA, CCF, GR, BIA, RG 75, NA.

[97] Wallahee to Meritt, Nov. 3, 1914, file 120088-14-115, YA, CCF, GR, BIA, RG 75, NA.

[98] 89 Wash. 479 (1916).

Bureau did not appeal, and instead suggested that Indians follow state law in all their off-reservation activities.[99]

By the 1920s, any Indian venturing off the reservation "for any purpose whatever" might, according to Agent Estep, "be arrested and fined under some charge or pretext."[100] Estep wrote that "when an Indian, claiming treaty rights, kills a deer off the reservation it is a very serious offense for which four or five men must be arrested, probably with considerable display of firearms and violence, and fined $100.00 each."[101] State officials made manifest in practice the subordination of tribal sovereignty inherent in both state and federal cases.

Martin Stahy, an Indian living at Lyle, Washington, described his experience after shooting a deer on off-reservation federal land:

> I killed the deer from between Skookum Meadow to Lewis River, which is all gov. land.... Game Warden met me on the Gov. Trail, the same place where I killed the deer. He took my whole family to Cultus Creek, where his car was parked. From There he took me to Stevenson, Wa. where he fined me $100.00 & gave me 30 da. in jail; he also sold my gun. Is there any way I can get my gun back, and I want to be able to hunt on gov. land without being molested.
>
> "I live here same as on reservation, pay no tax, and get no liscense [sic] for any thing. Does the 1855 Treaty for Yakima Indians include us? We have tho[ugh]t so.[102]

Stahy's experience was not uncommon; state officials routinely confiscated Indians' guns and usually sold them summarily.[103] State game officials usually

---

[99] Meritt wrote that the case made "it necessary for the Indians to comply fully with the laws of the State of Washington when hunting or fishing outside of their reservations. You must do this, or subject yourself to the penalties of the law. When on your reservation, you may hunt and fish without any regard of state law." Meritt to Warcomac, Feb. 12, RG 75, BIA.

[100] Estep to H. Sylvester Garvin, Asst. U.S. Attorney, Spokane, Jan. 12, 1925, "Hunting and Fishing, 1923-25" folder, box 81, General Correspondence, 1908-27, YA, BIA, RG 75, NA-Seattle.

[101] Estep to CIA, Nov. 13, 1923, file 89707-23-115, YA, CCF, GR, BIA, RG 75, NA, suggesting that some action be taken to make hunters obey the law or to prosecute people under the federal law. This was a long-term problem. See also statement of 'Tecumseh Yakatowit, "Indian Council Proceedings, Yakima Agency, Nov. 11, 1916, folder "Councils and Meetings (tribal) 1913-25," Tribal Records, 1897-1952, YA BIA, RG 75, NA-Seattle.

[102] Stahy to Yakima Indian Agency, Nov. 17, 1924, "Hunting and Fishing, 1923-25" folder, General Correspondence, 1908-27, box 81, YA, BIA, RG 75, NA-Seattle.

[103] For references to state authorities selling Indian guns, see Stahy to Estep, May 14, 1925, "Hunting and Fishing, 1923-25" folder, "General Correspondence, 1908-27," box 81, YA, BIA, RG 75, NA-Seattle; Estep to Prosecuting Attorney, July 24, 1925, same file; Estep to H. Sylvester Garvin, Asst. U.S. Attorney, Spokane, Jan. 12, 1925, same file; Stahy to Estep, Nov. 26, 1925, "Hunting and Fishing, 1923-25" folder, box 81, General Correspondence, 1908-27, YA, BIA, RG 75, NA-Seattle, noting that his brother and son were arrested, fined, and imprisoned, and their guns were confiscated for killing a buck deer for their own use on federal land. U.S. Park Service officials also confiscated Indian guns when they caught

also fined Indian hunters who either paid or "laid out" their fines in jail.[104] Selling guns and fines were two effective tactics that immobilized Indian hunters who generally were cash-poor.

To Yakama, hunting and gathering rights were treaty-based and therefore required no state licence, irrespective of what state and federal officials said to the contrary. Many Yakama continued to hunt off the reservation without licenses. "I do not want to do that [obey state game laws] for my own rights, as I want to have my old ways hunting and fishing with out the permission," Chief Wallahee wrote in 1915.[105] Similarly, Stahy wrote in 1925 that he did not "depend on State laws but hold the Government laws as I am a Government ward."[106] Without federal backing, however, the Yakama could do little more than state their beliefs and serve time in the county jails.[107]

During the 1920s, at least two Yakama cases gained local prominence, and brought the question of off-reservation hunting entitlements to the Washington courts for the first time. State officials were eager to legitimize their policy of denying off-reservation rights, and Indian hunters, obviously tired of waiting for officials to help them, were willing to try the courts on their own. Perhaps Yakama felt empowered by their military service during World War I and the 1924 Indian Citizenship Act.[108] In any case, they had nothing to lose.

Both cases centered on Yakama chiefs who had been long-time critics of federal policy and whose suits were unsuccessful.[109] Chief Saluskin and four

---

hunters within park boundaries. See Acting Dir. National Park Service to CIA, Oct. 18, 1917, file 97414-17-115, YA, BIA, RG 75, NA; Carr to CIA, Oct. 1, 1917, same file.

[104] Estep to Garvin, Jan. 12, 1925, folder "Hunting and Fishing, 1923-25," box 81, General Correspondence, 1908-27, YA, BIA, RG 75, NA-Seattle. See also C. A. Huntington, Deputy Game Warden, Lewis County, to Carr, July 11, 1914, folder "Permits, Hunting and. Fishing, 1913-23," General Correspondence, 1908-27 (Pol-Z), YA, BIA, RG 75, NA-Seattle.

[105] Wallahee to E. B. Meritt, Feb. 25, 1915, file 120088-14-115, YA, CCF, GR, BIA, RG 75, NA.

[106] Stahy to Estep, May 14, 1925, "Hunting and Fishing, 1923-25" folder, General Correspondence, 1908-27, box 81, YA, BIA, RG 75, NA-Seattle.

[107] In 1913, Yakama hired attorneys to press a tribal claim to the use of Trout Lake in the Columbia National Forest, but I do not know the outcome of their claim. See Acting CIA to Carr, Jan, 18, 1913, folder "Permits, Hunting and Fishing, 1913-23," box 85, General Correspondence, 1908-27 (Pol-Z), YA, BIA, RG 75, NA-Seattle; Carr to CIA, Jan. 24, 1913, ibid. Since the lake was off the reservation, CIA would not assist Yakama claimants.

[108] According to the Act of November 6, 1919, Indians who served in World War I could become citizens without changing their tribal property interests, Ch. 95, 41 Stat. 350. Under the Indian Citizenship Act of 1924, "all non-citizen Indians born within the territorial limits of the United States" were made U.S. citizens, again without affecting tribal property. Other Indians became citizens under the Dawes and Burke acts. Indian Citizenship Act, Ch. 233, 43 Stat. 253 (codified at 8 U.S.C. § 1401(b)).

[109] Burke to Estep, Dec. 19, 1923; for a summary of the Yakama position on the question of off-reservation deer hunting, see "Case Heard Here is Initial One; To Go to Superior Court," with a subtitle, "Charles Saluskin Admits Shooting Game Out of Season and Off Reservation but

others were found guilty of possessing deer meat out of season, after the group shot the animal for food while gathering huckleberries in the Gold hill district of the American River. Although Saluskin maintained that he would take the case to Superior Court, he failed to secure any federal support.[110] Chief Wallahee, who was arrested for shooting a doe "east of the summit of the Cascade Mountains" in Kittitas county, off the reservation, took his case to the Washington Supreme Court, and lost in 1927. Wallahee received no assistance from the Department of Justice because the U.S. Attorney at Spokane believed there were no treaty rights at stake.[111] The court, relying on the equal footing doctrine of *Towessnute*, found that the Yakama had no off-reservation treaty rights to hunt.[112]

The Yakima Council looked beyond the courts throughout the 1920s, but did not secure their subsistence treaty rights any better there. In 1925, the Council appealed to President Calvin Coolidge, asking for "justice and a square deal. We are infringed by the state law; our treaty unrecognized of June 9, 1855, with the government."[113] Council delegates such as Frank Selatsee, Saluskin, and Alva Cleparty took up their cause with Bureau's Washington, D.C. office on an annual basis during the '20s, but did not persuade the Bureau to assist them with either litigation or legislation.[114] On a local level, the Council tried to get the Yakima Agent to appoint more Indians to fill positions such as forest guards and range riders, in order to cut down on the apparent corruption among non-Indians who held those posts and to police the reserva-

---

Claims Treaty Guarantees Red Men Such Right," *Yakima Republic*, Sept. 25, 1923, clipping, enclosed in CIA to Estep, Nov. 13, 1923, in file 89707-23-115, YA, BIA, RG 75, NA.

[110] "Case Heard Here is Initial One." The *Yakima Republic* reported: "The Indians in the case are included among the oldest of the Yakima Indians."

[111] Jeffrey to Delle, Dec. 22, 1924, box 81, Hunting and Fishing, 1923-25, General Correspondence, 1908-27, YA, BIA, RG 75, NA-Seattle. See also Garvin to Estep, March 11, 1925, same file Agent Estep attempted to help Wallahee's case by offering to suspend the application of 4 Stat. 730, § 8 (1834) to non-Indians hunting on the reservation if the state would drop the charges. He also encouraged the prosecuting attorney in the case to set up a test case in Stevenson, Wash. which they would save until Wallahee's case was decided. Estep to Prosecuting Attorney, July 24, 1925, same folder as above; Estep to Delle, Dec. 10, 1924, same folder. See also Estep to CIA, Aug. 19, 1927, file 39001-24-115, YA, CCF, GR, BIA, RG 75, NA.

[112] *State v. Wallahee*, 143 Wash. 117, 255 P. 94, 94-95 (1927). The court in *Wallahee* erroneously relied on *Ward v. Racehorse* to support the assertion that Washington's enabling act did not recognize treaty rights, which, although true for Wyoming, was not true for Washington. 255 P. at 95; Wash. Const. art. XXVI, para. 2, 4.

[113] Louis Mann, corresponding secretary for Indian Council, White Swan, WA, to President Coolidge, Feb. 18, 1925, folder "Councils and Meetings (tribal) 1913-25," Tribal Records, 1897-1952, YA, BIA, RG 75, NA-Seattle.

[114] Selatsee statement in 1928 Delegation hearing; Burke to Noah James Saluskin, Frank Selatsee, Alva Cleparty, Feb. 4, 1928, file 6987-28-115, CCF, GR, BIA, RG 75, NA. See also Carr to CIA, Nov. 10, 1917, file 97414-17-115, YA, CCF, GR, BIA, RG 75, NA.

tion boundaries more effectively.[115] While the reservation was closed to non-Indian hunting completely beginning in 1924, enforcement remained problematic. "There were probably 2,000 such [federal hunting] violations every year during the hunting season," Agent Estep noted in 1929.[116]

If Yakama lost off-reservation rights, the Bureau seemed more willing to ensure that state authority over fish and game terminated at the reservation boundary.[117] Yakama who took deer, fish, and beaver on the reservation were not subject to state seasons and were immune to state prosecution. Yakama beaver trapping, because Washington prohibited it, was particularly annoying to state authorities who attempted to intercept pelts as soon as they left the reservation.[118] The Bureau assisted Yakama trappers in securing means of

---

[115] Yakima Council to Estep, Feb. 25, 1925, folder "Councils and Meetings (tribal) 1913-25," Tribal Records, 1897-1952, YA, BIA, RG 75, NA-Seattle. Estep observed that when whites were range riders they let their friends use the reservation to fish and hunt. "From personal observation I am of the opinion that there are altogether too many white men hunting on the reservation and it is probably true that a large number of them fish during the fishing season." Estep to CIA, Nov. 7, 1923, excerpt copy from file 87454-1923, filed in file 89707-23-115, YA, CCF, GR, BIA, RG 75, NA.

[116] Order approved April 12, 1924, Burke, CIA, to Estep, April 12, 1924, file 89707-23-115, YA, CCF, GR, BIA, RG 75, NA; Estep to CIA, Feb. 15, 1929, file 8940-29-115, YA, CCF, GR, BIA, RG 75, NA; Whitlock to Indian Office, Oct. 7, 1935, file 54939-35-115, YA, CCF, GR, BIA, RG 75, NA, requesting funds on behalf of tribal council to post no trespassing notices on reservation to keep off-reservation hunters and fishers away.

[117] Charles Burke to N. Sinnot, May 21, 1924, file 39001-25-115, YA, CCF, GR, BIA, RG 75, NA.

The Migratory Bird Treaty Act, as a case of federal jurisdiction over Indian hunters, applied to reservation Indians until the 1940s. See Solicitor's Opinion, June 15, 1934, holding that act was binding on Indians irrespective of where birds are found. Collier to Superintendents, March 17, 1936, file 13209-36-931, YA, CCF, GR, BIA, RG 75, NA. See also Supt. Johnson to CIA, Oct. 25, 1938, file 13209-36-931, YA, CCF, GR, BIA, RG 75, NA; in October 1941, Yakama hunters who allegedly violated the act appeared in federal court. Minutes of Yakima Council Meeting, Oct. 3, 1941, summary, file 9228-36-341, part B, YA, CCF, GR, BIA, RG 75, NA. See also "Minutes of Meeting of Indian Service Personnel in the Pacific Northwest to Discuss Indian Hunting, Fishing, and Trapping Problems," meeting held May 6-7, 1940, reported in OIA, Circular of Information to Superintendents, Wildlife Conservation Officers, etc., May 28, 1940, folder 115B "General Wildlife Correspondence and Circulars," box 351, Decimal Subject File 921, YA, BIA, RG 75, NA-Seattle [hereafter cited as Circular on Indian Hunting and Fishing, 1940], discussing cases against Indians for allegedly violating the Act. In *United States v. Cutler*, 37 F. Supp. 724 (E.D. Idaho, 1941), the court held that Shoshone Indians could not be prosecuted for violating the Migratory Bird Treaty Act where they had taken wild ducks on their reservation. On-reservation Indian hunting is exempt from federal regulation under the Act.

[118] 1919 Wash. Laws 155, provided that beaver trapped on reservation became subject to state control once it left the reservation, whether or not in the possession of the person who trapped it. On State policy to deem beaver taken on reservation as "within the state" for regulation purposes, see L. L. Thompson, AG, to J. W. Kinney, Supervisor of Game and Game Fish, Seattle, April 24, 1922, file 8940-29-115, YA, CCF, GR, BIA, RG 75, NA. The decision mirrored the state's position on salmon, see AG Opinion to L. H. Darwin, Supervisor of Fisheries, May 16, 1921, holding that salmon caught within on-reservation waters were taken

shipping the pelts off the reservation without incurring the wrath of state authorities. Beaver trapping was clearly market oriented, and consequently earned official favor.[119]

Conclusion: Subsistence and Sovereignty

By the early 1930s, state authority over Indian hunting and gathering was more entrenched than ever, both in Washington state and elsewhere.[120] In its *Wallahee* decision, the state court wrote, "[T]he Yakima Tribe was not an independent nation nor a sovereign entity of any kind, the Indians being mere occupants of the land...."[121] Clearly the Washington Supreme Court was no champion of Indian rights, but there was no reason it should have been: federal officials did not hold Indian off-reservation treaty rights as legitimate. Agent Estep reflected in 1924:

> [T]here seems to be a growing tendency in this State by the courts to gain a foothold on the reservations. If this is allowed to go on, or it be held that the State courts do have this jurisdiction, then the end of the Indians' rights and privileges is near at hand. The State courts would probably not go so far as to attempt to deprive him of his allotment but they are making an effort to tie up the products of his allotment and if they succeed in doing that

---

"within the waters of the state" and possession of them during the closed season was prohibited by 1921 Wash. Laws, Ch. 180, overruling, Ops. AG, 1901-02, 108, holding that elk killed on reservation was not killed "within the state." All opinions quoted in Thompson to Kinney, above.

[119] On federal attempts to secure Indian entitlements to trap, see Rhoads to S. F. Rathbun, state supervisor of game and game fish, May 9, 1930, and Rathbun to Rhoades, May 21, 1930, file 8940-29-115, YA, CCF, GR, BIA, RG 75, NA; Talbott Demmead, Acting U.S. Game Conservation Officer, to CIA, April 11, 1929, file 8940-29-115, YA, CCF, GR, BIA, RG 75, NA. On Agent's efforts to protect Indian trapping, see Estep to CIA, Feb. 15, 1929, file 8940-29-115, YA, CCF, GR, BIA, RG 75, NA; Paul G. Redington, Chief U.S. Bureau of Biological Survey, to CIA, Feb. 27, 1930, file 8940-29-115, YA, CCF, GR, BIA, RG 75, NA. See also Rathbun to Estep, Feb. 3, 1928, quoted in Estep to CIA, Feb. 15, 1929, file 8940-29-115, YA, CCF, GR, BIA, RG 75, NA, stating that as long as the pelts are taken on the reservation and shipped to a state whose laws permit importation of pelts, Indian trapping is permissible.

Beaver trapping presents the possibility of an interesting case study on tribal regulation of this on-reservation activity. See request by Supt. Johnson that Yakima Council restrict beaver trapping, in Yakima Tribal Council Meeting minutes, summary, October 3, 1941, file 9228-36-341, part B, YA, CCF, GR, BIA, RG 75, NA. The summary notes, "Several of the Councilmen expressed themselves as being opposed to any restriction to this trapping; however, it was agreed that the matter would be given further study." See also Circular on Hunting and Fishing, 1940.

[120] There were many grounds for state authority over Indian hunting. See summary in Appendix 3, "State Regulation of Off-Reservation Hunting and Gathering Rights, 1880-1940."

[121] *State v. Wallahee*, 143 Wash. 117, 255 P. 94, 95 (1927).

they had just about as well take the whole business and have it over.[122]

By the end of the period, in the realm of off-reservation subsistence rights, the "end of the Indians' rights and privileges" had come—at least for a while.

While the Yakima Council worked on closing the reservation to non-Indian hunters during the 1930s, as long as the political nature of treaty hunting and fishing rights remained unresolved, the tribe could not effectively protect even that space.[123] Indian allottees who did not own their land in fee were clearly exempt from state hunting laws while on the reservation, the Bureau asserted.[124] Indians who held their allotments in fee, however, did not enjoy such immunity and officials warned that they would be subject to state hunting and fishing laws.[125] That dichotomy presented an unresolved and potentially impossible enforcement problem because the reservation was, and remains, a patchwork of fee and trust lands.[126] Moreover, as long as public officials ignored the question of the nature of Indian sovereignty within the U.S. federal system, it was impossible to decide what rights non-Indian lessees and owners of Indian allotments would have. As lessees allowed their friends to come onto their land to hunt and fish or, worse, leased their lands to private gun clubs, there was no clear legal or moral basis on which to decide whether those activities were right.[127] If Indians were "mere occupants of the land" and

---

[122] Estep to CIA, Dec. 2, 1924, box 81, folder "Hunting and Fishing, 1923-25," General Correspondence, 1923-25, YA, BIA, RG 75, NA-Seattle. See also Estep to CIA, Feb. 15, 1929, file 8940-29-115, YA, CCF, GR, BIA, RG 75 NA.

[123] In 1935, Yakama requested signs prohibiting hunting, fishing, and trespassing on their lands, and one hundred dollars of tribal funds was appropriated for the project. Whitlock to BIA, Oct. 7, 1935, file 54939-35-115, YA, CCF, GR, BIA, RG 75, NA. The Bureau allocated money for printing such signs through at least 1940. (See same file.)

[124] See *Mason v. Sams*, 5 F.2d 255 (W.D. Wash., S. Div., Apr. 9, 1925) (Quinaielt fishers held exempt from state fishing regulations while fishing in on-reservation streams); *Pioneer Packing Co. v. Winslow*, 294 P. 557 (S.Ct. Wash., 1930) (state cannot interfere with Indian fishing right in Quinaielt River which crosses the reservation); *State v. Edwards*, 62 P.2d 1094 (S.Ct. Wash., 1936) (Swinomish Indians fishing between mean low water mark and extreme low water mark held to be fishing on reservation and state regulations held not to apply).

[125] Once Indians were made citizens, some Washington officials decided that state laws would apply to them. Estep to CIA, Dec. 2, 1924, "Hunting and Fishing, 1923-25" folder, General Correspondence, 1923-25, Yakima Agency, box 81, RG 75, BIA, NA-Seattle. Estep refused to give Indians who held patents in fee for their allotments authorization to trap beaver. See Estep to CIA, Feb. 15, 1929, file 8940-29-115, YA, CCF GR, BIA, RG 75, NA.

[126] Courts in other states, however, held that even if some reservation land had been allotted and subsequently purchased by non-Indians, state fish and game regulations would not apply. See, e.g., *State v. Cloud*, 179 Minn. 180 (1930), and *State v. Jackson*, 218 Minn. 429 (1973).

[127] Lessees were selling hunting privileges on lands that they leased for farming and grazing (to gunclubs) without getting agency approval. CIA noted that lessees did not have such

had no sovereignty as distinct nations, there was no justification for treating on-reservation users any differently from off-reservation users, or Indians from non-Indians. Many of those questions are still unresolved.

Not before the U.S. Supreme Court held in 1942 that Yakama fishers did not need to buy state licenses in order to fish did the state's grip on Indians begin to loosen. Significantly, legal developments that defined the nature of Indian subsistence rights occurred in cases involving fishing. Yakama during the period 1840 to 1933 retained a clear legal notion of their treaty rights to subsistence resources. Although they found little support for their rights at the state and federal level, they did not abandon their beliefs. They transmitted their understanding of their treaty entitlements to their children, and they continued to teach them the value of subsistence to being Yakama. In 1989, Agnes Tulee, curator of the Yakima Indian Nation Center Museum in Toppenish, explained that beautiful baskets of thin, curled, white camas root, and medicinal plants were too important to Yakama life to display in an ongoing exhibit about Yakama life and the earth. A "Meals on Wheels" program in Goldendale regularly serves roots, berries, and lichen in their senior lunch program.[128] Law did not yet protect, yet law had not destroyed, the culture of subsistence.

---

rights—only those that have been granted to them. Johnson to CIA, Ap. 29, 1937 and CIA to Johnson, June 7, 1937, both in file 13209-36-931, YA, CCF, GR, BIA, RG 75, NA.

[128] Helen Spencer, personal communication, Yakima, Wash., July 6, 1989.

10

CONCLUSION

> We Indians are Dispossessed and there always Exists big Evil by which we are tried to be blind folded and misrepresented into the hands of the Department of the Interior now let us all have same table to eat from white and red race there our great father wants to bring us into Civilized living ... if time is come you and me are dead and what will be good at the end of the next world to come why not be a good brothers and earn right way of living...?
> —Louis Mann (1916)[1]

In 1979, the U.S. Supreme Court upheld a lower court decision that granted to many Washington State tribes, including the Yakama, a significant share of the Columbia River salmon harvest. In its opinion, the Court reflected on more than seventy years of jurisprudence on the topic of Columbia River interracial fishing conflicts:

> The purport of our cases is clear. Nontreaty fishermen may not rely on property law concepts, devices such as the fish wheel, license fees, or general regulations to deprive the Indians of a fair share of the relevant runs of anadromous fish in the case area. Nor may treaty fishermen rely on their exclusive right of access to the reservations to destroy the rights of other 'citizens of the Territory.' Both sides have a right, secured by treaty, to take a fair share of the available fish.[2]

Although the Court's decision was couched in the seemingly neutral language of legal precedent, the clarity with which the justices viewed the case law was more the product of their consciousness of historical change than any visible thread running through the law.

The Court's decision was a recognition that Indian peoples had not assimilated obediently and merged their identities with Euro-Americans. The Yakama maintained their own subsistence and commercial fishery within the larger Columbia commercial fishery managed by Washington State and a score of federal regulatory agencies. That an Indian fishery continued to flourish in the Columbia River was a sore point with many state-licensed fishers who

---

[1] Louis Mann to Miles C. Poindexter, Feb. 2, 1916, box 76, folder 12, Miles C. Poindexter Papers, Accession no. 3828, University of Washington, Library Manuscripts Division, Seattle, WA [hereafter box:file, MCPP].

[2] *Washington v. Washington State Commercial Passenger Fishing Vessel Association*, 443 U.S. 658, 684-85 (1979).

would sooner have gone to war again against the tribes than allow them to practice ancient treaty-based rights.[3]

Yet the Court's decision also recognized that the future of the salmon fishery ultimately depended upon Native American and Euro-American cooperation in using the resource. Neither group had the right to destroy the fishery or to deprive the other of its share, and the determination of a "fair share" necessarily required the participation of both groups in decision-making.[4] In that process, Native Americans ideally would participate as a politically distinct group, neither manipulating nor being manipulated by Euro-Americans.

Yakama fought for their right to political and cultural independence throughout the period from 1855 to 1933. The idea of different peoples sharing the same resource while respecting their differences was not a new idea to them. Yakama Doctor Shea-wa recalled of the Indian subsistence fishery more than a half-century before, "The [Columbia] river, I might say, was a table for both sides of the river. It laid right in between them and they [Indian peoples] came and ate and were gone."[5] Louis Mann, writing in 1916, expressed similar hopes for the future of Yakama and Euro-American peoples when he advised, "[N]ow let us all have same table to eat from white and red race there our great father wants to bring us into Civilized living."[6] Civilized living, in Mann's definition, was the result of mutual respect for differences and economic and political freedom for all: "Let my people live in their own way," he wrote.[7] What, then, was the Yakamas' "own way"?

During the near century that is the focus of this study, Yakama life changed drastically. The ways of the old people no longer worked in the world dominated by Euro-Americans. By 1933, Yakama people no longer drew their sole support from subsistence activities. Now Yakama provided migrant labor in hops fields and orchards near the reservation and beyond. Many Yakama leased their allotted lands to non-Indian farmers who had the capital and political power needed to get water to the land and plant it. A few Yakama ran successful farms and ranching operations, but these were the exceptions, not

---

[3] For a description of inter-cultural salmon fishing conflicts and the response of state-licensed fishers to federal court decisions affirming Indian treaty rights to the fishery, see Fay G. Cohen, *Treaties on Trial: The Continuing Controversy over Northwest Indian Fishing Rights*, a report prepared for the American Friends Service Committee (Seattle: University of Washington Press, 1986).

[4] 443 U.S. 658, 684-85.

[5] Quoted in *United States v. Seufert Bros. Co.*, U.S. brief, March 16, 1916, file 93689-13-115, Yakima Agency, Central Classified Files, General Records, 1907-39, Records of the Bureau of Indian Affairs, Record Group 75, National Archives [hereafter cited as file, YA, CCF GR, BIA, RG 75, NA], p. 64.

[6] Mann to Poindexter, Feb. 2, 1916, 76:12, MCPP.

[7] Mann to Commissioner of Indian Affairs, n.d., but ca. 1916, quoted in Lucillus V. McWhorter, n.d., but ca. Feb. 1916, newspaper clipping in file 20332-16-115, YA, CCF, GR, BIA, NA.

the rule. Yet the transformation of Yakama peoples from subsistence gatherer-hunter-fishers to wage laborers, with the concomitant loss of economic independence is not the endpoint—or even most important theme—of their history.

During this period of rapid change, Yakama peoples centered their lives around values drawn from older generations. Subsistence remained an important part of Yakama life and the social organization of subsistence continued to provide the norms for many Yakama families. Men and women gave the products of their respective traditional subsistence work in ritualized gift exchanges that continued to mark important occasions, such as births marriages, and deaths. As metal cookware, guns, and manufactured clothing now found their way into these exchanges, gifts given by the previous generation increased in value: Beautifully woven berry baskets, beaded leather clothing, and dressed skins became treasured objects—both to give and to receive. Giving itself retained its significance in securing relationships among people; wealth flowed from giving, not from accumulating.[8]

Moreover, people hunted game, fished, and collected subsistence foods as an important component of their daily diets. In Washat, or Long House, worship and celebrations, subsistence resources, including water, berries, roots, and fish held sacred places: water was sipped before and after ceremonial meals; first foods feasts marked the appearance of berries, roots, and fish each year. Subsistence foods were scarcer, but they had taken on a heightened and sacramental importance to Yakama life. The Yakamas' treaty of 1855, with its promises of protection for land and subsistence resources, had come to hold a sacred place, too.

Although few of the headmen who signed the Yakamas' 1855 treaty viewed the agreement as beneficial, the treaty became the standard against which Yakama measured all U.S. actions affecting their resources. By law, Yakama were made subject to Euro-American laws and became objects of U.S. colonial policies. By necessity, Yakama learned to articulate their claims in a language that was not their own, and in that project, the 1855 treaty became their primary defense against federal and state attempts to mine their resources and silence their voices.

Yakama peoples were fortunate in some ways. They were not pushed west in front of an advancing tide of non-Indian settlement, only to be relocated in strange surroundings. The Yakama Reservation encompassed the homelands of several of the groups assigned to the reservation. Retaining even small pieces of ancestral lands—following allotment—meant that some Yakama families kept an important link with their history, a sense of place.

Further, Yakama were well organized politically. Despite the confusion and dislocation that must have followed the amalgamation of fourteen separate bands into one confederated tribe, people attempted to recognize the former independence of the different groups in creating their tribal govern-

---

[8] Helen Hersh Schuster, "Yakima Indian Traditionalism: A Study in Continuity and Change" (Ph.D. diss., University of Washington, 1975): 437-82ff.

ment, the Bureau's efforts to the contrary notwithstanding. When Congress passed the Indian Reorganization Act in 1934, which gave tribes a choice of whether or not to adopt Bureau-designed constitutions containing blueprints for government modeled roughly on the U.S. Constitution, Yakama voted against applying the Act to their tribe.[9] Yakama wanted to protect their own confederated tribal governing arrangement in which representatives from each of the original bands came together for decisionmaking.[10]

During the early twentieth century, the Tribal Council—and many individual Yakama—actively lobbied and petitioned federal and state officials to address problems faced by the tribe. Although not always successful, Yakama worked to protect the rights they did secure in the courts as well as to extend those rights into other areas. Yakama had no standing in court for most of the period, which made their efforts to gain federal advocacy for their cause even more important.

Yet the ultimate importance of the Yakamas' story lies not in whether they won their political and legal claims more often than not; rather it inheres in their continuing struggle to define themselves for themselves despite the tremendous pressure to assimilate to Euro-American culture. In 1840, to live a Yakama life meant to take part in one's community, and to respect and share the gifts of one's *wyakin*, thereby making manifest a particular consciousness of place as well as personal "location" in the community. In the 1930s, a Yakama life might be very similar, or it might mean working for wages and participating in the Washat religion, or it might mean living off the reservation as wholly a part of the Euro-American world. Those choices are the product of individual aspirations but also of the collective history of the Yakama people.[11]

The Yakama's collective history is one in which law and legal institutions play a crucial role. First, Euro-Americans regulated their relationship with Native Americans and with their environments primarily through the legal system. No resource of importance to Yakama subsistence escaped the touch of federal or state laws or Euro-American hands. Second, Euro-Americans wanted control over Native American resources but their law did not always aid them in that effort. As the Yakamas' history indicates, Native Americans learned to negotiate for themselves the legal system and employed it—sometimes successfully—to press their own claims.

The Yakamas' collective history, perhaps most importantly, is an environmental history, because without looking at the level of the daily interactions between nature and culture we cannot understand either the changes in or

---

[9] Ch. 576, 48 Stat. 984 (1934).

[10] J. M. Stewart to Caples Dave, June 14, 1935, file 31032-35-115, YA, CCF, GR, BIA, RG 75, NA; Schuster "Yakima Traditionalism," 266-68.

[11] For a more recent view of Yakima/Plateau life, see Eugene Hunn and J. Selam & Family, *Nch'i Wana: The Big River: Mid-Columbia River Indian People and Their Land* (Seattle: University of Washington Press, 1988).

continuities between Yakama subsistence life in the nineteenth and twentieth centuries. Euro-American concepts of private property, the market, and law radically transformed the ecology of the Yakamas' homelands.

Between 1840 and the present, the Yakima Basin and the larger Columbia River Basin underwent many changes, and the landscape bore the costs of economic development in many ways, foreseen and unforeseen. Sagebrush land became lucrative farms and orchards watered by a vast network of irrigation canals; the salts leeched from the earth were drained into the rivers by equally extensive artificial arteries. The Columbia River sustains a major commercial salmon fishery, its stocks increasingly maintained by hatcheries.[12] The river also supports a series of large hydroelectric projects that have turned the once free-flowing waters into a series of human-regulated lakes.[13] West and north of the reservation, the forested foothills and slopes of the Cascade Range bear the scars of clear cutting and provide a depleting source of fodder for the area's lumber mills.[14] North of Yakima, the Hanford Nuclear Power Reservation produced the plutonium used in the bomb dropped by the United States on Nagasaki, Japan, in the Second World War, and the plant now generates electrical power for the region—in addition to radioactive fallout.[15]

All these places were known first to Yakama and other Plateau peoples; the history of these changes belongs as much to Native American peoples as to Euro-Americans. Native American voices have stories to tell about these changes, but do Euro-Americans have ears to hear them?

A society's lack of economic and political independence does not indicate that it has lost cultural integrity or is no longer an actor in history. The Yakama people clearly did not cease to have a voice once they became federal wards and every tribal member and the tribe's collective resources became subject to U.S. oversight and management. Yakama history, too, does not end there or in the 1930s. During the more than half-century following this study, Yakama continued to litigate, lobby, and petition to protect their fishery, water, timber,

---

[12] See Bruce Brown, *Mountain in the Clouds: A Search for the Wild Salmon* (New York: Simon and Schuster, 1982).

[13] Gus Norwood, *Columbia River Power for the People: A History of the Policies of the Bonneville Power Administration* (Portland, OR: U.S. Department of Energy, Bonneville Power Administration, 1981); see also Wesley Arden Dick, "When Dams Weren't Damned: The Public Power Crusade and Visions of the Good Life in the Pacific Northwest in the 1930s," *Environmental Review* 13 (1989): 113-53; Lewis E. Queirolo and William A. McNamee, "The Columbia-Snake: Challenges for Multiple-Use River Management," *Pacific Northwest Bulletin* 212 (1981); Philip R. Wandschneider, "Control and Management of the Columbia-Snake River System," *Bulletin* no. 0937 (Pullman, WA: Agricultural Research Center, Washington State University, 1984).

[14] For the early history of lumber industry in this region, see John Fahey, *The Inland Empire: Unfolding Years, 1879-1929* (Seattle: University of Washington Press, 1986): 188-213.

[15] Michele A. Stenehjem, "Pathways of Radioactive Contamination: Examining the History of the Hanford Nuclear Reservation," *Environmental Review* 13 (1989): 94-112.

and other resources. By the 1950s, the Tribal Council was responsible for managing tribal land and resource use policies, including timber sales, subsistence and commercial fishing, the purchase of alienated ancestral homelands, reservation water use, and zoning.[16] The tribe's struggle for self-determination and economic independence continues into the present.

Louis Mann, like the U.S. Supreme Court in its 1979 decision on Native American fishing rights, envisioned a cooperative sharing in which all people would come together and neither Euro-American nor Indian headed the table. Yakama have been forceful advocates of this vision, despite legal and political institutions designed to erase their voices and independence. It is time for all peoples to work together as we learn "civilized living" in a world in which no one race or culture is the most well-informed or dominant player.

---

[16] For a discussion of tribal efforts in these areas, see Charles "Click" Relander, ed., *Treaty Centennial, 1855-1955: The Yakimas*, 1st ed. (Washington State Historical Society and Oregon State Historical Society, published by authorization of the Yakima Tribal Council; Yakima, WA: Republic Press, 1955).

APPENDIX I

CROP YIELDS AND LAND HOLDINGS STATISTICS, YAKAMA RESERVATION, 1898-1935

TABLE I:1

Principal Crops Grown By Acreage—Wapato Project, 1918

Indians	No. acres	Whites	No. acres
Alfalfa*	1,862	Alfalfa*	24,847
Wheat	662	Wheat	11,604
Pasture	243	Orchard	3,288
Barley	205	Potatoes	3,178
Corn	150	Sugarbeets	2,722
Oats	145	Pasture	2,075
Potatoes	136	Corn	2,051
Sugarbeets	98	Barley	1,867
Misc.	94	Clover	1,047
Timothy	57	Misc.	994

*Does not include crops grown on orchard floors.

Source: L.M. Holt to CIA, June 18, 1918, file no. 52639-18-341, YA, GR, CCF, BIA, RG 75, NA.

TABLE I:2

Principal Crops Grown By Acreage—Ahtanum Project, 1918

Indians	No. Acres	Whites	No. Acres
Wheat	298	Alfalfa	1,624
Alfalfa	216	Wheat	822
Barley	43	Potatoes	305
Misc.	36	Pasture	232
Pasture	32	Barely	176
Oats	13	Corn	134
Potatoes	12	Misc.	87
Clover	9	Orchard	86
Potatoes	7	Oats	64
Truck	2	Onions	25

Source: L.M. Holt to CIA, June 18, 1918, file no. 52639-18-341, YA, GR, CCF, BIA, RG 75, NA.

TABLE I:3

Principal Crops Grown By Acreage
Wapato Irrigation Project, 1935

Indians			Lessees			White Owners		
Crop	Value	Acres	Crop	Value	Acres	Crop	Value	Acres
Alfalfa	22.64	2570	Alfalfa	21.83	14772	Alfalfa	22.67	11338
Wheat	24.48	1143	Wheat	24.92	10127	Wheat	25.76	6429
Pasture	10.00	843	Pasture	10.00	7311	Pasture	10.00	4803
No crop	0.00	535	No crop	0.00	3990	No crop	0.00	2802
Oats	20.48	433	Potato	92.19	4640	Potato	95.71	2552
Potato	57.64	360	Oats	17.60	2272	Apples	338.92	2209
Barley	18.12	276	Corn	22.50	1409	Oats	18.11	1893
Corn	21.00	126	Barley	16.72	1271	Barley	21.00	1007
Garden-truck	45.00	124	Onions	144.90	1195	Sugar beets	68.50	950
Cantaloupe	91.80	107	Cantaloupe	124.00	858	Hops	247.26	876

Mean Value Per Crop-Acre		
$31.15	$47.47	$84.79

Value is given in dollars per acre.
Source: Crop Yield Report Wapato Project, Ahtanum Project, Toppenish-Simcoe Project, Calendar year 1935, file no. 39451-34-341, YA, RG, CCF, BIA, RG 75, NA.

TABLE I:4

Principal Crops Grown By Acreage
Ahtanum Irrigation Project, 1935

Indians			Lessees			White Owners		
Crop	Value	Acres	Crop	Value	Acres	Crop	Value	Acres
Alfalfa	14.95	267	Wheat	19.14	688	Alfalfa	21.48	280
Wheat	12.91	166	Alfalfa	19.50	525	Pasture	10.00	159
Oats	10.63	85	Oats	16.00	420	Wheat	19.60	101
Pasture	10.00	52	Pasture	10.00	349	Apples	364.20	86
Barley	6.59	51	Barley	13.64	214	Oats	17.92	80
Potato	199.66	50	Potato	17.40	84	Hay*	13.00	37
No crop	0.00	21	Hay**	13.00	69	Barley	9.68	34
Corn	12.00	5	Rye	23.40	49	Peaches	41.16	31
Orchard	***	5	Corn	16.00	47	Potato	36.00	25
			Beans	30.00	20	Corn	20.00	24

Mean Value Per Crop-Acre		
$29.64	$17.80	$53.50

Value is given in dollars per acre.
*Not alfalfa or clover.
**Not alfalfa.
***Non-bearing
Source: Crop Yield Report Wapato Project, Ahtanum Project, Toppenish-Simcoe Project, Calendar year 1935, file no. 39451-34-341, YA, RG, CCF, BIA, RG 75, NA.

TABLE I:5

**Principal Crops Grown By Acre--
Toppenish-Simcoe Irrigation Project, 1935**

Indians			Lessees			White Owners		
Crop	Value	Acres	Crop	Value	Acres	Crop	Value	Acres
Not Available			Wheat	17.60	180	Alfalfa	26.00	246
			Potato	72.80	94	Wheat	24.84	173
			Barley	20.00	63	Oats	19.43	130
			Alfalfa	19.50	57	Barley	12.00	104
			Oats	18.00	45	Pasture	10.00	71
			Pasture	10.00	38	Potato	120.00	36
			Corn	48.00	13	Clover	13.00	15
			Orchard*	84.00	2	Garden-Truck	84.00	10
						No Crop	0.00	7
						Beans	**	3
						Rye	24.50	3

Mean Value Per Crop-Acre		
Not Available	$36.24	$33.38

Value is given in dollars per acre.
*Includes small fruits and berries.
**Not given and not included in mean value calculation.
Source: Crop Yield Report Wapato Project, Ahtanum Project, Toppenish-Simcoe Project, Calendar year 1935, file no. 39451-34-341, YA, RG, CCF, BIA, RG 75, NA.

TABLE I:6a

**BIA Estimated Number of Leases of Allotted Lands
For Farming, Grazing, and Business
At Yakima Reservation, 1898-1928**

Year	Number	Type	Term (years)	Revenue ($0.00) per acre per year
1898	"a few"*		3	--**
1899	9	F,G	3	1.00-1.75
1900	--	--	--	--
1901	76***	F,G	1,5	
1902	145	F,G	3,5	0.50-420.00#
1903	230	F,G,B	--	0.50-25.00#
1904	335	F,G	3,5	0.50-1.00
1905	379##	F,G	--	0.50-5.00^
1906	410	F,G,B	--	0.50-5.00^
1907	138	F(only)	--	--
1908	114^^&	F,G,B,M		--
1909	93^^	F,G		--
1910	--	--	--	--
1911	632	F,G	--	1.75
1912	629	F,G	--	1.86
1913	710	F,G	--	2.10
1914	1426	F,G	--	1.72
1915	819	F,G	--	2.01
1916	1004	F,G	--	2.39
1917	1120	F,G	--	1.91-1.33
1918	1220	F,G	--	1.76-2.18
1919	1250	F,G	--	1.16-5.40
1920	1252	F,G	--	1.16-5.40
1921**				
1928	1300	F,G	3,5,7	--

F = farming; G = grazing; B = business; M = mining.
Generally, BIA kept separate compilations for mining leases of reservation lands and I have not included them here.
*CIA-AR, 1898, 305.
**No figures are available for this year, or for the period 1921-1928.
***15 leases were pending. All 76 leases approved were to whites.
#Farming and grazing leases averaged $0.50-2.00 per acre per year; business leases averaged much higher. In 1902, 3 of 79 leases were for business purposes; in 1903, approximately 4 of 230 leases were for business; 1906, 14 of 410 leases were for business. Farming and Grazing leases remained the majority of leases throughout the period.
##Another 14 were pending.
^Unimproved farm land was still rented at $0.50-2.00 per acre, while improved land rented for $2.50-5.00 per acre.
^^Includes only new leases approved that year; not total number of leases.
&Includes mining.
Sources: CIA-AR, 1898-1920; Estep to CIA, Nov. 4, 1928, file no. 52539-28-341, YA, CCF, GR, BIA, NA.

TABLE I:6b

Yakima Reservation Land Covered by Leases For Farming and Grazing for Selected Years

Year	Number of leases	Total Acreage Under Lease	Percent of Reservation (approx. 800,000 acres)
1904	335	27,338	.034
1905	379	28,559.37	.035
1906	410	30,034.39	.036
1911	632	45,697.95	.057
1912	629	44,121.11	.055
1913	710	48,122	.060
1914	1426	49,347	.062
1915	819	49,300	.062
1916	1004	60,400	.076
1917	1,120	69,500	.087
1918	1,220	74,500	.093
1919	1,250	86,389	.107
1920	1,250	86,389	.107

Source: CIA-AR, 1904-06, 1911-20.

APPENDIX II

COLUMBIA RIVER SALMON FISHERY COMMERCIAL CATCH,
1866-1934

TABLE II

Year	No. Columbia River Canneries	Total Pounds Caught	Total Cases Packed
1866	1	272,000	4,000
1867	1	1,224,000	18,000
1868	2	1,904,000	28,000
1869	4	6,800,000	100,000
1870	5	10,200,000	150,000
1871	6	13,600,000	200,000
1872	6	17,000,000	250,000
1873	8	17,000,000	250,000
1874	13	23,800,000	350,000
1875	14	25,500,000	375,000
1876	17	30,600,000	450,000
1877	29	25,840,000	380,000
1878	30	31,280,000	460,000
1879	30	32,640,000	480,000
1880	35	36,040,000	530,000
1881	35	37,400,000	550,000
1882	35	36,808,400	541,300
1883	39	42,799,200	629,400
1884	37	42,160,000	620,000
1885	37	37,658,400	553,800
1886	39	30,498,000	448,500
1887	39	24,208,000	356,000
1888	28	25,328,436	372,477
1889	21	21,072,180	309,885
1890	21	29,632,632	435,744
1891	22	27,128,804	398,953
1892	24	33,138,984	487,338
1893	24	28,279,568	415,876
1894	24	33,326,800	490,100
1895	24	43,159,328	634,696
1896	24	32,755,396	481,697
1897	2	38,025,028	552,721
1898	23	33,950,192	487,933
1899	17	24,003,632	332,744
1900	16	25,798,966	358,772
1901	13	29,832,444	390,183
1902	14	26,200,024	317,143
1903	16	30,488,736	339,577
1904	20	36,863,872	395,104
1905	19	37,800,064	397,273
1906	19	35,653,064	394,898
1907	19	28,720,628	324,171
1908	14	24,340,892	253,341
1909	15	24,535,328	274,087
1910	15	35,330,420	391,415
1911	15	49,480,008	543,331

Table II, continued

Year	No. Columbia River Canneries	Total Pounds Caught	Total Cases Packed
1912	15	27,530,198	285,266
1913	15	26,556,172	266,479
1914	17	38,501,303	454,621
1915	19	43,838,680	558,534
1916	20	42,746,340	547,805
1917	20	40,447,986	555,218
1918	20	44,125,423	591,381
1919	21	44,934,497	580,028
1920	22	36,311,560	481,545
1921	20	26,712,547	323,241
1922	23	30,152,657	392,174
1923	23	35,667,250	480,925
1924	22	38,167,054	500,872
1925	21	42,333,443	540,452
1926	21	35,566,659	479,723
1927	22	37,688,415	519,809
1928	24	33,127,066	446,646
1929	21	32,321,281	422,117
1930	21	31,923,399	429,505
1931	20	27,031,840	353,699
1932	15	23,330,217	296,191
1933	14	26,846,800	336,711
1934	13	27,901,937	362,721

Source: Courtland L. Smith, Salmon Fishers of the Columbia (Corvallis: Oregon State University Press, 1979): Appendix B, "Price and Quantity Data for Columbia River Salmon Fishery, 1866-1973."

APPENDIX III

STATE REGULATION OF OFF-RESERVATION HUNTING AND GATHERING RIGHTS

In its 1905 decision in *United States v. Winans*, the Supreme Court held that Washington could not bar Yakama fishers from using "usual and accustomed" off-reservation places. It was well within the tribe's power to reserve those locations, "Nor does it restrain the State unreasonably, if at all, in the regulation of the right," the Court stated.[1] The question of what constituted reasonable state regulation of Indian off-reservation subsistence entitlements, in fishing and elsewhere, proved a volatile question over which state courts differed widely. Why? Because the underlying question about the relative powers of states, tribes, and the federal government had not been resolved.

Between *Winans* and the 1940s, when federal courts became more active in determining the relative rights of Indian and state fishers, state courts justified their regulation of Indian off-reservation subsistence activities on any of the following eight grounds:

> (1) The regulating state was admitted on an equal footing with other states, and authority over game passes to the state upon statehood.[2]
>
> (2) Indians are on an equal footing with non-Indians once the state is admitted, and they lose any special, i.e. treaty-based, privileges.[3]
>
> (3) The state has conservation interest that overrides treaty promises.[4]
>
> (4) The state's conservation interest extends to regulating specific classes of people and to specific implements used to fish and

---

[1] 198 U.S. 371, 384 (1905).

[2] *Ward v. Racehorse*, 163 U.S. 504 (1896); *State v. Towessnute*, 89 Wash. 478, 154 P. 805 (1916); *State v. Meninock*, 115 Wash. 478, 197 P. 661 (1921); *State v. Wallahee*, 143 Wash. 117, 255 P. 94 (1927). While the Supreme Court rejected the equal footing doctrine in *Winans*, some state courts, including Washington's, seemingly were unaffected by that holding.

[3] *United States v. The James G. Swan*, 50 F. 108 (N.D. Wash., 1892); *State v. Meninock*, supra.

[4] *Ward v. Racehorse*, supra; *Geer v. Connecticut* 161 U.S. 519 (1896); *Winans*, supra; *Ex parte Crosby*, 38 Nev. 389, 149 P. 989 (1915); *New York ex rel. Kennedy v. Becker*, 241 U.S. 556 (1916); *Meninock*, supra.

hunt.[5]

(5) The state's conservation interest extends to regulation of proceeds of hunting and gathering in interstate commerce.[6]

(6) Once land passes out of Indian country status, states can regulate Indian activities thereon.[7]

(7) State regulations apply to those over whom the state has jurisdiction, irrespective of whether they are in Indian Country or not.[8]

(8) Location at issue is not a "usual and accustomed" place.[9]

Virtually every ground, except the eighth, results from striking the balance between state, tribal, and federal powers in favor of the states.

During the same period, there were a number of cases in which state and federal regulations of Indian subsistence activities failed. The cases rested upon the following grounds:

(1) Federal officials cannot compromise treaty stipulations by imposing regulations on Indian hunters and fishers after a treaty has been negotiated.[10]

(2) Congress cannot abrogate treaties by implied language and thereby terminate subsistence privileges.

(3) The federal government has exclusive jurisdiction over Indian wards living on reservation and over Indian Country and this precludes state regulation.[11]

(4) Off-reservation treaty fishing is protected by treaties which supersede state law.[12]

(5) The federal government has authority over interstate commerce, and therefore can protect the proceeds of Indian hunting

---

[5] *Patstone v. Pennsylvania*, 232 U.S. 138 (1914); *Becrav v. Sawtelle*, 88 P.2d 999 (Ariz. 1939).

[6] *LaCoste v. Dept. of Conservation*, 263 U.S. 545 (1924).

[7] *Eugene Sol Louie v. United States*, 274 F. 47 (9th Cir. 1921) [murder]; *State v. Monroe*, 83 Mont. 556, 274 P. 840 (1929) [manslaughter]; *State v. Johnson*, 212 Wis. 301, 249 N.W. 285 (1933) [manslaughter and hunting, on on-reservation, fee patented land].

[8] *Selkirk v. Stevens*, 72 Minn. 335, 75 N.W. 386 (1898); *Ex parte Crosby*, supra.

[9] *United States v. McGowan*, 2 F. Supp. 426 (1931), on appeal, 62 F.2d 955 (9th Cir. 1933); *United States v. Bakers Bay Fish Co.*, 2 F. Supp. 426 (S.D. Wash., 1931).

[10] *United States v. Carpenter*, 111 U.S. 347 (1884); *Mason v. Sams*, 5 F.2d 255 (S.D. Wash., 1925).

[11] *Jones v. Meehan*, 175 U.S. 1 (1899); *Cook v. United States*, 288 U.S. 102 (1933).

[12] *Winans*, supra; *Seufert Bros. Co. v. United States ex rel. Confederated Tribes of Yakima Indian Nation*, 249 U.S. 194 (1919); *McCauley, et al. v. Makah Tribe*, 128 F.2d 867 (9th Cir. 1942).

and fishing from state regulation while the goods are in transit.[13]

(6) Indians own fish and other resources on the reservation and are therefore not subject to state or federal jurisdiction.[14]

(7) Indians can hunt and fish to procure food on reservation, but if they do so for any other purpose, they are subject to state regulation.[15]

These cases fall out differently from the cases upholding regulation in that with the exception of number six, they strike the balance among states, tribes, and the federal government in favor of federal power, and not on the basis of any inherent tribal sovereignty over the subsistence activities.

In its 1942 decision in *Tulee v. State of Washington*, the U.S. Supreme Court indicated for the first time that state regulation of Indian off-reservation fishing had limits. The Court found that Washington could not require Yakama fishers to purchase state licenses to fish. While the state might regulate "the time and manner of fishing ... necessary for the conservation of fish," as it did for its other residents, the Court reasoned, it could not condition the Indians' exercise of their treaty rights upon the payment of a fee.[16] In no way, however, did the Yakamas' treaty preclude the state from regulating their entitlements. Thus, as in the pre-1942 decisions, tribes were not included in the federal-state relation as sovereign entities.

The Supreme Court addressed the issue again in a 1968 case involving Puyallup fishers who claimed that their operations should be exempt from Washington's regulations where state gear restrictions effectively would have eliminated the set net-based Indian fishery at Commencement Bay and the Puyallup River. The Court adopted a two-part test that allowed state regulation of Indian fishers where (1) "there is a need to limit the taking of fish" and (2) the state can show that the regulation at issue is "indispensable" to achieve limited takings.[17] Here again, state power over Indians was a given; the test focused on the nature of state regulations, and not tribal sovereignty. No one asked, for example, how Indian regulations of the fishery might figure in the state's regulatory process.

Not surprisingly, litigation over regulation of the Indian fishery did not diminish after *Puyallup I*, rather the state and federal courts went on to produce a bewildering array of case law as Indians in the Pacific Northwest and

---

[13] *Pioneer Packing Co. v. Winslow*, 159 Wash. 655, 294 P. 557 (1930).

[14] *Mason v. Sams, supra*; *State v. Edwards et al.*, 188 Wash. 467, 62 P.2d 1094 (1936); *United States v. Cutler*, 37 F. Supp. 724 (D. Idaho, 1941). Each of these cases rested on other grounds as well.

[15] *State v. Cooney*, 77 Minn. 518, 80 N.W. 696 (1899).

[16] *Tulee*, 315 U.S. 681, 684 (1942).

[17] Court citing *Maison v. Confederated Tribes*, 314 F.2d 169 (9th Cir. 1963), in *Puyallup Tribe v. Department of Game of Washington et al.*, 391 U.S. 392, 401 n.14 (1968) [this case became known as *Puyallup I*].

elsewhere took to the courts to settle claims—often on an incident-by-incident basis, with courts retaining continuing jurisdiction.[18]

Tribes have made places for themselves in the regulation of resources at the local level by creating their own regulatory agencies, licensing their members, and gaining scientific expertise. Yet in that respect they can do little more than adopt the language and customs of the dominant society and argue for a share in the decision-making process much as other interested groups do.[19] Real power remains illusory and cannot stem from anything less than a reconsideration of the place of tribes in the federal-state relationship.

---

[18] For an overview of this history, see American Friends Service Committee, *Uncommon Controversy: Fishing Rights of the Muckleshoot, Puyallup, and Nisqually Indians* (Seattle: University of Washington Press, 1970); and Fay G. Cohen, *Treaties on Trial: The Continuing Controversy over Northwest Indian Fishing Rights* (Seattle: University of Washington Press, 1986).

[19] According to the Northwest Electric Power Planning and Conservation Act of 1981, for example, the tribes' interests in conservation of fish and wildlife resources can be considered by the Pacific Northwest Power Planning Council (created by the Act) along with other interested federal and state agencies, and interest groups. The Council itself is composed entirely of state appointees: two from each Idaho, Washington, Oregon, and Montana. 16 U.S.C. § 839(b)(f)(3); § 839(b)(a)(2)(A)-(B).

SELECTED BIBLIOGRAPHY

MANUSCRIPT SOURCES

Bancroft Library, Univerisity of California, Berkeley:
 Rev. George Waters, Letters
 U.S. Office of Indian Affairs, Washington Superintendency, Scrapbook on Indians of the Pacific Northwest, 1846-1878

National Archives and Record Service, Washington, D.C.:
 Records of the Bureau of Indian Affairs, Record Group 75
 Records of the U.S. Court of Claims, Record Group 123
 Records of the Department of Justice, Record Group 60
 Records of the Supreme Court, Record Group 267

National Archives and Record Service, Seattle Branch:
 Records of the Bureau of Indian Affairs, Record Group 75

Yakima Valley Regional Library, Yakima, WA:
 Charles (Click) Relander Papers

University of Washington Libraries, Manuscript Collection, Seattle, WA:
 Miles C. Poindexter Papers, Accession no. 3828
 Henry J. Snively Papers, Accession no. 3095

Yakima Valley Museum, Yakima, WA:
 Files on Yakima Indian history

SECONDARY SOURCES

Ahern, Wilbert. "'The Returned Indians': Hampton Institute and its Indian Alumni." *Journal of Ethnic Studies* 10 (1983): 101-24.

American Friends Service Committee. *Uncommon Controversy: Fishing Rights of the Muckleshoot, Puyallup, and Nisaually Indians.* Seattle: University of Washington Press, 1970.

Anastasio, Angelo. "The Southern Plateau: An Ecological Analysis of Intergroup Relations." *Northwest Anthropological Research Notes* 6 (1972): 102-229.

Arval, Morris A. "Washington Water Rights—A Sketch." *Washington Law Review*

31 (1956): 243-60.

Baker, J. H. *An Introduction to English Legal History.* 2d ed. London: Butterworths, 1979.

Barnett, H. G. *The Yakima Indians in 1942.* Mimeograph. Eugene, OR: University of Oregon, 1942.

Barsh, Russel L. *The Washington Fishing Rights Controversy: An Economic Critique.* Rev. ed., Seattle: Graduate School of Business Administration, University of Washington, 1977.

——, and Henderson, James Youngblood. *The Road, Indian Tribes and Political Liberty.* Berkeley: University of California Press, 1980.

Bauer, Carl J. "Labor Without Brains: Water Development, Law, and Policy in Washington State, 1890-1935." M.S. thesis, University of Wisconsin-Madison, 1988.

Bell, Derrick A. *And We Are Not Saved: The Elusive Quest for Racial Justice.* New York: Basic Books, 1987.

Benedict, Ruth F. "The Concept of the Guardian Spirit in North America." American Anthropological Association *Memoirs* no. 29 (1923).

Bieder, Robert E. *Science Encounters the Indian, 1820-1880: The Early Years of American Ethnology.* Norman: University of Oklahoma Press, 1986.

Blanchet, Francis N. *Historical Sketches of the Catholic Church in Oregon During the Past Forty Years.* Portland, OR: Catholic Centennial Press, 1878.

Blumm, Michael, et al. "The Fish and Wildlife Coordination Act and Columbia Basin Water Project Operations." *Anadromous Fish Law Memo* 6 (1980): 1-9.

Bowden, Charles. *Killing the Hidden Waters: The Slow Destruction of Water Resources in the American Southwest.* Austin: University of Texas Press, 1977.

Bower, John Arthur. "The Hydrogeography of Yakima Indian Nation Resource Use." Ph.D. diss., University of Washington, Seattle, 1990.

Boxberger, Daniel L. *Handbook of Western Washington Indian Treaties: With Special Attention to Treaty Fishing Rights.* Contributions to Aquaculture and Fisheries, Occasional Paper 1. Lummi Island, WA: Lummi College of Fisheries, 1979.

—— "In and Out of the Labor Force: The Lummi Indians and the Development of the Commercial Salmon Fishery of North Puget Sound, 1880-1900." *Ethnohistory* 35 (1988) 161-90.

—— "The Lummi Island Reef Nets." *Indian Historian* 24 (1980): 48-54.

—— *To Fish in Common: The Ethnohistory of Lummi Indian Salmon Fishing.* Lincoln: University of Nebraska Press, 1989.

Boyce, W. T. and Boyce, J. C. "Acculturation and Changes in Health Among Navajo

Boarding School Students." *Social Science and Medicine* 17 (1983): 219-26.

Coulter, C. Brewster. "The Victory of National Irrigation in the Yakima Valley, 1902-1906." *Pacific Northwest Quarterly* 42 (1951): 99-122.

Brown, Bruce. *Mountain in the Clouds: A Search for the Wild Salmon.* New York: Simon and Schuster, 1982.

Browning, Robert J. *Fisheries of the North Pacific: History, Species, Gear and Processes.* Anchorage, AK: Northwest Publishing Co., 1974.

Brumberg, Joan Jacobs. "Zenanas and Girlless Villages: The Ethnology of American Evangelical Women, 1870-1900." *Journal of American History* 69 (1982): 347-71.

Buechner, Helmut K. "Some Biotic Changes in the State of Washington, Particularly During the Century 1855-1953." *Washington State College Research Studies* 21 (1953): 154-92.

Burns, Robert I. *The Jesuits and the Indian Wars of the Far Northwest.* Yale Western Americana Series. New Haven: Yale University Press, 1966.

Callicott, J. Baird. "Genesis Revisited: Murian Musings on the Lynn White, Jr. Debate." *Environmental History* 14 (1990): 65-90.

Campbell, Kate. "Ditch Tender Keeps the Water Flowing." *PG&E Progress* (Jan. 1990): 4-5.

Canny, Nicholas P. "The Ideology of English Colonization: From Ireland to America." In Stanley N. Katz and John M. Murrin, eds., *Colonial America: Essays in Politics and Social Development,* 3d ed. New York: Alfred A. Knopf, Inc. (1983): 47-68.

Chambers, Reid Peyton, and Price, Monroe E. "Regulating Sovereignty: Secretarial Discretion and the Leasing of Indian Lands." *Stanford Law Review* 26 (1974): 1061-96.

Childerhose, R. J. and Trim, Marj. *Pacific Salmon and Steelhead Trout.* Vancouver: Douglas & McIntyre, 1979.

Clark, Ella E. *Indian Legends of the Pacific Northwest.* Berkeley: University of California Press, 1953.

Coan, C. F. "The Adoption of the Reservation Policy in the Pacific Northwest, 1853-55." *Oregon Historical Quarterly* 23 (1922) 13-38.

Cohen, Fay G. *Treaties on Trial, The Continuing Controversy over Northwest Indian Fishing Rights.* Report prepared for the American Friends Service Committee. Seattle: University of Washington Press, 1986.

Cohen, Felix S. *Handbook of Federal Indian Law.* 1982 ed. Charlottesville: The Michie Company, 1982.

Coffer, William E. (Koi-Hosh). *Spirits of the Sacred Mountains: Creation Stories of the American Indian.* New York: Van Nostrand Reinhold Co., 1978.

Coleman, Michael C. *Presbyterian Missionary Attitudes toward American Indians, 1837-1893.* Jackson: University Press of Mississippi, 1985.

Conway, Jill. "Women Reformers and American Culture, 1870-1930." *Journal of Social History* 5 (Winter 1971-1972): 164-77.

Cook, S. F. "The Epidemic of 1830-33 in California and Oregon." University of California, *Publications in American Archaeology and Ethnography* 43 (1955): 303-25.

Commissioner of Fisheries Report. In *Bonneville Dam and Protection of the Columbia River Fisheries.* Sen. Doc. no. 87, 75th Cong., 1st Sess., July 22, 1937.

Corwin, Edward S. "The Basic Doctrine of American Constitutional Law." *Michigan Law Review* 12 (1914): 247-76.

Coulter, Calvin B. "The Victory of National Irrigation in the Yakima Valley, 1902-1906." *Pacific Northwest Quarterly* 42 (1951): 99-122.

Cronon, William. *Changes in the Land: Indians, Colonists, and the Ecology of New England.* New York: Hill and Wang, 1983.

Crosby, Alfred W. *Ecological Imperialism: The Biological Expansion of Europe, 900-1900.* Cambridge, Eng.: Cambridge University Press, 1986.

——— "Virgin Soil Epidemics as a Factor in the Aboriginal Depopulation in America." *William and Mary Quarterly*, 3d ser., 33 (1976): 289-99.

Crow Dog, Mary, and Erdoes, Richard. *Lakota Woman.* New York: Grove and Weidenfeld, 1990.

Crutchfield, James A. "Management of the North Pacific Fisheries: Economic Objectives and Issues." *Washington Law Review* 43 (1967): 283-307.

Dancey, William B. "Riverine Period Settlement and Land Use Pattern in the Priest Rapids Area, Central Washington." *Northwest Anthropological Research Notes* 10 (1976): 147-60.

Deioria, Vine Jr., and Lytle, Clifford M. *American Indians, American Justice.* Austin: University of Texas Press, 1983.

———, and ———. *The Nations Within: The Past and Future of American Indian Sovereignty.* New York: Pantheon Books, 1984.

Desmond, Gerald R. *Gambling Among the Yakima.* Washington: The Catholic University Press, 1952.

Dills, Gary. "Effects of Prescribed Burning on Deer Browse." *Journal of Wildlife Management* 34 (July 1970): 540-44.

Dobyns, Henry F. "Brief Perspective on a Scholarly Transformation: Widowing the 'Virgin' Land." *Ethnohistory* 23 (1976): 95-104.

——— "Estimating Aboriginal American Population, An Appraisal of Techniques with a New Hemispheric Estimate." *Current Anthropology* 7 (1966): 395-416.

—— *Their Number Become Thinned: Native American Population Dynamics in Eastern North America*. Knoxville: University of Tennessee Press in cooperation with the Newberry Library Center for the History of the American Indian, 1983.

Donaldson, Ivan J., and Cramer, Frederick K. *Fish Wheels of the Columbia*. Portland, OR: Binfords & Mort, 1971.

Drury, Clifford M. *Elkanah and Mary Walker: Pioneers Among the Spokanes*. Caldwell ID: The Caxton Printers, Ltd. 1940.

—— *Henry Harmon Spalding*. Caldwell, ID: Caxton Printers, Ltd., 1936.

Du Bois, Cora Alice. *The Feather Cult of the Middle Columbia*. General Series in Anthropology, ed. Leslie Spier, no. 7. Menasha, WI: George Banta Publishing Co., 1938.

Dunbar, Robert. *Forging New Rights in Western Waters*. Lincoln: University of Nebraska Press, 1983.

Dwight, Timothy. *Theology, Explained and Defended, in a Series of Sermons....* 5 vols. Middletown, CT: Clark & Lyman for T. Dwight, 1818-19.

Emmerich, Lisa Elizabeth. "'To Respect and Love and Seek the Ways of White Women': Field Matrons, the Office of Indian Affairs, and Civilization Policy, 1890-1938." Ph.D. diss., University of Maryland, College Park, 1987.

Fahey, John. *The Inland Empire: Unfolding Years, 1879-1929*. Seattle: University of Washington Press, 1986.

Fobes, Natalie. "The Saga of Salmon, an Epic Struggle to Survive Man." *Seattle Times*, special report, Nov. 22, 1987.

Foner, Eric. *Reconstruction: America's Unfinished Revolution, 1863-1877*. New York: Harper & Row, Publishers, 1988.

Friedman, Lawrence M. *A History of American Law*, 2d ed. New York: Simon & Schuster, 1985.

Fulton, L. A. *Spawning Areas and Abundance of Chinook Salmon (Oncorhynchus tshawytsha) in the Columbia River Basin—Past and Present*. Washington, D.C.: U.S. Department of the Interior, 1968.

—— *Spawning Areas and Abundance of Steelhead Trout and Coho, Sockeye and Chum Salmon in the Columbia River Basin—Past and Present*. Washington, D.C.: U.S. Department of the Interior, 1970.

Gabel, Peter, and Harris, Paul. "Building Power and Breaking Images: Critical Legal Theory and the Practice of Law." *New York University Review of Law & Social Change* 11 (1983): 369-411.

Garrand, Victor. *Augustine Laure, S.J.: Missionary to the Yakimas*. Trans. by Michael M. O'Malley. Fairfield, WA: Ye Galleon Press, 1977.

Gates, Paul W. *History of Public Land Law Development*. The Management of Public Lands in the United States Collection. Washington, D.C.: GPO, 1968; reprint ed. New York: Arno Press, 1979.

—— "The Homestead Act in an Incongruous Land System," *American Historical Review* 41 (1936): 652-81.

—— "Indian Allotments Preceding the Dawes Act." In J. Clark, ed., *The Frontier Challenge*. Lawrence: University Press of Kansas, 1971, 141-70.

Gay, E. Jane. *With the Nez Perces: Alice Fletcher in the Field, 1889-92*. Frederick E. Hoxie and Joan T. Mark, eds. Lincoln: University of Nebraska Press, 1981.

Geertz, Clifford. *The Interpretation of Cultures: Selected Essays*. New York: Basic Books, Inc., 1973.

Gibbs, George. "Report on the Indian Tribes of the Territory of Washington." In *Reports of Explorations and Surveys to Ascertain the Most Practicable and Economical Route for a Railroad from the Mississippi River to the Pacific Ocean*. 33d Cong., 1st Sess., 1855. H.R. Ex. Doc. 129, 419-66.

Gibson, Arrell Morgan. "Philosophical, Legal, and Social Rationales for Appropriating the Tribal Estate, 1607-1980." *American Indian Law Review* 12 (1984): 3-37.

Gile, Albion. "Notes on Columbia River Salmon." *Oregon Historical Quarterly* 56 (1955): 140-53.

Gordon, George W. *Report upon the Subject of the Fishing Privileges etc. Guaranteed by Treaties to Indians in the Northwest with Recommendations in Regard Thereto*, Jan. 19, 1889. U.S. Department of Interior, Branch of Fisheries, typed transcript, 1986.

Gordon, Robert W. "J. Willard Hurst and the Common Law Tradition." *Law and Society Review* 10 (1975): 9-55.

Gossett, Gretta. "Stock Grazing in Washington's Nile Valley, Receding Ranges in the Cascades." *Pacific Northwest Quarterly* 55 (1964) 119-27.

Gunther, Erna. "An Analysis of the First Salmon Ceremony." *American Anthropologist* 28 (1926): 605-17.

—— "A Further Analysis of the First Salmon Ceremony" *University of Washington Publications in Anthropology* 2 (no. 5) (1928): 129-173.

Haines, Charles Grove. "Vested Rights." *Texas Law Review* 2 (1924): 257-90, 387-421; and *Texas Law Review* 3 (1925): 1-43.

Haines, Francis. "The Northward Spread of Horses Among the Plains Indians." *American Anthropologist* 40, n.s., (1938): 429-37.

Harmon, Ray. "Indian Shaker Church The Dalles." *Oregon Historical Quarterly* 72 (1971): 148-58.

Hewes, Gordon W. "Indian Fisheries Productivity in Pre-Contact Times in the

Pacific Salmon Area." *Northwest Anthropological Research Notes*, 7 (1973): 133-55.

Higgins, E. L. "Smohalla, the Prophet of Priest Rapids." *Overland Monthly*, ser. 2, 17 (1891): 208-15.

High Country News. *Western Water Made Simple*. Washington, D.C.: Island Press, 1987.

Hobhouse, L. *Liberalism*. London: Oxford University Press, 1964.

Hopkins, Daniel R. *Princes and Peasants: Smallpox in History*. Chicago: University of Chicago Press, 1983.

Horowitz, Charles. "Riparian and Appropriation Rights to the Use of Water in Washington." *Washington Law Review* 7 (1932): 197-215.

Horwitz, Morton J. *The Transformation of American Law, 1780-1860*. Studies in Legal History. Cambridge, MA: Harvard University Press, 1977.

Hoxie, Frederick E. *A Final Promise: The Campaign to Assimilate the Indians, 1880-1920*. Lincoln: University of Nebraska Press, 1984.

—— "Towards a New North American Indian Legal History." *American Journal of Legal History* 30 (1986): 351-57.

Hulbert, Archer Butler, and Hulbert, Dorothy Printup, eds. *Marcus Whitman, Crusader: 1802-1839*, 3 vols. Colorado Springs and Denver, CO: The Stewart Commission of Colorado College and the Denver Public Library, 1936.

Hundley, Norris, Jr. "The Dark and Bloody Ground of Indian Water Rights: Confusion Elevated to Principle." *Western Historical Quarterly* 9 (1978): 454-82.

—— "The 'Winters' Decision and Indian Water Rights: A Mystery Reexamined." *Western Historical Quarterly* 13 (1982): 17-42.

Hunn Eugene. "On the Relative Contribution of Men and Women to Subsistence Among Hunter-Gatherers of the Columbia Plateau: A Comparison with Ethnographic Atlas Summaries." *Journal of Ethnobiology* 1 (1981): 124-34.

—— "Sahaptin Fish Classification." *Northwest Anthropological Research Notes* 14 (Spring 1981): 1-19.

——, and French, David H. "Lomatium: A Key Resource for Columbia Plateau Native Subsistence." *Northwest Science* 55 (1981): 87-94.

——, and J. Selam & Family. *Nch'i Wana: The Big River: Mid-Columbia River Indian People and Their Land*. Seattle: University of Washington Press, 1988.

Hurst, James Willard. *Law and the Conditions of Freedom in the Nineteenth-Century United States*. Madison: University of Wisconsin Press, 1956.

—— *Law and Markets in United States History: Different Modes of Bargaining Among Interests*. The Curti Lectures, the University of Wisconsin-Madison, April 1981. Madison: University of Wisconsin Press, 1982,

Hurt, R. Douglas. *Indian Agriculture in America, Prehistory to the Present.* Lawrence: University Press of Kansas, 1987.

Jackson, Curtis E., and Marcia J. Galli. *A History of the Bureau of Indian Affairs and Its Activities Among Indians.* San Francisco, R&E Research Associates, 1977.

Jacobs, Melville. "A Sketch of Northern Sahaptin Grammar." *University of Washington Publications in Anthropology* 4 (1931): 85-292.

—— "Historic Perspectives in Indian Languages of Oregon and Washington." *Pacific Northwest Quarterly* 28 (1937): 55-74.

Jacobs, Wilbur R. "The Tip of an Iceberg: Pre-Columbian Indian Demography and Some Implications for Revisionism." *William and Mary Quarterly*, 3d ser., 21 (1974): 123-32.

Jacobson, C. K. "Internal Colonization and Native Americans: Indian Labor in the United States from 1871 to World War II." *Social Science Quarterly* 65 (1984): 158-71.

Jensen, Joan M. *With These Hands.* Old Westbury, NY: The Feminist Press, 1981.

Johnson, Ralph. "The States Versus Indian Off-Reservation Fishing: A United States Supreme Court Error." *Washington Law Review* 47 (1972): 207-36.

Josephy, Alvin M., Jr. *The Nez Perce Indians and the Opening of the Northwest.* New Haven: Yale University Press, 1965; abridged edition: Lincoln: University of Nebraska Press, 1971.

Kairys, David. "Legal Reasoning." In David Kairys, ed. *The Politics of Law: A Progressive Critique.* New York: Pantheon Books (1982): 11-17.

Karamanski, Theodore J. *Fur Trade and Exploration, Opening the Far Northwest, 1821-1852.* Norman: University of Oklahoma Press, 1983.

Knack, Martha C., and Stewart, Omer C. *As Long as the River Shall Run: An Ethnohistory of Pyramid Lake Indian Reservation.* Berkeley: University of California Press, 1984.

Koppes, Clayton. "Public Water, Private Land: Origins of the Acreage Limitation Controversy, 1933-1953." *Pacific Historical Review* 47 (1978): 607-36.

Lauer, T. E. "The Common Law Background of the Riparian Doctrine." *Missouri Law Review* 28 (1963): 99-106.

—— "Reflections on Riparianism." *Missouri Law Review* 35 (1970): 1-25.

Llewellyn, Karl N., and Hoebel, E. Adamson. *The Cheyenne Way: Conflict and Case Law in Primitive Jurisprudence.* Norman: University of Oklahoma Press, 1941.

Limerick, Patricia Nelson. *Legacy of Conquest: Unbroken Past of the American West.* New York: W. W. Norton & Co. 1987.

Locke, John. *The Second Treatise of Government*. First published in 1690. Thomas P. Peardon, ed. New York: Macmillan Publishing Company, 1952.

Lohse, E. S., and Sammons-Lohse, D. "Sedentism on the Columbia Plateau: A Matter of Degree Related to the Easy and Efficient Procurement of Resources." *Northwest Anthropological Research Notes* 20 (1986): 115-36.

Lund, Thomas. *American Wildlife Law*. Berkeley: University of California Press, 1980.

MacKinnon, Catherine A. *Feminism Unmodified: Discourses on Life and Law*. Cambridge, MA: Harvard University Press, 1987.

Macpherson, C. B. *The Political Theory of Possessive Individualism: Hobbes to Locke*. New York: Oxford University Press, 1962.

McCool, Daniel. *Command of the Waters: Iron Triangles, Federal Water Development, and Indian Water*. Berkeley: University of California Press, 1987.

McCurdy, Charles W. "Stephen J. Field and Public Land Law Development in California, 1850-1866: Case Study of Judicial Resource Allocation in Nineteenth Century America." *Law and Society Review* 10 (1976): 235-66.

McEvoy, Arthur F. *The Fisherman's Problem: Ecology and Law in the California Fisheries, 1850-1980*. Cambridge: Cambridge University Press, 1986.

—— "Toward an Interactive Theory of Nature and Culture: Ecology, Production, and Cognition in the California Fishing Industry." *Environmental Review* 11 (1987): 289-305.

McLoughlin, William. *The American Evangelicals, 1800-1900: An Anthology*. Gloucester, MA: Peter Smith, 1976.

—— *Revivals, Awakenings, and Reform: An Essay on Religion and Social Change in America, 1607-1977*. Chicago: University of Chicago Press, 1978.

McNeill, William. *Plagues and Peoples: A Natural History of Human Infections*. Garden City, NY: Anchor/Doubleday, 1976.

McWhorter, Lucillus Virgil. *The Crime Against the Yakima*. North Yakima, WA: Republic Print, 1913.

—— (He-mene Ka-wan). *The Discards*. N.p. 1920.

—— *Yellow Wolf: His Own Story*. Caldwell: ID, Caxton Press, 1940.

Marshall, Alan G. "Nez Perce Social Groups: An Ecological Interpretation." Ph.D. diss., Washington State University, 1977.

Martin, Calvin. *Keepers of the Game: Indian-Animal Relationships and the Fur Trade*. Berkeley: University of California Press, 1978.

Mathes, Valerie Sherer. "A New Look at the Role of Women in Indian Society." *American Indian Quarterly* 2 (1975): 131-39.

Meinig, Donald W. *The Great Columbia Plain: A Historical Geography, 1805-1910*. Seattle: University of Washington Press, 1968.

Merchant, Carolyn. *Ecological Revolutions: Nature, Gender, and Science in New England*. Chapel Hill, University of North Carolina Press, 1989.

—— *The Death of Nature: Women, Ecology and the Scientific Revolution*. San Francisco: Harper & Row Publishers, 1980.

Miller, Christopher. *Prophetic Worlds: Indians and Whites on the Columbia Plateau*. New Brunswick, N.J.: Rutgers University Press, 1985.

Morgan, Edmund S. *American Slavery. American Freedom, the Ordeal of Colonial Virginia*. New York: W. W. Norton & Co., 1975.

Murphy, Mike. "Indian Water Accord." *Yakima Herald-Republic*, Feb. 21, 1979, p. 3.

Nash, Gary B. "The Image of the Indian in the Southern Colonial Mind." *William & Mary Quarterly* 3d ser., 29 (1972): 197-230.

Nash, Roderick. *Wilderness and the American Mind*, 3d ed. New Haven: Yale University Press, 1982.

Netboy, Anthony. *The Columbia River Salmon and Steelhead Trout: Their Fight for Survival*. Seattle: University of Washington Press, 1980.

—— *Salmon, the World's Most Harassed Fish*. Tulsa: Winchester Press, 1980.

Norwood, Gus. *Columbia River Power for the People: A History of the Policies of the Bonneville Power Administration*. Portland, OR, U.S. Department of Energy, Bonneville Power Administration, 1981.

Novak, Barbara. *Nature and Culture: American Landscape and Painting, 1825-1875*. New York: Oxford University Press, 1980.

O'Bannon, Patrick W. "Technological Innovation in the Pacific Coast Canned Salmon Industry, 1864-1924." Ph.D. diss., University of California, San Diego, 1983.

Oliphant, J. Olin. "Encroachments of Cattlemen on Indian Reservations in the Pacific Northwest, 1870-1890." *Agricultural History* 24 (1950). Reprinted in Paul Gates, ed., *The Rape of Indian Lands* The Management of Public Lands in the United States Collection. New York: Arno Press (1979): 43-58.

Pacific Salmon Commission. *Pacific Salmon Commission, Handbook*. Vancouver, B.C., Pacific Salmon Commission, 1988.

Pagels, Elaine. *The Gnostic Gospels*. New York.: Random House, Inc. 1979, paperback ed. New York: Vintage Books, 1981.

Pambrun, Andrew Dominique. *Sixty Years on the Frontier in the Pacific Northwest*. Fairfield, WA: Ye Galleon Press, 1978.

Pisani, Donald J. *From the Family Farm to Agribusiness: The Irrigation Crusade in California and the West, 1850-1931*. Berkeley: University of California Press, 1984.

—— "Irrigation, Water Rights, and the Betrayal of Indian Allotment." *Environmental Review* 10 (1986): 157-76.

—— "Reclamation and Social Engineering in the Progressive Era." *Agricultural History* 57 (1983):46-63.

—— "State v. Nation, Federal Reclamation and Water Rights in the Progressive Era." *Pacific Historical Review* 51 (1982): 265-82.

Proudhon, Pierre-Joseph. *What is Property? An Inquiry Into the Principle of Right and of Government*. Translated by Benjamin R. Tucker. New York: Dover Publications, Inc. 1970.

Prucha, Francis P. *American Indian Policy in Crisis: Christian Reformers and the Indians, 1865-1900*. Lincoln: University of Nebraska Press, 1976.

—— *The Great Father: The U.S. Government and the American Indians*. 2 vols. Lincoln: University of Nebraska Press, 1984.

Pyne, Stephen J. *Fire in America: A Cultural History of Wildland and Rural Fire*. Princeton, N.J.: Princeton University Press, 1982.

Queirolo, Lewis E. and McNamee, William A. "The Columbia-Snake: Challenges for Multiple-Use River Management." *Pacific Northwest Bulletin* 212 (1981).

Ramsey, Jarold, ed. *Coyote Was Going There: Indian Literature of the Oregon Country*. Seattle: University of Washington Press, 1977.

Ray, Verne. *Cultural Relations in the Plateau of Northwestern America*. Series Publications of the Frederick Webb Hodge Annual Publication Fund, 3. Los Angeles: The South Western Museum, 1939.

—— "Native Villages and Groupings of the Columbia Basin." *Pacific Northwest Quarterly* 27 (1936): 99-152.

—— "The Sanpoil and Nespelem: Salishan Peoples of Northeast Washington." *University of Washington Publications in Anthropology* no. 5 (1932).

—— et al. "Tribal Distribution in Eastern Oregon and Adjacent Regions." *American Anthropologist* 40, n.s. (1938): 384-415.

Reichwein, Jeffery C. "Native American Response to Euro-American Contact in the Columbia Plateau of Northwestern North America, 1840-1914: An Anthropological Interpretation Based on Written and Pictorial Ethnohistorical Data." Ph.D. diss., Ohio State University, 1988.

Reid, John Phillip. *A Better Kind of Hatchet: Law, Trade, and Diplomacy in the Cherokee Nation During the Early Years of European Contact*. University Park: Pennsylvania State University Press, 1976.

—— *A Law of Blood: The Primitive Law of the Cherokee Nation*. New York: New York University Press, 1970.

Relander, Charles (Now Tow Look). *Drummers and Dreamers: The Story of Smohalla the Prophet and his Nephew Puck Hyah Toot...*, with a foreword by

Frederick Webb Hodge. Caldwell, ID: The Caxton Printers, 1956.

——, ed. *Treaty Centennial, 1855-1955: The Yakimas.* 1st ed. Washington State Historical Society and Oregon State Historical Society, published by authorization of the Yakima Tribal Council. Yakima, WA, Republic Press, 1955.

Rich, Edwin Ernest. *History of the Hudson's Bay Co., 1670-1870.* With a foreword by Winston Churchill. 2 vols. Publications of the Hudson's Bay Record Society nos. 21-22. London: Hudson's Bay Record Society, 1958-59.

Rose, Carol M. "'Enough and as Good' of What?" *Northwestern University Law Review* (1984): 417-42.

—— "Possession as the Origin of Property," *University of Chicago Law Review* 52 (1985): 73-88.

Ross, Alexander. *Adventures of the First Settlers on the Oregon or Columbia River.* Milo Milton Quaife, ed. Lakeside Classics. R. R. Donnely & Sons, Inc., 1923.

—— *The Fur Hunters of the Far West.* Milo Milton Quaife, ed. Lakeside Classics. R. R. Donnely & Sons, Inc., 1924.

Rowley, William D. *U.S. Forest Service: Grazing and Rangelands: A History*, 1st ed. College Station, TX: Texas A & M University Press, 1985.

Ruby, Robert H., and Brown, John A. *Indians of the Pacific Northwest.* The Civilization of the American Indian Series. Norman: University of Oklahoma Press, 1981.

St. Hoyme, Lucile E. "On the Origins of New World Paleopathology." *American Journal of Physical Anthropology* 31 (1969): 295-302.

Sakurai, Atsushi. *Salmon.* New York: Alfred A. Knopf, 1984.

Sanger, David. "Development of the Pacific Northwest Culture Area, Historical and Environmental Considerations." In *Contributions to Anthropology: Ecological Essays*, National Museum, Canada, Bulletin, 230. Ottawa: Queen's Printer (1969): 15-23.

Sax, Joseph L., and Abrams, Robert H. *Legal Control of Water Resources: Cases and Materials.* American Casebook Series. St. Paul, MN: West Publishing Co., 1986.

Schalk, R. F. "The Structure of an Anadromous Fish Resource." In Lewis R. Binford, ed., *For Theory Building in Archaeology: Essays on Faunal Remains, Aquatic Resources, Spatial Analysis and Systemic Modeling.* New York: Academic Press (1977): 207-49.

Scheiber, Harry N. "At the Borderland of Law and Economic History: The Contributions of Willard Hurst." *American Historical Review* 75 (1970): 744-56.

—— "Property Law, Expropriation, and Resource Allocation by Government, 1789-1910." *Journal of Economic History* 33 (Mar. 1973): 232-51.

——. "Race, Radicalism, and Reform: Historical Perspective on the 1879 California Constitution." *Hastings Constitutional Law Quarterly* 17 (1989): 35-80.

——. "The Road to Munn: Eminent Domain and the Concept of Public Purpose in the State Courts." *Perspectives in American History* 5 (1971): 287-328.

——, and McCurdy, Charles W. "Eminent Domain Law and Western Agriculture, 1849-1900." *Agricultural History* 49 (1975): 112-30.

Schuster, Helen Hersh. "Yakima Indian Traditionalism: A Study in Continuity and Change." Ph.D. diss., University of Washington, 1975.

Scott, Leslie M. "Indian Diseases as Aids to Pacific Northwest Settlement." *Oregon Historical Quarterly* 29 (1928): 144-61.

Selvin, Molly. "The Public Trust Doctrine in American Law and Economic Policy, 1789-1920." *Wisconsin Law Review* (1980): 1403-42.

Shaw, Anna Morre. *A Pima Past*. Tucson: University of Arizona Press, 1974.

Simmons, William S. "Cultural Bias in the New England Puritans' Perception of Indians." *William & Mary Quarterly* 3d Ser., 38 (1981): 56-72.

Sizer, Sandra. *Gospel Hymns and Social Religion: The Rhetoric of Nineteenth Century Revivalism*. Philadelphia: Temple University Press, 1978.

Smith, Courtland L. *Salmon Fishers of the Columbia*. Corvallis: Oregon State University Press, 1979.

Smith, George Otis. *Geology and Water Resources of a Portion of Yakima County, Wash*. Water Supply and Irrigation Papers of the U.S. Geological Survey, no. 55. Washington, D.C.: U.S. Geological Survey, 1901.

Smith, Henry Nash. *Virgin Land: The American West as Symbol and Myth*. Cambridge, MA: Harvard University Press, 1950; reissued, 1970.

Smith, Michael T. "The History of Indian Citizenship." In Roger L. Nichols, ed., The *American Indian: Past and Present*, 3d ed. New York:. Knopf (1986): 232-41.

Smits, David D. "The 'Squaw Drudge': A Prime Index of Savagism." *Ethnohistory* 29 (1982): 281-306.

Smythe, William Ellesworth. *The Conguest of Arid America*. Americana Library Paperbacks. Seattle: University of Washington Press, 1970.

Spier, Leslie. *The Prophet Dance of the Northwest and its Derivations: The Source of the Ghost Dance*. General Series in Anthropology, ed. Leslie Spier, no. 1. Menasha, WI: George Banta Publishing Co., 1935.

——, and Sapir, Edward. "Wishram Ethnography." *Washington University Publications in Anthropology* 3 (1930): 151-300.

Splawn, A. J. *Ka-Mi-Akin: Last Hero of the Yakimas*. Portland, OR: Kilham Sationery & Printing Co., 1917.

Steen, Harold K. *The U.S. Forest Service: A History*. Seattle: University of Washington Press, 1976.

Stevens, Isaac Ingalls. *A True Copy of the Record of the Official Proceedings at the Council in the Walla Walla Valley 1855*. Darrell Scott, ed. Fairfield, WA: Ye Galleon Press, 1985.

——— "Letters of Governor Isaac I. Stevens, 1853-1854." With an introduction by John S. Richards. *Pacific Northwest Quarterly* 30 (1939): 301-37.

Stewart, Hiliary. *Indian Fishing: Early Methods on the Northwest Coast*. Seattle: University of Washington Press, 1977.

Strickland, Rennard James. *Fire and the Spirits: Cherokee Law from Clan to Court*. Norman: University of Oklahoma Press, 1975.

——— "Genocide-at-law: An Historic and Contemporary View of the Native American Experience." *University of Kansas Law Review* 34 (1986): 713-55.

Swindell, Edward G. *Report on Source, Nature and Extent of Fishing, Hunting, and Miscellaneous Rights of Certain Indian Tribes in Washington and Oregon*. Los Angeles, CA: U.S. Department of the Interior, Office of Indian Affairs, Divison of Forestry and Grazing, 1942.

Trafzer, Clifford. *Indians, Superintendents, and Councils: Northwestern Indian Policy, 1850-1855*. New York: University Press of America, 1986.

Trennert, Robert A. "From Carlisle to Phoenix: The Rise and Fall of the Indian Outing System, 1878-1930." *Pacific Historical Review* 52 (1983): 267-92.

Turner, Frederick Jackson. "The Significance of the Frontier in American History." In *The Frontier in American History*. New York: Holt, Rinehart, and Winston, 1947; reprint edition with a foreword by Wilbur R. Jacobs, Tucson: University of Arizona Press, 1986.

Uebelacker, Morris L. "Geographic Explorations in the Southern Cascades of Eastern Washington: Changing Land, People, and Resources." Ph.D. diss., University of Oregon, 1986.

——— *Time Ball: A Story of the Yakima People and the Land*. Toppenish, WA: Yakima Indian Nation, 1984.

Underhill, Ruth M. *Rainhouse and Ocean. Speeches for the Papago Year*. American Tribal Religions Series, vol. 4. Flagstaff, AZ: Museum of Northern Arizona Press, 1979.

——— *Singing For Power, The Song Magic of the Papago Indians of Southern Arizona*. Berkeley: University of California Press, 1938; California Library Reprint Series, 1976.

Unger, Roberto Mangabeira. *Knowledge and Politics*. New York: Free Press, 1975.

U.S. Bureau of the Census. *Indian Population in the United States and Alaska, 1910*. Washington, D.C.: Government Printing Office, 1915.

U.S. Department of the Interior, Bureau of Indian Affairs. *Annual Report of the Commissioner of Indian Affairs to the Secretary of Interior*. Washington, D.C.: Government Printing Office.

U.S. Department of the Interior, Census Office. *Report on Indians Taxed and not Taxed: 1890*. Washington, D.C.: Government Printing Office, 1894.

Utley, Robert M. *The Indian Frontier of the American West, 1846-1890*. Albuquerque, University of New Mexico Press, 1986.

Walker, Deward E., Jr. "Mutual Cross-Utilization of Economic Resources in the Plateau: An Example from Aborignal Nez Perce Fishing Practices." Washington State University (Pullman), Laboratory of Anthropology, *Report of Investigations*, no. 41 (1967): 15-39.

—— "New Light on the Prophet Dance Controversy." *Ethnohistory* 16 (1969): 245-55.

Waller, Otis L. "A Report on Irrigation Conditions in the Yakima Valley, Washington." *Bulletin* no. 61. Washington State Agricultural College and School of Science Experiment Station. Pullman, WA: Allen Bros., 1904.

Wandschneider, Philip R. "Control and Management of the Columbia Snake River System." *Bulletin* no. 0937. Agricultural Research Center. Pullman, WA: Washington State University, 1984.

Wardle, H. Newell. "Certain Rare West-Coast Baskets." *American Anthropologist*, n.s., 14 (1912): 287-313.

Washburn, Wilcomb E. *The Assault on Indian Tribalism: The General Allotment Law (Dawes Act) of 1887*. Philadelphia: J. B. Lippincott Company, 1975.

Weaver, Philip L., Jr. "Salt Water Fisheries of the Pacific Coast." *Overland Monthly*, 2d ser., 20 (1892): 149-63.

Weber, Max. *The Protestant Ethic and the Spirit of Capitalism*. Trans. by Talcott Parsons. Gloucester, MA: Peter Smith, 1988.

Wessel, Thomas R. "Agriculture, Indians, and American History." *Agricultural History* 50 (Jan. 1976): 9-20.

Whalen, Sue. "The Nez Perces' Relationship to Their Land." *Indian Historian* 4 (1971): 30-33.

White, Lynn, Jr. "The Roots of Our Current Ecological Crisis." *Science* 155 (1967): 1203-07.

White, Richard. "Native Americans and the Environment." In Swagerty, ed., *Scholars and the Indian Experience; Critical Reviews of Recent Writing in the Social Sciences*. Bibliographical Series. Bloomington, IN, published for the D'Arcy McNickle Center for the History of the American Indian, Newberry Library by Indian Press (1984); 179-204.

—— *The Roots of Dependency, Subsistence, Environment, and Social Change Among the Choctaws, Pawnees, and Navajos*. Lincoln: University of Nebraska Press, 1983.

Whitman, Narcissa Prentiss. "A Journey Across the Plains in 1836." Oregon Pioneer Association, *Transactions of the 19th Annual Reunion, 1891*. Portland, OR: A. Anderson & Co. Printers and Lithographers (1893): 40-68.

—— "Letters Written by Mrs. Whitman from Oregon to her Relatives in New York." Oregon Pioneer Association, *Transactions of the 19th Annual Reunion, 1891*. Portland, OR, A. Anderson & Co. Printers and Lithographers (1893): 79-179.

—— "Mrs. Whitman's Letters." Oregon Pioneer Association, *Transactions of the 21st Annual Reunion*. Portland, OR: George H. Himes & Co. Printers (1894): 53-219.

Whitner, Grant L. "Grant's Peace Policy on the Yakima Reservation, 1870-1882." *Pacific Northwest Quarterly* 50 (1959): 137-42.

Wilkinson, Charles F. *American Indians, Time, and the Law: Native Societies in a Modern Constitutional Democracy*. New Haven: Yale University Press, 1987.

—— and Anderson, H. Michael. *Land and Resource Planning in the National Forests*. Washington, D.C.: Island Press, 1987.

—— and Conner, Daniel Keith. "The Law of the Pacific Salmon Fishery: Conservation and Allocation of a Transboundary Common Property Resource." *Kansas Law Review* 32 (1983): 17-109.

Williams, Nancy M. and Hunn, Eugene, eds. *Resource Managers: North American and Australian Hunter Gatherers*. AAAS Selected Symposium 67. Boulder, CO: Wesview Press, 1982.

Williams, Robert A. "The Algebra of Federal Indian Law: The Hard Trail of Decolonizing and Americanizing the White Man's Indian Jurisprudence." *Wisconsin Law Review* (1986): 219-99.

—— "Documents of Barbarism: The Contemporary Legacy of European Racism and Colonialism in the Narrative Traditions of Federal Indian Law." *Arizona Law Review* 31 (1989): 237-78.

—— *The American Indian in Western Legal Thought: The Discourses of Conquest*. Oxford: Oxford University Press, 1990.

Wilson, Gilbert L., ed. *Buffalo Bird Woman's Garden*. St. Paul, MN: Minnesota Historical Society Press, 1987.

Wissler, Clark. "Ceremonial Bundles of the Blackfoot Indians." American Museum of Natural History; *Anthropological Papers* 7, pt. 2 (1912): 71-104.

Wollenberg, Elmer. "The Columbia River Fish Compact." *Oregon Law Review* 18 (1938): 88-107.

Worster, Donald. *Rivers of Empire: Water Aridity and the Growth of the American West*. New York: Pantheon Books, 1985.

Selected Legal Materials

Cases

Arizona v. California, 373 U.S. 546 (1963).

Benton v. Johncox, 17 Wash. 277, 49 P. 495 (1897).

Brendale v. Confederated Tribes and Bands of Yakima Indian Nation 492 U.S. 408 (1989).

Brown v. Chase, 125 Wash. 454, 217 P. 23 (1923).

California Oregon Power Co. v. Beaver Portland Cement Co., 295 U.S. 142 (1935).

Conrad Investment Co. v. United States, 161 F. 829 (9th Cir. 1908).

Department of Ecology v. Acquavella, 100 Wash. 2d 651, 674 P.2d 160 (1983).

Donnelly v. United States, 228 U.S. 243 (1913).

Fouke v. Mandel, 386 F. Supp. 1341 (D. Md. 1974).

Geer v. Conn., 161 U.S. 519 (1896).

Gibbons v. Ogden, 9 Wheat. 1 (1824).

Holly v. Totus, 655 F. Supp 548 (E.D. Wash. 1983).

Ickes v. Fox, 85 F.2d 294 (1936).

In re Ahtanum Creek, 139 Wash. 84, 245 P. 758 (1926).

In re Waters of Alpowa Creek, 129 Wash. 9, 224 P. 29 (1924).

Kittitas Irr. Dist. v. Sunnyside Irr. Dist. (E.D. Wa., So. Div., Civ. Action no. 21, 1945).

Kittitas Reclamation Dist. v. Sunnyside Valley Irrigation Dist., 763 F.2d 1032 (9th Cir. 1985).

Makah Tribe v. Schoettler, 192 F.2d 224 (9th Cir. 1951).

Mason v. Sams, 5 F.2d 255 (W.D. Wash., April 9, 1925).

Missouri v. Holland, 252 U.S. 416 (1920).

N. Y. ex rel. Kennedy v. Becker, 241 U.S. 556 (1916).

P.J. McGowan & Sons, Inc. v. Van Winkle, 21 F.2d 76 (D. Ore. 1927).

Pioneer Packing Co. v. Winslow, 159 Wash. 655, 294 P. 557 (1930).

Puyallup Tribe v. Dept. of Game (Puyallup I), 391 U.S. 392 (1968).

Seufert v. Olney, 193 F. 200 (E.D. Wash., So. Div., Nov. 8, 1911).

Seufert Bros. v. United States, 249 U.S. 194 (1919).

State v. Allen, 80 Wash. 83, 141 P. 292 (1914), *rehearing en banc*, 82 Wash. 698, 144 P. 294 (1914).

State v. Alexis, 89 Wash. 492, 155 P. 1041 (1916).

State v. Edwards, 188 Wash. 467, 62 P.2d 1094 (1936).

State ex rel. Liberty Lake Irr. Co. v. Superior Court of Spokane County, 47 Wash. 310, 91 P. 968 (1907).

State v. Meninock, 115 Wash. 528, 197 P. 641 (1921).

State v. Tiffany, 44 Wash. 602, 87 P. 932 (1906).

State v. Towessnute, 89 Wash. 478, 154 P. 805 (1916).

State v. Wallahee, 143 Wash. 117, 255 P. 94 (1927).

Thorpe, et al. v. Tenem Ditch Co., 1 Wash. 566, 20 P. 588 (1889).

Tulee v. Washington, 315 U.S. 681 (1942).

United States v. Ahtanum Irrigation District, 236 F.2d 321 (9th Cir. 1956).

United States v. Brookfield Fisheries. Inc., 24 F. Supp. (D. Ore. 1938).

United States v. Taylor, 3 Wash. Terr. 88, 13 P. 333 (1887).

United States v. McBratney, 104 U.S. 621 (1882).

United States v. McIntire, 101 F.2d 650 (9th Cir. 1939).

United States v. Rio Grande Dam Co., 174 U.S. 690 (1899).

United States v. Washington, 506 F.Supp. 187 (W.D. Wash. 1980).

United States v. Winans, 198 U.S. 371 (1905).

United States v. Winters, 207 U.S. 564 (1908).

Ward v. Racehorse, 198 U.S. 371 (1906).

Washington v. Washington State Commercial Passenger Fishing Vessel Association, 443 U.S. 658 (1979).

Whitefoot v. United States, 293 F.2d 658 (Ct. Cl. 1961), *cert. denied*, 369 U.S. 818 (1962).

Yakima Tribe v. United States, 4 U.S. Indian Claims Com'n *Decisions* 294 (1956).

Yakima Tribe v. United States, 5 U.S. Indian Claims Com'n *Decisions* 661 (1957).

Treaties

Treaty with the Yakima, June 9, 1855, 12 Stat. 951 (1863).

Statutes

An act to authorize the sale and disposition of surplus or unallotted lands of the Yakima Indian Reservation, in the State of Washington," 33 Stat. 595, Act of Dec. 21, 1904 (1904).

Dawes General Allotment Act, 24 Stat. 389 (1887).

Donation Land Act, 9 Stat. 496 (1853).

Newlands Act, 32 Stat. 388-90 (1902).

Visit us at *www.quidprobooks.com*.

CPSIA information can be obtained at www.ICGtesting.com
Printed in the USA
BVOW03*1323020415

394238BV00004B/19/P